INDIGENOUS EMPOWERMENT THROUGH CO-MANAGEMENT

GRAHAM WHITE

INDIGENOUS EMPOWERMENT THROUGH CO-MANAGEMENT

Land Claims Boards,
Wildlife Management, and
Environmental Regulation

UBCPress · Vancouver · Toronto

© UBC Press 2020

All rights reserved. No part of this publication may be reproduced, stored in a retrieval system, or transmitted, in any form or by any means, without prior written permission of the publisher, or, in Canada, in the case of photocopying or other reprographic copying, a licence from Access Copyright, www.accesscopyright.ca.

29 28 27 26 25 24 23 22 21 20   5 4 3 2 1

Printed in Canada on FSC-certified ancient-forest-free paper (100% post-consumer recycled) that is processed chlorine- and acid-free.

Library and Archives Canada Cataloguing in Publication

Title: Indigenous empowerment through co-management: land claims boards, wildlife management, and environmental regulation / Graham White.
Names: White, Graham, 1948- author.
Description: Includes bibliographical references and index.
Identifiers: Canadiana (print) 20190223103 | Canadiana (ebook) 20190223197 |
    ISBN 9780774863025 (hardcover) | ISBN 9780774863032 (softcover) |
    ISBN 9780774863049 (PDF) | ISBN 9780774863056 (EPUB) |
    ISBN 9780774863063 (Kindle)
Subjects: LCSH: Conservation of natural resources – Canada, Northern – Case studies. |
    LCSH: Community-based conservation – Canada, Northern – Case studies. | LCSH:
    Conservation leadership – Canada, Northern – Case studies. | LCSH: Advisory
    boards – Canada, Northern – Case studies. | CSH: Native peoples – Legal status, laws,
    etc. – Canada, Northern – Case studies. | CSH: Native peoples – Canada, Northern –
    Politics and government – Case studies. | LCGFT: Case studies.
Classification: LCC S934.C2 W45 2020 | DDC 333.720971–dc23

Canadä

UBC Press gratefully acknowledges the financial support for our publishing program of the Government of Canada (through the Canada Book Fund), the Canada Council for the Arts, and the British Columbia Arts Council.

This book has been published with the help of a grant from the Canadian Federation for the Humanities and Social Sciences, through the Awards to Scholarly Publications Program, using funds provided by the Social Sciences and Humanities Research Council of Canada.

UBC Press
The University of British Columbia
2029 West Mall
Vancouver, BC V6T 1Z2
www.ubcpress.ca

To Cathy ... always

Contents

Figures and Tables / ix

Preface / xi

Acknowledgments / xiv

Acronyms / xvi

Part 1: What Are Land Claims–Based Co-management Boards?

1 A New Species in the Canadian Governmental Menagerie / 3

2 Northern Governments, Land Claims, and Land Claims Boards / 20

Part 2: Specific Land Claims Boards

3 The Nunavut Wildlife Management Board / 55

4 The Yukon Fish and Wildlife Management Board / 98

5 The Mackenzie Valley Environmental Impact Review Board
and the Mackenzie Valley Land and Water Board / 152

6 The Mackenzie Valley Boards and the Regulatory
Improvement Saga / 209

Part 3: A Review of the Key Issues

7 Issues of Board Independence / 247

8 Traditional Knowledge in Claims-Mandated Co-management Boards / 266

9 Indigenous Influence through Claims Boards? / 297

Notes / 324

Selected Bibliography / 363

Index / 369

Figures and Tables

Figure

2.1 Map showing territorial land claims agreements / 31

Tables

2.1 Statistical data on the territories / 21

2.2 Finalized comprehensive land claims agreements in the territorial North / 30

2.3 Territorial land claims boards / 41

2.4 Membership of territorial land claims boards / 43

2.5 Cultural and gender profile of members of selected claims boards / 44

Preface

This book has been long in the making. It began in 1999 with a grant application to SSHRC's Federalism and Federations Research Program; the application was successful and serious research began in 2000. Over the following years, periods of intense work, especially fieldwork, were interspersed with fallow stretches during which I kept a watching brief on Northern co-management boards but focused my attention on other projects. While the resulting delays were frustrating, I like to think that they made for a valuable long-term perspective.

This book is based on personal interviews, primary documents, secondary literature, and observation of board meetings. The interviews were conducted in an unstructured format on a not-for-attribution basis, that is, respondents were promised anonymity for their observations. All but half a dozen interviews I conducted in person; the balance I did by telephone. Those interviewed were members, former members, and staff of various claims boards; officials of the federal and territorial governments; and elected and appointed officials of various Indigenous organizations. All told, I conducted nearly 130 interviews between 2000 and 2018, in Dawson City, Igloolik, Inuvik, Iqaluit, Cambridge Bay, Rankin Inlet, Ottawa-Hull, Yellowknife, and Whitehorse. About a dozen interviews involved more than one person. A number of respondents were interviewed more than once; some half-dozen were interviewed three or four times. In a number of instances additional information was obtained through follow-up telephone calls and e-mails. Direct quotations and paraphrases from those involved in board processes that are not otherwise attributed are taken from the notes of these interviews.

I attended meetings of the Inuvialuit Game Council and the Wildlife Management Advisory Council (NWT) in Inuvik in December 2001 and again in December 2006; meetings of the Nunavut Wildlife Management Board in Igloolik in September 2005, in Cambridge Bay in December 2007, in Iqaluit in March 2013, and in Rankin Inlet in December 2014; and meetings of the Yukon Fish and Wildlife Management Board in Whitehorse in February 2013 and December 2016. Members of both wildlife boards permitted me to remain during in camera meetings, for which I am most grateful. I attended public hearings held in Whitehorse by the Yukon Water Board in February 2003 and in June 2006, by the Mackenzie Valley Environmental Impact Review Board in Hay River in February 2004, and by the Mackenzie Valley Land and Water Board in December 2011 in Yellowknife. I also attended a Traditional Knowledge Workshop the Mackenzie Valley Environmental Impact Review Board organized in Yellowknife in November 2002; the direct quotations of participants' comments from this workshop, cited in various chapters, are taken from the notes I took there.

In addition to the formal interviews and the observation of board meetings, I gleaned a good deal of insight from casual conversations with various people familiar with claims boards. While these discussions significantly informed my thinking about boards, they were not recorded and none are quoted or cited in the book.

The secondary literature on Northern claims boards is far more extensive than might be thought, though little of it is explicitly directed to answering the questions this book addresses. The boards themselves produce extensive documentation. Virtually all publish annual reports as well as background and discussion papers; some publish minutes of meetings and related documents. The larger regulatory boards maintain extensive websites, which, among other things, offer full-text decisions and submissions received from proponents and opponents of proposed projects (these documents can be both lengthy and numerous) as well as the sometimes pointed formal exchanges between boards and ministers on the substance of recommendations.

I gathered a substantial number of documents in the course of the research, many of which are cited in the notes. A large proportion of them can be accessed through the internet; in those cases I have provided the URLs. Others were available online at some point but are no longer accessible. Still others were documents that were never publicly available in the sense of being "published," either in hard copy or online, though officials of boards and of public and Indigenous governments were usually willing to pass them on to me. Some of the older CBC News stories cited are still available online; URLs are provided for them. Other CBC stories from the same period are no longer available online. I have, or have had, in my possession hard or electronic copies of all documents and news stories cited in the notes.

Indigenous Empowerment through Co-management unfolds as follows. Chapter 1 sets the stage for subsequent chapters, arguing that the Northern claims co-management boards should be viewed as an important development in Canadian Indigenous-state relations, and offers a thumbnail sketch of the boards. It also explicates the two central components of the conceptual framework for the book, treaty federalism and co-management. Chapter 2 provides background and context for the analysis of Northern claims boards, offering brief accounts of the three territories and their political-governmental traits, the Indigenous organizations and governments so central to territorial governance, and the principal characteristics of comprehensive land claims. It also presents a wide-ranging general account of the organization and operation of claims boards. Chapters 3 to 6 examine a few specific claims boards in some detail. Chapters 3 and 4 focus on wildlife management boards: the Nunavut Wildlife Management Board and the Yukon Fish and Wildlife Management Board (as well as the Yukon Salmon Sub-Committee and the Regional Resources Councils). Chapters 5 and 6 look at two of the larger and more active of the environmental regulatory boards, the Mackenzie Valley Environmental Impact Review Board and the Mackenzie Valley Land and Water Board. Various dimensions of board independence are examined in Chapter 7, while Chapter 8 considers the capacity of claims boards to incorporate Traditional Knowledge into their operations, focusing on two boards, the Nunavut Wildlife Management Board and the Mackenzie Valley Environmental Impact Review Board, which have made especially concerted efforts in this regard. Chapter 9, the concluding chapter, draws together the strands of the earlier chapters, analyzing them in the context of the forceful critiques levelled against co-management boards by authors such as Marc Stevenson, Paul Nadasdy, and Hayden King.

Acknowledgments

Over the two decades since the initial grant application, more than one SSHRC grant was necessary to keep the project afloat. I am very grateful for that support. Thanks also to the editors of *Arctic* and *Canadian Public Administration* for allowing me to use material that first appeared in "Cultures in Collision: Traditional Knowledge and Euro-Canadian Governance Processes in Northern Land-Claim Boards," *Arctic* 59 (December 2006): 401–14; "'Not the Almighty': Evaluating Aboriginal Influence in Northern Land-Claim Boards," *Arctic* 61, Suppl. 1 (2008): 71–85; and "Issues of Independence in Northern Aboriginal-State Co-management Boards," *Canadian Public Administration* 61 (December 2018): 550–71.

Along the way a great many people proved uncommonly helpful sources of information, assistance, and advice. I owe enormous thanks to the many dozens of (current and former) board members, staff, government officials, and other knowledgeable Northerners who agreed to interviews – many more than once – follow-up calls, and e-mails as well as document requests. All were promised anonymity, and, accordingly, no attributions are made of quotations or paraphrases from the interviews.

Aside from the interviews, a number of people were especially helpful in various ways; none, of course are responsible for any errors or dubious interpretations. Special thanks to, in alphabetical order, Jason Akearok, Kirk Cameron, Vern Christensen, Christine Cleghorn, Mark Cliffe-Phillips, Will Dunlop, Michael d'Eça, Shelagh Montgomery, Zabey Nevitt, Jim Noble, Angela Plautz, Lorraine Seale, Diane Sheldon, Norm Snow, Stephen Traynor, Jesse

Trerice, Graham Van Tighem, Glen Williams, Bob Wooley, Gordon Wray, and Eric Yaxley. My late colleague Richard Simeon was enthusiastic and insightful in encouraging me to adopt a treaty federalism approach to the project. Gina Cosentino and Andrew McDougall provided first-rate research assistance. My ever-sage editor, Randy Schmidt, and his colleagues demonstrated once again why UBC Press is such a wonderful partner in academic publishing; thanks to Holly Keller for shepherding another sprawling manuscript through the production process and to Joanne Richardson for her deft hand at copyediting: not only did she do me the honour of only minimally revising my prose but she saved me from a goodly number of embarrassing errors. The anonymous reviewers were supportive of my work while constructive and thoughtful in their criticisms and suggestions for revision.

As ever, my most heartfelt thanks go to my wife Cathy for endless support and tolerance of my continuing inability to get the hang of retirement.

Acronyms

AANDC	Aboriginal Affairs and Northern Development Canada
AIP	Agreement in Principle
BNL	basic needs level
BQCMB	Beverly and Qamanirjuaq Caribou Management Board
BRS	Board Relations Secretariat
CEAA	*Canadian Environmental Assessment Act*
CIG	Claims and Indian Government Implementation Branch
CITES	*Convention on International Trade in Endangered Species of Wild Fauna and Flora*
COSEWIC	Committee on the Status of Endangered Wildlife in Canada
CWS	Canadian Wildlife Service
CYFN	Council of Yukon First Nations
CYI	Council of Yukon Indians
DAR	Developer's Assessment Report
DFN	Dehcho First Nations
DFO	Department of Fisheries and Oceans
DIAND	Department of Indian Affairs and Northern Development
DoE	[federal] Department of Environment
EA	environmental assessment

EIR	environmental impact review
EIRB	[Inuvialuit] Environmental Impact Review Board
ERM	environmental resource management
FJMC	Fisheries Joint Management Committee
FOI	freedom of information
FTP	flexible transfer payment
GLWB	Gwich'in Land and Water Board
GN	Government of Nunavut
GNWT	Government of the Northwest Territories
HTA	Hunters and Trappers Association
HTO	Hunters and Trappers Organization
IFA	*Inuvialuit Final Agreement*
IFMP	Integrated Fish Management Plan
INAC	Indian and Northern Affairs Canada (1990s)
INAC	Indigenous and Northern Affairs Canada (under J. Trudeau)
IPG	institution of public government
IQ	Inuit Qaujimajatuqangit
IRC	Inuvialuit Regional Corporation
IRWG	Implementation Review Working Group
ISR	Inuvialuit Settlement Region
JBNQA	*James Bay and Northern Quebec Agreement*
JEP	Joint Examination Project
KFN	K'atl'odeeche First Nation
KWB	Kivalliq Wildlife Board
MVEIRB	Mackenzie Valley Environmental Impact Review Board
MVLWB	Mackenzie Valley Land and Water Board
MVRMA	*Mackenzie Valley Resource Management Act*
NAP	Northern Affairs Program
NGOs	non-governmental organizations
NIRB	Nunavut Impact Review Board
NIWS	Nunavut Inuit Wildlife Secretariat
NLCA	*Nunavut Land Claims Agreement*
NMRWB	Nunavik Marine Region Wildlife Board

NPC	Nunavut Planning Commission
NTI	Nunavut Tunngavik Incorporated
NuPPAA	*Nunavut Project Planning and Assessment Act*
NWMAB	Nunavut Wildlife Management Advisory Board
NWMB	Nunavut Wildlife Management Board
NWT	Northwest Territories
PCO	Privy Council Office
REA	Report of Environmental Assessment
RIA	Regional Inuit Association
RRC	Renewable Resources Council
RWOs	[Nunavut] Regional Wildlife Organizations
SARA	*Species at Risk Act*
TAH	total allowable harvest
TEK	traditional ecological knowledge
TFN	Tungavik Federation of Nunavut
TK	traditional knowledge
UFA	[Yukon] *Umbrella Final Agreement*
WHB	Western Hudson Bay
WMAC (NS)	Wildlife Management Advisory Council (North Slope)
WMAC (NWT)	Wildlife Management Advisory Council (NWT)
YESAB	Yukon Environmental and Socio-economic Assessment Board
YESSA	*Yukon Environmental and Socio-economic Assessment Act*
YFWMB	Yukon Fish and Wildlife Management Board
YG	Yukon Government
YSSC	Yukon Salmon Sub-Committee
YTG	Yukon Territorial Government
YWMB	Yukon Wildlife Management Board

PART 1

WHAT ARE LAND CLAIMS–BASED CO-MANAGEMENT BOARDS?

chapter 1

A New Species in the Canadian Governmental Menagerie

Among the pressing problems facing the Canadian federation, those involving the accommodation of Indigenous peoples' rights, interests, and aspirations arguably raise the most fundamental and most difficult governance issues. Political accommodation of Indigenous peoples is especially problematic because, even in Canada's highly diverse society, they constitute the most distinctive cultural minorities. And, as the plural "minorities" suggests, great variations are evident among the many Indigenous nations and communities across Canada. Moreover, essential precepts of Indigenous political culture – ways of conceiving politics, political values, and understandings about how those values should play out in practical politics – often differ fundamentally from prevailing Euro-Canadian values and approaches.

Crucially, what sets Indigenous peoples apart from all other cultural minorities in this country is the essential and compelling fact that their position within the federation is founded on an explicit and unique constitutional framework: the treaties they have signed with Britain and with Canada. What has been termed "treaty federalism" is increasingly understood as a fundamental element of the Canadian constitutional order. The Royal Commission on Aboriginal Peoples put it this way: "the terms of the Canadian federation are found not only in formal constitutional documents governing relations between the federal and provincial governments but also in treaties and other instruments establishing the basic links between Indigenous peoples and the Crown."[1]

In principle, the governance provisions in these treaties – implicit and explicit – offer the means and the opportunity for accommodating Indigenous peoples within the Canadian political community. In practice, however, it is often uncertain how – or even if – relations between Indigenous peoples and the Canadian state are actually shaped by the treaties. In particular, the role of the treaties in advancing the Indigenous quest for self-determination is a matter of much empirical and normative dispute.

This book explores one important facet of treaty-based political accommodation of Indigenous people in Canada. It looks at the co-management boards established under the comprehensive land claims, which the Government of Canada recognizes as "modern treaties," finalized in the territorial North. These boards, which have become key players in a host of environmental, economic, and cultural issues across the North, represent a compromise between Indigenous peoples' desire for complete control over matters of crucial importance to them and the insistence of the federal government on established patterns of state control, exercised through the federal and territorial governments. Through the lens of treaty federalism, the book addresses the central question about these boards: *Have they been effective in ensuring substantial Indigenous influence over policies affecting the land and wildlife of traditional territories?*

Claims boards' capacity for protecting and advancing Indigenous interests has been cited as "contributing to the reconciliation process in Canada" and to the realization of the United Nations Declaration on the Rights of Indigenous Peoples, to which Canada is a signatory.[2] Article 18 of the declaration states: "Indigenous peoples have the right to participate in decision-making in matters which would affect their rights."

The thirty Northern claims boards are, in a term used mainly in Nunavut but applicable across all three territories, "institutions of public government."[3] Yet they are not federal or territorial boards, nor are they a species of Indigenous self-government. Rather, they exist at the intersection of the three orders of government within Canada: federal, provincial/territorial, and Indigenous. They do not constitute anything like a fourth order of government in any formal way, but they can and do wield significant power over policies and decisions affecting not only day-to-day life in the territories but also the long term development of the Canadian North. Claims-based co-management boards exist or are emerging in at least three provinces; this book, however, looks only at boards in Nunavut, the Northwest Territories (NWT), and Yukon.

Northern claims boards warrant a close look not simply because they are new and unique features of Canadian federalism. Nor simply because of their political clout in the territorial North, which, though small in population, constitutes close to 40 percent of Canada's land mass with vast stores of natural resources. These boards carry great significance in terms of their potential for accommodating Indigenous peoples' political interests and perspectives within the Canadian state. Yet political scientists have paid little attention to claims boards. Lawyers have written about various boards, explicating their jurisdiction and processes, usually from a technical, legalistic perspective, while scientists, geographers, and environmentalists have produced a substantial literature examining the boards' activities relating to the environment and wildlife. Political scientists, however, have conducted very limited research on the boards and their place within the structures and processes of the Canadian state; they have published only one book-length study and a handful of articles and chapters.[4] To the limited extent that social scientists have considered claims boards as vehicles for Indigenous influence, the work has been carried out mostly by anthropologists.[5]

Accordingly, an important objective of this book is to draw political scientists' attention to a new and potentially significant set of institutions in the ever-evolving domain of Canadian federalism. To this end the case study chapters provide extensive detail on the structures and processes of selected boards, highlighting their organizational development. These chapters examine the nature and causes of the changes that have characterized boards over the course of their relatively short lifetimes (the first boards were created in 1984; most date from the 1990s).

Claims Boards: A Thumbnail Sketch

Before proceeding, a brief sketch of Northern claims boards is necessary to provide context for the balance of the chapter. A more fulsome overview of comprehensive land claims and the boards established under them is provided in Chapter 2, while Chapters 3 to 6 look at several boards in detail.

Since the mid-1970s, the federal government, together with provincial or territorial governments, has been negotiating "comprehensive land claims" with various Indigenous organizations, almost exclusively in Northern Canada (the most notable exception being that of the Nisga'a of central British Columbia and the massive Algonquin claim in eastern Ontario). Agreements have been finalized in Labrador and in Northern Quebec, and with the Nisga'a, but they have been in areas literally peripheral to the provinces in which they are located. By contrast, the claims settled in the territories are of central political and economic importance to the people and governments "north of 60," not least because they cover all of Yukon and Nunavut and more than half of the NWT. As the name implies, comprehensive land claims encompass a wide range of provisions, many of which directly or indirectly impinge on governance. The boards examined in this book carry significant governance provisions.

The Northern comprehensive claims are remarkable achievements, particularly given the limited resources available to the small Indigenous communities and organizations pursuing them. In little more than three decades, the claims have transformed politics and administration across the territories. The co-management boards analyzed in this book are but one element of the claims, albeit an especially important element. A comprehensive assessment of the multifaceted components of the Northern claims and their far-reaching effects has yet to be done. Suffice it to say here that many aspects of the claims beyond the co-management boards have profoundly influenced the North and the place of Indigenous people in it.

Boards established under the comprehensive land claims differ fundamentally from the myriad non-claims boards and political institutions permeating Northern governance. As "modern treaties," comprehensive claims are constitutionally protected under section 35 of the *Constitution Act, 1982*. Accordingly, as integral components of the claims, the boards enjoy quasi-constitutional status. This status accords them importance and permanence far beyond that of run-of-the-mill boards.

The boards' jurisdiction is largely limited to wildlife, land, and environmental issues. Few boards' mandates extend more than marginally into more conventionally defined social and cultural policy such as education, health, and social welfare.

Claims boards fall into four broad categories. One group deals with wildlife management; its activities include advising on and setting policy as well as specific harvest levels for various species, directing and facilitating wildlife research and supporting local renewable resources councils and hunters' and trappers' organizations. The Nunavut Wildlife Management Board (NWMB) is an example. A second major set of boards is responsible for land use planning: such bodies as the Gwich'in Land Use Planning Board set the frameworks that govern economic development projects, location of transportation facilities, and the like. A third group, which is involved in regulating projects that might disturb or damage the environment, has two subsets. One subset, illustrated by the Mackenzie Valley Land and Water Board (MVLWB), issues licences and permits to projects ranging from small gravel pits to oil and gas pipelines. The other subset conducts environmental impact assessments on proposed projects, usually the larger ones, as part of the licensing process. The work of these boards is closely related to, though nonetheless separate from, the boards that issue permits and licences; an example is the Mackenzie Valley Environmental Impact

Review Board (MVEIRB). The claims boards that comprise a final group, represented by the Nunavut Arbitration Board, serve as dispute resolution bodies for claims-related issues. They have thus far been of little significance; some have yet to have any cases referred to them.

Wide variation in structure, mandate, and operation characterizes boards in the same fields across the three territories. The accounts of the wildlife management boards in Chapters 3 and 4 bring this home clearly. While a detailed analysis of the sources and implications of these variations is beyond the scope of this book, some attention is devoted to the factors shaping certain boards. Boards typically have between seven and ten members; a few are somewhat larger or smaller. All board members are nominees of one of the three parties to the claim (the Indigenous organization, the territorial government, and the federal government). In most instances the formal appointments are made by the federal government. Some boards are structured so that half the members are nominees of Indigenous governments or organizations and half are public government nominees.

Board members, however, are not (with a few exceptions) representatives or delegates of the parties that nominated or appointed them. Key to understanding the nature and role of the claims boards is the fundamental principle that they and their members are to act independently. The legal frameworks establishing some boards explicitly state that members are to act "in the public interest" and are not to take direction from the parties that nominated them. Like judges, members are expected to use their best judgment and to reach decisions on the basis of the evidence before them. As might be expected, however, the question of board independence is not so straightforward as this simple formulation would have it. Issues of board independence are examined in Chapter 7.

Save the little-utilized arbitration panels, the boards have permanent, full-time professional staff, some numbering only three or four, while others have a dozen or more. Many boards make extensive use of modern communications technology, for example, maintaining online registries containing the full text of submissions and technical reports pertaining to projects under review or webcasting public hearings.

Funding for claims boards – for large, active boards, several million dollars a year – comes almost entirely from the federal government (the territorial governments provide some funding, but by and large this is redirected federal money).

In a few cases, boards possess the legal capacity to make final, binding decisions on permits, harvest quotas, and the like. In most cases, however, and certainly in almost all matters with far-reaching implications, the boards have only advisory powers. They make recommendations to government, which need not follow the boards' advice. Put this way, the boards appear to wield little real clout since governments would seem free to ignore their recommendations. This appearance is deceiving, however, and the reality, considered in later chapters, is quite different.

Claims boards decide, advise, and recommend. As a rule they have no powers of inspection or enforcement and rely on federal and territorial officials – wildlife officers, environmental inspectors, and the like – to put their recommendations into operation and to police the licences and plans they issue. An important exception here is the Nunavut Impact Review Board, which both under the Nunavut land claim and the *Nunavut Project Planning and Assessment Act* has substantial inspection and monitoring powers. Recent amendments to the *Mackenzie Valley Resource Management Act* potentially entail a similar monitoring regime for environmental regulatory boards in the NWT; as of early 2019, however, the process was still being developed.

Certainly, in these and other ways, the powers of claims boards are constrained. The boards are, however, important and prominent players in Northern politics that attract constant media attention. Few issues of the main weekly newspapers in the NWT and Nunavut, *News/North NWT* and *Nunatsiaq News*, do not carry substantial stories about some claims board or other; the boards are also frequent subjects of CBC Radio news stories. Yukon boards also receive a good deal of media attention.

Treaty Federalism

"Treaty federalism" is an approach to Indigenous-state relations premised on the notion that treaties are defining elements of the Canadian federation. The concept was first articulated in Russel Barsh and James Youngblood Henderson's book *The Road*, which examines the relationship of American tribes to the United States government. Barsh and Henderson's central argument about US treaties runs as follows:

> Intent, interpretation and practice combine to make these instruments something more than "treaties" as they are understood in international law. They are political compacts irrevocably annexing tribes to the federal system in a status parallel to, but not identical with, that of the states ... Treaties are a form of recognition and a measure of the consensual distribution of power between tribes and the United States.[6]

This argument applies with equal force in Canada. In the words of one Indigenous scholar:

> First Nations in Canada formed treaty relations with several European
> nations which governed their intra-relations. Part of those intra-nation
> undertakings included the continuance of the right of First Nations govern-
> ance ... Treaty federalism stands for "Indian consensus" and "Indian consent"
> in regard to the manner and form of our co-existence with the Queen's white
> children under the Canadian constitutional framework ... In essence treaty
> federalism is a way of restoring the unique First Nations-Crown relations
> since earliest colonial times.[7]

The Royal Commission on Aboriginal Peoples put it simply: "Treaty federalism is an integral part of the Canadian constitution."[8]

The constitutional status of treaties is obviously central here, but so too is the *federal* nature of the relationship. In Canada, as a manifestation of Indigenous peoples' quest for self-determination, treaty federalism combines "identity politics and traditional territorial politics of federalism."[9] As Richard Simeon and Katherine Swinton remind us, "federalism is at once a set of institutions – the division of public authority between two or more constitutionally defined orders of government – and a set of ideas which underpin such institutions. As an idea, federalism points us to such issues as shared and divided sovereignty, multiple loyalties and identities and governance through multi-level institu-tions."[10] By positing a regime founded upon three distinct orders of govern-ment – federal, provincial/territorial, and Indigenous – treaty federalism is concerned with just such issues. As Henderson notes, in Canada "treaties created shared responsibilities rather than supreme powers."[11]

The Canadian treaty federalism literature is almost exclusively framed in terms of developing Indigenous self-government as a means of restoring the spirit and intent of the "historic" treaties signed by First Nations and the British and Canadian authorities. Kiera Ladner, for example, writes of treaty federalism as "an Indigenous vision of the future," arguing that the treaties "hold the solu-tion for the problems that we face today in restructuring and decolonizing the Aboriginal/non-Aboriginal relationship."[12] Thus treaty federalism is usually seen as operating through direct, government-to-government relationships. Yet it may also take the form of indirect relationships mediated by institutions such as the Northern claims boards. Like the historic treaties, comprehensive land claims are about establishing principles for land ownership and use and principles for political-governmental relations between Indigenous peoples and the Canadian state. Both are inherently constitutional in nature. It follows that settled comprehensive land claims comprise a central element of treaty federalism.

The Indigenous understanding of treaty federalism, according to Thomas Huegelin, "emphasizes mutualist and holistic values, and it operates through a process of coordination and compromise on the basis of consensus. It is meant to be an open-ended, horizontal and renewable partnership aiming at the autonomy and reciprocity of all participants ... [It] establishes a common bond of mutual obligations as well as organized self-determination."[13] Many of these phrases would fit comfortably in claims boards' mission statements, though a key question is how well the on-the-ground reality matches the rhetoric.

Just as the limited Canadian literature on treaty federalism relates mainly to the historic treaties, so too it tends to be abstract and conceptual rather than concrete and empirical. Few treaty federalism scholars have attempted to set out in any detail how the overarching principles they outline might play out in practical issues of governance. In offering an on-the-ground account of Northern claims boards, this book thus represents a departure from conventional treaty federalism literature. The hope is not only that a treaty federalism perspective will strengthen the analysis of claims boards but also that the conclusions drawn about the boards will advance and refine treaty federalism as a tool for understanding Indigenous-state relations.

Co-management

The term "co-management" came to prominence in the natural resource literature during the 1980s and 1990s. As leading co-management scholar Fikret Berkes writes:

> There is no widely accepted definition of co-management. The term broadly refers to various levels of integration of local- and state-level management systems ... A more precise definition is probably inappropriate because there is a continuum of co-management arrangements from those that merely involve, for example, some local participation in government research being carried out, to those in which the community holds all the management power and responsibility.[14]

Co-management principles and processes could presumably be applied to a wide range of governmental activities, such as health and education, but the vast co-management literature is almost entirely concerned with natural resources, typically common-pool resources in situations not characterized by regimes built on private property and individual rights.[15] Significantly, although co-management is not inherently about Indigenous peoples' involvement in natural resource policy making and implementation, a great deal of the literature, especially the Canadian literature, focuses on just that. As David Natcher and his colleagues observe, "co-management regimes are not only changing the way in which lands and resources are being managed, but are also restructuring indigenous-state relations more broadly."[16]

As summarized by Peter Usher, the contrast between the state wildlife management system and that of Northern Indigenous peoples is stark:

> The state system rests on a common property concept in which the state assumes exclusive responsibility for managing a resource equally accessible to all citizens. The state manages for certain levels of abundance on a technical basis, and then allocates shares of this abundance to users on an economic and political basis. The system of knowledge is based on a scientific accumulation, organization, and interpretation of data, and management problems are resolved in a technical, historical framework. The system of management is bureaucratic, which is to say hierarchically organized and vertically compartmentalized. Managers become distinct from harvesters, authority becomes centralized and flows from the top down. The environment is reduced to conceptually discrete components which are managed separately. As these separate management units take on a life of their own, management objectives diverge and become focused on specialized objectives: maximizing fur production, trophy production or recreational expenditures. Not least, the management of fish and wildlife resources becomes separated from the management of the lands and waters that sustain them ...
>
> The indigenous system rests on communal property arrangements, in which the local harvesting group is responsible for management by consensus. Management and harvesting are conceptually and practically inseparable. Knowledge comes from the experience of every aspect of harvesting itself – travelling, searching, hunting, skinning, butchering and eating. It is accumulated by every individual, and shared intimately and constantly within the household, the family, or whatever is the social unit of production. It is also shared and exchanged within the larger society, and handed down in the form of stories from one generation to the next. In sum, these observations, like those of the state system's, become coded and organized by a paradigm or a set of paradigms that provide a comprehensive interpretation of them. The

knowledge, so produced becomes the cultural heritage of these societies, just as what we call science is part of ours ... The indigenous system of management is a core feature of all Northern native cultures, and is therefore intimately linked with their values, ethics and cosmology, which are generally based on an integrated, non-compartmentalized view of the environment.[17]

Claudia Notzke rightly comments that "the two systems are based on and operate within two profoundly different social realities, the protagonists of which have held the other resource management systems in anything but high regard and commonly have failed to acknowledge the other as having any legitimacy."[18] Little wonder then that Berkes and others see the central challenge in making co-management work as getting the adherents of the two systems to accept that the other's perspectives and techniques can be merged into an effective system utilizing the best of both systems.

In contemplating how – or if – co-management can truly meld elements of the state and Indigenous wildlife management systems, it is well to recognize that, although elements of the Indigenous system persisted throughout the twentieth century, in most of Northern Canada the state system became overwhelmingly dominant. Accordingly, bringing the two together through co-management was not a process of blending two equally powerful systems but, rather, of replacing elements of the state system with significant aspects of the Indigenous system.

The co-management literature encompasses cases across North America and the globe, but, as Tracy Campbell, among others, has pointed out, co-management institutions created by the constitutionally protected comprehensive land claims agreements of the Canadian North are qualitatively more powerful and effective than others lacking such a foundation.[19] According to Natcher not only did the co-management provisions of the 1975 *James Bay and Northern Quebec Agreement* (*JBNQA*) depart significantly from established Canadian wildlife management regimes, as "the first viable alternative to state wildlife management in Canada," the *JBNQA* "also represented a clear shift in state policy, as wildlife management moved from the biological to the political."[20] Although the co-management regimes of the *JBNQA* and the 1984 *Inuvialuit Final Agreement* (*IFA*) in the Northwest Territories are often seen as lacking the clout for Indigenous people enshrined in subsequent land claims agreements, in 1989 Berkes commented: "the co-management provisions of these agreements are quite detailed, and provide for a level of user group participation in resource decision-making which is simply unparalleled in Canada and rarely achieved elsewhere."[21]

The Northern claims-mandated co-management boards are located towards the power-sharing end of Berkes's continuum and are generally understood to entail joint exercise of decision-making authority between, on the one hand, government and, on the other hand, Indigenous people and their organizations. A few Northern claims boards are indeed true co-management bodies in terms of formal sharing of decision-making authority. Some boards established by the *IFA* have members appointed by government and by the Inuvialuit who are explicitly designated as "representatives" of their appointing bodies.[22] Significantly, however, although on paper the formal structure of these *IFA* boards, as well as the orientation of their members, differs fundamentally from those of the other claims boards in the North, the reality is that they operate much like the other boards and their members relate to one another in similar ways.[23]

For Lars Carlsson and Fikret Berkes, co-management is more than a formal power sharing arrangement: it is "an approach to governance."[24] In studying co-management regimes, they argue, "by over-emphasizing the formal aspect of such power sharing arrangement, one might run the risk of disregarding the functional side of co-management which should be understood as a continuous problem-solving process."[25] They suggest that co-management "should be understood as a process in which the parties and their relative influence, positions and activities are continuously adjusted."[26] While it is important to look beyond the formalities of the claims-mandated Northern co-management boards to their effectiveness as natural resource problem solvers, the legal and procedural frameworks within which they operate are centrally important to their activities. Moreover, as they evolve, as do all institutions, their scope for continuous adjustment is subject to clear limits.

It will not have escaped the reader's attention that, as exemplified in the authorities just cited, both conceptually and empirically the co-management literature relates almost entirely to renewable natural resources. What then of claims-mandated boards engaged in environmental regulation, primarily involving non-renewable natural resources? At first blush they would not appear to be constructed on or operating according to co-management principles, which are largely concerned with allocation of common pool resources. On closer inspection, however, environmental regulatory boards, such as the Nunavut Impact Review Board (NIRB) and the MVLWB, are deeply engaged in issues pitting certain uses of land – perhaps the ultimate common-pool resource – particularly non-renewable resource extraction, against other uses, such as traditional Indigenous hunting, trapping, and fishing activities. Moreover, as set out not only in the claims that brought them into being but also in the self-image they have adopted, boards tasked with environmental regulation operate with an explicitly articulated co-management ethos.

Echoing observations of several people interviewed for this book, Natcher and his colleagues write that "co-management has more to do with managing human relationships than resources per se." Accordingly, they suggest, the success of co-management regimes "depends on the participants' abilities to engage rather than subvert differences in knowledge and cultural experiences."[27]

It is worth keeping in mind that the term "co-management" can mean quite different things to different people. During a 2003 interview an official in the Department of Indian Affairs and Northern Development (DIAND) Whitehorse office commented: "co-management is a very sensitive word; the First Nations like to think that they've negotiated co-management but the government thinks in terms of 'cooperative management' which means that the government runs the show and the buck stops with the minister."

Thierry Rodon's 2003 book, *En partenariat avec l'État: Les expériences de cogestion des Autochonones du Canada*, is the only major comparative study of Indigenous peoples' experiences with co-management in Canada. In it, he asks whether co-management is an instrument of control for integrating Indigenous peoples into the structure of the Canadian state or whether it is a way for them to regain mastery over their traditional lands and revive their power.[28] Rodon outlines four interpretive models ("scenarios") for understanding Indigenous peoples and co-management.[29] First, co-optation ("confiscation du pouvoir" – taking power away): "the institutions of co-management allow the Canadian state to promote the integration of Indigenous peoples."[30] "Participation of Indigenous peoples in resource management encourages them to accept scientific and administrative norms – in other words, the values and standards of the Canadian society."[31]

A second model, transaction ("partage du pouvoir" – power sharing), sees co-management in terms of intercultural transactions between Indigenous peoples and the representatives of the Canadian state. In this way "the institutions of co-management could allow each group to contribute its own values and objectives."[32] The third, "l'autonomisation" or empowerment ("reconquête du pouvoir" – reclaiming power), interprets co-management as "a way [Indigenous peoples] can take back control over their land, their resources, and ultimately their lives."[33] According to the final model, "le malentendu" or misunderstanding ("lutte pour le pouvoir" – struggle for power), "the institutions of co-management only reproduce the lack of political understanding between governments and Indigenous groups."[34] Though Rodon does not explicitly say so, it is clear both from their formulation and the way he uses them in his analysis that these interpretive models may be analytically distinct but are not entirely mutually exclusive. Accordingly, in a given jurisdiction, the co-management regime, as indeed individual boards, may exhibit elements of more than one model.

Empirically, Rodon examines five cases of Indigenous co-management, all of which involve renewable resources, mostly management of fish and wildlife; one deals with timber management. These cases are the three fish and wildlife co-management boards created by the *Inuvialuit Final Agreement*; the Hunting, Fishing and Trapping Coordinating Committee established under the *JBNQA*; the Nunavut Wildlife Management Board; the Beverly and Qamanir-juaq Caribou Management Board; and the Wendaban Stewardship Authority in Northern Ontario. Only the first three are claims-mandated boards. A more extensive account of Rodon's findings must await the final chapter; suffice it to say at this point that, with respect to the three claims-based case studies, overall he primarily found integration and misunderstanding ("malentendu"), with limited intercultural transaction and very little empowerment.

On balance the Canadian literature presents a somewhat more positive assessment of claims-mandated co-management (see Chapter 9), but, as discussed in the concluding chapter, several anthropologists, deeply familiar with Northern Indigenous peoples and co-management processes, offer profoundly negative assessments of Northern co-management regimes. According to one, "it would be difficult to conceive a more insidious form of cultural assimilation than co-management as currently practiced in northern Canada."[35]

Doubtless some Northern Indigenous people would agree, but many experienced Indigenous leaders, who are certainly not naive about the difficulty of maintaining cultural identity in the face of state power, saw – and continue to see – substantial possibilities for co-management as realized through boards established under the comprehensive land claims. To cite one notable example, Chesley Andersen, former vice-president of the Inuit Tapirisat of Canada (now Inuit Tapiriit Kanatami), supported co-management as a way to "bring together the traditional Inuit system of [wildlife] knowledge and management with that of Canada's. We knew that we could manage our resources in our own tradition, but we also recognized that the government's management system has something to offer. Our definition of co-management is the blending of these two systems of management in such a way that the advantages of both are optimised and the domination of one on the other avoided."[36]

Two final points about co-management. First, as mentioned at the outset of the chapter, co-management is not self-government. Myriad variations of self-government exist, but all entail some measure of exclusion of non-Indigenous people from governmental processes and/or from programs and services provided by government. Many Indigenous people would prefer that land and wildlife decisions be taken and policies set by self-governments rather than by co-management regimes, but for the most part co-management prevails. Second, this book is exclusively concerned with co-management through Northern land claims boards. Many other forms of Indigenous-state co-management regimes exist in the North and indeed elsewhere in Canada, including two of Rodon's cases. Some have proven highly successful; others less so. None, however, are considered in subsequent chapters; they deserve their own study.

Unpacking the Central Question

The central question informing the analysis in this book can be succinctly stated: Do claims boards enable Indigenous peoples to exercise substantial influence over the land and wildlife policies so crucial to them? Northerners have not been reluctant to express their views. Members and staff of Northern claims boards regularly make conference presentations lauding the boards' success in bringing Indigenous influence to bear on important land and wildlife questions. At the same time harsh critics are not hard to find. Jim Bell, the long-time editor of *Nunatsiaq News* and one of the North's most astute and experienced political observers, offers a no-holds-barred assessment of the Nunavut claims boards:

> [Inuit negotiators] pointed to the system of environmental management boards, and promised beneficiaries that these boards would give Inuit effective control of Nunavut's entire land base.
>
> We now know that this promise was a lie. Thirteen years later, the highly-touted board system at the heart of that lie now smells like a whorehouse on a Sunday morning.
>
> At best, it's a shared management system that allows Inuit, and the public, to be consulted on some issues. At the very worst, it's a system that surrenders effective control of the entire land base, for most environmental issues, to the federal government.[37]

Indigenous political scientist Hayden King, analyzing claims boards in the three territories from a theoretical perspective, concludes that "co-management regimes are one of the many facets of [Indigenous] disempowerment."[38]

Clearly, all views should be assessed with scepticism. The hardly surprising corollary is that answering the central question turns out to be a complex undertaking, involving several subsidiary questions. This complexity is reflected along several dimensions. In the first place, overall judgments must take into account considerable variation across claims boards. Their numbers are substantial, as is the range of their activities: some thirty exist in the territories, engaged in, among other things, wildlife management, land-use planning, and environmental regulation. As well, the socio-political contexts in which they operate vary a good deal across the three territories. So too, a temporal dimension comes into play: some boards have been up and running for two decades and more while others have barely begun their work. Over their histories several have experienced noteworthy changes in their performance, and not simply by virtue of gaining experience and developing expertise. Some have gone through conflict-ridden phases when they were clearly dysfunctional. Others, though not engulfed in conflict, nevertheless accomplished little for extended periods. Still others have been widely acknowledged as highly effective for long stretches of time.

Understanding, then, that assessing Indigenous political influence through claims boards necessarily involves generalizing across a substantial range of institutions and their experiences, what are the subthemes explored in subsequent chapters? The first is straightforward and easily addressed: Are Indigenous people appointed as board members in sufficient numbers to exert meaningful influence? The answer is unequivocal: invariably half or more – sometimes a good deal more – board members are Indigenous, and they are full and engaged participants in board work. Or perhaps one should say male Indigenous board members are full and engaged participants since, as detailed in Chapter 2, Indigenous women (as indeed non-Indigenous women) are seriously underrepresented on claims boards.

Indigenous people may be at the table with solid clout in board decision making, but do the boards themselves wield real power? The ability to influence meaningless decisions or readily ignored recommendations is worth little. In formal, legal terms, claims boards have limited capacity to render binding decisions and for the most part have advisory status only; the federal and territorial governments retain the final power. However, as is so often the case in more familiar realms of Canadian federalism, a substantial gap exists between legal technicalities and real-life governance so that claims boards can and indeed do exercise significant power and influence.

For Indigenous influence to be realized through claims boards it is necessary that they enjoy independence from the federal and territorial governments. Do they? Three distinct components of the independence issue require attention. First, with governments in most instances holding the power to make board appointments, is independence compromised? Second, since claims boards are all but entirely dependent on government for their funding, does the "golden rule of politics" – "he who has the gold rules" – prevail? If, in other words, boards are financially beholden to government, how independent can they be? Third, beyond control over appointments and finances, can governments bring into play other processes that adversely affect board independence? Federal legislation to eliminate the regional land and water boards in the NWT, examined in Chapter 6, certainly suggests that this can occur. A full treatment of board independence also requires a look at the relationship of Indigenous governments to the members they have nominated. The crucial question of board independence is examined in Chapter 7.

Indigenous influence via claims boards entails not only decisions and policies premised on Indigenous interests and preferences but also board procedures and operations that reflect Indigenous approaches and modes of thought. Accordingly, the analysis must extend beyond the substance of decisions to the nature of board activities and decision making. Here the most central – and most problematic – question involves the extent to which boards have incorporated "traditional knowledge'" into their operations. Chapter 8 looks in detail at this issue, with particular focus on two important boards.

The final question turns the others on their heads. Where the questions outlined above seek to determine whether claims boards have fulfilled the promise of enhancing Indigenous influence over land and wildlife policies, some observers ask whether the boards have not actually visited significant harm on Indigenous peoples. This line of thinking sees co-management as entailing the co-optation of Indigenous peoples into Euro-Canadian governance processes as antithetical to their cultures and ways of life to an extent far outweighing the limited influence they can wield via claims boards. From this perspective, it may be true that Indigenous peoples exercise influence through the boards, but it is not *Indigenous* influence – bringing Indigenous worldviews, culture, and processes to bear. The concluding chapter considers this critique.

Rodon sets out his co-optation/integration and autonomization/empowerment models of co-management, outlined above, as fundamentally antithetical. Indeed, the central issue his book addresses is whether co-management promotes the integration of Canadian Indigenous peoples into state structures or enhances their control over their traditional lands and resources. The central question animating *Indigenous Empowerment through Co-management* is whether Indigenous peoples in the territorial North are able to exercise substantial influence over land and wildlife decisions and policies through claims-mandated co-management boards. It is not posed in either/or terms with respect to the extent of Indigenous integration into state structures and processes. Rather, the assumption is that the very essence of co-management is integration into governance institutions for the purpose of exerting influence. By definition, co-management is very different from self-government. Where the proper balance lies between integration and influence is, to be sure, a matter of vital import. However, it is a normative issue that Indigenous people, not social scientists, should decide.

chapter 2

Northern Governments, Land Claims, and Land Claims Boards

This chapter offers background and context for understanding Northern land claims boards as well as a fuller account of the boards than presented in Chapter 1. In this overview, the territorial governments, as signatories to the claims and as important players in the political environments in which claims boards operate, warrant attention. In turn, these governments cannot be understood without an appreciation of the societies they reflect. Accordingly, the chapter begins with a quick look at the three territories, their governments, and their politics. A brief account follows of the Indigenous organizations and governments representing claimant groups. One aspect of their overall prominence in the Northern political landscape is that these organizations nominate or appoint members of the claims boards. Next the chapter turns to comprehensive land claims, outlining their principal features. With this backdrop in place, the boards themselves are brought into focus, though this account necessarily proceeds at a fairly high level of generality.

A word on terminology. The federal government has long played a key role in territorial governance, including with respect to land claims boards. One department has taken the lead not only on claims and self-government negotiations but has also (in previous decades) provided a wide range of programs and services. Once known as DIAND – the Department of Indian Affairs and Northern Development – by the 1990s it had become Indian and Northern Affairs Canada (INAC). During the Harper Conservative administration the department's name was changed to Aboriginal Affairs and Northern Development Canada (AANDC). The Trudeau government again changed the name, this time to Indigenous and Northern Affairs Canada (INAC), but in 2017 it divided this into a revamped Indigenous and Northern Affairs Canada (charged with high-level claims, self-government, and related issues) and Indigenous Services Canada (engaged in service delivery). As part of a 2018 cabinet shuffle, responsibility for federal-territorial relations was assigned to a minister of intergovernmental and Northern affairs and internal trade was supported by an intergovernmental secretariat in the Privy Council Office. Throughout all this, however, the department's legal name under the *Department of Indian Affairs and Northern Development Act* has remained the Department of Indian Affairs and Northern Development. For this reason, as well as to avoid acronym overload and because many Northerners continue to refer to it as DIAND, this is the acronym I use throughout the book.

The Territories and Their Governments

The three Northern territories share a number of features: minuscule populations spread across vast areas, harsh climates, underdeveloped infrastructure, inferior constitutional status, and so on. Yet they also vary a good deal in terms of climate, geography, demographics, economic underpinnings – and politics.[1] Table 2.1 presents some basic statistical data on the size, demographics, and public finance of the three territories.

TABLE 2.1
Statistical data on the territories

		Nunavut	NWT	Yukon
Area (000 km²)		1,878	1,172	483
Population, 2018		38,650	44,445	40,483
Indigenous proportion of population*		84.1	50.1	23.3
Capital's proportion of population*		20.5	46.7	75.8
Community size:	500**	5	18	8
	501–1,000	5	8	5
	1,001–2,000	12	2	1
	2,001–4,000	2	4	1
	>4,000	1	1	1
Expenditure budget, 2018–19 ($B)		2.20	1.73	1.38
Proportion of budgetary revenue from federal transfers, 2018–19		89.4	80.3	82.8

* Data are for 2016 or 2017.
** Excludes places with fewer than twenty inhabitants.
Sources: Demographic data from the territorial bureaus of statistics websites; budgetary data from territorial budget documents.

A word on the territories' constitutional position and their jurisdictional scope is in order. Territories differ from provinces principally in lacking formal independence from the federal government, in their more constrained jurisdictional ambit, and in their exclusion from certain constitutional processes.[2] As exemplified in the *Nunavut Act*, the federal government has the power to create new territories or to dissolve or substantially change existing ones. It also retains the legal authority to overturn any legislation passed by a territorial legislature. The great bulk of territorial government financing comes in grants from Ottawa. All this suggests that the territories exist as little more than subservient outposts of the federal government. This would have been an accurate assessment three or four decades ago but it no longer matches the reality.

Ottawa may indeed enjoy the formal authority to make and unmake territories, but it is inconceivable that it would do so without strong local support (as was evident in the creation of Nunavut). So too, the federal government's nominal power of disallowance over territorial legislation is arguably as dead a constitutional letter as its nominal power – still ensconced in black and white as section 90 of the *Constitution Act, 1982* – to disallow provincial legislation. The territories' financial dependence on Ottawa is certainly real, though it is important to recognize that virtually all federal transfer payments to the territorial governments come in the form of unconditional grants, which they may spend as they see fit. If and when complete devolution finally takes place, the territories' financial dependence on Ottawa will decline dramatically.

Over the past three decades, the federal government has gradually devolved almost all "province-like" powers to the territories, so that the territorial governments now have jurisdiction over health, education, social services, internal transportation, renewable resources such as forestry and wildlife, civil law, local government, and other fields. A few minor areas have yet to be turned over to the territories, such as labour relations and the Crown prosecutorial function. The one major power the federal government retains is ownership (and in Nunavut control) of non-renewable natural resources. Unlike in southern Canada, where Crown land is provincially owned, the federal government owns Crown land in the territories. This is critically important since, beyond the lands owned by Indigenous organizations through their land claims, the territories consist almost entirely of Crown land. In effect, the territories are in the same position as were the Prairie provinces prior to 1930, when Ottawa handed over to them ownership and jurisdiction over land and natural resources. One implication is that environmental protection has been primarily a federal rather than a territorial responsibility, though this is changing significantly under the devolution agreements in Yukon and the NWT. As well, federal ownership of the land and the non-renewable resources under it means that the vast royalties generated by oil and gas production and by diamond mining, as well as lesser monies from other mining activities, accrue mostly to federal coffers even under the devolution agreements.

Devolution of authority over land and resources occurred in Yukon through a massive transfer of jurisdiction and resources to the territorial government in 2005. Cynics argue that Yukon was able to affect such a deal before the other territories not because its negotiators were more astute but because they were willing to accept an inferior package and because Yukon generally lacks the valuable resources found in the NWT and Nunavut (diamonds, oil and gas), control over which Ottawa is loath to give up.

Devolution sat atop the Government of the Northwest Territories' (GNWT) agenda for years, but demands from Indigenous organizations and governments for involvement in the process and for access to the financial benefits made for difficult negotiations. In 2014, a wide-ranging devolution agreement between Ottawa and the GNWT came into force, with provisions quite different from those of the earlier Yukon deal, primarily in terms of financial transfers to Indigenous organizations and governments. For the purposes of this book, an important aspect of both devolution deals has been a significant – but by no means total – shift in the final governmental decision-making power with respect to claims boards recommendations from Ottawa to the territories.

Prime Minister Paul Martin pledged in 2004 to see devolution in Nunavut completed by 2008,[3] but progress thus far has been glacial. A protocol setting out a negotiation framework was signed by Ottawa, the Government of Nunavut (GN), and Nunavut Tunngavik Incorporated (NTI, the Inuit land claims organization) in 2008, but a chief federal negotiator was not appointed until 2012. Having accomplished little if anything, he was replaced by a new chief federal negotiator late in 2014 who was, in turn, following a long fallow period for negotiations, replaced in summer 2016. The process grinds on.

While federal ownership of land and natural resources and Ottawa's primacy in collecting resource revenues stand out as obvious and important exceptions, the territories exercise almost all the day-to-day powers of the provinces. (This includes taxation: the territories can levy the full range of taxes available to the provinces, including personal and corporate income tax.) And Canadian provinces rank among the strongest subnational governments in the world. Otherwise put, while the territories fall somewhat short of the full range of powers held by the provinces, they have nonetheless developed into strong, autonomous jurisdictions, firmly in control of their own affairs.

A final general point. As is evident from Table 2.1, all three territories are extraordinarily dependent on Ottawa financially, each government receiving between 80 and 90 percent of its funding in federal transfers, most of which are unconditional. In addition, Ottawa directs substantial amounts of money to various social and economic programs essential to the North. Thus territorial societies rank among the most heavily subsidized on the planet. To an extent, the territories' heavy dependence on the federal government reflects their continuing lack of control of natural resource revenue, but it is also a function of the weakness of the private sector and the high costs endemic across the North, which affects everything from food to construction.

Nunavut

Nunavut, the realization of the long-held dream of the Eastern Arctic Inuit, came into existence in 1999, following Parliament's passage of the *Nunavut Act* in 1993. The largest jurisdiction in Canada – roughly the size of Western Europe – and lying entirely north and east of the tree line, it endures the longest and harshest winters and has the least developed infrastructure of the three territories. None of its twenty-five communities is connected by road to much beyond the local airstrip, nor do any of them have docks or wharves able to accommodate even moderate-sized ships. Pangnirtung has the best facilities, a small-craft harbour (a substantial facility is in the planning stage for Iqaluit). The total population is roughly 39,000, with some 7,500 living in the capital, Iqaluit; only a handful of communities has as many as 1,500 residents. Roughly 84 percent of the population is Inuit. The non-Inuit population is concentrated in the larger centres, so that many communities are more than 95 percent Inuit. A related noteworthy demographic fact about Nunavut is its age profile: according to Statistics Canada data for 2018, whereas the median age of all Canadians was 40.8, with 16.1 percent of the population under 15, the median age in Nunavut was 26.1 and nearly a third of the population (31.8 percent) was under 15. By contrast, a sixth of Canadians (17.2 percent) were 65 or older compared with fewer than 1 in 25 Nunavummiut (3.9 percent), the people of Nunavut, having reached 65.[4] The implications for public policy priorities are as profound and difficult as they are obvious.

Tensions regularly surface among the three administrative regions of Nunavut, but they largely reflect perceptions of political inequities rather than cultural differences. Regional dialects exist, most notably Inuinnaqtun in the Kitikmeot region, written in Roman orthography rather than syllabics, but all Inuit in Nunavut are well able to comprehend one another's Inuktitut.

Economically, Nunavut remains heavily dependent on government, both for employment and for supporting large numbers of people through social assistance. Non-renewable natural resources hold enormous potential but the logistical difficulties in extracting them and getting them to market are formidable. To cite but one example of Nunavut's checkered experience of resource extraction, the territory's first diamond mine came on stream in 2006 but within a few years had been abandoned as uneconomic. The service sector – transportation, construction, tourism, and so on – is important, but the potential for growth is limited. The traditional economy – hunting, fishing, and trapping – contributes little by way of monetary infusion but remains of considerable importance for many households and is of great cultural significance.

Government in Nunavut largely follows the model inherited from the NWT, which exhibits certain Indigenous features but ultimately is very much a standard Euro-Canadian government. The twenty-two-member Legislative Assembly conforms to the Westminster model of cabinet-parliamentary relations, with the government led by a premier and cabinet. It departs from the political arrangements familiar elsewhere in Canada, save in the NWT, by virtue of its "consensus government" approach, reflecting the absence of political parties. The premier and the cabinet, chosen by secret ballot of all members of the Legislative Assembly (MLAs), operate as something akin to a permanent minority government. All told, however, as is the case in the NWT, despite the distinctive institutional arrangements characterizing the legislature, which appear congruent with traditional Northern Indigenous culture, the Nunavut Legislative Assembly is best understood as a modification of the Westminster system rather than as a fundamental departure from it.[5] MLAs and ministers are overwhelmingly Inuit.

The administrative arm of the Government of Nunavut is even more conventional and decidedly less Inuit. Hierarchical departments, headed by deputy ministers and assistant deputy ministers, closely resemble those in provincial governments in both structure and process. The GN is committed to establishing Inuktitut as the working language of government and in imbuing both policy and process with Inuit Qaujimajatuqangit (IQ – roughly, "that which has been long known by Inuit": Inuit values and ways of behaving, sometimes rendered as "Inuit social values"), but opinion is divided on how realistic these goals may be. The fact that most of the senior managers in the GN and almost all of the technical specialists are non-Inuit, few of whom speak Inuktitut, stands as a major impediment. Front-line government services, forms, and other documents are generally available in Inuktitut, but internal government communications are mostly conducted in English. Perhaps the most distinctive feature of the GN is the degree to which it is "decentralized," not only in the sense of maintaining departmental field offices in all but the smallest communities but also in having dispersed to small communities throughout the territory organizational units that, in other governments, would be located in the capital. On this initiative as well, opinion as to its success is mixed.[6]

Yukon

On several dimensions, the contrast between Yukon and Nunavut is substantial. Yukon's climate is generally more moderate, evidenced by the thick forests that cover all but its northernmost reaches. Infrastructure is substantially more developed, as exemplified by the good all-weather highway system connecting every community but one (Old Crow, in the far north). Demographically, Yukon is predominantly non-Indigenous; citizens (as they are called) of First Nations constitute only about a quarter of the population and are principally found in the small communities outside the capital, Whitehorse. Aside from Whitehorse and Dawson City, no community in the territory has more than a thousand residents, and most have fewer than five hundred (see Table 2.1). Three out of four Yukoners live in Whitehorse, which dominates the territory economically and politically far more than do the capitals of the other territories. Mining, once the mainstay of the economy, is making something of a comeback but remains of lesser importance than public-sector activity and the service sector, most notably tourism.

Fourteen First Nations, most numbering only a few hundred, inhabit Yukon, exhibiting, among other things, significant cultural and linguistic differences. In 1993, an umbrella final agreement was reached covering the entire territory. The Yukon *Umbrella Final Agreement* (*UFA*), however, is not per se a finalized land claim; rather, it provides a framework within which individual First Nations can settle their claims and realize their self-government aspirations. Both the economic resources and the political sophistication of the First Nations vary a good deal.

Politically, Yukon is the closest territorial analogue of a province. Elections and legislative politics are conducted on the basis of a well-developed party system, featuring familiar options: the Liberal Party, the New Democratic Party, and the Yukon Party (effectively the local Conservative Party). With numerically small ridings, the first-past-the-post electoral system can transform minor shifts in public opinion into wild swings in the composition of the nineteen-member House; in recent years, all three political parties have held power.[7] With the Yukon Party notably less sympathetic to First Nations aspirations and less accommodating of their political demands than the NDP or the Liberals, transitions from one party to another are of substantial consequence to Indigenous peoples in Yukon.

Save accommodations necessitated by the scale of operations, the bureaucratic apparatus of government closely follows the standard provincial model. At the same time, the emergence of self-government regimes since finalization of the *UFA* is reshaping governance in important ways, though First Nations governments have generally been measured in taking up the jurisdictional responsibilities currently exercised by the territorial government to which they are entitled under the *UFA*. Given Yukon's demographic makeup, both the elected members of the Legislative Assembly (and, by extension, the cabinet) and the territorial bureaucracy are largely non-Indigenous.

The Northwest Territories

The NWT occupies the middle ground, literally and figuratively, between Yukon and Nunavut. Like the other territories it swings between periods of heady economic growth fuelled by a diamond boom, extensive oil and gas development, and anticipation of a Mackenzie Valley pipeline, and periods of economic doldrums characterized by slowdowns in the oil and gas sectors and in diamond mining and by a stagnant or declining population. A third of its thirty-three communities, all small and predominantly Indigenous, are not accessible by all-weather road; some have ice road access in the winter. In overall terms, the territorial population is evenly split between Indigenous and non-Indigenous residents. This rendering, however, masks deep cultural and political divisions across Indigenous groups, evidenced by the number of settled land claims and ongoing negotiation processes. The Inuvialuit of the Mackenzie Delta and the Arctic islands are linguistically and culturally close to the Inuit of Nunavut and Alaska but not to the Dene (the First Nations) of the NWT. The Dene are split into several tribal groupings, marked by linguistic differences and on occasion by sharp political antagonisms. In some regions, the substantial Métis population is closely integrated politically with the Dene, but elsewhere distance and discord mark Dene-Métis relations.

The NWT is easily the most politically complex territory. Various First Nations have adopted very different postures towards land claims, self-government, and relations with the federal and territorial governments. Only two self-government agreements have been finalized, in the Tlicho region and in the small community of Deline; other self-government proposals are at various stages of negotiation. Despite long-standing efforts, no constitutional arrangement has been reached for territory-wide governance that would accommodate both the Indigenous and non-Indigenous communities, though it is evident that what amounts to a federal system is emerging.[8] All this is overlaid with tensions between Yellowknife and the smaller communities, between Dene and Métis, and between those with differing perspectives on resource development projects. And while settled land claims cover more than half the NWT, in the "unsettled" areas, negotiations on claims and self-government aspirations have been long underway, but resolution is nowhere in sight.

As in Nunavut, the legislature operates without political parties as a "consensus government." Most MLAs are Indigenous and all premiers since 1991 have been Indigenous. Positions in the upper echelons of the bureaucracy are predominantly held by non-Indigenous people and, despite the NWT's having six official Indigenous languages (in addition to English and French), Indigenous language government services are very limited, likely reflecting the rapidly declining numbers of Indigenous people fluent in their own languages.

Northern Indigenous Governments and Organizations

The Indigenous organizations involved with the Northern claims boards are not mere interest groups. They are, in a very real sense, governments controlling great swaths of land and considerable financial resources, providing important programs and services to their members – indeed, defining who is and who is not a member – and interacting with territorial and federal governments on a government-to-government basis. Where they have been finalized, the land claims assign these organizations specific rights and responsibilities for claims implementation. The monies that form part of the claims settlements are paid to them, and they are the legal title holders to the lands and mineral rights returned to claim beneficiaries.

Organizational arrangements vary a good deal, though community- and regional-level representation is an important element in each. The Inuvialuit Regional Corporation (IRC), for example, is run by a chair/chief executive officer, chosen by the chairs of the six Inuvialuit community corporations who, in turn, are elected by the beneficiaries in their communities. Nunavut Tunngavik Incorporated, by far the largest land claim organization, with close to one hundred staff, has an eight-member board of directors. The president and the vice-president are elected by universal vote of all claim beneficiaries, with the balance of the board composed of the elected presidents and vice-presidents of the three regional Inuit associations. The Council of Yukon First Nations (CYFN) is essentially a federation of eleven of the fourteen Yukon First Nations (with the Gwich'in of the NWT represented through one of the member

First Nations). With individual claims and self-government agreements defined along regional lines, CYFN lacks the same level of authority to act on claims and other issues as other organizations in the territories, though the very small populations of some Yukon First Nations render them heavily dependent on it. The grand chief is elected by the CYFN General Assembly, composed of the member First Nations, and works with the Leadership – an executive committee composed of the vice-chief, the chiefs of all member First Nations, and a representative of the Elders' Council.

The southern NWT is without settled land claims, but while the Indigenous organizations there lack the powers and resources available to those with finalized claims, they are nonetheless important players in the political and economic life of the territories. That they are seen by federal and territorial governments as more than interest groups is suggested by Ottawa's appointment, in the late 1990s, of an "emissary" to the Dehcho First Nations (DFN) of the southwest NWT in an effort to get treaty/land claim negotiations on track. In addition to the DFN, the Akaitcho Treaty 8 Dene and the Northwest Territory Métis Nation represent Indigenous peoples in the areas of the NWT without settled claims.[9]

These Indigenous organizations and governments are involved in far more than claims implementation (which includes but is not limited to dealings with claims boards). They mount cultural and educational ventures, provide services such as hunter and trapper support programs, and interact with other governments on all manner of issues. Some, such as the IRC, have become aggressive and sophisticated business operators, while others maintain an arm's-length relationship with the "birthright corporations" (airlines, construction companies, real estate enterprises, and the like) they own.

Northern Comprehensive Land Claims

In 1921, with the signing of Treaty 11 in the Northwest Territories, centuries of treaty making between the original inhabitants of this land and the Canadian state and its British forbears ceased. This despite the fact that great tracts of Canada, including most of the territorial North, had never been covered by treaties or other agreements with the Canadian or British authorities. In the mid-1970s, following the landmark *Calder* decision from the Supreme Court of Canada, the federal government effectively resumed treaty making by opening negotiations on a series of far-reaching "land claims."[10] The first "comprehensive land claim," the *James Bay and Northern Quebec Agreement* (*JBNQA*) with the Inuit and Cree of Northern Quebec, was signed in 1975. Lacking the urgency that propelled the *JBNQA*, the pressing need for a clear legal footing to allow the massive James Bay Hydro project to proceed, subsequent negotiations on other claims stretched out over much longer spans of time.

Federal policy distinguishes "comprehensive land claims" from "specific claims." The latter are essentially allegations by First Nations that the Crown has failed to live up to the commitments made when treaties were signed. They often centre on questions of land ownership and compensation for land or other First Nations resources; governance issues are not usually involved in a significant way. By contrast, comprehensive land claims relate to territory never subject to treaty or situations in which existing treaties are so fundamentally flawed, principally by virtue of federal government failure to implement key treaty provisions, that new agreements are warranted.

The issues are complex, the stakes are high in terms of power and resources, and the positions of the Indigenous organizations and the federal government are often diametrically opposed. Accordingly, claim negotiations are typically protracted affairs; some have extended over two decades.[11]

The Government of Canada explicitly terms comprehensive land claims as "modern treaties," and it is critical to understand the implications of treaty status. Treaties are not simply real estate deals or routine contractual arrangements. They are solemn undertakings – not for nothing do Indigenous people use the word "sacred" when referring to their treaties – between sovereign entities setting out, among other things, political and governmental relationships between these entities. In line with the tenets of treaty federalism, section 35 of the *Constitution Act, 1982,* recognizes comprehensive land claims as embodying "treaty rights" and affirms their constitutionally protected status.

Table 2.2 lists the comprehensive land claims that have been finalized in the territorial North. As the accompanying map illustrates, these agreements cover most of Yukon, all of Nunavut, as well as northern and central NWT. Negotiations have been under way for agreements in the remainder of the NWT but

TABLE 2.2

Finalized comprehensive land claims agreements in the territorial North

Finalized land claim	Date	Responsible Indigenous organization
Inuvialuit Final Agreement	1984	Inuvialuit Regional Corporation
Gwich'in Comprehensive Land Claim	1992	Gwich'in Tribal Council
Sahtu Dene and Métis Comprehensive Land Claim	1993	Sahtu Secretariat Incorporated
Nunavut Land Claims Agreement	1993	Nunavut Tunngavik Incorporated
Yukon Umbrella Final Agreement	1994	Council of Yukon First Nations
Tlicho Land Claims and Self-Government Agreement	2005	Tlicho Government

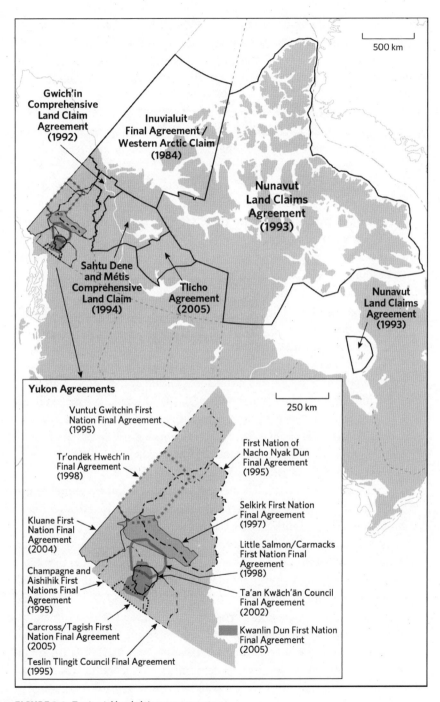

FIGURE 2.1 Territorial land claims agreements

remain far from completion. By the end of 2006, eleven Yukon First Nations had finalized claims and self-government agreements under the *UFA*. In the intervening years none of the remaining First Nations have settled; some have abandoned claims negotiations and are pursuing other means of attaining their political goals.

Each settled claim has unique provisions, but certain features are found in all claims. In return for relinquishing Indigenous title to their traditional lands (but not other Aboriginal rights) to the Crown, claimant groups receive:

1 *Cash compensation:* Ottawa pays substantial amounts of money over a specific period ($1.14 billion over fourteen years in the case of the Nunavut claim) for the land, including for past usage. These monies are paid to the organization representing the claim beneficiaries and invested in trust funds and economic development projects. The interest generated is used to fund social, cultural, and political activities.

2 *Title to land:* Ownership of specific parcels of land is formally vested in the Indigenous organization (again, to be held in common for all beneficiaries). Total land quantum ranges from about 15 percent to nearly 30 percent of the total "settlement area." A proportion of this land includes subsurface rights; this is significant since land ownership in Canada does not normally include rights to the subsurface. Specific lands are selected by the claimant group in negotiations with government, on the basis of economic potential, cultural and spiritual importance, environmental sensitivity, and related factors.[12]

3 *Access and harvesting rights:* The rights of claim "beneficiaries" to travel on and to hunt and fish throughout their traditional lands is affirmed, subject to conservation measures, safety issues, and the like.

4 *Governance commitments:* For the first two decades of the comprehensive land claims process, Ottawa refused to negotiate land claims and self-government concurrently despite claimant groups' repeated insistence that these were two sides of the same coin. The Chrétien government reversed this policy so that the *Tlicho Agreement*, which was finalized after the policy changed, incorporates both standard land claims provisions and self-government arrangements. Prior to this, settled claims typically included only federal commitments to negotiate wide-ranging self-government regimes and general frameworks for the negotiations. In the case of Nunavut, where the Inuit were not pursuing self-government, Article 4 of the claim, "Nunavut Political Development," committed the federal government to establish a Nunavut territory, the specifics of which were to be contained in a separate political accord. The entire article is less than a page long.[13]

5   *Co-management boards:* Each settled claim provides for the establishment of a suite of tripartite boards; specifics vary a good deal across claims.

In addition, each claim includes a host of miscellaneous provisions and benefits, ranging from royalty arrangements to preferential hiring in government to guaranteed participation in the creation and management of national parks.

The claim documents themselves are substantial tomes, some running to hundreds of sections and subsections, many of which are couched in all but impenetrably convoluted legalese. In turn these are supplemented with massive "implementation contracts" or "implementation agreements/plans" setting out in extensive detail which party to the claim (federal government, territorial government, Indigenous government/organization) is responsible for implementing specific provisions of the claim, timelines for implementation, funding arrangements, and related issues. In some instances, tripartite implementation panels or committees, comprised of senior representatives of the three parties, meet regularly to review the progress of implementation, resolve disagreements, and work on developing the next implementation contract. Some panels publish annual reports, the tone and substance of which can range from anodyne to redolent of bitter conflict. Some claims make provision for large-scale reviews of the implementation status of the claims for their first five or ten years. In some instances, such as the Gwich'in claim, these reviews have been conducted by representatives of the parties to the claim in essentially the same fashion as the annual reviews; in other cases, Nunavut being an example, independent consultants were engaged to do the work. These reviews, which are published, can be blunt about failures in claim implementation.

Implementation contracts typically have a ten-year term; their renegotiation can prove highly problematic as this is an opportunity for the parties to seek to correct what they regard as oversights or errors in the initial contracts or to force those whom they believe to have reneged on important commitments to live up to their responsibilities. The most notable instance of such conflict has been in Nunavut, where the initial implementation contract expired in July 2003 and negotiations on a new contract collapsed. No less a personage than Justice Thomas Berger was called in to serve as a conciliator to get the deadlocked negotiations back on track. Much of his interim report focused on funding and other support for claims boards.[14] His efforts failed to resolve the impasse, and in 2006 NTI launched a $1 billion lawsuit against the federal government for failing to live up to its implementation obligations. That NTI had a strong case was confirmed in early 2015 when Ottawa and NTI agreed to a $255 million out-of-court settlement, which included substantial funding increases for claims boards.[15]

The settled land claims across the territorial North are sweeping in their scale and implications. It is scarcely possible to overstate how important they are to governance processes and to many aspects of Indigenous peoples' lives. However, while many laud the progress that the claims represent, significant currents of Indigenous discontent with the claims are also evident. Important elements within the Indigenous leadership and at the community level have been unwilling to accept the compromises entailed in signing on to a land claim agreement. Some proposed claims settlements, such as the Dene-Métis agreement-in-principle of the late 1980s in the NWT, fell apart completely, and others were either temporarily or permanently defeated in authorizing referenda. As well, Indigenous governments and organizations with claims in place continuously voice serious criticism of what they see as Ottawa's failure to fully and properly implement the claims. Indeed, a prominent Indigenous organization has emerged, devoted to pressuring the federal government on implementation issues: the Land Claims Agreements Coalition, which includes most Indigenous territorial organizations with settled claims. The extent and depth of discontent with the claims is all but impossible to gauge.

Northern Claims Boards

Origins

Although specifics vary from one claim to the next, the boards' common origin lies in political compromise. Indigenous negotiators wished to maximize Indigenous control over as many facets of land use, environmental protection, and wildlife management as possible and wanted to enshrine whatever was achieved in the text of the claims themselves. The federal government was adamant that the public interest required public government capacity to set and implement policies for public lands and for certain aspects of Indigenous-owned lands. Thus emerged the essential political compromise that saw the creation of public government bodies with strong Indigenous representation.

"When we were negotiating the land claim agreement," observed former Nunavut premier Paul Okalik, who was on the Inuit negotiating team, "we were trying to put as many constraints as possible on ministerial authority."[16] Another Inuit leader commented: "Our main goal in the [land claim] negotiations on natural resources has been to obtain as much control as possible over what happens to the land, fresh water, ocean and animals in Nunavut. We've been using our claim to conserve and protect all of the land in Nunavut, whether we end up owning it or not."[17] One of the key First Nations negotiators on the Yukon claim offered a similar recollection: "The whole essence of the claim was to decentralize authority from Ottawa to the territory; the boards were an important part of that." When asked about the origin of the NWT co-management boards, Bob Overvold, one of the lead negotiators on the Dene-Métis claim in the 1980s, recalled:

> The [impetus for] co-management boards didn't come from the Dene-Métis. The feds had no self-government policy and weren't willing to negotiate self-government in the claim. We wanted as much control over lands, resources, and wildlife as possible but we were hitting a brick wall and eventually gave in and accepted the creation of the co-management boards to maximize the influence we'd have.[18]

A First Nations leader involved in one of the regional NWT claims also mentioned the need to compromise in order to reach a deal: "we didn't get as much in the claim as we wanted, but I'm a realist; I didn't want another 25 years before things were finalized ... you settle for the best you can settle for."

This compromise reflected Ottawa's initial policy requiring that land claims and self-government be negotiated and settled separately. One long-time official who worked on claims on behalf of Indigenous organizations in the (present-day) NWT argued that "the boards were a way of getting around the fact that the federal government's claims policy excluded self-government. Under a sensible federal policy, boards would have been negotiated under self-government rather than as part of claims ... If, at the beginning, the federal government had had a vision and an acceptance of Indigenous rights and Indigenous self-government, we wouldn't have seen anything like the boards we have now."

In Nunavut, compromise of a different sort prevailed. Because the Inuit were pursuing a public government model, Ottawa's concerns about losing control to self-government regimes did not arise. Nonetheless, the boards represented a compromise for the Inuit, rooted in their uncertainty about the prospects of finalizing their land claim. Several interviewees, who served on both sides of the table during the negotiations, commented that the boards represented for Inuit a hedge or "contingency plan" against the possibility that they would ultimately fail to obtain a Nunavut territory and government. Had Ottawa committed early on to creating Nunavut, which would (eventually) control land and resources, the need for the boards would have been largely obviated. Inuit interest in creating boards also reflected a desire for defences against potential resource mega-projects, which were all the rage during the early stages of the negotiations.

Although Inuit negotiators understood that the federal government's willingness to cede control over natural resources was limited, they were unwilling to settle for unsatisfactory co-management arrangements. "We are not prepared to settle for just advisory bodies, as has been the case in other land-claim settlements," said Chief Negotiator Bob Kadlun, "we are already up to our ears in advisory bodies."[19]

A federal official who spent much of the 1980s working on land claims commented that Ottawa's approach varied a good deal from claim to claim, and hence the nature of the claims boards also varies substantially: "[There was] no overall basic philosophy across the North; it was more a question of what was pragmatic and possible in a given claim. In terms of resource management, there was no fundamental underlying principle guiding how boards were established, though having said that, it was clear that the central idea was opening opportunities for Indigenous people's input and involvement in deciding resource management questions."

Thus not only do boards with similar functions differ substantially across the various Northern claims in terms of structure and mandate, the suites of co-management boards established by the claims vary widely in their fundamental organization. Under the Inuvialuit claim, for example, separate boards exist for fish (the Fisheries Joint Management Committee) and game (the wildlife management advisory councils),[20] whereas in Nunavut one board – the Nunavut Wildlife Management Board – has jurisdiction over both. Yukon nominally follows the Nunavut model, but management issues relating to salmon (by far the most important aquatic species in Yukon) are dealt with by the Yukon Salmon Sub-Committee, technically a subcommittee of the Yukon Fish and Wildlife Management Board but in reality a largely separate entity. Land use planning boards exist under the Nunavut, Gwich'in, and Sahtu claims but are absent in the Inuvialuit and Tlicho claims. In Yukon, the Land Use Planning Council oversees and coordinates temporary regional land use planning commissions. All Northern claims provide for boards to regulate water use, but under the Gwich'in, Sahtu, and Tlicho agreements these boards also consider and issue land use permits, while in Nunavut, Yukon, and the Inuvialuit region, land use permits are issued by DIAND or by local authorities.

Not everyone in the federal government bought into the principle of substantially enhancing Indigenous participation in resource management processes, thereby reducing federal control. As is no less true today than when the claims were being negotiated, "Ottawa" is hardly an undifferentiated monolith, with all component parts agreed on either ends or means. One of the negotiators for the Inuit on the Nunavut claim has maintained that, while the federal claims negotiators had accepted the Inuit proposal for a wildlife management board "with teeth," progress on this front was halted when "a couple of the federal departments ... just dug in their heels and refused." These departments, he contended, were unwilling to countenance the "sharing of control" that must lie at the heart of a successful land-claims process.[21]

Legal Foundations

The formal legal bases on which claims boards operate vary a great deal, even within a single claim. In Nunavut, for example, the structure, mandate, and other essential provisions of the Nunavut Wildlife Management Board are detailed in the text of the *Nunavut Land Claims Agreement*, leaving little need for enabling legislation.[22] Other Nunavut boards for some time owed their existence to a default position in the claim (Article 10.1.1), which required creation of several "institutions of public government" (commonly known as IPGs) within two years of the claim's ratification, even if the enabling legislation had not been passed by Parliament. As it turned out, it was nearly a decade following the claim's ratification in 1993 before Parliament passed the legislation setting the Nunavut Water Board and the Nunavut Surface Rights Tribunal on an explicit legal footing. In the interim, considerable friction was evident between the Nunavut Water Board and the federal government, principally over what Ottawa saw as the board's unacceptably wide interpretation of its mandate and the board's insistence, supported by NTI and the GN, that the claim legitimized its position that its decisions did not, as Ottawa insisted, require ministerial approval.

It took even longer, and with more false starts, before the *Nunavut Planning and Project Assessment Act* (*NuPPAA*) provided legislative footing for the Nunavut Planning Commission (NPC) and the Nunavut Impact Review Board (NIRB). The absence of legislation for these boards had been less problematic than in other instances, in part because the twenty-page article in the claim that established NIRB set out its roles and procedures to a substantial degree and in part because NIRB did not adopt the confrontational, expansionist stance vis-à-vis the federal government that characterized the Water Board. Passed by Parliament in 2013 and proclaimed in force in 2015, *NuPPAA* not only confirmed and clarified the NPC's and NIRB's roles and processes, it also made significant changes to the overall regulatory regime, in line with the Conservative government's policy of "streamlining" environmental regulation.

In the NWT, some boards only came into being with passage of federal legislation several years after the Gwich'in and Sahtu claims were finalized. The Gwich'in had resorted to legal action to prod the process along, citing a provision in their claim committing Ottawa to legislate the boards into being within two years of passage of legislation ratifying the claim – that is, by December 1994. It was only in 1998 that the Mackenzie Valley Land and Water Board, along with two regional boards, the Gwich'in Land and Water Board and the Sahtu Land and Water Board,[23] and the Mackenzie Valley Environmental Impact Review Board were created by the *Mackenzie Valley Resource Management Act* (*MVRMA*), along with the Gwich'in and Sahtu land use planning boards.[24]

No specific legislation supplements the rather brief provisions in the Inuvialuit claim for the various *IFA* boards. The *IFA* regulatory boards must abide by the processes and requirements of various federal and territorial statutes, but this is qualitatively different from the extensive legal frameworks set out in federal acts specifically addressed to boards such as the Nunavut Water Board and MVEIRB. Until the 2014 devolution package, the Northwest Territories Water Board operated under the federal *Northwest Territories Water Act*, with jurisdiction only over that part of the Inuvialuit Settlement Region (until passage of the *MVRMA*, its remit had been the entire NWT). Since devolution, the board, renamed the Inuvialuit Water Board, operates under the territorial *Waters Act*. It is mentioned in this section as part of the regulatory regime, but – unlike all the other boards discussed – it does not derive from a settled land claim.

All three Yukon regulatory claims boards – the Yukon Environmental and Socio-economic Assessment Board, the Yukon Water Board, and the Yukon Surface Rights Board – are established and governed by their own acts.

Federal and territorial statutes empowering claims boards take two forms. The first, the most prominent examples of which are the *MVRMA* and the *Yukon Environmental and Socio-economic Assessment Act*, creates boards that did not previously exist. The second fleshes out the legal framework for boards already in existence. This second type of legislation goes into far more detail than the provisions of the claim under which the boards operated prior to the legislation, though it cannot contravene or override claims. By way of illustration, the four and a half pages outlining the functions of the Nunavut Surface Rights Tribunal in the Nunavut claim are expanded fourfold in the *Nunavut Waters and Nunavut Surface Rights Tribunal Act*.

Legislation establishing or confirming boards pertains in almost all instances to those with regulatory or arbitration functions. Of the wildlife management boards, only the Nunavut Wildlife Management Board has anything like a legislative foundation (in the Nunavut *Wildlife Act*), and even in that case the legislation essentially repeats the language in the claim. The wildlife boards operate on the basis of the provisions set out in the claims.

That certain claims boards are based on acts of Parliament raises the question as to whether their continued existence, if not precarious, is nonetheless subject to future federal legislation that might fundamentally alter them or abolish them altogether. A partial answer is that, given the constitutionally protected status of the claims, should Ottawa abolish a board it would be required to establish a replacement board fulfilling the same functions. Until recently it was widely believed that while the federal government had the technical power to make substantial changes to the powers, structures, and operations of claims boards, it would do so only with the agreement of the other parties to the claims, and in particular the Indigenous claimant groups.

This view was fundamentally challenged by federal legislation introduced during the later part of the Harper Conservative government's final mandate. The 2014 federal *Northwest Territories Devolution Act* (Bill C-15) made a number of significant changes to the *MVRMA* and would have made fundamental changes to the environmental regulatory regime had certain provisions been implemented. The most notable change, though by no means the only one of moment, was to have been the abolition of the three regional land and water boards, whose functions were to be folded into a massively revamped Mackenzie Valley Land and Water Board. The GNWT acquiesced in these changes, it was widely believed, as Ottawa's price for going ahead with devolution. Indigenous governments and organizations, however, vehemently objected to altering the boards, arguing that doing so would constitute a fundamental abrogation of the spirit and intent of the settled claims, noting that the objectionable *MVRMA* amendments had nothing to do with devolution. They challenged the proposed changes to the boards in court and won a legal battle halting the changes shortly before they were to come into force. This landmark episode is recounted in some detail in Chapter 6.

In Yukon, the federal government, again over the vociferous objections of First Nations, in 2015 proposed legislation, Bill S-6, which would have substantially affected the powers and operations of the Yukon Environmental and Socio-economic Assessment Board. This legislation was also challenged in court. Following the October 2015 federal election, the Liberal government abandoned the proposed changes in both the NWT and Yukon that had raised Indigenous hackles. The politics around Bill S-6 are examined in Chapter 7.

Mandates and Jurisdiction
All boards fall clearly into one of the four principal categories of boards identified in Chapter 1: wildlife management, land use planning, environmental regulation, and arbitration. None spans the boundaries of two groupings. A

strict reading of the claims could lead to the conclusion that the arbitration boards have neither the co-management ethos nor the governance responsibilities of the other claims boards and thus are not properly included with them. These bodies have had little or nothing to do, though some are influential despite a lack of overt activity[25] and, accordingly, receive little attention in this book, so that this is not an issue requiring resolution here.

Not surprisingly, given the varying circumstances of their creation, significant variations exist in board mandates. Northern claims boards deal primarily with wildlife, land, and environmental issues. Few boards' mandates extend more than marginally into social and cultural policy such as education, health, and social welfare. Significant exceptions do occur, such as the MVEIRB, whose legislation stipulates that "impact on the environment" is to include "any effect on the social and cultural environment," with the result that in conducting environmental assessments it "has the authority to consider socioeconomic impacts and impacts on the cultural well-being of the residents and communities in the Mackenzie Valley."[26] Similarly, as its name proclaims, the Yukon Environmental and Socio-economic Assessment Board also has a broad remit to examine social and economic issues. Other claims boards can also become at least indirectly involved with socioeconomic and cultural issues, but according to an "Environmental Audit" of the NWT, which focused on the work of the regulatory boards such as the MVEIRB, by and large this has not happened. "One of the guiding principles of the MVRMA," the report notes, "is that it have regard to the 'social, cultural and economic well-being of residents and communities in the Mackenzie Valley' (s. 115). Despite this requirement, the framework for MVRMA regulatory instruments focuses almost exclusively on biophysical impacts."[27]

Other examples of variations in board mandates would include the extensive monitoring carried out by the Nunavut Impact Review Board, which is unmatched in other environmental regulatory boards (though under the 2014 changes to the *MVRMA*, the MVEIRB will likely acquire a monitoring function), and the contrast between the land and water boards of the Mackenzie Valley and the water boards of Nunavut, Yukon, and the Inuvialuit region, which deal only with water.

Table 2.3 lists all the claims-based co-management boards across the three territories, classifies them according to function, and indicates the size of their membership. The *IFA* wildlife management boards are fundamentally different – in conception, if not necessarily in operation – from the other claims boards. Members of all other co-management boards in the territories are required to act independently of the parties that nominated them, reaching decisions on their own best judgment, "in the public interest." By contrast, the members of certain *IFA* boards are explicitly appointed as representatives of their parties and are understood to speak on their behalf. As discussed in other chapters, this is less of a hard and fast distinction than this formalistic rendering might suggest. Nonetheless, it is an important and unique feature of the *IFA*.

TABLE 2.3
Territorial land claims boards

	Board	Type	Members
Nunavut	Nunavut Planning Commission	LUP	5*
	Nunavut Impact Review Board	ENV	9
	Nunavut Water Board	ENV	9
	Nunavut Wildlife Management Board	WILD	9
	Nunavut Surface Rights Tribunal	ARB	5
NWT	Sahtu Land Use Planning Board	LUP	5
	Gwich'in Land Use Planning Board	LUP	5
	Mackenzie Valley Environmental Impact Review Board	ENV	9
	Environmental Impact Screening Committee	ENV	7
	Environmental Impact Review Board	ENV	6
	Mackenzie Valley Land and Water Board	ENV	5
	Sahtu Land and Water Board	ENV	5
	Gwich'in Land and Water Board	ENV	5
	Wek'èezhìi Land and Water Board	ENV	5
	Sahtu Renewable Resources Board	WILD	6
	Gwich'in Renewable Resources Board	WILD	6
	Wek'èezhìi Renewable Resources Board	WILD	9
	Wildlife Management Advisory Council (NWT)	WILD	7
	Wildlife Management Advisory Council (NS)	WILD	5**
	Fisheries Joint Management Committee	WILD	5
	Inuvialuit Arbitration Board	ARB	11
	Gwich'in Arbitration Panel	ARB	8
	Sahtu Arbitration Panel	ARB	8
	NWT Surface Rights Board	ARB	5***
Yukon	Yukon Land Use Planning Council	LUP	3
	Yukon Environment and Socio-economic Assessment Board	ENV	7
	Yukon Water Board	ENV	9
	Yukon Fish and Wildlife Management Board	WILD	12
	Yukon Salmon Sub-committee	WILD	10
	Yukon Surface Rights Board	ARB	5

* Article 11.4.5 of the *Nunavut Land Claims Agreement* specifies that membership shall be at least five but does not specify an upper limit.

** Article 12 (47–48) of the *Inuvialuit Final Agreement* specifies that membership shall be at least five but does not specify an upper limit.

*** Up to nine board members may be appointed.

Structure and Membership

Northern claims boards exhibit a dizzying array of structural designs and membership configurations. Accordingly, no attempt is made in this section to be comprehensive. Rather, the intent is to convey some of the boards' basic organizational features and the nature of their membership, along with a sense of the myriad variations to the main models.

Most boards have seven to nine members, though some have as few as four or five; the Yukon Dispute Resolution Board has but three. The unique structure of the Mackenzie Valley Land and Water Board, which includes all members of the three regional land and water boards, makes for twenty members; no other Northern claims board is nearly so large. The larger boards commonly employ panels of three or five members for specific undertakings. For a few boards, such as the Nunavut Planning Commission and the Wildlife Management Advisory Council (North Slope), minimum membership is specified – usually five – but no upper limit is set. These boards typically operate with the minimum number of members.

More important than size is composition. Almost all boards follow one of two models. The vast majority have half their members nominated by Indigenous organizations and half by government. For a few others, each of the parties to the claim nominates one-third of the members; the Yukon Land Use Planning Council is an example. (These membership proportions are exclusive of the chair; the various procedures for selecting a chair are discussed below.) The Nunavut Surface Rights Tribunal and the NWT Surface Rights Board are outliers in that they are not formally structured along co-management lines. Neither the relevant claims nor the enabling legislation entitle any Indigenous organization or government to nominate members to these boards, although both include Indigenous members. In both cases, the legislation does stipulate residency requirements; for example, the NWT board members are to be resident in each of the four land claim areas. As well, "considerable knowledge ... [of] traditional Aboriginal knowledge" is a criterion for appointment.[28] Legislation establishing the Yukon Surface Rights Board follows more conventional co-management procedures, requiring half the members to be CYFN nominees.

Table 2.4 contains data on membership of all territorial claims-based co-management boards, showing numbers of total members, Indigenous and non-Indigenous members, as well as vacancies, as of February 2018. Significantly, eighteen of twenty-nine boards had more Indigenous than non-Indigenous members, and another four had equal numbers.[29]

Table 2.5 presents data on all members of selected boards (two each in Nunavut, the Inuvialuit Settlement Region [ISR], the Mackenzie Valley, and

TABLE 2.4
Membership of territorial land claims boards (February 2018)

	Board	Members			
		Total	Indigenous	Non-Indigenous	Vacant
Nunavut	Nunavut Planning Commission	5*	4	0	1
	Nunavut Impact Review Board	9	6	0	3
	Nunavut Water Board	9	6	2	1
	Nunavut Wildlife Management Board	9	9	1	3
	Nunavut Surface Rights Tribunal	5	2	3	0
NWT	Sahtu Land Use Planning Board	5	5	0	0
	Gwich'in Land Use Planning Board	5	3	1	1
	MV Environmental Impact Review Board	9	6	2	1
	Environmental Impact Screening Committee	7	4	3	0
	Environmental Impact Review Board	6	4	2	0
	MV Land and Water Board	5	1	1	3
	Sahtu Land and Water Board	5	2	1	2
	Gwich'in Land and Water Board	5	3	1	1
	Wek'èezhìi Land and Water Board	5	4	1	0
	Sahtu Renewable Resources Board	6	3	1	2
	Gwich'in Renewable Resources Board	6	2	2	2
	Wek'èezhìi Renewable Resources Board	9	4	4	1
	Wildlife Management Advisory Council (NWT)	7	4	3	0
	Wildlife Management Advisory Council (NS)	5**	2	3	0
	Fisheries Joint Management Committee	5	2	3	0
	Inuvialuit Arbitration Board	11	1	7	3
	Gwich'in Arbitration Panel	8	0	0	8
	Sahtu Arbitration Panel	8	1	2	5
	NWT Surface Rights Board	5***	3	2	0
Yukon	Yukon Land Use Planning Council	3	1	2	0
	Yukon Environment and Socio-economic Assessment Board	7	2	3	2
	Yukon Water Board	9	4	3	2
	Yukon Fish and Wildlife Management Board	12	6	5	1
	Yukon Salmon Sub-committee	10	7	3	0
	Yukon Surface Rights Board	5	2	2	1

* Article 11.4.5 of the *Nunavut Land Claims Agreement* specifies that membership shall be at least five but does not specify an upper limit.

** Article 12 (47–48) of the *Inuvialuit Final Agreement* specifies that membership shall be at least five but does not specify an upper limit.

*** Up to nine board members may be appointed.

Yukon) since their creation (or, in the case of the Yukon Water Board, since it was transformed into a claims-based board under the *UFA*). It shows that members of the two Nunavut boards have been overwhelmingly Inuit, that membership of the two Mackenzie Valley boards has been predominantly Indigenous, and that in Yukon and the ISR, non-Indigenous members have marginally outnumbered Indigenous members. If Indigenous people have been well represented among the members of these boards, the same cannot be said for women. Overall, 81 percent of members on the eight boards were men, with only one board – the MVLWB – having marginally more than 30 percent women members over its history. The proportion of Indigenous board members who were women, 22 percent, is slightly higher than that of non-Indigenous board members, 15 percent. That this imbalance has not reflected lack of interest on women's part is suggested by the experience of Madeleine Redfern. Redfern, who went on to earn a law degree and become mayor of Iqaluit, recalls unsuccessfully applying to serve as a board member on several Nunavut IPGs.[30]

On the Indigenous side, for some boards the regional emanations of the principal Indigenous organization or government make the nominations. Several of the Nunavut boards, for example, have one member nominated by each of NTI and the three regional Inuit associations. Similarly, the Sahtu and Gwich'in claims require that at least one member of the Mackenzie Valley Environmental Impact Review Board be a nominee of the Gwich'in Tribal Council and that another be a Sahtu Secretariat nominee. In addition to the four permanent members of the Yukon Salmon Sub-Committee, First Nations in each of three

TABLE 2.5
Cultural and gender profile of members of selected claims boards (number of members to March 2018)

	Indigenous			Non-Indigenous		
	Men	Women	Total	Men	Women	Total
Wildlife boards						
Nunavut Wildlife Management Board	42	3	45	7	0	7
Yukon Fish and Wildlife Management Board	20	6	26	22	5	27
Environmental boards						
Nunavut Impact Review Board	21	9	30	3	0	3
MVLWB	24	12	36	11	4	15
MVEIRB	13	8	21	11	2	13
EIRB	12	3	15	17	1	18
Yukon Water Board*	17	6	23	21	7	28

* Post-UFA.

river drainage basins are entitled to nominate two members who are to participate only in matters affecting salmon in their drainage basins.[31]

On the government side, positions on some boards are designated for nominees of particular government departments or agencies. Though not specified in the text of the *IFA*, it has come to be understood that government positions in the Inuvialuit boards are to be filled by representatives of specific government units, such as the Canadian Wildlife Service (CWS) or the federal Department of Fisheries and Oceans (DFO). The Nunavut claim explicitly sets aside positions on the Nunavut Wildlife Management Board for nominees of the DFO minister and the minister responsible for CWS.

The wildlife management boards under the *IFA* and the Gwich'in and Sahtu claims are distinctive in having official alternate members who participate in board activities should regular members be unavailable. On the NWMB, the Makivik Corporation, the land claim organization for the Inuit of Nunavik (Northern Quebec), nominates two alternate board members, who are entitled to take part in board processes for issues affecting Nunavik, but this is quite different from the alternates on the *IFA*, Gwich'in, and Sahtu boards. The legal framework for other boards, such as the MVEIRB, makes provision for alternate members, but none have been appointed. A distinctive provision of the Nunavut claim recognizes the vast geographic scale of the Nunavut Planning Commission's mandate by permitting the Inuit organization responsible for nominating members to substitute alternate members for those on the commission "in order to ensure appropriate representation from the region for which planning is being conducted."[32]

Public servants sit as members on a number of Northern claims boards. As noted, positions on some wildlife management boards are effectively designated for employees of specific governmental organizations; for others, the practice may not be so explicit but public servants are nonetheless routinely appointed as members. For still other boards, such as the Nunavut Planning Commission, the claim or the enabling legislation prohibits public servants from sitting as board members. That government employees serve on boards has obvious implications for their independence (this issue is examined in Chapter 7). A less obvious consequence derives from what are widely seen as inadequate per diem payments for board members. Board members who must take time off work for board meetings and other activities may lose money by serving on claims boards or they may not be prepared to put sufficient time into preparation for meetings because of their financial constraints. As well, potential members may decline invitations to serve on boards for financial reasons. Public servants, whose board activities form part of their normal jobs, face no such constraints.

For most boards, members nominated by Indigenous organizations or territorial governments are formally appointed by the federal government. Inevitably, exceptions exist: from the outset, the Yukon Government made the appointments to the Yukon Fish and Wildlife Management Board. With devolution, the Yukon Government now makes the appointments to the Yukon Water Board, though a third of the members are federal nominees. A measure of Ottawa's reluctance to give up control over important boards is that, even after devolution, the federal government still appoints members of the MVEIRB and the MVLWB in the NWT and the Yukon Environmental and Socio-economic Assessment Board. In a few instances, Indigenous governments make board appointments directly. The wildlife management boards and the environmental regulatory boards established under the *Inuvialuit Final Agreement* are examples.[33] So too, the Tlicho Government directly appoints members to boards established by the *Tlicho Agreement*, and the Inuit organizations make appointments to the Nunavut Wildlife Management Board (but not to the other Nunavut IPGs – a measure of the board's importance to Inuit). In Yukon, under the *UFA*, when the territorial government makes board appointments it must accept the nominees of the Council of Yukon First Nations, conveying to it effective appointment power. The Government of Nunavut makes appointments to the Nunavut Impact Review Board and to the NWMB but not other IPGs; the Government of the Northwest Territories does not appoint any members to claims-based co-management boards. The distinction between nominating and appointing members may seem insignificant but, as noted in Chapter 7, Ottawa is not averse to rejecting nominees – and provides no explanation when it does so.

In accordance with Article 38.1.4 of the Nunavut claim, lack of agreement among the parties once resulted in a superior court judge appointing the members of the Nunavut Arbitration Board.[34] Board members usually live in the territory or region over which their boards have jurisdiction. For the most part, board members are not subject to residency requirement, though again exceptions exist. By way of illustration, a majority of both the CYFN and Yukon Government nominees to the Yukon Fish and Wildlife Management Board must be Yukon residents, while the chair of the Yukon Environmental and Socio-economic Assessment Board is to be a Yukon resident, and a majority of the members of regional land use planning commissions in Yukon must be Yukon residents "with a long term familiarity with the region or regions being planned."[35] In Nunavut at least half of the Nunavut Planning Commission members must live in the Nunavut Settlement Area, but no other residence restrictions affect members. No formal restrictions on residency exist for boards in the NWT (including the *IFA* boards), but the GNWT has adopted an informal practice of not renominating members who no longer live in the territory.

Chairs of Northern claims boards can wield substantial power. Some chairs work on board business on close to a full-time basis and thus are able to take the lead in directing staff, setting board directions, and interacting with government and other outside organizations. Chairs' pay and perks tend to be significantly better than those of board members, who are involved only on a part-time basis and typically have full-time jobs unrelated to board activities. Selection and appointment processes for chairs vary widely. On the *IFA* boards, chairs are appointed by government or the Inuvialuit with "the consent" of the other parties.[36] Chairs of some boards, such as the Nunavut Wildlife Management Board, are appointed by the federal minister "on nomination" by the board, implying that the minister could reject a nomination but not impose a chair on the board against its wishes.[37] The chair of the Nunavut Arbitration Board is chosen by the board from among its members.[38] A distinctive provision applies to the *IFA* Environmental Impact Screening Committee (but, curiously, not to the Environmental Impact Review Board): in case of a deadlock among the parties the chief justice of the NWT or the chief justice of Yukon is given the power to appoint a chair.[39] On other boards, the federal government has effectively unfettered power to appoint the chair. As outlined in Chapter 5, a major political contretemps ensued when Ottawa exercised this power to reject the shortlist of candidates prepared internally by the MVLWB and to appoint instead a controversial figure as chair.

Removal of a chair is a largely untested area with much leeway for conflicting interpretations. Certainly, however, in the two most prominent instances in which boards attempted to depose their chairs, at the Nunavut Planning Commission and at the Mackenzie Valley Environmental Impact Review Board, Ottawa's clear authority to appoint the chairs trumped the boards' wishes.

An extended enquiry into the political implications of board appointments must await Chapter 7, but one point is worth noting at this juncture. Not only is the issue of *who* is appointed to claims boards significant but so too is the question of *when* they are appointed. A serious continuing issue is the protracted delay that frequently characterizes appointments, occasionally leaving boards with vacancies that last for years, in turn creating operational problems, including difficulty meeting quorum requirements. Table 2.4 shows that, as of February 2018, more boards had vacancies than had a full complement of members, with no fewer than six boards short at least three members. In one extreme case, the Gwich'in Arbitration Panel, all eight board positions were vacant and had been for many months. The table does not show the length of time certain vacancies persist, which can be considerable, stretching into years.

Board appointments are normally for three years, though on a handful of boards the term is four or five years. Few if any boards have any restrictions about the number of terms members (or chairs) may serve; members routinely serve for two or more terms.

Boards, especially those engaged in environmental regulation, may be required to rigorously follow detailed procedures in dealing with governments, local communities, individuals, corporations, and so on. Generally, however, they enjoy wide scope to determine their internal procedures. One critical exception involves board quora. While it is not unusual for an organization's founding legal framework to set its quorum, it is highly significant that quorum for many Northern claims boards must include not just a specific number of members but also at least one member nominated or appointed by government as well as one nominated or appointed by the responsible Indigenous organization. This is a strong indication of the co-management ethos underpinning the boards.

Members' Pay and Benefits

Board members' financial compensation has generated controversy, both for being too high and for being too low. Inevitably, the media have zeroed in on a few chairs whose pay far exceeds $100,000 a year.[40] By contrast, those charged with assessing boards have identified low rates of pay as a significant impediment to their effectiveness. The Second Five Year Review of the Nunavut claim echoed the concerns of Justice Berger in his Conciliator's Report that the chair and members of the NWMB were significantly underpaid at $325 and $225 a day, respectively.[41] Though the gap has since narrowed, in 2001, while they were often asked to take on similar tasks, members of the MVEIRB received $200 a day while members of the Canadian Environmental Assessment Agency were paid $575 a day.[42]

Early in 2002, Ottawa brought in a new schedule of payments for members of Northern claims boards (some reflecting reclassifications of boards across the categories into which the Privy Council Office slots boards and agencies). Members of some boards, such as NIRB and the MVEIRB, saw their honoraria almost doubled, from $200 to $375 per day, while others, most notably those serving on the wildlife management and land use planning boards, received far more modest increments, typically from $200 to $225 per day.[43] Since their compensation comes in the form of honoraria, board members receive no benefits. Moreover, with the high cost of living in the North, the rates are, in real terms, decidedly less munificent than they might seem to non-Northerners. No surprise, then, that indifferent rates of pay are often cited as a problem in attracting and retaining high-quality board members. One board executive director put it succinctly: "the honoraria suck." In late 2017, a senior DIAND official told a gathering of board members and staff that the minister had commissioned a study of board honoraria with a view to increasing them.[44]

Staff, Office, and Meeting Locations

Staffing arrangements vary a good deal, as do levels of staff support. Aside from the little-used arbitration boards, which require no more than occasional part-time support, boards normally have at least five or six full-time staff; larger and more active boards, such as the Nunavut Planning Commission and the Nunavut Impact Review Board, may have staff complements of twenty or more. The staff of the Yukon Environmental and Socio-economic Assessment Board is exceptionally large, numbering forty-one as of early 2019.[45] Boards rarely have lawyers on staff, but many retain outside counsel, some of whom have been with their boards for many years. Some boards make extensive use of consultants to provide technical or specialized expertise on all manner of concerns.

Most boards would not countenance the notion of relying on government departments, especially DIAND, for staff support, even of a technical nature. A few exceptions do exist; section 11 (23) of the *IFA*, for example, specifies that the federal government is to provide staff for the Environmental Impact Review Board (EIRB). Similarly, the *Umbrella Final Agreement* specifies that the federal Department of Fisheries and Oceans is to provide "technical and administrative support" to the Yukon Salmon Sub-Committee and that the sub-committee's executive secretary, its highest ranking official, is to be a senior DFO bureaucrat.[46] (As discussed in Chapter 4, however, the sub-committee has come to rely primarily on its own dedicated staff.)

Save staff of the federal government, who provide support on a part-time basis for EIRB and the Yukon Salmon Sub-Committee, for the most part board staff are employees of their boards; nothing more, nothing less. Again, however, exceptions occur. Staff of the Yukon Water Board, who had been federal government employees prior to devolution, are employees of the Yukon Government,

Most boards have complete control over their human resource policies and processes, from hiring to pension plans. Few if any boards have reciprocal arrangements with governments, public or Indigenous, to accord employees preferential hiring or seniority privileges, such as the right to be considered for "internal" job competitions. Boards occasionally second staff from the federal or territorial governments for specific projects.

As they do in so many other respects, the *IFA* boards differ from other boards in terms of staff support. In a unique arrangement, a Joint Secretariat provides staff support to all *IFA* boards, save the Wildlife Management Advisory Council (North Slope) (WMAC[NS]), which has a small stand-alone secretariat in Whitehorse, plus the Inuvialuit Game Council, an arm of the Inuvialuit government. Some staff are assigned full-time to specific boards with purely administrative functions, such as finance and payroll, purchasing, and the like, handled by a common staff pool. The very substantial funding increase the Joint Secretariat received in late 2017 enabled it to expand its capacity substantially, through the creation of new positions, in areas such as communications and support for hunters and trappers committees, and through enhanced professional development for staff. As of early 2019, Joint Secretariat staff numbered twenty.[47] This has proven a highly effective arrangement, but it has no analogue in other claims boards. Attempts in Nunavut to realize economies through pooling of resources to develop common services such as printing and purchasing have been fruitless.

The Yukon Environmental and Socio-economic Assessment Board has its main office in Whitehorse plus six "Designated Offices" in communities across the territory (including one in Whitehorse) that conduct virtually all project evaluations – all but 2 of 202 in 2017–18.[48] Other Northern claims boards with branch offices are the Nunavut Planning Commission and the Wek'èezhìi Land and Water Board; the wildlife management boards have extensive links with local Hunters and Trappers Organizations, regional resources councils, and, in Nunavut, regional wildlife boards. Generally speaking, offices of boards with wide-ranging geographic mandates are located in the territorial capitals; offices of boards established under regional claims are generally found in the largest communities in the settlement areas. The *IFA* and Gwich'in boards, for example, are all headquartered in Inuvik. Exceptions exist, such as the Wek'èezhìi Renewable Resources Board, which works out of offices in Whatì, a small Tlicho community. The Nunavut Wildlife Management Board's offices are in Iqaluit, but the other active Nunavut IPGs have their offices outside the capital: the Water Board in Gjoa Haven, the Planning Commission and the Impact Review Board in Cambridge Bay.[49] After the passage of the *Mackenzie Valley Resource Management Act*, the NWT Water Board (renamed the Inuvialuit Water Board in 2014) had jurisdiction only over the Inuvialuit Settlement Region, but its office remained in Yellowknife for an extended period. Despite occasional pressure for it to relocate to Inuvik, this occurred only recently, in part because the *Northwest Territories Water Act* required the board to maintain its "main office" in Yellowknife and in part because of resistance from a former chair, a businessman and former NWT cabinet minister who lived in Yellowknife. Following the 2014 devolution agreement, the board is now subject to the NWT *Waters Act*, which specifies that the board office be in Inuvik.

Though it is expensive, the wildlife management boards make a point of holding some of their regular meetings in communities throughout their jurisdiction. This is partly symbolic but also has the significant value of promoting direct contact between the boards and the local hunters, trappers, and fishers through well-attended informal community gatherings. The regulatory boards routinely hold both formal public hearings and informal visits in communities that stand to be affected by proposed developments the boards are reviewing.

Funding

The chapters on specific boards examine their funding in some detail. Suffice it to say for now that Northern claims boards are all but totally dependent on government, primarily the federal government, for their funding and that board funding, in terms of both process and level, has long been a major point of contention between the boards and the federal government. A substantial increase in levels and duration of funding for NWT boards in late 2017 has gone some way to reducing friction over finances,[50] as did the enhanced IPG funding in Nunavut that came as part of the settlement of NTI's billion-dollar lawsuit in 2015.

From Preliminaries to Case Studies

In addition to setting out basic contextual information about politics and government in the three territories, this chapter provides an overview of the origin, nature, legal foundations, mandates, structure, and membership of Northern claims boards. In so doing, it makes clear that, while certain essential features are found in all boards, extensive variation characterizes the boards. Different claims produced boards that are structured and operate in distinctive ways, including those engaged in similar functions, such as land use planning or wildlife management.

The image of claims boards provided in this chapter is essentially static, with only limited attention devoted to whether and how boards change. To be sure, fundamental mandates and structures have largely remained unchanged for most boards. However, as the case studies in the following chapters demonstrate, boards have changed and developed, and continue to develop, as they have matured and gained experience. Particularly notable is how boards' relations with governments – federal, territorial, and Indigenous – have evolved.

Beyond the quantitative data on board membership, which show strong to very strong Indigenous representation among board members, the chapter offers little evidence one way or another on the central question animating this book: Do Northern Indigenous people wield significant influence over wildlife and environmental policies through claims-mandated co-management boards? With the concepts of treaty federalism and co-management defined in Chapter 1, and an overview of board characteristics outlined in this chapter, the stage is set to look in detail at a few specific boards in the next four chapters. The first to be examined is the Nunavut Wildlife Management Board.

PART 2
SPECIFIC LAND CLAIMS BOARDS

chapter 3

The Nunavut Wildlife Management Board

The Nunavut Wildlife Management Board stands out as a major success story in the oftentimes uneven implementation of the *Nunavut Land Claims Agreement*. Where the other major Nunavut institutions of public government – the Nunavut Planning Commission, the Nunavut Impact Review Board, and the Nunavut Water Board[1] – have all experienced, mostly in their early days, high-profile scandals or periods of serious dysfunction, the NWMB has earned a reputation for competence and professionalism. The strong relations it enjoys with Inuit hunters and Inuit organizations and with the federal and territorial governments enable it to take on controversial issues and render tough decisions while maintaining the respect of its wildlife management partners. The independent review of the first five years of the *NLCA* listed the board as one of the "best successes" of the claim, describing it as "a good example of how implementation bodies can be well-organized administratively, properly focussed on obligations and objectives, and operate within the spirit and intent of the Agreement."[2] In its listing of "key accomplishments," the second independent review of the claim gave prominent place to the NWMB and several of its main projects.[3]

To be sure, it has not been entirely smooth sailing for the board, which on occasion has found itself in conflict with both the federal and territorial governments, and, less frequently, with Nunavut Tunngavik Incorporated, the powerful Inuit organization responsible for overseeing implementation of the claim. Most disputes have been over individual decisions or issues, though some have been ongoing. Nor have its relations with the three regional wildlife organizations

(RWOs) and with the local hunters and trappers organizations (HTOs) always been amicable or cooperative. And, from time to time, undercurrents of discontent regarding the board's policies and procedures, some minor, some substantial, are evident among Inuit beneficiaries.

With only minor exceptions, the NWMB has avoided internal discord in members' dealings with one another or in relations between members and staff. Nor has it undermined its credibility with Inuit beneficiaries and governments by engaging, as did other Nunavut IPGs in their early years, in foolish and expensive boondoggles such as overseas trips of dubious value.

Creation of a powerful, effective body through which Inuit would strongly influence wildlife policy and administration was a top priority for the Inuit leaders negotiating the claim. Prior to the claim, "Inuit were relegated, at best, to the margins of the decision-making process" on wildlife issues; their limited advisory status was "more often than not ... very unsatisfactory to them. The strong feeling among Inuit was that others were in control of their destiny; that those others did not understand them; and that they had little interest in hearing from them."[4]

One of the federal government negotiators on the Nunavut file recalled that more time was spent on the boards than on any other topic and that Inuit were determined that the claim include a strong management regime for wildlife and the environment in which Inuit were front and centre, noting that "Inuit were adamant that they wouldn't accept boards without 'teeth.'" The Inuit assessment was that the wildlife bodies and processes in the Inuvialuit claim – an obvious model – lacked the legal and political authority they sought for wildlife management. According to Terry Fenge, a key advisor to the Inuit negotiators, "government negotiators insisted that ministers be identified as the locus of final, ultimate decision-making authority. Inuit eventually accepted this proposition but insisted, in turn, that ministerial authority to override decisions made by the ... [claims boards] be confined to circumstances and procedures defined in the agreement."[5]

Inuit determination bore fruit in the agreement on wildlife, which became Article 5 in the claim. This was the first article to be initialled by the negotiating teams, more than a decade before the claim was finalized. Numerous changes were made to the article over the years, some barely weeks before finalization.[6] Certain federal departments involved in wildlife issues, such as the Department of Environment, adamantly opposed the terms of the agreement for giving away altogether too much of their power to Inuit and to land claim organizations. A good deal of time and political pressure, as well as some compromise, was required before these objections were overcome. One important issue involved the board's role with respect to habitat. "Government seemed to fear that an expansive board [habitat] mandate might hinder decisions on the disposition of rights to develop and use sub-surface resources" and thus insisted on a clause (Article 5.2.36) significantly limiting the board's ability to manage habitat.[7] Some involved with the board maintain that certain departments – the Department of Fisheries and Oceans is often cited in this regard – have yet to fully accept the board's legitimacy and continually attempt to undermine it and, by extension, the claim.

A telling indication of the importance of the NWMB in realizing Inuit political aspirations is found in the claim's Preamble. Included in the four enumerated objectives is the need "to provide Inuit with wildlife harvesting rights and rights to participate in decision-making concerning wildlife harvesting."[8] Article 5 provides the institutional means for reversing the exclusion of Inuit from wildlife decision making, primarily through the creation and empowerment of the NWMB. Article 5's principles are nothing if not explicit about the centrality of Inuit to wildlife management:

> The legal rights of Inuit to harvest wildlife flow from their traditional and current use ... There is a need for an effective system of wildlife management that complements Inuit harvesting rights and priorities, and recognizes Inuit systems of wildlife management that contribute to the conservation of wildlife and protection of wildlife habitat ... There is a need for an effective role for Inuit in all aspects of management including research.[9]

"Effective role" was not, however, to mean control; the final principle of Article 5 is that "Government retains the ultimate responsibility for wildlife management."[10] To a substantial extent, of course, it is the Inuit-dominated Government of Nunavut that is responsible for wildlife management.

Still, the claim did go a considerable distance towards entrenching Inuit influence in wildlife management. Article 5, by far the longest in the claim, sets out the composition and responsibilities of the NWMB in sufficient detail that, unlike many other claims boards in Nunavut and elsewhere, no enabling legislation was necessary to bring it to life or to specify its roles and procedures.[11] As well, Article 5 renders the NWMB unique in a number of important ways. Alone among the Nunavut IPGs, Inuit organizations directly appoint members to it. At the other boards, Inuit organizations nominate prospective members, but the federal government decides whether to accept and appoint them. The board is also unique in the primacy it affords Inuktitut, in terms of both formal status and reality, as well as in being the only Nunavut IPG with a privative clause, saving its decisions from appeals (though in certain circumstances, judicial review of board decisions is possible). Its funding may not be unique, but by comparison with all other wildlife management boards in the North, the NWMB is very well funded.

In terms of "teeth," the NWMB is distinctive – unique at the time – in the "negative option" respecting government authorization of its decisions. In most instances, when the board makes a decision, which it passes on to government, the government has only a relatively short time period to reject the decision, typically sixty days in the case of federal ministers, thirty days for GN ministers. Otherwise the decision automatically comes into force. It was this provision that Paul Quassa, one of the Inuit leaders whose signature is on the claim, was referring to when he proclaimed: "Now we've got a Nunavut Wildlife Management Board that will have decision-making powers. And we've got a disallowance clause that will help to guarantee that government cannot automatically override decisions relating to Inuit share of wildlife. This is what we have spent five years fighting for."[12]

The NWMB is distinctive among Nunavut IPGs, and indeed among all claims-mandated boards, for the high priority it accords traditional Indigenous knowledge, referred to in Nunavut as Inuit Qaujimajatuqangit. Sometimes rendered as "things long known by Inuit," a better definition is "the Inuit way of doing things: the past, present and future knowledge, experience and values of Inuit society."[13] The board has not found it easy to incorporate IQ into its activities and decision-making processes or to reconcile it with Western science. Nevertheless, the board's commitment to IQ is genuine and noteworthy.

In terms of the conventional definition discussed in Chapter 1, in which co-management entails the sharing of decision-making power between public governments and Indigenous governments and organizations, the NWMB is not, strictly speaking, a co-management board. However, like all of the other claims-mandated boards in the territorial North, the NWMB describes itself in co-management terms and refers to its "co-management partners." The board *Governance Manual* puts it this way:

> The Board is an independent administrative tribunal ... The NWMB acts as the primary decision-making agency within a co-management system of wildlife management. Co-management refers to a system of partnerships in which the partners – Inuit and Government – work co-operatively to assist the Board to make particular decisions, to conduct and commission research, and to provide approvals, advice, recommendations and information.[14]

At the same time, the board also refers to its role in the decision-making process as "co-jurisdictional" with the territorial and federal governments.[15]

Early Days

Reflecting the Inuit leadership's unwillingness to leave key claim implementation measures to the federal government's discretion, the *Nunavut Land Claims Agreement* required establishment of the NWMB immediately upon ratification of the claim via passage by Parliament of the enabling legislation. This provision underlines the priority accorded the NWMB by the Inuit negotiators; the deadline for creating the other major IPGs was two years after ratification. The wisdom of this approach was brought home by a holdup of several months in getting the board up and running, owing to a delay on Ottawa's part in appointing members.[16] Still, it is noteworthy that the board was operational more than five years before the Nunavut Government came into being.

The first set of board members, sworn into office in January 1994, had to oversee the hiring of staff and the logistical arrangements surrounding the creation of a new organization, develop policies and procedures, and begin preparations for the many tasks assigned the NWMB by the claim. They also had to overcome the unhappy legacy of the Nunavut Wildlife Management Advisory Board (NWMAB). This was a transitional agency "intended to operate according to the spirit and goals of the agreement in principle of the Nunavut land claim,"[17] comprised of four Inuit-appointed members and four government appointees and an independent chair. With insufficient funding to do much more than hold meetings, the NWMAB lacked the analytic and research capacity to evaluate reports and proposals put to it by government. Little known or understood by Inuit hunters, it lacked popular legitimacy. Its decision, prompted by the federal Department of Fisheries and Oceans, to severely restrict beluga quotas in three South Baffin communities put it at odds with the communities, which thought the restrictions unjustified. Following a brief occupation of the DFO office in Iqaluit – a remarkable occurrence given the long-standing Inuit aversion to such confrontational tactics – Inuit organizations formally disavowed the NWMAB as having any connection to the as yet unborn NWMB.[18] The Tungavik Federation of Nunavut (TFN), NTI's predecessor, was unequivocal in asserting that the NWMB, on which such hopes rested, had nothing to do with the NWMAB: "it's TFN's view that the Nunavut Wildlife Management Advisory Board is a government body established for interim purposes and bears no resemblance or has no connection to the NWMB."[19]

In short order, the NWMB was able to establish itself as credible and legitimate. In part this reflected the substantial resources at its command, which accorded it an independence unknown at the NWMAB and allowed it to become known in the communities, not least by flowing money to the three RWOs and to the local HTOs. The board's credibility also reflected its early decisions and activities, including the decision to license the harvest of one bowhead, the first in many years. Strong support from NTI also enhanced the board's stature.

In addition to holding meetings where routine decisions and issues were processed, the board organized workshops and meetings throughout Nunavut to inform local hunters of its mandate and activities. By the end of its second year, the NWMB was well established, with staff, policies, and procedures in place; two large and critically important research projects under way or planned; the Nunavut Wildlife Research Trust created; and good relations established with key wildlife stakeholders. A major strategic planning exercise, finalized in May 1996, served to chart the board's next five years.[20]

Structure and Operations

The NWMB has nine members. As noted, unusually, both in Nunavut and the other territories, Ottawa cannot filter or reject nominees since it does not make the actual appointments, save its own. NTI and the three regional Inuit associations (RIAs) each appoint one member. For the first few years, the RIAs often did not consult the RWOs when making appointments,[21] and to the RWOs' annoyance, this situation still occurs on occasion. The Government of Nunavut appoints one member, while the federal government appoints three: one nominated by the minister of fisheries and oceans, one nominated by the minister responsible for the Canadian Wildlife Service (CWS) – to this point, always the minister of the environment – and one nominated by the DIAND minister "in consultation with" the GN. The DIAND-nominated member, but no other member, must be resident in Nunavut.[22] The chair is nominated by the board and appointed by the federal government. Thus, unlike other boards, while Ottawa could refuse the NWMB's nominee, it could not impose its own choice for chair on the board, although it has on more than one occasion dragged its feet for an extended period before making an appointment. On one occasion, the board submitted a nomination for the chair and Ottawa asked for a list of nominees; the board stood firm and eventually its nominee was appointed. Until 2012, the chair was formally a board employee, engaged in board business on a full-time basis, serving as chief executive officer. This duality of roles twice led to the bizarre situation, lasting for months, in which the CEO – and chair-designate – participated in, and indeed ran, board meetings but could not vote because Ottawa had not formally appointed the board's choice as chair.

Terms are for four years and are renewable. An unusual provision permits the appointing body to remove "its'" member from the board for cause. This has never happened, though on at least one occasion a board member seemed likely to be recalled; some observers suggest that the Inuit cultural disinclination to engage in personal criticism has been a factor here. The board itself can, by majority vote, recommend to the appointing body that its member be removed. As with other claims boards, delays in formalizing appointments can cause problems. With the board quorum set at five, when the board has two vacancies, as has happened, if more than one or two members are absent the validity of a meeting is jeopardized. For a period in 2013, four of the nine board posts were vacant so that none of the five members could miss a meeting lest quorum be lost. Most often it is federally appointed positions that remain vacant for extended periods. By way of illustration, from early 2004 to mid-2007 either the DIAND-nominated position or the DFO-nominated position was vacant. Not long after those positions were filled, the CWS-nominated position fell vacant for over four years.

The overwhelming majority of board members have been Inuit: as of early 2018 only seven of the forty-two board members (17 percent) have been non-Inuit.[23] Women have been even less in evidence than non-Inuit; only three women, all Inuit, have been board members, though during 2001 and 2002 the three served simultaneously. It has been over a decade since a woman has been on the board. Virtually all Inuit members are experienced hunters; for many, hunting has been their main occupation. They thus bring extensive on-the-land expertise to board deliberations. Non-Inuit have typically been public servants or former public servants with years of practical field experience, who recognize the Inuit members' traditional knowledge and are in turn accepted by the Inuit as bringing valid perspectives to the table.

One of the more interesting non-Inuit appointments was the DFO's appointment of Daniel Shewchuk in 2014; only a few years earlier, Shewchuk had been GN minister of the environment, with authority to approve or reject NWMB decisions (and, prior to that, he had appeared before the board as an employee of the GN Department of Sustainable Development, the predecessor of the Department of Environment). When Ben Kovic resigned as chair in early 2016, the board chose Shewchuk to serve as acting chair; he was appointed chair in 2018. Prior to Shewchuk's tenure all chairs and acting chairs were Inuit. The claim is silent on the characteristics of the chair but the board has made clear its preference that the chair be a beneficiary fluent in both Inuktitut and English, thus almost guaranteeing that the chair would be an Inuk.[24] Shewchuk's facility in Inuktitut is limited.

Although precise data on NWMB members' ages are not available, the typical member is at least well into his fifties, meaning that he can draw on a wealth of practical, on-the-land experience.[25] Particularly in the board's first years, some members served for extended periods; founding chair Ben Kovic served for ten years and Canadian Wildlife Service appointee Kevin McCormick was a member from the outset in 1994 to 2009. More recently, turnover rates have increased, to the point where GN and federal officials who deal with the board cite lack of continuity in membership as a significant problem. Such complaints are more than slightly ironic since the GN and the federal government are responsible for nominating or appointing more than half the members and since they seem, in recent years, to have adopted a "give-someone-else-a-turn" approach to board appointments. Perhaps the most extreme example of wholesale turnover may be found in the fact that, in late 2014, only one member had been on the board eighteen months earlier, though one of the "new" members was Kovic, who had returned as chair after a decade away from the board.

Fish and marine mammals in the waters between Nunavut and Nunavik, the Inuit region of Northern Quebec, are subject to NWMB management as well as to management by the Nunavik Marine Region Wildlife Board (NMRWB). Accordingly, Makivik, the Nunavik land claim organization, appoints two members to the board who replace two of the members appointed by Nunavut Inuit organizations when issues affecting what are termed "areas of equal use and occupancy" come before the board. The NWMB has adopted a fairly narrow interpretation of this provision of the claim, involving the Makivik-appointed members only on matters that apply uniquely to areas of "equal use and occupancy." The Makivik members don't often attend regular board meetings but are present at hearings dealing with overlap or with issues of mutual concern and take part in conference calls when such matters come up. The NWMB and NMRWB have held joint public hearings.

The board office is in Iqaluit. In its first year, the board invited proposals from a number of communities to house its office; Pond Inlet, Pangnirtung, Igloolik, and Arviat responded but their submissions were deemed "incomplete," so no move was made.[26] Early on, regional offices were established in Arviat and in Kugluktuk, staffed by regional liaison officers. These offices were closed and the positions, which primarily involved running the Nunavut Harvest Study, were eliminated in 2003–04. For some years, the board occupied space in a building with NTI's head office literally down the hall from the NWMB office, but no one imagined that this proximity in any way compromised its independence.

At full complement the board has a dozen staff, plus part-time support from a private practice lawyer. Until 2018 Michael d'Eça, an Ottawa-based lawyer, was with the board from its creation, attending board meetings, drafting important documents, and representing the board at meetings. Jim Noble served as chief operating officer (retitled executive director in 2012) for over twenty years until his retirement in early 2015. In no small measure, the continuity and expertise that Noble and d'Eça provided, along with Kovic's guidance over the board's first decade, were factors in its success.[27] Significantly, both Kovic and Noble had extensive field experience as wildlife officers prior to joining the board.

In terms of continuity among technical staff, the record is mixed. The board has benefited from significant continuity of tenure among those who have held the top technical position, director of wildlife; three persons each served in that post for close to five years, though others' tenure was shorter. Turnover and vacancies in the junior biologist ranks have been constant problems. The board's 2018 strategic plan identified lack of human resource capacity – primarily vacancies – as an important risk to effective functioning and in need of mitigation. The organization chart in the plan shows four biologists plus the director of wildlife.[28] Rarely has the board had three junior biologist positions staffed, and it has occasionally found itself with a single junior biologist. As of early 2019, however, four biologists were working for the board, though the director of wildlife position was vacant.

During the board's early years, the issue of the representativeness of its staff arose. At a May 1996 meeting, a member pointed out that "there are concerns in the communities that the composition of the board's staff may not reflect the Nunavut population."[29] The board discussed staff issues again a few weeks later, raising the question of the board's compliance with Article 23 of the claim (mandating "representative" levels of Inuit hiring in government throughout Nunavut) and also considering the number of women holding staff positions.[30] Although consideration was given to a trainee program, this did not materialize, and, largely owing to the lack of Inuit with the university training required for the board's technical positions, little progress has been made on this front. No Inuk has ever been director of wildlife or held a biologist position. Many of the lower-ranked administrative positions have been held by Inuit, and the board's translators have all been Inuit. Noble's replacement as executive director, Jason Akearok, is an Inuk with a master's degree in biology. Akearok had previously worked for the Canadian Wildlife Service and had briefly been a board member himself. Women have been reasonably well represented among staff biologists; two women have served as director of wildlife.

The board holds regular quarterly meetings, typically lasting two or three days, plus as many as three public hearings a year focusing on specific issues; these are also usually two or three days long. Until 2006, the board called what are now termed public hearings "special meetings," though in the early years special meetings were much less frequent and often simply dealt with routine business. The first actual public hearing, on GN-proposed harvest restrictions, took place in 2006. Agendas and submissions, in Inuktitut and English, are posted on the board's website in advance of meetings. Public hearings may take place in conjunction with regular meetings or independently. Finding that public hearings were, as one person at the board put it, "getting out of hand" – increasing in frequency and becoming cumbersome and expensive – the board began to hold what it calls written public hearings in which interested parties, including members of the public, are invited to submit documents but no public meeting takes place. The board may hold several written public hearings a year – 2015 saw six – on narrowly defined questions, such as proposed *Species at Risk Act* listings of particular species, total allowance harvests (i.e., quotas in certain areas), and so on.

In its early years the board frequently met outside Iqaluit, including in small communities such as Kimmirut and Coral Harbour, seeing this as valuable for maintaining its connections with hunters and for ensuring that people in the communities were aware of and involved in the board's activities. Over the course of its first two decades, the board met in seventeen of Nunavut's twenty-five communities; a handful of meetings have been held outside Nunavut (in Yellowknife, Winnipeg, and Ottawa). In its first six years only five of twenty-five regular meetings were held in Iqaluit. More recently, meetings have usually taken place in Iqaluit: as of early 2019, thirty-four meetings had been held since 2009, only eight outside Iqaluit, all in larger communities such as Rankin Inlet and Cambridge Bay. The board scaled back on community meetings for financial and logistical reasons. Some public hearings take place in communities directly affected by the subject of the hearings. However, since only the larger communities have the accommodation and meeting facilities the board requires for public hearings, most are held in Iqaluit. On an issue of special importance to a particular small community, the board may hold what amounts to a pre-hearing consultation in the community, gathering evidence to be used in the actual hearing in Iqaluit. When the board held a public hearing on Southampton Island caribou, it carried out this type of consultation in Coral Harbour. Board members and staff travel frequently to communities to consult with local hunters and fishers on specific wildlife issues and to attend meetings of the RWOs. As the second five-year review approvingly noted, the board "consults with each and every community."[31]

Article 5.2.17 of the claim specifies that "the NWMB shall conduct its business in Inuktitut and, as required by legislation or policy, in Canada's official languages." Few if any other claims boards are mandated to operate in an Indigenous language; even Nunavut's other major IPGs are to operate in Canada's official languages (English and French), though any member can request that Inuktitut be used. Board meetings are conducted in English and Inuktitut; simultaneous English-Inuktitut interpretation is provided at meetings by the board's two staff translators/interpreters. This is essential since typically one or two board members are effectively unilingual in Inuktitut. Almost all of the oral presentations and other interventions by board staff and from officials of the federal government and the GN are in English; most of the questions from and discussions among board members are in Inuktitut, as are many of the contributions from NTI representatives. Documents going to board members, most of which are prepared in English, must, with certain exceptions, be available in both languages, with the responsibility for translation resting on the governments and organizations providing documents.[32]

An indication that the translation requirement is taken seriously was the postponement of a special meeting on regulations to implement the new territorial *Wildlife Act*, an important and contentious matter, for several weeks because Inuktitut translations of key documents were not ready. On the board's website, all material is available in Inuktitut and English. Technical and senior administrative staff of the board have overwhelmingly been non-Inuit with minimal facility in Inuktitut. This limitation has been somewhat mitigated in that, save one, all those who have served as chair or acting chair have been fluently bilingual. Still and all, translation of technical scientific terms into Inuktitut can be problematic, as can translation of Inuit ideational concepts into English. As well, Inuit board members occasionally complain about the quality of translation.

For the past few years, board members have been provided with laptop computers that enable them to find and follow documents under discussion at meetings more easily than had been the case previously, when they had to rely on bulky, unwieldy binders. As well, documents are projected onto large screens at the front of the room – one in Inuktitut, one in English.

Representatives of NTI, the GN (usually from the Department of Environment), and the federal government (usually DFO and the Canadian Wildlife

Service/Department of Environment) attend all board meetings and frequently contribute to discussions. For the first decade or so, everyone save board members and staff were asked to leave when the board went in camera to consider decisions. Subsequently, once "NTI started getting snotty about process," as one person put it, the board has allowed a limited number of "non-voting observers" to remain when the board meets in camera. This should have been the practice from the outset since, under sections 5.2.2 and 5.2.3 of the claim, observers representing the federal or territorial governments, NTI, and the three regional Inuit associations have the right to remain once the board goes in camera, though the board determines if and how they participate in the meeting. These observers are not permitted at what the board terms an "internal in camera meeting," at which internal administrative and operational matters are considered and, on occasion, especially sensitive policy matters. Others, from NGOs, RWOs, and other organizations, are also occasional attenders. Most meetings draw few members of the public, though certain issues, such as polar bear quotas, generate substantial public interest and attendance.

Functions and Activities

The claim assigns the NWMB a wide range of functions, requiring it to take on more diverse and extensive activities than most other claims-mandated wildlife management boards, though its financial and staff resources far exceed those available to the other boards. In one way, however, the board has a narrower remit than other Nunavut IPGs. A provision of the *Nunavut Land Claims Agreement Act*, the federal legislation implementing the claim, explicitly states that the NWMB is not an agent of the Crown. Among other things, this means that the board is not responsible for conducting consultations on behalf of the Crown.[33] No other IPG is mentioned in the act, in this or any other way.

The board's decision-making authority covers the entire Nunavut Settlement Area as defined by the claim – that is, virtually all of the Territory of Nunavut,[34] plus a twelve-mile offshore zone. Beyond twelve miles, the board has only advisory powers, unless Ottawa delegates authority to it, as it has in allocating certain fish and shrimp quotas established by the federal government.

Probably the most significant, and typically the most contentious, board responsibility is to establish, subject to ministerial approval, "basic needs levels'" (BNLs) and "total allowable harvests" (TAHs) for marine mammals (walrus, narwhal, and various species of whale), terrestrial mammals (caribou, polar and grizzly bear, muskox, etc.), birds, fish, and plants (though the board devotes little attention to plants). Considerably simplified, total allowable harvest refers to the numbers of a species to be harvested that the board considers to be sustainable. The basic needs level refers to the numbers of a particular species that Inuit may harvest for their needs. The claim provides that, if the board establishes a TAH, it must also set a BNL, meaning that harvesting by Inuit, which may occasionally include commercial harvesting, gets first priority and that, should the TAH equal the BNL, then all harvesting is reserved for Inuit.

Establishing TAHs and BNLs typically entails setting regional quotas for particular species.[35] RWOs allocate quotas among communities, and the actual distribution of quotas via "tags" to individual hunters is carried out by the local HTOs. The board has the authority to establish BNLs and TAHs for all species found in Nunavut, but it has concentrated on a relatively small number of especially important or seriously threatened species. Despite the importance of seal hunting in Inuit culture and traditional economy, the board has not sought to regulate the seal harvest. No person or organization has suggested that this might be necessary.

Section 5.6.25 of the claim required the board to set BNLs for beluga, narwhal, and walrus within a year of being established. In most cases, it was over two decades before this was done, and indeed, in some cases, it has yet to be done. Initially, the board was waiting for data from the Harvest Study (see below) before proceeding. As the Second Five Year Review put it in 2006: "with very little scientific data available on the populations of these species during the 1990's, and all of the harvests already being taken by Inuit ... the NWMB felt it was pointless – even irresponsible – from a wildlife management perspective to essentially guess at the basic needs levels for Inuit."[36] Subsequently, the board, in concert with DFO, established community-based management of beluga and narwhal in several communities and later a community-based monitoring network that, to some extent, obviated the need for the board to set BNLs.[37] As of the Second Five Year Review, the parties acknowledged that, although the board's obligation under section 5.6.25 had not been met, they were "in agreement with the actions taken in respect to this Section."[38]

The NWMB also sets "non-quota limitations": restrictions on harvesting other than those on TAH, such as public safety, season of harvest, method of harvest, and the like. Under the claim, the board has a limited mandate to deal with habitat issues, but it has as yet only occasionally been active in this area – for example, in setting a quota on harvesting of kelp in one region of Hudson Bay.[39]

Other board activities include: reviewing and approving management plans for wildlife and habitat, most frequently in species-at-risk processes; approving and setting conditions for HTO applications for sport hunts for walrus; deciding on occasional requests for "live capture" of animals either for research purposes

The Nunavut Wildlife Management Board

or for display at zoos or aquariums (given the Inuit distaste for such practices, which are seen as disrespectful to animals, the board has consistently opposed live capture); approving the transfer of tags between HTOs if no TAH is in place for a species (if a TAH exists, transfer of tags is determined by the HTOs and RWOs); allocating quotas for commercial harvesting of fish, such as turbot and shrimp, once the federal DFO minister has established the quotas; evaluating and funding applications from government agencies and HTOs for wildlife research; and, with DFO approval, sanctioning the emergency harvest of animals, usually beluga or narwhal, entrapped by adverse ice conditions, with no hope of surviving.

The board also participates in *Species at Risk Act* (*SARA*) processes for designating certain animal and plant species as "endangered," "threatened," or "of special concern." Aside from the oftentimes differing perspectives of, on the one hand, the board and, on the other hand, the *SARA* scientists and bureaucrats, this is an area of significant jurisdictional friction. Whereas the act says that claims-mandated wildlife management boards, such as the NWMB, are to be *consulted* in the *SARA* process,[40] the board's view is that under the claim it retains decision-making authority, subject to ministerial approval. The relationship got off to a rocky start when the board refused to consider an early proposed listing of grizzly bear and wolverine as species of special concern because the process had been insufficiently consultative and lacked an Inuit Qaujimajatuqangit component.[41]

In its first few years, the board found its staff overburdened with screening applications to other IPGs for land and water use permits and licences, commenting on research applications to the Nunavut Research Institute, DFO, and the GN Department of Sustainable Development. This occurred since virtually every application for a licence or a permit has wildlife implications. By 1999, the board took a policy decision to cut back substantially on such functions to allow its staff to concentrate on their regular duties.[42] The premise of this change was that the other Nunavut IPGs, such as the Nunavut Impact Review Board and the Nunavut Water Board, were better equipped for such screening and, indeed, were more appropriate for the task. On occasion, the board does involve itself in potentially significant development applications. In a strongly worded March 2016 press release, for example, the board weighed in opposing proposed mining development in an important caribou calving ground in the Kivalliq Region "after having considered available Inuit Qaujimajatuqangit and western scientific information regarding the negative impacts of human land-use activities on calving caribou and habitat."[43]

The NWMB runs a modest conservation education program aimed primarily at children. Among its initiatives have been activity and colouring books, books on Nunavut wildlife, and donations to conservation projects run by other organizations.

Prior to the creation of the Nunavut Inuit Wildlife Secretariat in 2005 (discussed below), the board on several occasions sent staff or hired consultants to sort out administrative disasters at RWOs and HTOs. For a period in 2011, NWMB staff looked after the financial and administrative needs of the Nunavut Surface Rights Tribunal as it righted itself from serious organizational disarray.

Decision-Making Process[44]

The NWMB consistently insists that, in its main functions, it is a decision-making rather than an advisory body, and indeed the claim categorizes the board's activities as "decisions" (as well, the board does have a number of clearly advisory responsibilities). In a few instances, primarily in distributing research funds, allocating fish (including shrimp) quotas that have been set by the federal government (but only within the Nunavut Settlement Area), and in structuring internal operations, the board has complete authority. Most of its decisions, however, are sent to ministers, who have the power to reject or modify them. Decisions about terrestrial mammals, most notably polar bears, caribou, and muskox, go to the GN minister of environment. Within thirty days, the minister must either reject the decision or request more time to consider the matter, which the board usually grants; otherwise, the decisions stand. Federal ministers have similar authority, though they have sixty days before board decisions automatically take effect. The DFO minister deals with board decisions on fish (including freshwater fish) and marine mammals, primarily walrus, beluga, narwhal, and bowhead whales, while the minister of environment is responsible for decisions pertaining to migratory birds. *SARA* authorizes the federal minister of environment to become involved with terrestrial mammals.

NWMB decisions that are to go to ministers are made in camera. What the board terms "non-voting observers," public servants and representatives of Inuit organizations who are not board members, are entitled to remain during the in camera sessions when decisions are made, though they are bound by the claim's confidentiality provisions. They are not to participate in the discussion unless board members ask for information or for their opinion.

The claim prohibits the board from making public an initial decision sent to a minister until the minister has accepted it, either explicitly by letter to the board or implicitly by letting the time run out, or rejected it. While understandable from a government perspective, this provision can be problematic for the board's co-management partners. For example, since it will usually have had a representative at the in camera meeting when the decision was taken, NTI will know about the decision but will be unable to communicate it to RWOs, HTOs, or beneficiaries.

Board decisions as well as ministerial responses to them may only restrict or limit Inuit harvesting for specific reasons. When this occurs it is almost invariably for "valid conservation" purposes or for reasons of "public health or public safety." Of course, perceptions as to what constitutes a valid conservation purpose or a matter of public health and safety may vary widely.

Ministers who disallow board decisions must provide reasons in writing. Should a minister reject an NWMB decision, the board must reconsider the issue and render what the claim terms "a final decision," which is sent to the minister. In such cases the board practice is to forward the minister's decision to its co-management partners on a confidential basis and to seek their views before responding to the minister. A final board decision can accept the minister's reasons for overturning the initial decision. The board has the discretion to make its final decision public. Ministers can accept or reject final board decisions or, unlike with initial decisions, can vary them. Significantly, no deadlines constrain ministerial responses to final board decisions; for the most part, ministers respond with moderate dispatch, but the process can occasionally drag on for an extended period. The board has no formal recourse against ministerial responses to its final decisions.

The claim permits a minister to take a "reasonable interim decision" to limit harvesting in "urgent and unusual circumstances." In such cases the board is to conduct a "full review" of the matter as soon as possible. This provision was most recently employed in early 2015 by the GN minister of environment to impose a complete moratorium on harvesting caribou on Baffin Island, in response to alarming data showing a precipitous decline in caribou numbers (the moratorium was subsequently modified to allow very limited hunting).[45]

NTI has long complained that the process is lacking in transparency and that the NWMB needs to do more to improve access to board decisions and ministerial responses. NTI recognizes that the confidentiality requirements in the claim must be respected but argues that oftentimes no one other than the board or the minister knows the outcome of the process in a timely fashion. This is not simply, according to NTI, a matter of good policy, but it would also avoid abrogating the right of Inuit and their organizations to seek judicial review of board or ministerial decisions since such proceedings must be started within thirty days of the decision in question. Although the board recognizes the need for timeliness, it is not concerned about Inuit losing the right to pursue a judicial review; this is because the thirty-day period only begins when a party is informed of a decision, not when the decision is made.

NTI has recommended that the board should routinely post on its website the content of board decisions and ministerial responses once the 30/60-day period has expired.[46] The NWMB *Governance Manual*, dated 2012, states:

> The NWMB maintains an up-to-date Decision Registry, available for viewing on its website. The Registry includes every NWMB resolution made pursuant to NLCA Article 5, and includes the names of the mover and the seconder for each resolution. NWMB decisions are only placed in the Registry after they are no longer confidential ... For each resolution, the Registry also posts the Board's final decision letter to the Minister, as well as the Minister's reply correspondence that accepts, varies or rejects the NWMB decision.[47]

The board's 2018 strategic plan indicated a June 2018 target date for making the decision database available. A section of the board website is titled "Decisions," but, as of early 2019, it had no content available to the public.

A good deal of board business is conducted via conference call. While this offers efficiency, especially for matters requiring quick action, considerable criticism of the board's extensive use of conference calls has been voiced by NTI, among others. Many of the issues discussed and decided in conference calls are minor, including internal administrative matters; however, others are of substantial import, such as quota allocations and policy positions vis-à-vis federal and territorial departments and NTI. Although representatives of government and NTI are permitted to take part in conference calls, including in camera decision-making sessions, the reality is that the board's co-management partners are not usually aware of upcoming conference calls nor do they have the documents to be discussed; the board website does not list planned conference calls or post the relevant documents as it does for regular meetings and for public and written hearings. According to published minutes, at only three of the board's first fifty conference calls were non-board participants involved. Participation by DFO and NTI representatives, and to a lesser extent GN representatives, became more frequent after 2001, though it was still the case that neither DFO nor NTI staff were involved in as many as half of the conference calls between 2002 and 2010. For some time, conference calls have been treated as in camera meetings so that minutes are no longer published.

Budget and Funding

Beyond specific commitments for government funding of research, the claim is largely silent on board finances. Like other comprehensive claims, the *NLCA* was accompanied by a detailed implementation contract setting out roles and responsibilities of the parties to the claim and specifying levels of government funding for various claim-mandated activities. Thus funding for the NWMB was set at $3.74 million annually (in 1992 dollars, with an annual increment based on a complex formula) in the implementation contract that covered the first decade of the claim (1993–2003).[48] Despite the critical importance of the implementation contract to the smooth functioning – and assured funding – of the claim, no second contract was established. Negotiations between NTI and the federal government reached a stalemate over both funding levels and implementation principles. Conciliation efforts by highly respected former jurist and Indigenous rights champion Thomas Berger came to naught. Berger devoted the bulk of his interim report to IPG funding, and in his analysis of NWMB funding he also addressed funding for HTOs and RWOs. Berger recognized the need for adequate, stable, and predictable funding for the NWMB but did not recommend a specific level; he did, however, recommend a "substantial increase" in federal funding for HTOs.[49] His final report dealt mainly with non-IPG issues but did note that, following the release of the interim report, although no overall agreement had been reached on a new implementation contract, the Nunavut Implementation Panel, the tripartite body responsible for claim implementation, did agree to an overall increase of roughly $2 million per year for IPGs until 2013. This figure reflected Canada's standing offer for IPG funding, which was substantially lower than the boards themselves (and NTI) had proposed.[50] For the NWMB, this amounted to an annual budget of approximately $5.6 million at the start of the time period.

The failure of Canada, the GN, and NTI to agree to a second implementation contract was one of the factors that, in 2006, led NTI to launch a $1 billion lawsuit against the federal government for failing to meet a range of implementation responsibilities under the claim. Of the many alleged breaches of the claim set out in NTI's statement of its case, the first listed was significant underfunding of the IPGs, including the NWMB, and the HTOs.[51] Years of research, legal manoeuvring, and negotiation culminated in a settlement early in 2015 under which Ottawa committed to pay $255.5 million to NTI and to provide enriched funding to the IPGs and, via the NWMB, to RWOs and HTOs.[52]

In the 2016–17 fiscal year, the board received roughly $10.8 million from Ottawa, though well more than half ($6.4 million) was distributed to the RWOs and the HTOs, leaving the board with some $4.4 million for operating expenses; it actually spent $3.9 million for a surplus of $543,000 (these figures exclude grants paid out of the Nunavut Wildlife Research Trust [see below]). The largest single expenditure was, unsurprisingly, wages and benefits ($1.6 million) followed by board meeting costs ($344,000) and office rent ($342,000); other substantial expenses included the cost of the community-based monitoring network, contracted services, and professional fees.[53]

Initially, Ottawa funded the board through annual "contribution agreements." These are contracts, typically used by government in financing limited-term projects or in providing annual funding to First Nations bands, and normally entail returning unspent funds at the end of the agreement period. As early as the board's first meeting in January 1994, members complained that such a mechanism was inappropriate for an ongoing board mandated by the land claim.[54] This was a continuing source of aggravation for several years. In early 1997, DIAND proposed a number of revisions to the contribution agreement, which, according to Executive Director Jim Noble, "would seem to have the effect of significantly eroding the nature and independence of the NWMB."[55] Two conference calls were held on this matter during the first week of April. In the first, the board, believing that the proposed changes contravened the land claim, agreed to seek NTI's help, asking it to write a strongly worded letter to the DIAND minister and pushing for immediate interim financing for the board.[56] In the second, "Board Members considered that new and intrusive powers of access to NWMB financial information would be inappropriate for application to an institution of public government (IPG). This seemed especially unreasonable given that no complaints or observations regarding NWMB financial performance have been made by DIAND to date. A provision for unilateral cessation of funding would be tantamount to provision for unilateral termination of the Board, existence of which is established and guaranteed under no less authority than the Canadian Constitution." The board opted to seek, in concert with NTI, a judicial review of the proposal.[57] Eventually, a modus vivendi was reached, but hard feelings persisted.

The board's submission to the first five-year review of the claim pulled no punches in its criticism of DIAND:

> At each of its last three fiscal year ends, the NWMB has been subjected to enormous last-minute pressure by the Department to sign an unacceptable document, or face having no operational funding. Each year, the Board has reluctantly signed an interim agreement, amidst assurances that necessary changes are imminent ... [In correspondence] the Minister has strongly

indicated her wish to make the necessary changes to the document ... Nevertheless, once again this spring, the NWMB was delivered – just days before its fiscal year-end – an entirely inappropriate contribution agreement ... The NWMB is understandably frustrated by such intransigence, and bewildered that certain elements within the DIAND bureaucracy can apparently overrule the wishes of the Minister.[58]

The authors of the five-year review agreed with the criticisms of the NWMB and the other IPGs about contribution agreements, commenting that, "as long as appropriate and practical accountability mechanisms are in place, restrictive financial administrations seem unnecessary."[59] Executive Director Noble had used more direct language during the 1997 funding flap: contribution agreements, he told *Nunatsiaq News*, are a "Mickey Mouse way of getting funds every year."[60]

In 2000, DIAND agreed to adopt a different funding mechanism, a "flexible transfer payment" (FTP), which did not entail automatic lapsing of unspent funds at year end. A staff briefing described the provisions of FTPs as "very significant improvements" over contribution agreements. The FTP imposed new reporting and accountability requirements that were "onerous ... [but] not beyond what a responsible agency should be ready and able to provide."[61] So long as they are earmarked for purposes approved in previous workplans, the board is entitled to retain funds unspent at the end of the year. Tellingly, shortly after the FTP was instituted, a veteran GN bureaucrat with no connection to the NWMB argued that the main reason DIAND moved to adopt FTPs was to improve its relationship with the powerful Treasury Board Secretariat, the federal government's central agency responsible for overseeing public spending. According to this interpretation, "DIAND has had to do all kinds of questionable things [in funding IPGs and other claims implementation matters] that fly in the face of everything Treasury Board stands for ... The FTPs were first and foremost to get Treasury Board off their backs and let DIAND play the games it wants ... The FTPs were not a great gift of DIAND to the IPGS; the first consideration was for DIAND's position."

Indeed, for a short period the new FTP arrangements worked to the board's satisfaction, but within not much more than a year DIAND began to unilaterally impose conditions that in the board's view contravened both the spirit and the letter of the FTP. Some years later, a board staff person, reflecting on the FTP, commented that, while it was an improvement over contribution agreements in terms of the flexibility to move money around and to keep it at year end, the improvement is one of degree rather than kind in that the FTP imposes too many conditions. Nor were the supposed virtues of FTPs always in evidence. In 2007, the board found it necessary to write the minister objecting to a DIAND decision rejecting a request to carry forward unused funds, arguing that this contravened the conditions of the FTP and "objecting to this retroactive, unilaterally-imposed change in policy and ... to the lack of notification of, and opportunity to respond."[62] The second five-year review, in 2006, offered no comment on the funding mechanism for the NWMB.

A related source of friction between the board and Ottawa in the early years was the "reprofiling" of IPG monies – the shifting of one board's surplus funds to another board. When the Implementation Panel unilaterally transferred money from the NWMB to the Nunavut Impact Review Board in 1999, the board expressed its displeasure, noting that, while the panel had authority to do this, it should not do so "capriciously."[63] It is worth noting that the Implementation Panel included GN and NTI representatives, so that the decision was not entirely Ottawa's doing. No "re-profiling" has occurred since this episode.

In these financial contretemps with the federal government, the board dealt with DIAND's Implementation Branch but assumed that the impetus for Ottawa's actions came from the Treasury Board Secretariat, which, like so much of Ottawa officialdom, had little appreciation of the distinctive nature of the IPGs established under the land claim or indeed of the claim itself. One NTI official simply observed: "DIAND is terrified of Treasury Board."

The board is often approached for subsidies and donations for various projects (beyond the wildlife research discussed below). It has traditionally been open to such requests; aside from supporting meetings and activities directly connected to wildlife, "these kinds of small donations are a common tradition in the North," as one person involved with the board put it. Donations, typically between $5,000 and $60,000, have gone, among other purposes, to support wildlife symposia and workshops sponsored by NTI; to local HTOs for planning of bowhead whale hunts; to the Nunavut Implementation Commission for celebrations around the April 1, 1999, creation of Nunavut; to Nunavut Sivuniksavut, a well-regarded Inuit post-secondary education institution in Ottawa to assist students "to visit a new land and its people and to act as ambassadors for Nunavut";[64] to Nunavut Arctic College for development of a bookkeeping course that would be beneficial to HTO staff; and $10,000 for a "Safety in Bear Country" video.[65] Among requests turned down by the board have been those from the Nunavut Help Line; a men's hockey team (for travel to a tournament); Inuit Language Week; and, most notably, from HTOs for such projects as building cabins for hunters, cleaning up campsites, and purchase of a trailer for additional office space.

In 2000, DIAND informed the board that it would no longer accept budgets or audits containing an item for "donations," stating that they were "not an admissible expense under expenditures funded by DIAND and not considered as part of an obligation to be met under the NLCA." The board complied with this directive but did not fundamentally alter its practices; rather, "the Board decided that it would be appropriate to re-structure its 'Donations Policy,' with provision to contribute funding by way of 'Conservation Education' or 'Advertising and Promotion' to externally-sponsored initiatives that were relevant to the mandate of the NWMB or to its operations."[66]

NWMB and Wildlife Research

The Nunavut Wildlife Management Board is unique for its role in developing and running large research projects and in funding research.[67] The first implementation contract earmarked some $11 million for the board's use to promote wildlife research on the part of the federal or territorial governments in Nunavut. Early on the board established the Nunavut Wildlife Research Trust to disburse the money, with board members as trustees, and an outside firm to manage investments. Only projects conducted or sponsored by the federal or territorial governments are eligible for funding, though the actual work can be contracted out to consultants or academics, and only for "research that is of high priority to the NWMB."[68] No draws were made on the fund for its first three years, and, with astute investment decisions, it had grown to over $23 million by 2015, enabling the board to provide federal and territorial departments with hundreds of thousands of dollars annually for research; each year at least $500,000 is distributed with the total sometimes exceeding $900,000.[69] These are substantial amounts and have the notable effect of reversing the usual funding dependency relationships, in that federal and territorial departments rely on the board for financial support of important projects.

The board also uses operating funds to support smaller-scale research by non-governmental agencies, primarily HTOs. Overall amounts distributed under this NWMB Studies Fund rubric vary substantially; $40,000 to $50,000 is routine, but in some years grants exceed $100,000 and on one occasion totalled more than $200,000, though in this instance some funded projects did not go ahead and the money was refunded.

These programs are entirely separate from the landmark Nunavut Harvest Study and the Inuit Bowhead Knowledge Study. Both of these massive projects were explicitly written into the claim and were to be organized and managed by the NWMB. Funding was guaranteed: $500,000 was allocated for the Inuit Bowhead Knowledge Study while the Harvest Study was to be "fully funded by Government." The bowhead study drew heavily on traditional Inuit knowledge, in the form of systematic recording of hunters' sightings set against elders' recollections of the frequency of sightings in previous decades. Findings from the harvest study provided essential baseline data used by the board to determine basic needs levels and total allowable harvests. Carried out over five years, the Nunavut Harvest Study was the largest such research project ever undertaken, with more than six thousand hunters and elders interviewed, often monthly, by fieldworkers as to the location, size, sex, and age of the animals they harvested. Costing $7.3 million,[70] the survey employed nearly forty people at its peak. Reports from both the Harvest Study and the Inuit Bowhead Knowledge Study were widely distributed and remain available, in Inuktitut and English, on the board's website.

Over the years, the board frequently discussed the possibility of mounting a second harvest study and earmarked significant funds for it. However, it became clear that the board was unlikely to be able to secure adequate funding and the idea fell into abeyance.

NWMB and Inuit Qaujimajatuqangit

Given its powers and responsibilities, it is hardly surprising that Inuit Qaujimajatuqangit is of central importance to the NWMB. The language of the claim underlines the importance of IQ principles in the board's operations, requiring, for example, that the wildlife management regime "recognizes Inuit systems of wildlife management" and the "need for an effective role for Inuit in all aspects of wildlife management, including research."[71] Thus the board's vision statement: "conserving wildlife through the application of Inuit Qaujimajatuqangit and scientific knowledge."[72] The 2018 strategic plan placed IQ as the board's second (of five) strategic goals, behind only wildlife management.[73] Only a brief overview of the board's experience with IQ is presented here. Chapter 8 looks in more detail at how the board has fared in its efforts to have IQ guide its operations and meetings.

In considering IQ it is essential to recognize that equating it to "traditional" knowledge, in the sense of information about and understandings of the past, is highly misleading. IQ does of course entail Inuit experiences of the past, but it is by no means static, constantly evolving as conditions and circumstances change: "this knowledge is not restricted to traditional knowledge in the meaning of 'old knowledge passed down from previous generations'; it also includes knowledge acquired by the current generation."[74]

From the outset, the NWMB has highlighted the importance of IQ in research, such as the bowhead study, and in the information and values on which the board bases its decisions. It has devoted considerable attention to ways of ensuring that IQ is adequately incorporated into decision making – for example, by routinely seeking advice and information from elders and hunters in its public hearings, especially those called to consider TAHs.

Still, many Inuit, unconvinced that Western science is willing to take IQ seriously, believe that the NWMB privileges Western science over IQ in its decision making. Scientists, said one IQ elder at the Rankin Inlet meeting described below, only pretend to use IQ "to look good" and don't actually use it. Another added: "Qallunaat [white people] don't trust anything they don't see in writing." Even board members express scepticism about science. At one meeting a member commented, "I tend to believe the information from Inuit more than I do from the Qallunaat departments," while another added, "instead of doing our homework in the office, we should do it in the communities ... we've been the hunters for hundreds of years."[75]

An NTI official quoted by Dominique Henri voiced both frustration and hope about the board's use of IQ:

> You need resources to collect IQ, you need commitment and set time aside to do it properly. Other than that you do a disservice to people ... I am tired of lip service about IQ. Everything is done for science. It's applied, it's documented, it's recorded, it's put into place, it's made into law. I want IQ to have the same value, legitimacy and impact as science does. Science and IQ need to be at the same level ...There is a lot of work to be done in documenting IQ. I think to some extent people have tried it but it's not there yet.[76]

In seeking to give full and proper consideration to IQ, the board has established an IQ coordinator position, created the IQ Research Fund, and adopted both formal and informal procedures encouraging the use of IQ. The 2018 strategic plan includes detailed actions and performance indicators for enhancing IQ in the board's operations and decisions, such as staff training "in the Inuit way of life."[77] As discussed in Chapter 8, these and other measures have enabled the NWMB to integrate IQ into its work to a significant degree, though at the same time substantial limits to its use arise from the Western bureaucratic nature of its structure and operations.

RWOs and HTOs

Nunavut's three Regional Wildlife Organizations and the Hunters and Trappers Organizations found in all communities play key roles in wildlife management and interact continually with the NWMB. Inuit-only bodies formally recognized in the *Nunavut Land Claims Agreement*, RWOs and HTOs exercise substantial authority, most notably in allocating and enforcing board-established quotas and in regulating harvesting practices. They also provide advice and information to the board and to other governmental agencies. RWOs and HTOs have their own by-laws and limited, usually part-time, staff; the claim requires the board to provide "adequate funding" to them.[78]

HTOs are overwhelmingly male institutions. According to former NWMB member Joan Scottie, in the 1970s women were not allowed to belong to HTOs.[79] A survey conducted in 2004–05 found that fewer than 10 percent of HTO board members in the Baffin (Qikiqtaaluk) region were women;[80] this situation is unlikely to have changed significantly in the intervening years. "Most HTOs," another study maintains, "are composed of harvesters from the older generations, who find resource management threatening."[81]

To say that relations between the board and the RWOs and the HTOs have sometimes been difficult is a gross understatement. One board staff member put it succinctly: "27 HTOs, 27 disasters" (in addition to the twenty-five legally constituted communities, two very small "outpost camps" have their own HTOs). Lack of capacity lies at the root of many HTO problems. With their limited budgets and often limited local talent pools, HTOs have difficulty recruiting and retaining competent staff, resulting in endemic financial and administrative troubles. The creation of the Nunavut Inuit Wildlife Secretariat (NIWS) and the substantial increases in government funding of HTOs has improved the situation markedly, though rough spots remain. Minutes of early board meetings are replete with references to serious problems at HTOs, usually related to financial matters. On several occasions the board sent staff "to clean up the HTO's accounting," as the minutes of one board meeting put it.[82] When it came to light that one HTO was $200,000 in debt, including $100,000 owed to Revenue Canada, the minutes recorded a remarkable pronouncement: "the Board expressed its usual dismay about the kinds of financial revelations that are emerging in this particular case."[83]

Nor were the RWOs immune from administrative woes. In 2004, the board's director of finance and administration was seconded to sort out matters at the Qikiqtani Wildlife Board, where both the executive director and the finance person had quit and no filing had been done for a year. That same year the NWMB was told that a joint review by its staff and NTI Department of Wildlife and Environment staff led to a decision to close the Kivalliq Wildlife Board office until its books could be updated and audited.[84] These administrative issues were serious in and of themselves but entailed more than the fact that the RWOs were not operating smoothly: they also meant that the RWOs were failing to perform their primary functions as part of the wildlife management system. A long discussion was held at a November 1999 board meeting on what to do about the RWOs and the HTOs, in part because of pressure from NTI for the board to do more, including financially, to help them. The position espoused by board chair Ben Kovic is worth quoting at length:

> NTI has not shown much imagination or initiative in addressing the problems. The only advice that the NTI President ever had for the NWMB in this matter was to increase the effort devoted to training ... The NWMB could focus hard on accountability, but the ultimate lever for that approach has to be the threat of shutting down an organization that is persistently delinquent or in arrears. The NWMB, as an institution of public government, does not consider that it has the authority to even contemplate such action against an Inuit organization. Now and increasingly, the slightest inclination of a hardening line by the NWMB is met by claims that the problems derive from inadequate funding.[85]

In 2004, the NWMB and NTI jointly engaged a consulting firm to review the operation of the RWOs and HTOs. The report did not sugar-coat these organizations' woes:

> In practice, the demands placed on wildlife management organizations far exceeds the vision of the Claims negotiators who established initial statements of responsibility and levels of funding. Given difficulties within the Government of Nunavut, both NTI and the RWOs have had to take on much more responsibility than originally intended. HTOs, which, for the most part, are one-person operations are responsible for a much broader range of obligations, programs and services than originally conceived, but without a concomitant increase in resources, staffing, training or policy support. Expectations and demands are growing: neither resources nor capacity, by and large, are keeping pace.[86]

Adapting recommendations from the consultants' report, with significant prompting from the board, NTI created the Nunavut Inuit Wildlife Secretariat to provide RWOs and HTOs with centralized support for basic financial and administrative functions. Formally established in October 2005, NIWS is responsible to a board composed of the chairs and vice chairs of the RWOs and is funded by NTI and the RWOs. Its main office is in Rankin Inlet but it also has staff in regional centres; it typically has three to five staff members. NIWS provides payroll and bookkeeping services to the RWOs and HTOs and a range of other minor administrative functions, such as travel arrangements and assistance with project management. It has developed policy and operational manuals for HTOs.

In March 2006, the NWMB agreed to a NIWS request for $160,000 to assist in its early work. However, the board was not prepared to support the secretariat's rather grandiose initial plans for wide-ranging involvement in wildlife issues, including working directly with federal departments on consultation and policy development.[87] In September 2007, the board's response to a NIWS request for additional funding was "to compliment NIWS for work done to date and to advise them that no additional financial support is available at this time."[88] Three years later, the board was less diplomatic in turning down a NIWS request for $350,000: "The Board recommended that NIWS review their own budget and decide how to find the necessary funding from within the organization."[89] NIWS subsequently adopted a more low-key posture and scaled back its aspirations to routine financial and administrative support to HTOs and RWOs.

Some HTOs bring in significant monies through sports hunting, guiding, and related activities. A few have fared very well financially by virtue of fishing endeavours: Baffin Fisheries, also known as the Baffin Fisheries Coalition, a joint venture of five Baffin HTOs, runs a substantial commercial fishing operation, with a fleet of four large vessels. Most HTOs, however, are hard-pressed for funding.

Core funding for HTOs comes from the NWMB, though this is essentially a transfer of money received from DIAND. The NWMB has no role in setting the level of funding, though it is involved in accountability processes. In 1999, each HTO annually received $60,000 from the board, plus a top-up of roughly $10,000 from the GN; by 2006, it was $74,000 plus the GN top-up; in 2014, the level had risen substantially to $140,000, and, under the 2015 settlement between NTI and the federal government, it was raised to roughly $200,000 with a built-in yearly escalator (half that to the two outpost camp HTOs). The GN contribution has essentially remained stable. With NIWS relieving the HTOs of administrative responsibilities, especially with respect to finances, the hope is that the new level of funding will enable them to operate more effectively.

Early in 2019, the federal government, through the Canadian Northern Economic Development Agency, announced one-time-only funding of $216,000, supplemented by $54,000 from NIWS, to Nunavut HTOs "to assist with the development of tools to update their governance system."[90] The money was earmarked for training materials, relating to accounting, human resources, governance procedures, and the like, to be delivered by NIWS.

Independence and Co-management

Members of boards such as the NWMB are explicitly appointed to serve "in the public interest" and are to act independently of the entities that nominated or appointed them. They are not to be delegates or representatives. Accordingly, the NWMB is not, by the conventional definition, a co-management board. Yet it describes itself as engaging in co-management in concert with what it terms its "co-management partners." And, indeed, the NWMB has been able to square the independence-co-management circle.

The independence of members is taken seriously. New board members swear to perform their duties "faithfully, truly, *impartially* and honestly,"[91] and to drive the point home on such occasions, the chair, Ben Kovic, "stressed that NWMB members do not and cannot represent any particular group or agency."[92] Members' independence has been a constant theme of board activities from early days, when, for example, during a conference call, "Gordon K[oshinsky] reminded the Board that his appointment is 'to represent the public interest,' and that neither he nor the Department considered that it was his role to represent DFO."[93] Similarly, during one of the first board considerations of a proposed *SARA* listing, "It was felt it would be best if the DOE [federal Department of Environment] nominee would step aside when these [*SARA*] issues are dealt with, to avoid conflict of interest."[94] This step came at the instigation of Kevin McCormick, the DOE/CWS nominee; since McCormick left the board only one DOE/CWS employee has served on the board, and that briefly, so that the issue has not arisen.

At the same time, an important basis for appointing members has always been their personal experience and expertise in wildlife issues, raising the question of where the line lies between providing useful information derived from involvement in an appointing agency and promoting the views and interests of the agency. A case in point arose at the first board meeting during which the regional director of the federal Department of Environment told the board that its appointee, Kevin McCormick, "will be the CWS representative and he will have full authority to speak for that agency."[95] In subsequent meetings,

McCormick declared conflicts of interest on certain items and recused himself, and at other times noted that, in contributing to discussions, he was "putting my CWS hat on" to provide the board with insights into government perspectives.[96]

To be sure, board members' approaches to the independence question vary a good deal, both for public servants and appointees of Inuit organizations. One board official commented in an interview that, "on the government side, one [federally appointed] member is almost reporting minute by minute to his DG [director general]; another seems to have very little communication with his department." Nor, according to this person, were such tests of independence confined to public servants: one regional Inuit association was "up their nominee's nose if he doesn't perform as they want," while another refused to reappoint a person because "they expected him to be at all their board meetings and to take instructions from them." At one meeting I attended a member appointed by an Inuit organization, in explaining his annoyance at not being invited to a particular RWO meeting, said "each and every one of us [board members] has been mandated to represent our regions and our people."[97] All told, however, it is fair to conclude that the board and its members respect and carefully guard their independence, as symbolized by the formal enquiry, at the start of every meeting, if members have any conflicts of interest to declare.

If the NWMB's strong commitment to independence is logically incompatible with conventional understandings of co-management, its approach to its duties is very much in the spirit of co-management. "We think it's co-management," said one person associated with the board, "the board members are independent, but you're seeing a trend towards appointing the heads of the regional wildlife organizations to the board, bringing their perspectives as Inuit leaders – how much closer to co-management can you get?" The board's reference to its "co-management partners" is more than empty rhetoric, as evidenced by the board's long-standing policy of not deploying its subpoena power to obtain information or to force particular individuals to appear before it. Such hard-nosed tactics, in the board's view, would sour the cooperative relationship it seeks to foster with government and with Inuit organizations. The board has occasionally discussed the possible use of subpoenas and could well resort to using them in particular circumstances. While it is prepared to take tough, forthright stands in its dealings with its partners, it is reluctant to resort to outright confrontation. This was evident at a board meeting at which members were seriously displeased by what they saw as DFO's failure to live up to an important commitment. One member – interestingly, a former federal public servant – argued that the board should "put DFO's feet to the fire" through tough legal means. The board, however, decided on a less aggressive stance, reflecting its preference for civility in its relations with the department.[98] In other instances, NWMB minutes confirm that it typically chooses a moderate, though by no means supine, approach when it has differences with its partners.

Relations with Government and NTI

At the federal level the NWMB deals mainly with three departments: DIAND, usually the Implementation Branch within the Treaties and Aboriginal Government Division; the Department of Fisheries and Oceans; and the Department of Environment (DoE), primarily the Canadian Wildlife Service. The board's relations with DIAND have been almost exclusively confined to the realm of finance and administration. As noted above, the NWMB has often found itself at loggerheads with DIAND over what the board sees as intrusive and improper demands from the department, which some at the board attribute to high staff turnover and an inability or unwillingness to push back against Treasury Board Secretariat policies and procedures that are inappropriate for a constitutionally protected IPG. Still, it would be misleading to suggest that conflictual relations are the norm; many routine matters are settled without issue.

Substantive board decisions, on quotas, non-quota limitations, proposed *SARA* listings, and the like go either to DFO or the DoE. Board members and staff are quick to point out that they have long gotten on well with local DFO staff who are knowledgeable about conditions and circumstances in Nunavut. Especially in the early days, this positive assessment did not extend to DFO headquarters, which was often seen as uncooperative and condescending. "DFO seems determined to ignore or override the claim," was how one board employee put it. Although it took place some time ago, those associated with the board still cite as typifying the fraught relationship an instance when DFO requested the board's advice about an important shrimp quota issue on a Friday, demanding a response by the following Monday.[99]

As with DIAND, not all board dealings with DFO involve conflict and hard feelings, but many do. Problems have occurred with the *SARA* process. In June 2004, the NWMB found itself discussing a *SARA* listing that DFO had already made prior to even contacting the board about it. Given the board's view that its decision-making authority under the *NLCA* supersedes the *SARA* requirement for Ottawa to consult land claims boards, this was an especially galling snub, which resulted in a stern letter to the minister.[100] Another contretemps involved a DFO request for a *SARA* decision with a very short time line; the board refused to consider the request, commenting: "There is no time for procedural fairness or public consideration of this matter."[101]

Nor was the board's opinion of DFO improved when, as discussed above, after years of being challenged by Inuit hunters and elders, the department admitted that its critically important estimate of the bowhead whale population was off by several orders of magnitude. Hunting bowhead in the Eastern Arctic had been illegal since the 1970s (and believed by many Inuit to have been declared illegal long before), but the claim authorized a TAH of one bowhead, subject to ministerial approval. This number was thought by DFO to be sustainable, based on its studies, which estimated the entire stock of Eastern Arctic bowhead at roughly 350 animals.[102] As the bowhead study confirmed, it was widely believed among Inuit that bowhead were far more numerous and that the population was growing. The bowhead study did not attempt an estimate of total bowhead numbers, so that in setting the TAH for bowhead at one every second year, the board had little choice but to rely on DFO figures, despite considerable scepticism about them.

In 2007, DFO made public a revised estimate of the bowhead population: 14,400 (within very wide confidence limits, 4,810 to 43,105).[103] Given that bowheads reproduce slowly, it was evident that Inuit IQ had been far closer to the mark than had been the scientists. Based on these numbers, the board increased the annual TAH to five.

Perhaps the most contentious DFO-related set of issues for the NWMB involves quotas for fish and shrimp in the waters off Nunavut, where the board has only advisory powers. Decisions as to how much fish and shrimp are available for harvest in these waters and how much of the quota goes to Nunavut-based fishers rest entirely with the DFO minister (the board distributes quotas assigned to Nunavut). Although Nunavut interests have gradually gained access to higher tonnages, the board and Nunavut fishers have long complained that discriminatory politics have told against them. With DFO ministers usually representing ridings in Newfoundland and Labrador or Nova Scotia, it is crass politics that leads them, so the allegation runs, to favour southern-based companies when quotas are distributed.

Board officials have indicated that in recent years, especially but not entirely since the 2015 federal election, which brought a Liberal government to power, relations with DFO have improved markedly. Following the election, Nunavut MP Hunter Tootoo was appointed fisheries minister but resigned after only a few months; no significant policy changes affecting Nunavut occurred on his watch.[104] Within a few months of Tootoo's resignation, however, Fisheries Minister Dominic LeBlanc, who represented a New Brunswick riding, announced a significant change that substantially favoured Nunavut fishing enterprises by doing away with the so-called northern shrimp "last-in-first-out" quota policy, which had given significant advantage to non-Nunavut firms.

Under the claim, the DFO minister is required to give special consideration to the advice of the NWMB on quota allocations for waters adjacent to Nunavut and to consider the interests and needs of Nunavut fishers when setting quotas. For nearly a decade, the board, along with NTI, argued vociferously that the minister failed to respect the claim in decisions about turbot in the waters between Nunavut and Greenland. NTI twice took the federal government to court on the issue, winning once but losing a subsequent case. Eventually Nunavut Inuit acquired a sufficiently large turbot allocation to make reasonable scale commercial fishing possible but only through extensive lobbying and political pressure.[105] Early in 2017, Nunavut fishers were given a substantial boost when LeBlanc allocated almost all of a large turbot quota increase to Nunavut. All told, between 2001 and 2017, the proportion of turbot quota for waters adjacent to Nunavut allocated to Nunavut interests increased from 27 percent to 74 percent,[106] in no small measure due to the board's efforts.

A significant source of the tension between the NWMB and DFO has been the lack of appreciation on the part of the department's headquarters staff for the import and status of the board and the land claim that created it. "People laugh at you when you say that the claim overrides the *Fisheries Act*," commented one DFO official with long familiarity of land claims and claims-mandated boards such as the NWMB. This attitude is not limited to DFO; rather, it is a broad government-wide failing. As board lawyer Michael d'Eça told a parliamentary committee, "most of Ottawa doesn't have a clue about land claims."[107]

The board's principal interactions with DoE/CWS involve proposed *SARA* listings and the management plans required for species deemed to be threatened or endangered. By and large, the board's relations with the department have been cooperative and agreeable, though on occasion, as was the case with Peary caribou, serious discord emerges.[108]

Normally, Ottawa's powerful central bureaucratic agency, the Privy Council Office, has no direct or indirect dealings with the NWMB, but on one issue of both substantive and symbolic importance, the board has found itself in direct, frustrating conflict with it. According to Article 5.2.20 of the *NLCA*, "Each member shall be paid fair and reasonable remuneration for work on the NWMB." However, authority to set payment levels for board members rests entirely with the PCO, which has consistently shown itself oblivious to the nature of the board and the scope of its responsibilities. The PCO has established brief criteria for determining which of four categories of pay scales are applicable for agencies, boards, and commissions with part-time federal appointees, such as the NWMB. When the board was created, the implementation contract set NWMB per diems at $200. A few years later the PCO categorized the board as a Category IV agency, the lowest on the pay scale. A board-initiated access to information request turned up no documents at the PCO analyzing the board's remit or justifying its categorization.[109]

From the outset, per diem rates were a source of dissatisfaction among board members who felt that it undervalued their important work, which required substantial expertise, though not necessarily in the form of formal credentials. Nor was $200 a day especially munificent, given Nunavut's sky-high living costs. As early as 1995, the board was seeking an increase in per diems but was stonewalled by the federal government. When the Nunavut Implementation Panel considered the NWMB's request "Canada's member indicated that he was unable to support an increase based on Roger Tassé's report. Canada indicated that the Tassé report could not be made available to NTI."[110]

Repeated requests for reclassification and thus higher per diems came to naught, though the rate was raised to $225 a day in 2002, as part of a general increase for claims boards.[111] In frustration, the board submitted a twenty-two-page (plus appendices) brief to the PCO arguing that the range and importance of the board's responsibilities warranted a reclassification as a Category II agency. The report pointed out that other Nunavut IPGs ("none of greater complexity, diversity, scope or impact than the NWMB") had recently been upgraded from Category IV to Category II, resulting in their members receiving per diems 67 percent higher than those paid NWMB members.[112] It further noted that the board's classification equated it to the Oshawa Harbour Commission. No explicit statement was made as to the insult this represented: none was necessary – the inference was obvious.[113]

The PCO refused to accept the report's recommendation to reclassify the board as a Category II agency. At the board's request, NTI sought a judicial review of the PCO's refusal. In rejecting NTI's submission, the Federal Court did not engage the basic issue of whether the prevailing NWMB per diems were "fair and reasonable" but instead concluded, through tortuous legal reasoning, that its refusal was not subject to judicial review since the PCO lacked the statutory authority to set the NWMB's remuneration.[114] In his 2005 *Conciliator's Interim Report,* Thomas Berger described the board's anomalous pay rates as "an aberration that must be corrected,"[115] and the Second Five Year Review concurred;[116] however, as of 2019, the PCO's categorization of the NWMB and the attendant per diems remain unchanged. The board's 2018 strategic plan sets out "fair and equitable remuneration" for board members as an item requiring attention.[117] Little wonder that its dealings with the PCO leave the board sceptical about Ottawa's professed good intentions.

Most board decisions about terrestrial mammals (including polar bears), birds, and habitat involve the GN's Department of Environment (formerly Department of Sustainable Development). Board members and staff often have long-standing personal links to GN staff and to the minister. These personal relationships can be important in facilitating interaction, but they by no means guarantee agreement on wildlife issues. Though territorial ministers have turned down few NWMB decisions, significant conflict has emerged on occasion. Perhaps the most notable clashes occurred during the development of the territorial *Wildlife Act* and the enactment of regulations implementing it. As discussed in more than half a dozen conference calls during 2003, the board had numerous significant concerns about provisions in the draft act, most of which were eventually resolved to its satisfaction, though not without difficult negotiations. As well, although the act was passed in 2003, it took over a decade to put the critically important regulations in place, owing in large measure to disagreement among the GN, the NWMB, and NTI.

The NWMB has extensive, close relations with NTI, marked by generally good cooperation interspersed with occasional tensions. Wildlife issues are among NTI's central concerns, but the links go beyond a mutual interest in, and usually similar perspectives on, wildlife. Not only do NTI and the regional Inuit associations appoint members to the board, but the appointees are sometimes senior figures in the Inuit organizations. Perhaps the most notable illustration, though hardly the only one, was Raymond Ningeocheak, who simultaneously served as NTI vice-president responsible for wildlife and as a member of the board.

Over the years the board has clearly and consistently taken the stance that, although its activities and decisions primarily affect Inuit, its mandate does not extend to promoting Inuit interests per se. NTI, which does represent Inuit and their interests, accepts the NWMB's position but doesn't always agree with the way the board puts it into practice. One long-time observer comments that some tension arises because NTI, a very political organization, wants and expects the board to be its political ally, but the board is generally unwilling to enmesh itself in politics.

To be sure, aside from behind-the-scenes frictions, NTI and the RWOs have been known to voice serious criticism of the NWMB in public settings. By way of illustration, at one public meeting, NTI took the board to task for lacking in transparency and sought a board policy that would notify the public whenever ministers accepted, varied, or rejected a board decision so that aggrieved persons or organizations could instigate a judicial review.[118] At an NWMB meeting I attended, an NTI official vociferously criticized a position the board had adopted and was in turn upbraided by a board member who demanded an apology for what he termed a "diatribe." More civil language soon prevailed, though no apology was forthcoming.

Such episodes, however, are the exception. The essentially cooperative relationship between the NWMB and NTI is symbolized by the board's frequent financial contributions to NTI projects – wildlife symposia, training programs, and the like – and by the board's support for an NTI legal action against the DFO minister's reduction of turbot quota, which extended to sharing the cost.[119] For NTI's part, it is telling that in more than one instance it contemplated taking the NWMB to court over board decisions to which it was opposed but decided against doing so in order to maintain good relations. One NTI official commented that "NTI tends to identify with IPGs – we're partisan on their behalf, for example in working to secure funding."

Two of the key themes underpinning the board's 2018 strategic plan, significantly titled *Connect and Collaborate*, are the need for close cooperation between the board and its partners – the federal and territorial governments, NTI, the RWOs, the HTOs, and so on – and the importance of effective communications with the partners and with the public.[120]

Major Contentious Issues

The Nunavut Wildlife Management Board makes dozens of decisions every year. Most are routine and uncontroversial. Others, however, are of substantial importance and generate significant controversy and confrontation. This section looks at several especially noteworthy and conflictual issues: the bowhead hunt, the proposed traditional polar bear hunt, and polar bear quotas.

The Bowhead Hunt
Bowhead whales, which typically reach fourteen to eighteen metres in length, were nearly hunted to extinction by commercial whalers in the nineteenth century. In 1979, their depleted numbers led to federal legislation banning their killing without a licence; in the Eastern Arctic no licence applications were made until 1995, as sanctioned by the *Nunavut Land Claims Agreement*. In negotiating the claim, the Inuit placed a high priority on restoring their

Aboriginal right to harvest bowhead. Accordingly, an unusual provision of the claim (Article 5.6.18) requires the NWMB to establish a total allowable harvest of at least one bowhead, subject to DFO ministerial approval.

Board planning for the bowhead study, also required by the *NLCA*, began in 1994, as did the process for setting a bowhead TAH. However, a major problem arose for the board in the form of an illegal bowhead harvest by three Inuit hunters near Igloolik in September 1994. Accounts varied as to the circumstances: the whale was dying and the hunters didn't want the meat to be wasted; they wanted to accommodate a respected elder's desire to taste bowhead muktuk (blubber) before passing away; they misunderstood the claim's provisions about the bowhead hunt. Whatever the reason, the board was caught between the figurative rock and a hard place. The leading Inuit organizations – NTI, the Baffin Region Inuit Association, and the Inuit Tapirisat of Canada – "moved from a unanimous condemnation of the Igloolik hunters' actions to a mitigated support of their cause once they saw that a trend had emerged in Inuit communities to sympathize with the hunters. Finally, NTI and BRIA declared their support for the hunters and stated that they would cover their legal costs."[121] Thus the board could either condemn the hunters, thereby antagonizing Inuit organizations and people in the communities, or it could undermine its authority and credibility by supporting the hunters. Chair Ben Kovic sent out a press release on the board's behalf, calling the episode "regrettable" in that "it did not follow or adhere to the terms of the NLCA."[122] In the end, DFO dropped the charges, after the board suggested that it do so, arguing that it would be better to expend energy and money on conservation education than on an "adversarial, divisive and very expensive" trial.[123] Although he welcomed the decision, Kovic emphasized that "this process is not the right way" and that Nunavut hunters should follow the provisions set out in the land claim, provoking an angry exchange with NTI president Jose Kusugak.[124]

The board had little trouble deciding on a TAH of one bowhead, though the DFO minister waited until the second last day of the sixty-day period to indicate approval. As with polar bear quotas, it was widely believed that international, especially US, anti-harvest pressure weighed heavily on Ottawa's perspectives and actions. The first hunt, near Repulse Bay in August 1996, did not go well, largely owing to inexperience, but with more extensive planning and training and better equipment, subsequent hunts proved successful. Indeed the bowhead hunt has taken on considerable symbolic importance, underlining the value of the claim for the protection of traditional Inuit practices.[125] As well, the hunt provides substantial amounts of meat and muktuk, which are distributed across Nunavut.

Nevertheless, the bowhead hunt continues to generate conflict. With DFO accepting that bowhead stocks are far larger than thought when the claim was negotiated, it concluded that "human induced mortality" (which includes harvest, ship collisions, and net entanglements) of up to eighteen whales a year is sustainable, though it cautioned against raising the quota to anywhere near that level.[126] By contrast, based on DFO's numbers, NTI recommended that the board simply remove the TAH – in other words, do away with the quota altogether.[127] While the board did raise the bowhead TAH to three per year in 2009 and five in 2015 (with ministerial agreement), NTI was unsatisfied and continued to press the board vigorously for a higher (or no) TAH.

Traditional Polar Bear Hunt

In 1997, Noah Kadlak, an experienced hunter from Coral Harbour, applied to the NWMB to conduct a polar bear hunt using traditional methods: a dog team and a spear. Board permission was needed because the NWT *Wildlife Act* only allowed hunters to use rifles and crossbows in bear hunting.[128] Kadlak planned to have the hunt filmed. The board decided to approve the hunt, subject to a number of conditions – for example, that Kadlak be accompanied by a hunter with a rifle. NWT minister of resources, wildlife and economic development Stephen Kakfwi rejected the board's decision on a variety of grounds, including concern for public safety. This was the first NWMB final decision to be overturned. The board quickly reaffirmed its initial decision, but in November 1998 the minister informed the board that he would not make a final decision but would punt the issue to the Nunavut Government, which was to be in operation within a few months. (The resulting delay did not contravene the provisions of the claim since no timelines constrain ministers' final decisions.)

In October 1999, after pressure from the board to resolve the issue, GN sustainable development minister Peter Kilabuk rejected the board decision on the grounds that the hunt posed "an unacceptable risk to public safety."[129] NTI president Paul Quassa disputed the minister's decision, claiming "the minister was basing his decision on the fact that this might not look very well with animal rights groups [because of the proposed filming] ... Noah (Kadlak) was going to do this in a very safe manner and I don't care what animal lovers think. I only worry about Inuit rights."[130] NTI sought and won a judicial review of Kilabuk's decision, which sent the matter back to the minister for reconsideration. Justice Robert Kilpatrick of the Nunavut Court of Justice ruled that the minister lacked evidence for his decision and thus unjustifiably infringed Inuit rights under the claim.[131] Kilabuk's successor, Olayuk Akesuk, rejected the hunt, citing the advice he received from eleven elders: "the elders told me that such a hunt is very dangerous and Kadlak's proposal is not a very safe one. Because of that, they could not support the hunt."[132] For his part, Quassa charged that the minister had manipulated the elders and promised that NTI would, in concert with the NWMB, continue to fight on Kadlak's behalf.[133]

The issue petered out, however, in part because NTI's priorities shifted to other matters and in part because the process dragged on for so long that Kadlak found himself unable to conduct the hunt in the way he had originally envisaged. Although it is impossible to cite evidence one way or the other, a reasonable speculation would be that the NWMB's highly publicized support for Kadlak's proposed hunt played well among Inuit hunters and other beneficiaries.

Polar Bear Quotas

No decision or set of issues has so directly challenged the co-management ethic of the NWMB or posed as stark a contrast between Western science and IQ as the continuing disputes over polar bear TAHs. Polar bears have become iconic symbols for climate change activists, who maintain that global warming has already done grievous harm to the bears' habitat in that the disappearance of sea ice renders it increasingly difficult for the bears to hunt seals, their prime food source. Fears that worsening conditions could lead to the extinction of polar bears promote very strong conservation sentiments. Western science provides a more nuanced assessment but overall sees severe threats to the health of polar bear populations resulting from continued global warming.[134]

For Inuit, polar bears are important not just as a source of food and income from what has come to be termed "conservation hunting." While Inuit culture demands respect for all animals, polar bears hold a special, profound place in Inuit culture and cosmology. Polar bears, which are like humans in their role as top predators, their ability to stand upright, and their facility in constructing snow houses, are seen as sentient and, indeed, as possessing "superior mental powers to humans in that they are psychic and can read human thoughts and intentions."[135] As well, "traditionally, hunting was thought to influence the [size of] the population only by the manner in which it was carried out. Disrespectful hunting would drive animals away, while respectful hunting could draw animals to humans."[136] Such beliefs continue to underpin the stance of many Inuit to polar bear management.[137] Whereas Western science has generally found polar bear populations to be stable or in decline, Inuit in many areas are convinced that polar bear numbers have increased substantially in recent times.

Like Alaska and Greenland, but unlike other Arctic countries, Canada permits Indigenous hunting of polar bears but is unique in sanctioning conservation (i.e., sport) hunting by non-Indigenous people. In that twelve of the world's nineteen recognized polar bear subpopulations are in Nunavut, international influences on polar bear hunting are especially significant for management policy and practice. This entails not only anti-hunting public opinion and activism but also legally binding directives from institutions such as the United States Fish and Wildlife Service and the *Convention on International Trade in Endangered Species of Wild Fauna and Flora (CITES)*.[138]

The NWMB has not hesitated to make tough decisions on polar bear quotas, for example, at one point imposing a complete moratorium on hunting in the M'Clintock Channel.[139] With few exceptions, in setting TAHs the board has found itself caught between scientific and governmental recommendations for reduced quotas and strong Inuit pressure to raise or even eliminate quotas. This dynamic has repeatedly surfaced with respect to the Western Hudson Bay (WHB) polar bear population.

The NWMB held a public hearing on the WHB TAH in Rankin Inlet in December 2014, which I attended. This was not the first public hearing or regular meeting on this issue. Although the WHB bear population is likely the most studied polar bear population in the world, uncertainty and disagreement have surrounded not only overall numbers but also the condition of the bears. Thus the quota set by the board and accepted by the GN fluctuated widely in the years leading up to the 2014 meeting, from 47 in 2002 to 56 in 2004, 38 in 2007, 8 in 2009, and 24 in 2011. The higher quotas reflected deference to IQ assessments of polar bear populations; the lower quotas emerging from scientific assessments of polar bear numbers plus pressure from the United States Fish and Wildlife Service, which criticized the GN for its failure to systematically document IQ.[140] The hearing came in response to ongoing pressure from HTOs and the Kivalliq Wildlife Board (KWB) to raise the existing TAH of twenty-four, which the board and the minister had reaffirmed that fall.[141]

In order to bring IQ into the decision-making process as effectively as possible, the board invited to the hearing, and paid the expenses of, representatives of the five communities that share the WHB TAH: Arviat, Rankin Inlet, Chesterfield Inlet, Baker Lake, and Whale Cove. The five HTO chairs, each accompanied by an elder, took part in the meeting and were seated at the table with board members, as were representatives of the KWB, NTI, and an "IQ elder" from Iqaluit and the GN deputy minister of environment (who had only recently left his position as director of wildlife at NTI).

GN and Environment Canada polar bear specialists made presentations of recent population studies, the gist of which was that the WHB subpopulation was stable. Environment Canada's land-based study estimated the number at 806 bears, while a GN aerial survey produced an estimate of 1,030.[142] On this basis the GN proposed maintaining the TAH at twenty-four bears (plus eight from Manitoba).[143]

The HTO chairs and the elders, supported by the KWB and NTI, insisted that the number of bears had increased substantially in recent years. A limited survey of people in the five affected communities conducted in early 2012 found that the majority of residents believed that polar bear numbers were at all-time highs and that there were too many bears.[144] Whereas they rarely saw bears when they were young, the elders said, bears were now so plentiful as to be constant safety threats in communities and to be causing serious food security issues because they were taking so many seals. For extended periods, it was pointed out, Arviat had to employ full-time watchmen to patrol the community to deal with wandering bears and had to take unusual precautions, such as ensuring that children did not go trick-or-treating outside at Halloween for fear of bear attacks. One elder spoke of a close relative who was killed and eaten by a polar bear.

Palpable hostility towards the scientists and disbelief with regard to their findings marked the meeting. It was not simply that local Inuit were convinced that the number of bears was much higher than the scientists claimed. Community representatives simply did not accept that the scientists had the expertise to support the conclusions they reached; one described the government researchers as "people who don't know what they are doing because they didn't grow up in our environment." Others voiced deep scepticism, if not outright rejection, of the scientists' methods: "I'd believe them if they came around every year rather than every 30 years" said one, while others questioned how a supposedly comprehensive survey could be completed in a few days. "What is your goal," one elder asked, "why are you always counting and surveying?" The scientists' explanations of their sampling techniques and their response that Environment Canada does run annual WHB polar bear surveys left Inuit unconvinced.[145] Whereas the scientists' work was rooted in a concern for a species under significant environmental pressure, the Inuit were not worried about the long-term prospects for polar bears, various community representatives commenting: "I have no idea why scientists think polar bears won't survive ... they are survivors"; "polar bears can adapt to any climate"; "I'm not worried about polar bears because they can survive better than me."

NTI and Environment Canada supported the GN's proposal to leave the TAH at twenty-four plus eight. The HTO chairs and the elders asked that it be raised to seventy-five. In the end the board decided on a TAH of thirty-eight, plus the eight "Manitoba" bears, though the confidentiality provision in the claim meant that this decision was not known for some time. In the end, the GN minister approved an increase of only four bears, generating a good deal of local resentment.[146]

During most of the hearing the entire audience, save the author, consisted of representatives of governments, Inuit organizations, or communities, though the meeting had been widely advertised as a public hearing. Towards the end, two members of the public did attend for a period. Members of the public are permitted to speak and to ask questions at public hearings, though not at regular meetings, but very few do.

In April 2007, Dominique Henri attended an NWMB public hearing in Arviat, called in response to a "ministerial management initiative" from the GN minister of environment proposing various options for the WHB polar bear quota, all involving reductions. As with the Rankin Inlet hearing seven years later, representatives from the five affected HTOs participated in the meeting, as did KWB officials, local elders, and, of course, scientists and NTI staff. Many of her observations apply with equal force to the public hearing in Rankin Inlet. She concluded, for example, that the conflict pitting Inuit against scientists, the GN, and to some extent the NWMB reflected not only the actual level of the TAH "but also (and most importantly) the ways in which quotas had been derived."[147] As for the meeting itself, "although substantial efforts and resources were allocated to the translation of oral and written material into both English and Inuktitut, the degree to which various actors could understand the concepts presented, as well as constructively engage with the formal setting of a hearing varied greatly according to their level of experience and preparation."[148] Moreover, despite the board's emphasis on co-management and its efforts to facilitate it, "a divisive logic of confrontation pervaded this trial-like consultative exercise."[149]

In Henri's estimation, the hearing process did enable Inuit influence on the nature of the debate and the policy questions under consideration but only limited influence on the central issue, the setting of a TAH for WHB polar bears.[150] In both the Arviat and Rankin Inlet hearings, the process, the dialogue, and the outcomes all demonstrated a wide gap in worldviews between Inuit and Western science that the NWMB, for all its efforts and good intentions, was unable to bridge. As George Wenzel put it, "stochastic models of polar bear ... population dynamics appear to be as metaphysical to Inuit as Inuit beliefs about replenishment through hunting appear to biologists."[151] Little wonder that "some Inuit consider the human-polar bear relationship to be threatened by the very existence of the quota system."[152]

Inuit Influence through the NWMB

Thierry Rodon's early assessment of the NWMB was ambivalent. He concluded that the NWMB experience was clearly a process of integration into state institutions. Has co-management, he asked, enhanced Inuit autonomy? If the criterion is Inuit capacity to make decisions within a framework Inuit have developed, his answer is no. If the criterion is Inuit ability to make decisions within a governmental system, his answer is yes.[153] My reading of the evidence presented in this chapter is that Inuit unquestionably exert significant influence through the NWMB. Whether this should be understood as advancing Inuit autonomy is a separate question, the answer depending, as Rodon suggests, on the criteria applied.

Prior to the creation of the Nunavut Wildlife Management Board, Inuit in the Eastern Arctic had virtually no formal involvement in establishing and administering wildlife policy and little more informal influence. As one of the key institutions of the land claim, the NWMB has clearly brought substantial Inuit influence to bear on both overall policy and specific government decisions affecting wildlife. Although in most areas its decisions can be rejected by government, in practice this only happens infrequently – and often at some political cost to the government that overturned the decision.

The board's influence reflects the respect it enjoys in the government departments with which it interacts (for the federal government, the respect is evident among officials in Nunavut if not always among their superiors in Ottawa). The NWMB's positive reputation is built on its thoroughly researched and well thought out decisions; its cooperative, co-management-premised approach in dealings with its partners; and its strongly Inuit character, all reinforced by the board's status as under the constitutionally protected land claim. For its part, although NTI is not always in agreement with the board, sometimes believing that it is not as vigorous in promoting Inuit interests as it might be, overall, it sees the board as an important ally and is a strong supporter.

The Inuit character of the board is evident to anyone attending one of its meetings. The overwhelming majority of its members are Inuit, with extensive first-hand knowledge of the land and wildlife; much of the discussion is in Inuktitut, with simultaneous interpretation available for presentations and interventions in English; a requirement that documents prepared for it in English be accompanied by Inuktitut translation is rigorously enforced; and serious attention is given to IQ.

None of this is to suggest either that the board has been problem-free or that its continuation as an effective, influential mechanism for bringing Inuit perspectives to bear on wildlife issues is assured. Retaining its reputation and influence has been and remains a challenge. Among the difficulties the board continues to face are a lack of understanding – or, in some instances, acceptance – in senior Ottawa circles of the land claim and the board's status under it; prolonged government delays in filling membership vacancies; problematic provisions of the claim that constrain the board (e.g., the lack of a deadline for government responses to "final" board decisions); staff turnover; and the difficulty of incorporating IQ into board decisions and processes.

These challenges are not new, and over the years the board has, by virtue of strong, stable leadership, high-quality staff, and substantial levels of funding, successfully fulfilled its mandate and, in so doing, brought a strong Inuit voice into wildlife management in Nunavut.

Afterword

Since the December 2014 Rankin Inlet hearing described above, the issue of polar bear numbers and quotas in Western Hudson Bay has continued to generate controversy and has been the subject of additional board hearings and meetings.[154] The demands of local Inuit for increased quotas took on a special urgency following the tragic killing of an Arviat man by a polar bear near the community in July 2018[155] and the death of a hunter from Naujaat as a result of a polar bear attack a few weeks later.[156] Shortly after the first attack, five polar bears were found shot to death, without tags and without their meat being harvested, near Arviat.[157] Inuit MLAs forcefully criticized the entire polar bear management approach, calling for an end to quotas and warning of possible civil disobedience on the part of hunters.[158] A GN submission to the NWMB calling for significant modifications to the existing polar bear co-management regime downplayed the scientific community's concerns about the effect of climate change on polar bears, favouring instead Inuit views that polar bear numbers have been growing.[159]

chapter 4

The Yukon Fish and Wildlife Management Board

A reasonable assumption about the Yukon Fish and Wildlife Management Board (YFWMB) would be that it is structured and operates in much the same fashion as its Eastern Arctic counterpart, the Nunavut Wildlife Management Board. To be sure, similarities exist, but the differences are manifold and far-reaching. Some are simply idiosyncratic, but others reflect substantial differences between Nunavut and Yukon: the distinct political contexts in which the two boards are embedded, including significant differences between the Nunavut claim and the Yukon *Umbrella Final Agreement*; the different demographic makeups of the two territories; the nature of the territories' government regimes – party-based in Yukon versus "consensus" in Nunavut; and differences between the wildlife and the habitat in Nunavut and Yukon (e.g., Nunavut effectively has no roads while Yukon has an extensive network of highways and heavily used resource roads affecting wildlife habitat). Moreover, in looking at the YFWMB it is necessary to extend the analysis to include the Yukon Salmon Sub-Committee, which has no Nunavut equivalent, as well as to the local Renewable Resources Councils (RRCs), which differ fundamentally from Nunavut Hunters and Trappers Organizations in composition, mandate, and influence. It is also worth bearing in mind that the budget of the Nunavut board is several times that of its Yukon counterpart.

The *UFA* between the Council of Yukon Indians (CYI; now Council of Yukon First Nations [CYFN]), the Government of Canada, and the Yukon Government (YG), was finalized in 1993 after two decades of off-and-on negotiations. As noted in Chapter 2, the *UFA* is not per se a land claim (though it is often described as such) but, rather, a framework under which individual First Nations negotiate and finalize land claims and self-government agreements.

The YFWMB was established by Chapter 16 of the *UFA* as, in language familiar from other claims, "the primary instrument" of fish and wildlife management in Yukon.[1] Each settled land claim – currently eleven – repeats Chapter 16 of the *UFA* with supplementary provisions to reflect local circumstances and preferences. The board has no additional legislative foundation; it is, for example, not mentioned in the Yukon *Wildlife Act*, though it is very much involved in the policy framework set out in the act.

The YFWMB's jurisdiction covers fish and wildlife in the entire territory with two notable exceptions. First, on the North Slope, a broad strip of land along the Arctic coast, wildlife management is the responsibility of the Wildlife Management Advisory Council (North Slope) (WMAC [NS]), a co-management board established under the *Inuvialuit Final Agreement*. Thus the YFWMB does not deal with marine mammals and, for the most part, does not make recommendations for wildlife in the North Slope area of the Inuvialuit Settlement Region. Section 2.6.2.5 of the *UFA* specifies that in any conflict or inconsistency between the *UFA* and the *IFA*, the *IFA* is to prevail. Beyond this stark admonition, how the two claims-mandated boards are to relate to one another is ambiguous. Since, as one public servant commented, "the IFA is blind to the UFA," the board has little contact with WMAC (NS).

Second, management of salmon, the most important aquatic species in Yukon, falls to the Yukon Salmon Sub-Committee (YSSC), nominally a subset of the YFWMB but in fact a largely separate entity.

Also formally outside the board's remit are what the definitions chapter of the *UFA* describes as "Exotic species or Transplanted Population"; bison and elk fall into this category, as do farm animals such as cattle and domestic sheep.[2] Nonetheless, the board does take an interest in the health and maintenance of farm animals out of concern that contact between domesticated animals and wildlife could spread disease to wildlife. In deference to the Porcupine Caribou Management Board, a non-claims board, the YFWMB generally does not deal with the Porcupine Caribou herd.

Another key limit on the board's jurisdiction, again very different from the wildlife management regime in Nunavut, is that its policy is to make recommendations that apply only to non-Indigenous people and to members of First Nations on lands outside their traditional territories. Section 16.7.11 of the

UFA leaves no doubt that the board has the authority to make recommendations to First Nations, but it has consistently declined to do so. To some extent this is because many First Nations lack legislation that would enable them to implement recommendations other than beyond urging voluntary compliance. Some, however, such as the Champagne and Aishihik First Nations, have passed their own wildlife acts that could serve as the basis for implementing board recommendations that the First Nation accepted. More fundamental, however, is the board's long-standing policy of entirely avoiding recommendations to First Nations governments. Indeed, the board has never made such a recommendation. Although First Nations subsistence harvests and wildlife management issues on First Nations lands are sometimes discussed, board members see these as, in one person's words, "a bit taboo" and refrain from addressing them directly. This self-imposed limitation on the board's remit means, according to one public servant, that the board works "with one eye closed." The implications of this policy are discussed in this chapter's conclusion.

In sharp contrast to Nunavut, where the wildlife article of the claim was the first to be negotiated, Chapter 16 of the *UFA* was the last element to be finalized. One interpretation has it that the hurried completion of Chapter 16 is evident in some of the loose and problematic wording about the roles, responsibilities, and relations of the board and the RRCs.

Mandate and Structure

A glance at some of the objectives of Chapter 16 of the *UFA* offers a clear sense of the balancing act the board is expected to perform:

- to ensure Conservation in the management of all Fish and Wildlife resources and their habitats;
- to preserve and enhance the renewable resources economy;
- to preserve and protect the culture, identity and values of the Yukon Indian People;
- to ensure the equal participation of Yukon Indian People with other Yukon residents in Fish and Wildlife management processes and decisions;
- to guarantee the rights of Yukon Indian People to harvest and the rights of Yukon First Nations to manage renewable resources on Settlement Land;
- to integrate the management of all renewable resources;
- to integrate the relevant knowledge and experience both of Yukon Indian People and of the scientific communities in order to achieve Conservation;

- to develop responsibilities for renewable resource management at the community level;
- to honour the Harvesting and Fish and Wildlife management customs of Yukon Indian People and to provide for the Yukon Indian People's ongoing needs for Fish and Wildlife;
- to deal fairly with all Yukon residents who use Fish and Wildlife resources in the Yukon; and
- to enhance and promote the full participation of Yukon Indian People in renewable resources management.[3]

While the guarantees provided "the Yukon Indian People" for participation in wildlife management are noteworthy, no comprehensive claim in the territorial North is so pointed in emphasizing the rights of non-Indigenous people in wildlife policy and decisions. This is, to be sure, not surprising given the numerical preponderance of non-Indigenous people in Yukon (most big game outfitters in the territory are non-Indigenous) and the resistance at the time in some quarters of the non-Indigenous community to the settlement of the *UFA*. Still, the contrast with Article 5 of the *Nunavut Land Claims Agreement*, which repeatedly emphasizes the primacy of Inuit and Inuit rights while scarcely alluding to non-Inuit, is striking.

Structurally, the YFWMB has twelve members, appointed by the Yukon Government. Half the members are to be nominees of Yukon First Nations (in practice, the CYFN) and half are "government" nominees. One of the government nominees is to be appointed "in consultation and concurrence" with the federal government,[4] but otherwise, unlike for wildlife management boards in Nunavut and the NWT, Ottawa has no role in nominating or appointing members. According to a former board member, at one point the federal government did attempt to influence board appointments, but the territorial government held firm and the pressure dissipated.

Under the *UFA*, a majority of both government nominees and of First Nations nominees must be Yukon residents. Today, the need for this provision is less than obvious in that few if any non-residents have ever been appointed to the board. However, a strong sentiment emerged during negotiations on the *UFA* that boards should be structured so as to prevent the recurrence of a scenario all too familiar to Yukoners, both First Nations and non-First Nations: outsiders would be sent by Ottawa, fly in, stay only briefly, and make bad decisions because they did not understand the local situation. One long-time Yukon politico contends that the non-resident provisions of the *UFA*, which also apply to other boards, "was a really strong unifying argument between First Nations and white people in getting on with the claim."

Board appointments are for five years and are renewable. In recent years members have generally not remained on the board as long as members did in its early years, leading to concerns about excessive turnover and loss of corporate memory. The territorial government makes the actual appointments, though an unusual, perhaps unique, provision in the *UFA requires* it to appoint the First Nations nominees to the various boards established under the agreement, including the YFWMB (2.12.2.4). One former minister of environment did indicate in an interview that he believed that he had the power to refuse to appoint a First Nations nominee but had never done so. Aside from occasional eye-rolling when a particular name comes forward as a potential nominee, neither the government nor the CYFN attempts to influence the selection of nominees from "the other side." Board members may be removed by the minister "for cause" following consultation with the nominating party. The *UFA* implementation plan contemplates a board advising the minister to remove a board member, but interviewees indicated that no members have been removed, though a few "came close." In at least one instance, as recorded in its minutes, the board directed the chair to write to a member who was frequently absent asking him to indicate his "intentions in terms of being an active Board Member";[5] the person in question had resigned by the next board meeting.[6] Members of the YFWMB may not be on an RRC, though many board members previously served on RRCs.

According to one *UFA* negotiator, the federal government's initial preference had been to structure the board on the Inuvialuit model: members explicitly designated as representatives of the party that nominated or appointed them, with government members usually drawn from the ranks of public servants. The YG rejected this approach and, from the outset, adopted an informal policy of not appointing public servants to the YFWMB. Those familiar with board history confirm that no deviation from this policy has occurred, though a number of former public servants have served on the board. The CYFN initially refrained from nominating its staff or staff of individual First Nations, but it has backed away from a hard and fast policy in part because of the difficulty of securing good people to serve on boards.

Women have been far more in evidence as YFWMB members than as Nunavut Wildlife Management Board members. Since its creation, eleven of the fifty-three YFWMB members have been women (21 percent). The number of women on the board has never fallen below two; at any given time, it is likely to have three, occasionally four, women members. Two women have served as board chair. In its early years, the board designated one of its members as a "youth representative."[7] This practice ended some time ago.

The board chooses its chair from among its members; the government must accept the board's choice. If the board has not selected a chair sixty days after the position becomes vacant, the territorial government can step in and appoint one of the board members as chair. This has never happened. Chairs typically serve two-year terms. An informal understanding sees the chairship alternate between First Nations members and non-Indigenous members; when the chair is First Nations, the vice-chair is non-Indigenous and vice versa. Initially, this practice was written into the operating procedures the board adopted.

An executive comprised of the chair, the vice-chair, and the executive director keeps YFWMB's work moving along collaboratively. Among other things, the executive deals with logistics such as organizing board agendas; it also engages with persons or groups involved with wildlife, such as the Yukon Outfitters Association, the Yukon Conservation Society, and the Yukon Fish and Game Association, as well as with ministers and other senior government officials. In addition, at any time the board has half a dozen or more "working groups" or special working committees. Their subject matter has varied a good deal over the years. Special working committees, such as the Personnel Committee, focus on internal board matters. Working groups are involved with both far-reaching issues such as traditional knowledge and narrowly defined concerns such as "meat management" – meat care and handling practices in the outfitting industry. Some working groups consist entirely of board members; others comprise members from a range of governmental and private organizations.

In a typical year the board holds five meetings lasting three days, mostly in Whitehorse, though at least one meeting a year is held "on the land"; this sometimes means in a community or a lodge, but for the most part it entails tents and rudimentary cabins on the land. Board members hold conference calls but not as an alternative to in-person meetings. With the majority of board members living in Whitehorse or nearby, commuting to meetings is not an issue for most members, though some members from fly-in or distant communities require long commutes. Members' busy schedules can make scheduling meetings difficult.

Similar to the model of the Nunavut Wildlife Research Trust, the YFWMB members also serve as the trustees for the Yukon Fish and Wildlife Enhancement Trust, a charitable foundation established by the *UFA*, with assets of roughly $4.9 million as of 2017. The trust supports research, education, and other projects aimed at protecting and enhancing fish and wildlife populations and their habitat; trustees allocate funds on the basis of an annual public call for proposals.

Board staff work out of a small suite of offices in downtown Whitehorse. In recent years, staff members typically number only three: an executive director, an office manager, and a third position whose function has varied over the years (most recently it has been a communications and information specialist). In earlier years staff were more numerous, though some were part-time.[8] At one point the board employed three "community stewards" whose positions were not covered by the board's core funding from government. The community stewards program proved highly successful and was subsequently taken over by First Nations who sought out funding and hired local stewards. From the board's perspective, the program ended on a high note and built capacity for First Nations in terms of fundraising and program operation.

The *UFA* requires the YG director of fish and wildlife to serve as an "advisor" to the YFWMB and to "ensure that technical support is provided to the Board."[9] This unusual provision is more than a vague commitment: the board works closely with the Yukon Department of Environment (formerly the Department of Renewable Resources), and the director of fish and wildlife attends board meetings, frequently briefing members on wildlife issues and policies at in camera sessions. Although it lacks extensive technical research capacity, the board only occasionally engages consultants for technical research. Consultants are hired for administrative tasks such as minute taking, information technology, and records management. The board's expectation is that, through the guidance of the director of fish and wildlife, the YG environment department will provide the technical research required to make informed recommendations. The board has no regular source of legal expertise; on occasion it has sought legal advice or opinions from private practice lawyers. The trust's part-time manager is not on the board payroll but is paid by the trust.

Early Days

The *Umbrella Final Agreement* and the first four First Nations final and self-government agreements came into effect February 14, 1995; the initial meeting of the Yukon Fish and Wildlife Management Board was held a month later in Whitehorse. Although a new entity, the YFWMB was able to draw on the experience of various predecessor boards. The Yukon Wildlife Management Board (YWMB) began operation in March 1988, replacing the Wildlife Management Advisory Council. A pre-implementation board was established in late

1990, taking over the work of the YWMB and preparing the way for the *UFA* board. Several of the first members of the YFWMB had served on either or both the YWMB and the pre-implementation board and brought with them firm ideas about what the new board should and should not do.

According to members of the YWMB, the Advisory Council had a poor record, in large part because it was viewed as lacking influence. The Yukon minister of renewable resources commented that it "was not given sufficient authority to be effective."[10] The YWMB saw its mission as providing advice to the minister based on gathering of information and public opinion and developing recommendations in a thorough and independent manner.[11] It did not, however, have any illusions that it was anything other than, as the minutes of one meeting put it, "an arm of the government."[12] The minister himself chaired the first meeting, pending the board's selection of a chair; it was understood that the minister would "determine which issues the Board will deal with."[13] The board secretariat consisted of the YG director of fish and wildlife and a secretary from his branch. And, on at least one occasion, to the consternation of some board members, when the chair was unavailable to speak to the media, the minister directed that a government employee speak on the board's behalf.[14]

Half the members of the YWMB were First Nations; half were non-Indigenous. Although the board had discussed with the minister the possibility of appointing non-Indigenous and First Nations co-chairs, the board unanimously decided that "race should not be an explicit criterion ... for determining the co-chair positions."[15] In order "to make the profile of the Board much more Yukon wide" than that of its predecessor, the board developed the practice of holding meetings in communities across the territory.

The first day of the initial YFWMB meeting was actually a joint meeting of the board and the pre-implementation board. The YFWMB's importance was highlighted in the speeches from Mickey Fisher (Yukon minister of renewable resources) and Judy Gingell and Albert James (chair and vice-chair, respectively, of CYI) that opened the meeting. The minister's address was upbeat if anodyne: "mutual support and cooperation are necessary for progress ... time and patience may be required ... honesty, openness, tolerance and patience on the part of all would create trust."[16] Gingell was also positive about the board but forthright:

> She stressed the need for protection of the interests of the ten First Nations who were still negotiating their agreements. Members were left with the clear impression that they have a special responsibility to respect the interests of these First Nations and their traditional territories in the absence local [sic]

RRCs ... Ms Gingell encouraged the Board to draw upon the wisdom of the elders. She observed that First Nations people had survived in the Yukon for countless generations by following that wisdom.[17]

At their joint meeting, members of the pre-implementation board offered a range of practical advice to the new *UFA* board, most notably a strong recommendation that board members receive cross-cultural training, including involvement of First Nations elders. Astute advice was also proffered that "members need to learn about 'bureaucratic' culture and the procedures and assumptions which are followed by the scientists and managers who have guided government management of wildlife."[18] Like the minister, though in a less platitudinous manner, pre-implementation board members emphasized the importance of genuine exchange of views and compromise, pointing out that not once had they resorted to a formal vote. They also warned that the development of regulatory proposals through public consultation had proven "problematic" because the Department of Renewable Resources had been too deeply involved in the process, especially in the form of its internal Regulations Review Committee that members saw as sometimes "working at cross purposes to those of the Board."[19] One member of the pre-implementation board observed that "the Board is like a marriage – members will be working together very closely. Since its [sic] a mixed marriage, members will have to work extra hard to make it work."[20]

The YFWMB quickly got down to work, emphasizing thrift, effectiveness, and transparency and demonstrating considerable political sensitivity. In short order it confirmed the contract of consultant Graham MacDonald as executive secretary, continuing the role he performed for the pre-implementation board; it provided members with fax machines, answering machines, long-distance calling cards, and file cabinets; and it leased an office in downtown Whitehorse. Thoroughgoing frugality was evident in the board's approach to these routine administrative matters. Initially, members were uncertain whether a full-time administrator, let alone support staff, was really needed (a secretary-receptionist was hired several months later), and one member cautioned that, should the board open an office, costs might spiral out of control.[21] When the office leased proved slightly larger than the board needed, the excess space was rented out for storage.[22]

Early in 1996, the board hired a First Nations woman, Pearl Callaghan, as executive director. After five years, Callaghan left and was replaced by Kelly Hayes, who remained with the board for three years. Christine Cleghorn, who later became YG director of fish and wildlife served briefly as executive director.

In 2006, Graham Van Tighem, who had been with the board in various capacities for several years, was appointed executive director and was still in that position at the time of writing.

The board's first annual report pointed out that the pre-implementation board "constantly found itself overloaded by issues ... [so that] there never seemed to be an opportunity to step back and put things in perspective." Accordingly, it "deliberately shelved issues for its first few months of operations to allow itself time to put together a system to avoid the same sense of overload that frustrated previous Board members."[23] An elaborate screening system was developed to highlight priorities and avoid duplication. All potential topics for board attention were subjected to a thorough assessment that sought a clear statement of the problem – if indeed it was a problem – and asked who was concerned about it and why and, most important, "is it really the Board's business?"[24] Significantly, whereas many newly formed boards seek to widen their mandates, if not outright empire build, the board took the stance that it needed to be careful not to usurp the role of the RRCs.

Demonstrating the YFWMB's commitment to transparency, the report not only devoted several pages to outlining and explaining the screening process in non-technical language as a guide for anyone wanting the board to address an issue but also included the full text of the board's operating procedures. Many were unremarkably routine. Some, however, were notably distinctive, such as the one-year limit to the chair's term and the requirement that if the chair were a government nominee – in effect non-Indigenous – the vice-chair would be a First Nations nominee and vice versa. Decisions were to be made by consensus wherever possible; failing consensus a two-thirds majority was required to pass a motion, and this meant not two-thirds of members present (assuming a quorum, which was set at eight) but eight of the twelve members. The operating procedures set out in extensive detail both the screening process and the creation and operation of "issue working teams," board subcommittees struck to review and report on specific issues. A section of the operating procedures devoted to "Use of Lawyers" revealed a distinct lack of enthusiasm for involving the legal fraternity in the board's work. Its first provision: "As a general principle, legal opinions will not be sought by the Board on internal matters or recommendations."[25]

The board's political sensitivity was evident in how it dealt with CYI and in its avoidance of controversial issues in the early going. Well aware of CYI's suspicion of the territorial government, the board went out of its way to show CYI that it understood co-management to mean working effectively with both the YG and CYI. As a practical step in this direction, the board asked CYI to appoint a liaison person.[26] When it came to light that the implementation process did not include CYI in negotiations around provisions of the contribution agreement that would fund it, the board refused to sign the agreement until CYI indicated its satisfaction with the contribution agreement.[27] Similarly, a confidentiality provision in the *UFA* that the board could not tell CYI about recommendations to the minister led it to seek (without success) a protocol with the minister that would enable it to keep CYI informed.[28] In response to CYI concern about what it saw as an inappropriate comment the minister had made at the initial board meeting about wishing to attend at least part of each board meeting, the chair sought out the minister, who assured the board and CYI that he only wished to demonstrate "openness and availability ... not to dictate its [the board's] agenda" and had no intention of regularly attending board meetings.[29]

From the outset, game farming and ownership of outfitting operations loomed as highly controversial issues that the board would have to confront. It wisely decided to hold them in abeyance and instead work on less contentious issues in order to build up credibility and support across the range of interests and organizations with which it would be interacting. On game farming the board declared it "had no appetite to get into a potentially divisive issue right off the start."[30] On outfitting ownership, it noted "general agreement that the Board was not equipped to deal with the issue in the immediate future and concern that the Board should place priority on processes to deal with issues before taking on controversial subjects."[31]

On several occasions in their first year, board members were briefed by federal, CYI, and YG officials on the principles and details of the *UFA*, especially but not exclusively Chapter 16 on fish and wildlife. Cross-cultural training sessions were held, attempts were made to involve First Nations elders in the board's work, and repeated commitments were made to incorporate traditional knowledge into board information gathering and decision making. The board developed positions on the proper discharge of its responsibilities, concluding, on the one hand, that it had the right to "intervene" in areas of federal jurisdiction such as forestry because of possible habitat implications, and, on the other hand, that it would tread carefully in areas without RRCs, ensuring that community support and consensus was present for any board action on wildlife management.[32]

Signals from the territorial government on its approach to the YFWMB were generally positive. The director of fish and wildlife disbanded the Regulation Review Committee that had exercised the pre-implementation board, promised to "not attempt to influence any of the [board's financial] detail," and offered the opinion that, while the minister retained final decision-making authority, "the Board can exert great influence and cause the Minister major political grief if he chooses to go against Board advice."[33]

Although the YFWMB spent a good deal of time in its first year working out processes, operating procedures, and the like, it did engage with and act on a significant number and range of substantive issues, from rebuilding caribou herds to outfitter quotas – itself a touchy issue – to proposed amendments to the federal *Yukon Quartz Act* and *Placer Mining Act* relating to wildlife habitat.[34] Significantly, in setting out its top priorities, the first was habitat protection; the others were wildlife recovery and effective co-management.[35]

The introductory message to the board's third annual report from Chair Gerry Couture was titled "Nobody Said It Was Going to Be Easy." In it he celebrated notable board successes, such as its "Two Eyes: One Vision" traditional knowledge conference and its successful campaign to pressure the territorial government to proclaim critical sections of the *Wildlife Act* pertaining to habitat. Couture also acknowledged the board's difficulty in dealing with controversial, divisive issues: "Board Members will be the first to admit that this year has sometimes been difficult. Their respect for each other and tolerance for differing views along with devotion to getting the job done has allowed us to get through some sessions that were often filled with controversy and on occasion led to tears. Like the public, the Board in itself reflects many diverse and strongly held views."[36]

For "differing views" one had to look no further than the quotations from board members published in the first few annual reports. Whereas in the second annual report First Nations nominees spoke of "respect for animals," "our Elders' dreams and visions," and so on, the government nominees generally emphasized "all Yukon residents," "all Yukoners," "all members of the public," with one commenting that the board "is working hard for the people of the Yukon. But under present trends, the train of thought and the transition we are going through, the non-native folks are not getting fair representation in regard to game management."[37] The following year, while First Nations nominees were stressing the inclusiveness of Chapter 16 of the *UFA* and of the board, some government nominees spoke of "traditional knowledge as a partner with science," noting "we are but a small part of the intricate ecosystems we all cherish." One YG nominee complained, "I feel very strongly that the White Portion of the Yukon population is not being represented fairly in regards to game management."[38]

In 2000, a five-year review of the implementation of the *UFA* and the first four First Nations land claim and self-government agreements was published.

Its brief comments about the board were quite positive. The review, conducted by an implementation review working group (IRWG) comprising representatives of the governments involved, in contrast with the independent, outside reviews of implementation of the Nunavut claim, concluded that the board had "performed well," taken on a range of important issues, developed strong ties with the RRCs, and kept government and the public well informed about its activities.[39] Better yet, "First Nation IRWG representatives have noted particular satisfaction with the role that the Fish and Wildlife Management Board (FWMB) and the local Renewable Resources Councils (RRCs) have played in giving local communities a voice in renewable resource management decisions."[40] The review offered neither criticisms of the board nor recommendations for amending the *UFA* provisions relating to it. The review did identify significant problems faced by the RRCs and the Yukon Salmon Sub-Committee (these are discussed later in this chapter). Doubtless the board was pleased with this assessment, though the "no-one-said-it-was-going-to-be-easy" theme was reiterated by the 2001–02 chair, Doug Urquhart, in his introduction to the seventh annual report: "The Board and the Renewable Resources Councils entered this new [*UFA*] age brim full of energy and enthusiasm only to find that it was all much harder than anyone imagined."[41] As did the Five Year Review, Urquhart expressed concern about the challenges faced by the RRCs.

Finances

In 2016–17, the YFWMB's budget was $693,000. Roughly 85 percent of the board's revenue came via the basic grant from the territorial government, funded in turn by federal implementation money. The balance was largely made up in one-time-only government grants earmarked for specific projects.[42] Until a few years ago, the board supplemented its government funding with grants from foundations and private-sector agencies such as Ducks Unlimited, the Walter and Duncan Gordon Foundation, and the Shell Environmental Fund. This distinctive feature of the YFWMB, uncommon among other claims-based wildlife management boards, saw board staff devoting substantial time and energy to fundraising in order to finance essential board functions. The ten-year review of *UFA* implementation warned that fundraising could be "disruptive to mandated work," recommending that boards – the YFWMB was not the only *UFA* board engaged in fundraising – should be funded by government at a level "that eliminates the need for Boards to engage in fundraising activities to meet the financial requirements of their mandate."[43] The Yukon Government was said to be displeased with the board's fundraising that facilitated activities, such as the Community Stewards program, outside its mandate. Not long after the review was published the board scaled back its fundraising, though on occasion it seeks outside funding for special projects, such as the "Yukon Fish and Wildlife – A 20:20 Vision" exercise in 2008–09, which was funded by the board, the Salmon Sub-Committee, and the Canadian Wildlife Service.

The territorial government reviews and approves the board budget, but, according to one senior territorial official, "we don't mess with it": if the budget looks reasonable there is no micromanaging. Not all board members agree that the government's financial review is so benign or hands-off. In 2014, at Ottawa's direction, the territorial government moved to deal with the surpluses that the board and some RRCs had built up, giving it three years to spend the money. The original implementation plan did not address the question of carryover; a 2015 amendment to the plan authorized the board to retain up to 15 percent of its annual transfer from YG, with the balance returned to the government.[44]

Activities

The board's work falls into two broad categories. The first involves reviewing policy and legislation/regulations. This remit includes a regular formal process for assessing and recommending changes to government regulations under the territorial *Wildlife Act*. It also includes development of broad policy proposals such as changes to government legislation and management plans for certain species. These frequently entail formal recommendations to governments. The second category encompasses a wide range of activities such as gathering and disseminating information, which sometimes involves policy papers or wildlife management plans; advising and receiving advice from RRCs and facilitating their work; and engaging with First Nations, the territorial government, the Yukon Salmon Sub-Committee, and wildlife stakeholders on all manner of issues. Some of these activities produce official documents or processes, such as a major conference on the integration of Western "scientific" knowledge with traditional knowledge,[45] a study of the environmental effects of off-road vehicles,[46] an extensive habitat protection program,[47] and a small program to boost the economic potential of trapping.

Under the *UFA* the YFWMB has "standing as an interested party in the public proceedings" of any government agency dealing with issues affecting fish and wildlife and their habitat (16.7.13). This remit includes other *UFA* boards, such as the regional planning councils, but far and away the board's most extensive interaction is with the Yukon Environmental and Socio-economic

Assessment Board (YESAB) since so many of the project proposals that come before it entail potential harm to fish and wildlife or their habitat. YESAB is required to circulate applications to a wide range of organizations, including the YFWMB. For some time the board attempted to keep on top of the many projects going through the YESAB process, but this proved a significant drain on staff time and was not particularly effective. In recent years, the executive director, as mandated by the board, keeps a watching brief on only the most significant applications, making more time available for matters of prime significance to the board. According to one person at the board, "we tend to focus on projects that are at the executive [i.e., highest] level screening through YESAB. This way we can avoid diluting the mandate of the RRCs who are the local experts when it comes to assessing and commenting on projects."

At that, the board's relation with YESAB has at times been fractious. At a recent YFWMB meeting I observed, YESAB officials briefed the board about a forthcoming environmental assessment of the Casino Mine project, heralded as potentially the largest mine in Yukon history. Testy exchanges with YESAB staff made it clear that certain board members had little confidence in YESAB's capacity to evaluate possible threats to wildlife habitat. The same meeting revealed, apparently not for the first time, significant lack of agreement between the board and YESAB as to the practical implications of the board's standing as an "interested party" in the YESAB process.

Whereas in Nunavut a good deal of the wildlife management board's work involves recommendations to government on harvest licences and community harvest quotas, the YFWMB does not generally engage in such activities. It can and does propose changes to the territorial government in *Wildlife Act* regulations to open or close hunting or fishing of particular species in designated areas or lakes, to vary hunting seasons, to sanction or prohibit certain hunting and fishing techniques (such as barbless hooks or drone-assisted hunting), and so on. However, regional or community wildlife quotas are simply not part of the board's mandate. Chapter 16 of the *UFA* gives the board power to establish, modify, or remove total allowable harvests and basic needs levels for fish and wildlife, but it has never been asked to deal with either.

The YFWMB is deeply involved in the analysis, review, and reformulation of the territorial government's wildlife policies. One especially noteworthy aspect of this involvement is its regular cycle of regulation review and recommendation. The board has spent considerable time in recent years assessing and revamping the regulation process. Currently, it unfolds as follows.[48]

The YFWMB annually solicits suggestions for changes to the regulations under the Yukon *Wildlife Act* from the YG, First Nations, RRCs, interest groups, and individuals.[49] Proposals must be submitted by April 30th. An individual or group proposing a regulation change fills out a simple form, which can be submitted online or by mail. Proponents are asked to specify the requested change and the rationale for it and to provide supporting information. On the premise that regulatory changes can be complex and have unintended consequences, proponents are expected to have discussed their ideas with Environment Yukon officials. Results of these discussions are to be specified on the form, as are outcomes of consultations with potentially affected parties such as First Nations, RRCs, and industry. Unless "substantial changes" have occurred since a rejected proposal was first submitted, it will not be accepted for a second review.

The board's executive director assists groups and individuals in clarifying and improving their proposals. In the fall a screening committee, composed of board staff and YG staff, reviews proposals and prepares a report for the board's October meeting. At that meeting the board assesses the proposals on the basis of the screening committee report and decides which should go forward for public review. Proposals are assessed in terms of both substance and jurisdiction: some are deemed to be local management issues and are forwarded to RRCs, others are referred to other boards or agencies. Until recently, proposals for regulatory change were designated either as "substantive," requiring public review, or as "administrative," which, if supported by the board, went directly to the minister without public review. Court decisions have convinced the YG that it has to be more careful about consultation processes, so that all proposals now are subject to public review, but "administrative" proposals tend to receive only limited review.[50]

A public review document is produced and circulated widely. These documents are models of how to facilitate public engagement: written in plain language, they are produced as inexpensive workbooks in which the issues are set out succinctly and with space for comments. In recent years this process has mostly unfolded online, though hard copies are available for return to the board. Some RRCs print copies of the document to make them available to local residents who lack internet access. Throughout October and November the board seeks comments from individuals and organizations and holds public meetings, usually in Whitehorse, but in other communities as well if interest is high. Comments can come in the form of oral presentations at meetings, written documents, or online submissions.

The ease of submitting proposals and of commenting on them online is noteworthy, though at a recent meeting one board member expressed concern that the new process privileges a high-tech elite while those most in need of information and the opportunity to weigh in on possible regulatory changes, such as trappers, lack the equipment and the skills to participate in the process via the internet.

A "what-we-heard" report goes to the YFWMB for its December meeting, where decisions are made as to which proposals warrant formal recommendations to the minister. It is quite common for the board to decline to send proposed regulatory changes forward to the territorial government. This could be because of public opposition or adverse effects on First Nations interests, or it could simply reflect the board's judgment about the proposed change or a lack of clarity or sufficient information in the proposal. Nor is the board averse to recommending that the minister vary or reject proposals originating from the minister's own department. So too, the board may expand the scope of a proposal that it recommends to the minister.[51]

The vast majority of recommendations go to the territorial minister of environment, but very occasionally recommendations are forwarded to the federal government, to First Nations governments, or to RRCs. A high proportion of the board's formal recommendations to government are generated through this process.

According to section 16.8 of the *UFA*, once the board makes a formal recommendation, the minister of environment has sixty days to accept, vary, replace, or set aside – reject – a board recommendation, with a further thirty-day extension possible. If the minister takes no action in this period, a recommendation is deemed to have been accepted. If the minister rejects or amends a recommendation, it is sent back to the board with reasons. The board then has thirty days to revise or reiterate its position; should it do so, the minister has forty-five days to reach a final determination, with, again, the absence of a contrary decision being equivalent to acceptance. Unless the minister directs otherwise, until a final disposition has been made of the recommendation, the process is subject to strict confidentiality. Over the years, with the notable exception of the captive wildlife imbroglio discussed below, the great majority of regulatory changes proposed by the board have been accepted by the YG.[52]

The YFWMB's annual report summarizes each proposed regulation change and outlines the board's analysis of it, which often makes reference to the public review and indicates the position the board has adopted on it. In the early years, the annual report included the minister's response to the board, usually verbatim; this is no longer the case. Many recommendations accepted by the minister give rise to government-to-government consultations between First Nations governments and the YG.

For recommendations about *Wildlife Act* regulations, the process might seem to be effectively finished once the minister has accepted, actively or passively, a board recommendation. Such is not the case.

The *UFA* (section 16.8.7) says: "Government shall, as soon as practicable, implement ... all recommendations and decisions of the Board that are accepted by the Minister." This includes recommendations that have been varied or that have been deemed accepted because no ministerial response has been received within the prescribed time limits. These provisions would seem to leave little room for interpretation; however, from the outset, the YG has followed a different process – one that rests on the distinction between "minister" and "government." On the premise that the minister lacks authority to render final decisions, the territorial government insists that board recommendations follow the usual route for proposed regulatory changes, including an internal vetting by the public service and a formal review by cabinet. This procedure not only lengthens the time from ministerial acceptance to actual implementation, sometimes by several months, but, more significantly, it holds the potential to undermine the board's authority.

One YG official argues that routing accepted board recommendations through cabinet allows "the capital-G Government the opportunity to have the benefit of comments from other departments" and that enhanced emphasis on the duty to consult requires the territorial government to consult potentially affected First Nations on the proposed regulatory changes. So too, before putting regulations into effect, the argument runs, the government needs to render most board recommendations into formal legal language.

These are all legitimate points, yet if various government departments are allowed to bring their perspectives and interests to bear, and if cabinet exercises its regulation-making authority in this way, the very real possibility exists that the regulation eventually passed to implement a board recommendation will subvert the intent of the recommendation, perhaps in a minor way, perhaps in a major way. Over the years, the board has acquiesced in this process: a diagram in its first annual report shows "cabinet approval of change" as a step in the board's review and revision of regulations.[53] The time the government takes to deal internally with accepted recommendations has been increasing; the diagram on the board's website illustrating the process as of early 2019 indicates that approximately twelve months is required from the time a recommendation is submitted to the minister to the time cabinet approves it.[54] The time required for its recommendations to come into effect has become a concern to the board.

The Yukon Fish and Wildlife Management Board

A recent change to the process irritated the board. For most of its first two decades, the YFWMB recommendations to the territorial government were considered annually. The YG now operates on a two-year cycle in terms of both proposing regulations to the board and in taking board recommendations to cabinet. Thus one year the board will receive no proposed regulatory changes from the government, while the next year it may face a large number. Proposals from RRCs, First Nations, individuals, or organizations are also in effect subject to the two-year cycle. The board may deal with their proposals the year they are received, but if it recommends acceptance, the minister will only bring them to cabinet the following year. According to one YG official, in seeing this as a way of downgrading the board and its work, the YFWMB is reading too much into this change. The move to a two-year cycle was driven by a lack of capacity for dealing with an increasing regulatory workload on the YG's part. Moreover, of all territorial legislation, the *Wildlife Act* – "an anomaly in the Yukon legislative landscape" – is the only one with an institutionalized regulatory process that the board continues to use to good advantage.

Meetings[55]

Most YFWMB meetings take place in Whitehorse. In the five years ending in 2018, aside from the annual "on-the-land" meetings, only two of twenty meetings occurred in communities outside the capital. Although Whitehorse has several hotels with suitable meeting facilities, a disproportionate number of meetings occur at the First Nations-owned Yukon Inn. The board also occasionally holds its meetings in the Kwanlin Dün Cultural Centre in Whitehorse. Attendance at meetings is good: rarely are more than one or two board members absent, though it is often the case that one or two of the twelve board positions are vacant. Quorum is seven members (having been scaled back from the original eight). The three staff members are present throughout the meeting, as is a contract minute-taker. When board members meet as trustees for the trust, the trust manager is present.

The territorial government's director of fish and wildlife attends virtually all meetings, often accompanied by technical staff. Territorial officials are routinely permitted to remain when the board goes in camera to discuss potential recommendations or other matters, though they are expected to refrain from participating unless asked to comment. Representatives of RRCs, usually chairs or executive directors, are accorded the same privilege. RRC chairs are invited to attend and participate in the April board meeting and all or most do. Specific RRCs may also be invited to other meetings or ask to attend. Over the course of a three-day meeting the board will usually have a "members-only" session, with only members and staff present. Only very rarely are staff excluded from meetings.

Members and staff sit at a rectangular table; the director of fish and wildlife and any RRC chairs present join them at the table. Deputants, who could include territorial or federal public servants; officials from CYFN; individual First Nations, consultants, researchers, or stakeholders (such as representatives of the Yukon Fish and Game Association); and so on, sit with the audience and come to the table when making presentations. Members frequently turn to Graham Van Tighem, the executive director, who has been with the board for nearly two decades, for advice and information; in turn, he frequently participates in discussions.[56] Meetings held in communities or meetings dealing with controversial issues can attract members of the public, but normally attendance by those not involved in the meeting is sparse to non-existent. Save in camera sessions, meetings are open to the media, but reporters and cameras are few and far between. It is not out of the ordinary for the territorial minister of environment or the federal MP to put in an appearance at board meetings, the latter usually by phone. This contrasts markedly with the Nunavut board, at whose meetings ministers and MPs are rarely, if ever, present.

Meetings begin and end with a prayer. Board-provided tablets containing all necessary documents have replaced bulky binders, though not all members are fully comfortable with computers. Throughout the board's history, members have been fully fluent in English, so that although the *UFA* contemplates translation of board proceedings and documents, the board does not do so. Indeed, the YFWMB has never provided translation at a meeting or translated a document. Meetings I attended were orderly, with members waiting to be recognized by the chair before speaking. At the same time, meetings were not stilted or excessively formal: serious discussion was often interspersed with light-hearted comments and wisecracks. Differences of opinion, be they between First Nations members and non-Indigenous members or between non-Indigenous members, are aired clearly and sometimes forcefully, but in a fashion respectful of the views of other members. Indeed, one public servant with extensive experience of the board observed that a key element in its success has been the respect members show one another. To a significant degree this respect reflects members' recognition that, while specifics vary a good deal, each member has extensive, first-hand experience with the land and wildlife.[57] On occasion the chair may manage proceedings with a view to avoiding serious divisions among members. This was evident at one meeting in the way the chair and the board handled the highly contentious issue of land use planning in the Peel watershed.

Given the range and depth of the members' experience, supplemented by the expertise available from board and government staff, plus at times from representatives of First Nations, private-sector organizations, and NGOs, discussion typically unfolds at a high, well-informed level, even on fairly technical matters.

"Representation" by Members of First Nations and Non-Indigenous Interests

As is the case with most boards established under the Northern comprehensive claims, members of the YFWMB, along with all other *UFA* boards, are to act "in the public interest."[58] The *UFA* explicitly declares that board members "shall not be delegates of the parties who nominate or appoint them,"[59] although in reference to the board, it requires that "the majority of *representatives* of Government and the majority of *representatives* of Yukon First Nations shall be Yukon residents."[60] In an interview, one of the government *UFA* negotiators in retrospect expressed uncertainty as to whether it might have been wiser to have board members explicitly act as "representatives." "The process now," he commented, "has just become excessive" in that in determining how to respond to board recommendations the YG is careful to solicit the views of affected First Nations, not only slowing things down but often leaving the board in an ambiguous position. An opposing view holds that if the First Nations board members were actually "representatives," they would have to consult their communities and organizations before taking a position on the board, which could lead to long delays. As well, given the nature of First Nations politics in Yukon, pressure would be felt from all fourteen First Nations to have representatives on the board.

This is not to deny that board members speak and act in ways that protect and promote the interests of, on the one hand, First Nations, and, on the other hand, non-Indigenous Yukoners, but neither does it imply that they are behaving as formal representatives. To be sure, one former public servant familiar with the board commented: "First Nation members have a hard time taking off their First Nation hats." At a meeting I observed, a board member introduced herself to deputants as "a CYFN rep." This does not mean, however, that members take direction from CYFN or from individual First Nations. One CYFN official commented that CYFN nominees on *UFA* boards "are there as representatives of CYFN but we can't really tell them what to do." Another person at CYFN was more blunt about some highly independent board members: "it would be a political nightmare trying to meddle with them."

Far more significant than what might be construed as "representative" behaviour on the part of board members are their orientations and experiences. Most members come to the board with well-formed understandings of fish and wildlife and of proper ways of dealing with them. Given the often dramatically different cultural attitudes and beliefs of those from First Nations and non-Indigenous heritage, it is hardly surprising that their responses to issues before the board should reflect those attitudes and beliefs. If anything, what is surprising about the board is the frequency with which First Nations and non-Indigenous members find common ground.

Long-time board observers suggest that it took some time for CYFN and YG nominees to be able to work together effectively. Some of the First Nations members had been *UFA* negotiators and tended to approach board issues as negotiators, whereas early on some non-Indigenous members came to the board either not understanding or accepting the *UFA*, and thus wanting to pursue issues already settled in it or simply having, as one person put it, "axes to grind." Over the years a more mature attitude has emerged, well captured in the observations of a former member who had been an outfitter: in the early days non-Indigenous board members had concerns about the board's powers but it is now generally understood by board members that the YFWMB is there "to represent the animals." That this sentiment should be expressed by an outfitter is notable in light of the long-standing conflict within the board over issues affecting outfitters.

Relations with the Yukon Government

The board's relations with the territorial government have ranged from close and collegial to abrasive and confrontational. A veteran First Nations leader put it this way: the YFWMB is "one of those boards that goes through highs and lows depending on the appointments; it's very political. Right now [June, 2010] it's doing well because they've had some strong appointments."

After a slightly rocky first few years, as the YFWMB and the YG sorted out what was for both a new and uncertain situation, the relationship matured into one marked by cooperation and mutual respect. Board members and staff worked closely with officials in the (then) Department of Renewable Resources to the point at which bureaucrats in other departments occasionally accused them of being too close to the board. A former minister spoke of being able to sort out concerns through informal communications: "if I didn't clearly understand an issue that the board was making a recommendation on ... out of courtesy and respect for the board, I'd ask them to explain their reasoning." This positive and generally productive relationship was unaffected by the political stripe of the government, with both the NDP and the Liberals holding power in this period. The election of a Yukon Party government in 2002, however, led to a marked change in the YG's dealings with the board, as evidenced in a major dispute over captive wildlife (sometimes referred to as "game farming").

The issue of wildlife in captivity, in fur farms, wildlife viewing facilities, commercial food production enterprises, and so on has been highly divisive in Yukon, as elsewhere in the North. Concerns exist about the potential for the spread of disease and about humane treatment of captive animals, but the most vociferous criticisms come from First Nations for whom it is deeply offensive and disrespectful to keep non-domestic animals such as Dall sheep, moose, and caribou in captivity. It was in this context that the YG proposed a series of changes to *Wildlife Act* regulations affecting captive wildlife, generally in the direction of loosening restrictions on so-called "game farms," several of which had been operating for years. After what the board termed "an extensive public review" that produced "an unprecedented number of responses from Yukoners," it forwarded thirty-four recommendations to the minister of environment. Initially, the minister rejected most of the recommendations, but following formal written exchanges with the board, his final response was to accept sixteen recommendations, vary another twelve, reject six, and indicate that he planned to amend the act to allow for private ownership of wildlife on game farms, an especially contentious issue.[61]

The minister's stance elicited an unusually blunt and public response from the YFWMB. The chair was quoted in the press criticizing the minister for providing only one-sentence explanations for rejecting or varying some recommendations, for putting wildlife at risk to serve the financial interests of a few individuals, and for threatening the integrity of the *Wildlife Act* with the proposed amendment.[62] Despite a limited rapprochement when the government purchased the most problematic captive wildlife facility, tensions remained. Shortly after this conflict erupted, several board members' terms expired. In short order a new slate of government nominees was appointed, nominees closely attuned to the government's ideological approach; one was a game farmer and another was the former president of the Yukon Party. "You don't get much more blatantly obvious than that" in terms of political interference was how one close observer of the board put it. Notably, however, another long-time observer, who most certainly has no Yukon Party sympathies, suggests that, while the appointees may have had particular views about wildlife management, they were independent minded and not the sort to take direction from the government. In his introductory message to the board's 2003–04 annual report, Chair

Ed Kormendy, in referring to the host of new appointments, felt it necessary to comment that "both Yukon First Nations and the Yukon Government have a duty to continue to appoint those individuals with the ability to represent the interests of all Yukoners, not personal or political interests."[63]

At about the same time came a shakeup in the Department of Environment that saw board allies fired or moved out of their positions; according to a public servant involved, "the government did what they could to castrate the Department of the Environment." All told, the government's actions confirmed a widely voiced suspicion that the government was consciously attempting to undermine the board. By 2005, the board was being described as dysfunctional even by supporters.

By this time things had become, as one public servant put it, "pretty ugly" between the board and the government. A former board member recounted in an interview a number of episodes that marked the "bad blood" suffusing the relationship. The board's annual reports in that period contained remarkable language. Every year the report would list the board's top priorities, as determined in annual strategic reviews. Although features of board operations would occasionally appear on the list, typical highlighted priorities were habitat protection, community stewardship, and support for RRCs. In 2005–06, however, the board's top priority was: "Establish an improved relationship with the Minister of the Environment, which will enable the Board to move forward in our work."[64] The following year the language was even more direct: "Strive to have meetings with the Minister of the Environment with an aim to opening communication, building rapport, and establishing trust."[65] In addition, the report noted, the board chair and/or vice-chair would henceforth hand deliver all correspondence to the minister.[66] Complicating an already difficult situation was the fact that, in December 2005, Premier Dennis Fentie himself assumed the environment portfolio, which he held until July 2008.

The "strive-to-have-meetings" language reappeared in annual reports as late as 2011–12, though as lower priority, but by 2006 things had begun to turn around for the board, in terms of both internal dynamics and relations with government. With a new chair and a new executive director in place (the third to hold each post in as many years), a cathartic mid-year retreat helped the board set a new course, so that, in 2008, the chair was able to report "our relationships with government and RRCs have improved."[67]

A key spur to the YFWMB's development of a clear vision of its mandate and objectives, which in turn assisted in improving its dealings with government, was an extensive consultation and reflection process in 2008–09, "Yukon Fish and Wildlife – A 20:20 Vision." This initiative was aimed at providing the board with a comprehensive picture of "what Yukon residents think about the current state of these [fish and wildlife] resources and what their vision is for the future." This would enable the board to formulate, in partnership with the RRCs and the Yukon Salmon Sub-Committee, a framework for providing "long range advice and recommendations" to territorial, First Nations, and federal governments.[68]

A discussion paper was developed and circulated widely to provide background and stimulate debate. In addition to commissioning a territory-wide public opinion survey, the board held a two-day symposium in Whitehorse, a number of community meetings, and made school presentations. The result was a rich store of data, quantitative and qualitative, on residents' activities relating to fish and wildlife and their attitudes on a wide range of management issues. The public documents summarizing the data provided breakdowns on certain questions according to age, gender, and First Nations memberships. The board had access to more extensive breakdowns.[69] Knowing in some depth and precision what Yukoners thought about issues before the board, one person commented: "we're comfortable as a board that in pushing sustainability and working to protect habitat we're on solid ground as far as the public thinks."

Board chair Don Hutton summarized the outcome of the "20:20" exercise as follows:

> The results of this initiative have prompted the Board to look even closer at our own mandate, vision and mission and to begin realigning ourselves to work together more with Yukoners and to become the voice for fish, wildlife and Yukoners in our interactions with the Regulators. It seems most Yukoners, including the Board, are looking for, and want involvement in, a more planned and proactive approach to the management of fish, wildlife and their habitat.[70]

Towards these ends, at an "on-the-land" meeting in June 2008, the board moved away from its annual reformulation of its strategic goals to a longer-term analysis, setting out priorities to guide its work for a five-year period. This approach continues.

Throughout the board's history, relations with the YG, whether with ministers or bureaucrats, have varied widely. In addition to the ideological stance of the government – though this has hardly been invariant, even among Yukon Party ministers – several of those involved in the process stress that the personality and background of the minister is a key factor. By way of illustration, the fact that Pauline Frost, appointed Liberal minister of environment following the 2016 election, was well known to the board, including as a former chair of the Yukon Salmon Sub-Committee, could hardly fail to affect relations. Much depends on how respectful the minister is towards the board and board processes, not least because this affects how aggressive the board is in its dealings with government. The board's relations with the public service range from close and cooperative to suspicious and hostile. Over the years the board has usually seen the director of fish and wildlife in the Department of Environment as an ally and a source of valuable information and advice. Experienced board members, however, maintain that the director's influence within the department has waned, pointing out that where once the director of fish and wildlife was one of three department directors, currently some ten directorships exist. "You ride roughshod over the board at your peril" was one public servant's appreciation of the relationship, but board members saw the bureaucrats' attitudes differently. In interviews, current and former board members voiced considerable animosity towards the bureaucrats, accusing them of blocking access to the minister, "playing games," and lacking respect for the board. A public servant responds that, while it is easy and perhaps politically advantageous to rail against government, board members, whose understanding of government is sometimes superficial, fail to appreciate how it can corrode relations with bureaucrats to the board's disadvantage. Adds a former public servant, the Department of Environment is "miles ahead" of other YG departments in terms of respecting and implementing the claim.

In the YFWMB's formative years, a board representative served on the interview panel when a new director of wildlife was being hired. More recently the board has had no involvement in the selection process, prompting it to question the minister on this point when he appeared before it following the appointment of a new director in early 2016. Government officials indicated at that meeting that the board should have been involved and would be in future.[71]

For the most part, the board's attitude towards the YG has been characterized by healthy scepticism and low-grade irritation rather than dysfunctional hostility, making for a generally productive and cooperative, if occasionally strained, relationship. The political stripe of the government has made a difference, with Yukon Party ministers more likely to find themselves seriously at odds with the board than NDP or Liberal ministers, though some Yukon Party ministers got along with the board far better than others.

Given the Yukon Salmon Sub-Committee's remit on salmon, the board has little to do with the federal government. On occasion, issues arise involving Ottawa. Typically, these entail the board objecting to actions that it sees as contravening the spirit or the letter of the *Umbrella Final Agreement*. An example of the latter was the Department of Fisheries and Oceans' failure, as required by the *UFA*, to consult the board on the far-reaching revisions to the federal *Fisheries Act* in 2012–13. The board, it was widely agreed, had an open and shut case against Ottawa in this instance. However, it saw little point in devoting financial and political resources to pursuing the matter for what would have been a largely symbolic victory.

The board did weigh in on the Harper government's proposed Bill S-6, which would have significantly altered the environmental assessment and regulation process established by the *Yukon Environmental and Socio-economic Assessment Act* in ways vehemently opposed by the Council of Yukon First Nations and others. Specifics of S-6 are discussed in Chapter 7; suffice it to say here that, after meeting with the premier, whose government supported the bill, the board, citing the importance of "upholding the Spirit and Intent of the Umbrella Final Agreement and the First Nation Final Agreements," went on record opposing amendments to the act that had not been agreed upon by the parties to the *UFA*. The board's submission to the House of Commons Standing Committee on Aboriginal Affairs called for a number of far-reaching sections of S-6 to be set aside.[72]

More recently, the board's relations with the federal government improved substantially. To some extent this has been a reflection of personnel changes at the local office of the DFO. Also notable was a board-hosted meeting in Whitehorse with a key federal agency, the Committee on the Status of Endangered Wildlife in Canada (COSEWIC). Some board members commented that relations with Ottawa are now better than those with the YG.

Traditional Knowledge

The only reference in the *UFA* to "traditional knowledge" (TK) is in relation to heritage issues and the mandate of the Yukon Heritage Resources Board.[73] The *UFA* does make occasional reference to the role played in governance processes by "the knowledge and experience of Yukon Indian People."[74] One of the objectives of Chapter 16, the fish and wildlife chapter, is "to integrate the relevant knowledge and experience both of Yukon Indian People and of the scientific communities in order to achieve Conservation."[75] Neither traditional knowledge, as it pertains to heritage issues, nor First Nations "knowledge and experience" is defined.

The YFWMB makes frequent reference to TK in its documents and board members, mostly but not uniformly First Nations members, regularly allude to it during meetings. One of the board's early accomplishments was a major conference about TK with special attention to its role in wildlife management.[76] The board unquestionably makes serious efforts to bring TK to bear on its work, but, like other claims boards, has difficulty knowing how to go about it. Accordingly, views, including among First Nations observers, as to how successful the board has been in incorporating TK into its activities are mixed.

Paul Nadasdy cites the difficulty the board encountered in dealing with the contentious issue of "catch-and-release" fishing as illustrative of the limits to the board's ability to reconcile the Euro-Canadian/scientific mindset with the ethical-cosmological elements of First Nations TK. Whereas non-Indigenous people tend to evaluate catch-and-release in terms of conservation, economics, and humane treatment of fish, the very idea of catch-and-release is deeply offensive to First Nations peoples, repudiating as it does their fundamental beliefs about human-animal relations.[77]

The Trust

Chapter 27 of the *UFA* establishes the Yukon Fish and Wildlife Enhancement Trust and designates all members of the YFWMB as trustees, though the trust and the board are separate legal entities. Whereas initial funding for the Nunavut Wildlife Research Trust came entirely from Ottawa, for the Yukon trust, the federal and territorial governments and CYI all contributed equal amounts, slightly more than a million dollars each. In order to build up the fund, no payments were made for the first two years; by 2017, the trust had grown to just under $5 million. Although all board members are trustees, an executive committee composed of a chair and at least two other trustees effectively runs the trust, supported by a part-time manager. A southern financial firm provides the trust with investment advice.

A call for proposals goes out early each year, with applications assessed by the trust's Technical Review Committee composed of trustees, the trust manager, and, if necessary, persons with specialized expertise, including territorial government staff and others outside government. Trustees bring a wide range of knowledge and experience to the process and, for the most part, are able to reach decisions on their own without outside assistance.

Whereas a substantial proportion of funds allocated by the Nunavut trust go to federal or territorial government agencies, public government receives few if any Yukon trust grants.[78] The list of funded projects on the trust website covering five years ending in 2015 shows no funds going to agencies of the federal or territorial governments. Governments are not explicitly ineligible, but trustees, guided by section 27.6.6 of the *UFA* ("Expenditures from the Trust are not intended to duplicate or replace Government expenditures on Fish and Wildlife management"), have been unwilling to fund public government projects. Those eligible for funding include individuals, including academics, businesses, NGOs, and educational institutions. Projects that restore, protect, or enhance fish and wildlife populations and their habitat are encouraged. Grants may cover up to 100 percent of project costs, and, although applicants may seek any level of funding, trust guidelines encourage requests of $15,000 or less; most grants are in the range of $10,000 to $15,000. Among the criteria trustees apply to project applications is a requirement for support from First Nations, RRCs, communities, and the public.

As a registered charity, the trust is legally required to disburse minimum amounts of money; its target is 3.5 percent annually.[79] In recent years, the trust has given out grants totalling between $86,000 and $180,000 to a wide range of applicants, including RRCs, First Nations, the Yukon Outfitters Association, the Yukon Fish and Game Association, the Yukon Conservation Society, the Society of Yukon Bird Observatories, and several individuals. Whereas a high proportion of grants from the Nunavut trust support research on various fish and wildlife species, the Yukon trust funds many non-research projects, on topics such as trapping education, habitat cleanup, off-road vehicle monitoring, and youth mentoring programs.

The trust welcomes but receives few donations, most of which are small. In 2012–13 six donations, from First Nations, First Nations development corporations, and private-sector firms, totalled less than $9,000. In some years no donations are received.

Reviewing the Board

Late in 2018, the Yukon Forum, which brings the YG cabinet and First Nations chiefs together on a regular basis, announced a review of the YFWMB. An outside consultant was to be engaged to "evaluate success and effectiveness of this important Chapter 16 entity," with completion of the study expected sometime in 2019.[80] According to government officials, the review was not generated by serious concerns or problems but, rather, reflected a recognition both by the YG and First Nations that the board plays a key role in wildlife policy and thus that attention to ensure it is working well was warranted. As well, the review was designed to address or clarify a range of issues, such as the relation of the RRCs to the board and the application of *UFA* boards in areas without settled claims. One official commented: "everything else in the UFA has been reviewed." A less sanguine interpretation came from a long-time board observer who said the impetus for the review came out of a CYFN general assembly marked by griping about the board and the Yukon Salmon Sub-Committee. According to this person, some First Nations leaders had been voicing discontent with the board because it interpreted its mandate as working in the public interest, as per the *UFA*, rather than giving priority to First Nations rights.

The board's response was not defensive. Its twenty-four-page brief explained its mandate and operations and put forward suggestions for clarifying its role and improving its effectiveness. The board reiterated several long-standing concerns and recommended various formal and informal changes to its relations with the YG, First Nations, and the RRCs. Inevitably, it sought enhanced funding, noting "aside from inflation adjustment, the Board has not seen an increase in our annual budget since 1993."[81] Among its recommendations were legal changes bringing the *Wildlife Act* into line with the *UFA* so as to provide the RRCs with the ability to establish bylaws, as intended by the *UFA*. The board also asked for clarification on various role and relationship issues. These included "whether it is expected that the Board should be more proactive in internally determining community issues and bringing them to Yukon Government and First Nations, as opposed to waiting for information (from Yukon Government, First Nations, RRCs, etc.) to make recommendations"; "improved communication between the parties on expectations regarding fish and wildlife issues"; and "clarification of Board's role in areas where First Nations are not signatories to the UFA."[82]

At the time of writing, a consulting firm had been engaged and had begun work, including through an online survey seeking opinions about the board from "rights holders, stakeholders and interest groups that are knowledgeable about fish and wildlife management in the Yukon" (though anyone, including non-Yukoners, could participate). The review ran for the first three months of 2019.[83] When complete, the final report of the review was to be made public.

Renewable Resources Councils

Renewable Resources Councils are integral components of the co-management system as mandated by the *UFA* and the land claim and self-government regimes established under it. They thus differ fundamentally from the Hunters and Trappers Organizations in Nunavut that at first blush they might seem to resemble. RRCs are structured very differently: they exercise a far wider range of functions and they play a more influential role in wildlife management than the HTOs. HTOs exist in every Nunavut community and long pre-date the *Nunavut Land Claims Agreement*. Membership in Nunavut HTOs is limited to local Inuit hunters and trappers, who elect executives from among themselves. In contrast, RRCs are structured on classic co-management lines: appointments are made by the territorial minister of environment, subject to cabinet approval, with half of the members nominated by the local First Nation and half by the government.

The tasks faced by RRCs are at once crucial and challenging. As a training handbook for members published by one RRC puts it:

> Implementation of the Umbrella Final Agreement (UFA) has proven much more difficult than anyone realized. The numerous Boards, Councils and Committees created by the UFA are each challenged to the limit to fulfill their mandate. Nowhere is this more evident than the expectations placed on the Renewable Resources Councils.[84]

Origin, Membership, and Organization

The *UFA* mandates an RRC "in each Yukon First Nation's Traditional Territory" once the First Nation has settled its claim.[85] RRCs are explicitly designated as institutions of public government, "acting in the public interest."[86] The RRCs came about as a result of pressure from First Nations eager to maximize local control over land and resources and deeply suspicious of the territorial government. As well, a few far-sighted non-Indigenous people recognized the potential for RRCs to bridge the gap between First Nations and non-Indigenous people. Tony Penikett, Yukon premier and lead territorial negotiator on the claim, has written how RRCs emerged as a means of reconciling two largely incompatible wildlife regimes: the Yukon Government's authority, under the *Yukon Act*, to regulate hunting and fishing and the First Nations' long-standing right to hunt for food on the 90 percent of the territory that qualified as unoccupied Crown land.[87] According to a former Yukon claims negotiator, until late in the negotiations it was planned that the RRCs would report to the YFWMB, but at the eleventh hour it was decided that they should report to the minister.

One veteran First Nations political figure suggests that the RRCs embody the philosophy suffusing the *UFA*: that community decision making, in matters relating to wildlife as in other spheres, should be paramount. Thus it followed that the design principle was that "everything was local; only the leftovers should go to the central board." This view is echoed by federal bureaucrats involved in negotiating the *UFA* who saw the RRCs as extremely valuable for the way that they "pull decisions out of the ivory towers in Whitehorse into the communities," as one put it. Another commented that the RRCs "embody the true spirit of the UFA."

The territorial government makes all RRC appointments, half on the basis of nominations from the local First Nations. CYFN has little involvement in RRC nominations.

Eight of the ten RRCs have six members; the Teslin RRC has ten to accommodate the clan structure of the Teslin First Nation; the Laberge RRC has eight members reflecting the involvement of two First Nations, the Ta'an Kwäch'än Council and the Kwanlin Dün First Nation. Most RRCs also have one alternate member nominated by government and one by the First Nation. Members serve three- or five-year terms and must live in the territory over which the RRC has jurisdiction. RRC chairs, who typically serve one- or two-year terms, are chosen by their members; most RRCs operate with co-chairs, one a First Nation nominee, one a government nominee. The territorial government has no involvement in the chair selection process unless the members fail to fill a vacancy within thirty days and, at that, can only appoint a sitting RRC member as chair. Typically, an RRC maintains a small office run by a single staff person. Recruiting and retaining good staff has been a perennial difficulty for RRCs from the outset, largely because of their limited financial resources. RRCs generally meet monthly, a few twice a month. Most meetings are open to the public.

Women are somewhat more in evidence in RRCs than they are in Nunavut HTOs, but the numbers are hardly overwhelming. A 2012 study by David Natcher found women held 15 percent of RRC positions.[88] A follow-up study of five RRCs by Kiri Staples and Natcher found that a third of RRC members (33 percent) were women, with women holding five of six positions at one RRC.[89] According to data on RRC membership on the government website as of October 2017, sixteen of seventy-three RRC members, including alternates (22 percent), were women. A somewhat higher proportion of First Nations nominees (27 percent) than government nominees (17 percent) were women, though, given the high turnover in RRC membership and the highly variable overall proportion of women members, too much should not be read into this (the Natcher and Staples-Natcher studies did not break membership down by nominating party). Even these nominal levels of participation, according to one long-experienced observer, overstates women's roles in RRCs, with women often marginalized to administration and discussions of berry picking.

Mandate and Activities
The *UFA* stipulates that the RRC serves as "a primary instrument for local renewable resources management,"[90] and it accords it power to make recommendations

to the YG, the local First Nation government, the YFWMB, and the Yukon Salmon Sub-Committee. RRCs take prime responsibility for local outfitter harvest quotas and for trapline allocations, which can be highly contentious. Section 16.6.10.6 of the *UFA* gives RRCs authority to make bylaws under the territorial *Wildlife Act* with respect to "management of Furbearers" such as beaver, fox, wolf, and marten. However, this remains an unrealized power since the requisite amendments to the act have never been made. A territorial official suggested that the government's failure to bring in appropriate amendments comes not from concern about empowering RRCs in this way but from deep reluctance to "open the act" to amendment since any changes are bound to be politically contentious. Local issues relating to basic needs levels and total allowable harvests also fall within the ambit of RRCs, though, like the board, they have never had to deal with them.

One person at the YFWMB commented that, "in some ways[,] they [RRCs] have more authority than we do." Although this may be true on paper, the reality tends to be somewhat different for a variety of reasons. Membership on an RRC calls not just for a significant time commitment but also for an unusual skill set: extensive first-hand knowledge of the land and the animals, capacity to understand and utilize complex technical reports, appreciation of local politics and sensibilities, plus at least moderate familiarity with administrative processes. RRC members receive honoraria, but few take on the job for the money; indeed, the reverse is more common since for many the pay cannot compensate for the time and energy the position requires. Accordingly, attracting and retaining good members can be difficult. Particularly given the relatively small number of Yukon First Nations citizens, it has been a constant challenge for First Nations governments to find good nominees for RRCs. "Without a doubt," Yukon First Nations lawyer and claims negotiator Daryn Leas points out, "the limited capacity of the Yukon First Nations is taxed to nominate committed and knowledgeable people" to serve on the many *UFA* and non-*UFA* boards and committees.[91]

Unsurprisingly, RRC members and staff often have only limited familiarity with the *UFA*, both its formal provisions and its actual operations, leading, among other things, to uncertainty as to possible recommendations to government and the process for making them. Lack of corporate memory is often a contributing factor. So too, RRCs have long been constrained by lack of financial resources, though recent increases in the transfers they receive from the YG have enhanced their capacity.

As is common among local communities and organizations in the North, RRCs' effectiveness is undermined by the sheer press of business confronting them, not all of which relates to fish and wildlife management. Several respondents observed that because of their strong links to the local communities and their ready availability, RRCs are overburdened by government consultations to the point of interfering with their *UFA*-mandated work. As well, as a territorial bureaucrat familiar with RRCs put it, "the resource councils are individuals that have to live in these small communities. They don't want to be seen as making decisions that are going to piss off people in the community because they have to live there. As a result, when it comes to making really hard decisions, they avoid them and pass the buck."[92]

None of this is to suggest that the RRCs are failures. Far from it. As with all real-world governmental institutions, RRCs' ability to realize their potential is significantly affected by resource constraints, human and financial, and by organizational and political realities. For all their limitations they are important, influential players in the co-management of fish and wildlife in Yukon. According to Penikett, "only with the final settlement of the Yukon land claim in 1992 and the establishment of local renewable-resource councils did community control of significant game-policy decisions become a reality."[93]

The range of RRC activities relating to fish and wildlife and their habitat is evident in the presentations they make at the annual meeting of the board to which all RRCs are invited. A sampling of the activities mentioned by RRCs at the board's April 2016 meeting includes, in addition to numerous meetings with organizations such as the Yukon Salmon Sub-Committee, the Yukon River Panel, departments of the territorial government, and, of course, the YFWMB:

- moose management programs;
- development of trapping guidelines;
- bison hunting workshops;
- funding a local school program to enable students to develop land-based skills;
- participation in research evaluating nutrients and contaminants in trout in a major lake;
- a wolf trapping workshop;
- meetings and consultations about off-road vehicle use;
- participation in YESAB processes;
- a bird-banding project;
- a wire recovery program (to locate and remove fencing and other wiring in which wildlife can become entangled);
- a timber supply analysis and a related review of vegetation analysis tools.[94]

As this list of just some of their activities illustrates, RRCs engage in a wide variety of short- and long-term projects. In addition to exercising prime authority over allocation of traplines, for which the *UFA* sets a target of 70 percent First Nations ownership (though the target is not reached in all instances),[95] RRCs develop, in concert with the local First Nations and the territorial environment department, detailed integrated fish and wildlife management plans. These documents contain both general principles and specific action plans that set out who is responsible for which aspects of the plans, timelines, and measures of success. They may also make recommendations to the YG, the YFWMB, and the local First Nations.[96]

RRCs vary a good deal in terms of their capacity, interests, and methods. Some are hard pressed to get on with their basic work and operate via quite basic administrative techniques. Others are deeply engaged in a wide range of issues and gather information by means of online surveys.

Like the board, the RRCs strive to incorporate traditional knowledge into their deliberations and decision making. In addition, RRCs call on what is termed "local knowledge": a recognition that long-time non-Indigenous people with extensive land experience also possess valuable insight into the land and the animals. An RRC member quoted by Kelly Hayes in her study of RRCs put it this way: "there are a lot of areas that we don't know or we don't have knowledge about, but we can refer to older members of the council, whether they are First Nation or non-First Nation people. They have a lot of local and traditional knowledge that they provide for us."[97] At the same time, a distinction is usually drawn between local knowledge, which is based on observation, and traditional knowledge, which is culturally based, limited to First Nations, and may have profound cosmological elements.

Initially, RRCs had to deal not only with territorial bureaucrats but also with DIAND officialdom since it was only in 2003 that jurisdiction over forestry and other fields affecting fish and wildlife was devolved from the federal government to Yukon. A territorial official interviewed by Hayes summarized what was apparently a widely held view: "there is no federal acceptance of the role of resource councils."[98] More recently, especially with Environment Canada, relations between RRCs and the federal government have improved substantially.

Finances

Funding for the RRCs is administered by the YG, which, in turn, receives federal government money for this purpose. As territorial officials are quick to point out, levels of RRC funding are specified in the *UFA* Implementation Plan. These arrangements differ from what is found in Nunavut, where HTO funding is provided by Ottawa on a more ad hoc basis and is channelled through the Nunavut Wildlife Management Board. Initially, each RRC received $75,000 annually with a small annual increment.[99] Occasional small increases to the base followed but still left RRCs in a financially straitened condition. The *Five-Year Implementation Review* was forthright, stating that "the number one implementation issue for all four RRCs [was] inadequacy of funding," and noting that full-time staff support was essential if RRCs were to fulfill their mandates but that, at the prevailing funding levels, this was unaffordable. The YG Department of Renewable Resources agreed that RRC funding was inadequate, despite the fact that First Nations had been subsidizing RRCs with low rent and use of office equipment.[100] The review recommended that Ottawa reassess RRC funding and that governments and RRCs collaborate to clarify priorities in order to reduce RRC workloads.[101] If a reassessment took place it did not result in significantly increased funding. Some RRCs thus turned to additional funding sources – private foundations as well as various federal and territorial programs – in order to undertake important projects. For several years, the Association of Yukon Renewable Resources Councils worked on and was able to coordinate RRC forestry activities; however, when its private funding dried up, the association came to an end.

A former RRC chair suggested that, while time-consuming and difficult, such fundraising activities were useful exercises in capacity building for the RRCs. Be that as it may, the *Ten-Year Implementation Review*, as it did with the YFWMB, recommended that RRCs be adequately funded so as not to have to rely on fundraising, which was described as "disruptive to mandated work."[102] The YG looked askance at such activities and called a halt to them, though the prohibition was subsequently lifted to some extent. The *Ten-Year Implementation Review* did not directly address RRC funding but it did make a number of recommendations aimed at rationalizing RRC priorities and reducing their workloads to enable them to live within their budgets.

According to Nadasdy, RRC financial concerns were not limited to the level of their funding. In addition, RRCs found the budgetary oversight of the YG burdensome and inappropriate. "The Yukon government's role in approving RRCs' budgets and line items," he writes, "gives its officials an important role in defining and regulating the activities in which RRC members can engage."[103] During the ten-year review of the *UFA*, in which Nadasdy participated as a First Nation representative, "RRCs complained that territorial officials were using the required [by the YG] work plans to interfere with council activities."[104] In particular, the territorial government did not accept that RRCs' mandates included identifying and attempting to fill gaps in wildlife research. Still, "the

RRCs did not submit passively to Yukon officials' efforts to dictate to them the terms of their own mandates." Some just went ahead with funding research and endured after-the-fact scolding from the government; others resorted to fundraising from private-sector foundations.[105] A YG official counters RRC complaints about heavy-handed financial scrutiny by arguing that Ottawa's increasing preoccupation with accountability leaves the territorial government on the hook for RRC spending deemed inappropriate by federal officials.

In 2015, the base for RRC funding was significantly increased; most RRCs now receive $144,657, in 2014 dollars, with a few receiving up to $160,000 to take their special circumstances into account. Like the board, RRCs are permitted to retain up to 15 percent of their annual payments. When the government cracked down on accumulated surpluses in 2014, whereas the board was given three years to spend the money, all RRC surplus funds were clawed back and reallocated to a special ten-year projects fund to which all RRCs could apply. Several respondents maintained that the territorial government exerts close, indeed restrictive, control over RRC financial affairs – to the point of constraining their activities.

Relations with the YFWMB

RRCs work closely, and generally harmoniously, with the YFWMB, though issues of roles and responsibilities are never far below the surface. The language of the *UFA* contributes to a lack of precision regarding jurisdictional boundaries, specifying as it does that the board is "the primary instrument of fish and wildlife management in the Yukon" while designating the RRC as "a primary instrument" for local renewable resource management. In 2007, the ten-year review noted continuing uncertainty on the part of the board and the RRCs as to their respective roles, recommending that the three parties to the *UFA* "develop orientation materials" that would clarify roles and responsibilities.[106] Little seems to have come from this. Early on the board worked out a protocol with the RRCs aimed at ensuring that "the Board will not attempt to deal with regional matters unless asked to by a [RR] Council."[107] The *UFA* requires that the board meet annually with RRC chairs; the board typically reserves the first day or two of its April meeting to hear from RRCs; board representatives also attend the annual meeting of RRCs. These meetings have proven valuable for the exchange of ideas and information and for focusing board support for the RRCs.

RRCs are frequently hard pressed to fulfill their responsibilities in light of frequent staff turnover, occasioned in no small measure by financial constraints, lack of orientation and training opportunities for members, overloaded agendas, and endless requests to participate in consultation exercises. The YFWMB has in response devoted substantial resources to supporting the RRCs through training, logistical assistance, and associated initiatives. "We're not here as a big brother, but as a resource network," was how one person formerly associated with the board put it, "we don't control their budgets or tell them what to do," although with respect to *UFA* processes, lack of training for RRC members means that "no one tells them what to do or how to do it or what the UFA means; it's not our job to do that but since no one else is doing it we try to help out." The board provides not just substantive advice to RRCs but also administrative support, though not at all on the scale of that provided to Nunavut HTOs by the Nunavut Inuit Wildlife Secretariat. At board meetings I attended, despite differences in opinion between First Nations and government nominees, the degree to which all members supported RRCs against the territorial government was striking. That the RRCs recognize and appreciate the support is suggested in the training handbook cited earlier: "basically the Board is one of your best friends."[108]

The board works closely with RRCs on both local and territory-wide issues but is reluctant to intervene when an RRC has initiated a proposal to the YG. Similarly, early on the board and the RRCs agreed "that the Board should hesitate to act as umpire when there is a split in community views on a management issue and should encourage resolution at the community level."[109] Significantly, the board would be entitled to step in to deal with local issues that arise in areas without RRCs but usually doesn't, so that the affected First Nations and communities deal primarily with the territorial government on fish and wildlife concerns.

Relations with the Yukon Government

RRC relations with the territorial government tend to be decidedly less amicable than they are with the YFWMB. Funding is a perennial source of friction, both its level and the YG's close oversight over how RRCs spend it, though complaints have lessened since the across-the-board increase in 2015. RRCs can and do receive government funding for special projects and sometimes receive payment for the consultation exercises that the YG asks them to take on. A close observer of RRCs maintains that the territorial government micromanages some RRCs' finances, in part in overreaction to some early inappropriate RRC spending: "YG clamped down pretty hard and applied a 'lowest common denominator' approach in which everyone had to abide by standards set to handle the worst problems ... They're quite picky as to what RRCs can spend money on."

As well, deep-seated suspicion of and hostility towards Whitehorse bureaucrats on the part of residents of small communities is rarely far below the surface, and it is worth recalling that all Yukon communities outside the capital are small. More generally, the *Ten-Year Implementation Review* commented on the need for more trust between government and RRCs.[110] Unsurprisingly, RRC members draw a distinction between the government's regional biologists and other technical people, with whom they work closely and whom they find to be helpful and supportive, and senior officials in Whitehorse, who are often seen as out of touch and controlling. One First Nation member of an RRC put it this way:

> I find with both YTG and DIAND, there are people in there who are excellent to work with. I think the problem comes from the regional managers and the director generals, you know. The higher-ups. That's where we have the problems. When it comes down to the biologists or the technicians, we all work well together. So there is co-management at the lower levels, but there isn't much co-management at the higher levels.[111]

Relations between RRCs and the YG have not been helped by occasional perceptions that the government used its appointment power to interfere with RRCs and was responsible for problematic delays in making appointments. That such allegations were more than the grousing of malcontents is suggested by the analysis and recommendations of the *Ten-Year Implementation Review*. Although it noted that delays and inappropriate appointments characterized all *UFA* boards, the review was especially forthright about RRC appointments:

> RRCs in particular noted that inattention to community sensitivities or personal dynamics among individuals when making appointments has been detrimental to their ability to function effectively ... In more than one instance the required FA [final agreement] 16.6.4.3 process did not occur before Yukon confirmed RRC appointments. Those oversights undermined the goodwill between Yukon and the affected YFN and reportedly affected how the RRC was subsequently viewed in the community.[112]

It is important to add that, on occasion, the YG has nominated First Nations citizens to serve on RRCs, just as First Nations have sometimes nominated non-Indigenous people.

RRCs and "Traditional Territory"
Overall, as will be seen, RRCs are positive influences on fish and wildlife management in Yukon. However, even aside from issues of funding, capacity, and

mandate uncertainty, fundamental deficiencies characterize the RRC regime. Many reflect the highly problematic concept of traditional First Nations territory. As Paul Nadasdy has demonstrated, the Euro-Canadian administrative requirement that First Nations delineate precisely their "traditional territories" contradicts not only ethnographic realities but also important cultural norms:

> [Establishing boundaries of traditional territories] requires Yukon Indian people to do something they have never done before: construct firm political boundaries between themselves and their neighbours (who are, often enough, close kin). The notion of a contiguous line separating "us" from "them" flies in the face of important cultural values of kinship and reciprocity, which continue to structure social relations among Yukon Indian people ... Any well-defined territorial boundary between First Nations must necessarily be cross-cut by kinship relations and inconsistent with both historical and contemporary patterns of use and occupancy.[113]

Moreover, Nadasdy points out, "there was little coordination among First Nations in mapping their territorial boundaries," as well, First Nations took different approaches to designating their territories: "some took an inclusive approach, drawing their boundaries as widely as possible to capture the historic land use of all their members; others were more conservative, giving up their claim to certain areas in an apparent effort to minimize potential overlap with other First Nations."[114]

Yet another territorial complication arises from unsettled transboundary disputes involving First Nations whose lands extend into British Columbia.

The process for designating traditional territories produced both a number of substantial overlaps between adjacent First Nations and a few areas not included in any First Nation's territory. Processes exist for resolving overlap issues; however, until a resolution is reached – and some are still outstanding – no RRC has jurisdiction in the area of overlap. In some instances a high proportion of a First Nation's traditional territory overlaps with those of other First Nations, hamstringing the work of the RRC. In some instances, informal arrangements between First Nations have been made as to overlap situations.[115]

No new final agreements have been reached with Yukon First Nations since 2005, and the prospects that the First Nations without final agreements will settle anytime soon, if ever, are limited (some are pursuing land and governance arrangements outside of the *UFA* process). Since RRCs only come into existence after a final agreement has been reached, the territories of these First Nations have no RRCs.

All told, wide swaths of the territory have no RRCs. To a limited extent, formal mechanisms are in place to deal with matters that RRCs would deal with, such as a forestry co-management agreement between the YG and Kaska First Nations. Overall, however, the territorial government deals with renewable resource issues in the areas without RRCs on a case-by-case basis. According to a territorial official, this approach has generally proven satisfactory. Another knowledgeable observer is less sanguine, pointing out that, without an RRC, it is often unclear just what the issues are, adding that a disproportionate number of lawsuits launched by First Nations against the territorial government arise in the areas where no RRCs exist. Still others suggest that in areas without RRCs, the territorial government plays "a disproportionate role in wildlife management,"[116] in part because, absent a finalized land claim and self-government agreement, the local First Nations lack the financial resources available to First Nations that have settled under the *UFA*.

Natcher and his colleagues studied one RRC in depth a few years after its creation. They commented that the Yukon minister seldom overrode RRC recommendations, provided they demonstrated "competence, credibility and effectiveness," adding that "by whose criteria competence and credibility are measured is becoming a point of increasing contention."[117] Their assessment of the RRC they examined is essentially one of promise as yet unfulfilled because of what they call the "cultural distance" between First Nation and non-Indigenous council members, which "has proven to be a formidable obstacle to reaching consensus on management issues."[118] Thus "the ultimate success of the CRRC [Carmacks Renewable Resources Council] will depend on members' ability to engage rather than subvert differences in knowledge and cultural experiences."[119] More than a decade later, a person familiar with (but not a member of) this RRC indicates that the early misgivings and misunderstandings have given way to cooperative relations among all council members and that these undergird a highly effective organization.[120] Such intercultural transactions, to use Rodon's term, are essential to the success of any Indigenous-state co-management arrangement.

Still, conflicts and unrealized promise notwithstanding, as with the YFWMB, the RRCs have unquestionably enhanced First Nations influence over wildlife and habitat issues, but their significance extends a good deal further. Indeed, some respondents argue that the real import of the RRCs lies in how they have increased local influence, non-Indigenous as well as First Nations, in these areas. In turn, this line of thinking suggests that the ability of non-Indigenous people to actively participate in resource management through RRCs has contributed substantially to legitimizing the *UFA* throughout Yukon.

The Yukon Salmon Sub-Committee

Mandate and Membership

All claims boards are unique in their own ways, but the Yukon Salmon Sub-Committee is especially distinctive in several respects. Its mandate is narrow, though to be sure, the various species of salmon are vitally important economically and culturally to Yukon First Nations and, to a lesser extent, to commercial non-Indigenous fishers. It has an unusual relationship to government, in this instance the federal Department of Fisheries and Oceans, which, until recently, gave rise to serious questions about its independence. No other claims board is as extensively involved in relations with another country (Yukon salmon migrate vast distances and spend much of their time in the Pacific and/or in Alaskan rivers). Finally, few if any claims boards have undergone shifts in their activities and their relations with government as substantial as those experienced by the YSSC.

The *UFA* establishes a "sub-committee" of the YFWMB to act as "the main instrument of Salmon management in the Yukon."[121] Normally a sub-committee is composed entirely of members of a larger body, but in this case only two members of the board, a First Nations nominee and a YG nominee, serve on the YSSC. Two other members are appointed by the federal minister of fisheries and oceans. Another six members, two nominated by First Nations in the drainage basins of three important salmon rivers – the Yukon, Alsek, and Porcupine – take part in deliberations affecting their regions; on occasion, First Nations have nominated non-Indigenous people to these positions. Appointments for members of the YFWMB are for the time remaining in the members' board appointments; the balance are for five years. According to section 16.7.16.6 of the *UFA*, although the nominal membership is ten, no more than two of the members from the drainage basins may vote at a time. Recently, however, the YSSC has permitted all members present to vote on all issues relating to drainage matters, in the interests of promoting inclusivity and encouraging attendance.

The chair is elected by the YSSC for a two-year term with re-election a possibility. Unlike at the YFWMB, no formal or informal expectation exists that a government nominee will be vice-chair if the chair is a First Nations nominee and vice versa, though this is often the case. An executive consisting of the chair, vice-chair, and financial secretary organizes the sub-committee's work. Under the *UFA*, YSSC members serve on the Yukon River Panel (YRP), the body formed by the governments of Canada and the United States to implement the *Yukon River Salmon Agreement*, an annex to the *Pacific Salmon Treaty*. The YRP is an international advisory body, which makes recommendations to management entities on both sides of the border concerning the conservation and management of salmon originating in Canada. Eight members of the sub-committee are appointed to the YRP; four serve as the main members, the other four are alternates. The *UFA* mandates that the majority of the Canadian section of the YRP must be made up of YSSC members.

For most of its existence the YSSC had a staff of three or four. All were DFO employees with other responsibilities who served on a part-time basis, so that in full-time equivalents the staff complement was about two and a half persons. More recently, the sub-committee's full-time executive director and an occasional part-time administrative assistant have not been DFO employees and have been selected by the sub-committee. Whitehorse-based DFO staff provide technical and administrative support to the sub-committee as part of their duties, most notably YSSC's executive secretary. On occasion, consultants are hired to conduct research or to provide administrative services such as facilitating strategic planning sessions and project management.

Activities

Regular sub-committee meetings are held three or four times a year for two or three days. In the past, meetings were more frequent but shorter: four to six a year, sometimes as many as a dozen a year. The executive committee meets between meetings as needed. Occasionally YSSC members participate in workshops, conferences, and other salmon-related activities. Most meetings are held in Whitehorse. It was long the case that occasional meetings took place in communities on the major salmon rivers, especially if the chair lived in one of the communities. More recently the sub-committee explicitly decided to hold more of its meetings in communities throughout the territory in order to improve public knowledge about the YSSC and its work. Meetings are open to the public, save for occasional in camera sessions, but few members of the public attend, at least in Whitehorse. Meetings of the three regional working groups, which take place on at least an annual basis, are usually held in affected communities. These engagement sessions and activities are closely tied to development of sub-committee recommendations to the minister on salmon management and allocations. Recommendations accepted by the minister are incorporated into the Integrated Fish Management Plan (IFMP) for the Yukon River, which DFO produces yearly. An unusual provision of the *UFA* (16.7.17.12 [f]) requires – rather than authorizes – the YSSC to recommend harvest allocation levels across regions for First Nations and for non-Indigenous commercial and recreational fisheries. Throughout its history, the sub-committee has consistently won ministerial approval for its recommendations.

The sub-committee makes recommendations beyond what goes into IFMPs. Recent examples include proposed changes to the federal *Fisheries Act*, funding levels for DFO's Yukon Area, and nominations for Canadian representatives on the Yukon River Panel.

Through both formal participation in the work of the Yukon River Panel and less formal interactions with government agencies and Indigenous peoples in Alaska, the sub-committee has extensive contact with representatives of American interests, though it is very much an adjunct to DFO's leadership on international fisheries files.

Other boards across the North that deal with fish tend to focus their efforts on setting harvest levels. This is indeed a crucially important function of the sub-committee, which occurs principally through development of the annual regional IFMPs, which it formally recommends to the DFO minister for adoption and enforcement. Compared to other boards with fish or wildlife remits, however, the YSSC directs a substantially higher proportion of its energies to other issues. Assessment, protection, and rehabilitation of salmon habitat are central sub-committee concerns, consuming a good deal of time and energy and involving it, as advocate rather than as decision maker, in a wide range of processes, from the regulation of placer mining to licensing of sewage facilities and responsibility for fuel spills. Like the YFWMB, under the *UFA* the sub-committee has standing at proceedings of agencies such as the Yukon Environmental and Socio-economic Assessment Board and the Yukon Water Board when salmon and salmon habitat may be at issue. The issues that command the YSSC's attention reflect the precarious health of salmon stocks. To a significant extent the sub-committee's central task is not so much managing the salmon fishery as ensuring that there will continue to be a salmon fishery.

Thus the YSSC is actively involved in various public education and outreach measures designed to raise awareness of issues relating to fostering of salmon stocks and to managing the salmon fishery. Included in these activities are public consultation and information sessions and regular public updates during salmon season as to the size and timing of the runs of various salmon species. At one point the sub-committee held youth contests and ran other untraditional activities, but after pressure from DFO, which saw these as beyond its mandate, they were halted.

The sub-committee attempts to maintain good communications with the RRCs, passing along correspondence and minutes, involving them in the IFMP process, and attending the annual meeting of all RRCs. Overall, however, the RRCs' direct involvement with the YSSC is limited, likely because they are so overburdened.

As is the case with other Northern wildlife management boards, the sub-committee's work is informed by both conventional scientific research and traditional knowledge. The sub-committee has commissioned some of this research itself.

Relations with the YFWMB

From the outset the "sub-committee" chafed at its designation as subordinate to the YFWMB; in the words of one participant, the two "never meshed." Not only did they have distinct mandates, but the board was oriented towards issues arising in relation to the territorial *Wildlife Act*, whereas the sub-committee dealt primarily with the federal Department of Fisheries and Oceans. Almost from its beginning the sub-committee called itself the Yukon Salmon Committee, distancing itself substantively and symbolically from the board, though the chair attended YFWMB meetings, and, of course, two of the sub-committee's members were also board members. The *Ten-Year Implementation Review* found the YSSC's situation unacceptable on several dimensions: "The SSC has not been operating according to the administrative provisions of the UFA and UFA IP [implementation plan] ... Despite the UFA provisions, the SSC has had little if any relationship with the FWMB." The review noted that the sub-committee was just that – a sub-committee of the board – but the requirement for the board to appoint the sub-committee chair was not being followed and the board had not seen a YSSC budget in a decade.[122]

Both symptom and cause of the sometimes difficult relations between the board and the sub-committee was the occasional clash between strong-willed chairs. In this, as in so many other aspects of Northern politics, individuals and their personalities loom large.

The *Ten-Year Implementation Review* had even more pointed criticisms of the sub-committee's relations with DFO, and these are discussed below. The review led to major changes in the orientation of the YSSC entailing, among other things, significantly improved relations with the YFWMB, evidenced by the move of the sub-committee office into space within the board's premises, rented from the board. It no longer refers to itself as the Yukon Salmon Committee: the "sub"-committee terminology has become the norm. Links between the sub-committee and the board extend beyond the two YFWMB members on the YSSC. In addition to routine exchanges of information, a standard agenda item at board meetings is a report from the sub-committee, and the board reviews and approves the sub-committee budget. Although this is usually a pro forma exercise, some members of the sub-committee find it annoying. The sub-committee choice for its chair must be approved by the board, but this, too, is largely done pro forma: no prospective chairs have been turned down. Overall, while communications are good between the board and the sub-committee, especially since they now share office space, the two tend to operate quite separately.

Relations with the Department of Fisheries and Oceans

The unique circumstances of the YSSC give rise to unique problems, mostly relating to perceptions of a lack of independence from DFO, though these have lessened substantially in recent years. One former negotiator called the *UFA* provisions relating to the sub-committee, which long bedevilled its work, as "weird." According to this person, DFO "simply declared this was how it's going to be; that's their standard MO" in order to retain control of salmon regulation. The YSSC is one of only three claims boards in the territorial North whose staff are federal government employees (the others are the Environmental Impact Review Board and the Arbitration Board in the Inuvialuit region).[123] It is the sole claims board required by its claim to be staffed in this way. Section 16.7.17.10 of the *UFA* specifies that DFO "shall provide technical and administrative support to the Sub-Committee ... and a senior official of the department in the Yukon shall serve the Sub-Committee as Executive Secretary." Typically, the sub-committee's executive secretary has major responsibilities in the department unconnected to sub-committee work.

One person familiar with the sub-committee in its early days suggested that some of the difficulty in DFO-YSSC relations arose from how the department viewed the sub-committee. "Initially," this person said, "DFO naively assumed that the salmon committee represented First Nations," perhaps because six or seven of the ten members were Indigenous. The sub-committee made it clear that, if DFO had issues to raise with First Nations, it should deal directly with them. Longer lasting and more problematic was the fact that "DFO saw the salmon committee as a board of convenience ... It [the YSSC] could front changes to management programmes or consultation processes without DFO having to take responsibility." Even more serious were the perception and the reality of the sub-committee's independence from DFO.[124]

For the first decade and a half of its existence, the sub-committee's offices were located in a federal government building on the outskirts of Whitehorse mostly occupied by DFO and generally known as the DFO building. Meetings frequently took place in the DFO boardroom. When it required legal advice, the YSSC usually relied on a DFO staff lawyer. It is now no longer assumed that the sub-committee would only seek legal advice from the DFO. All told, for most of its existence, it was widely believed that the YSSC was, if not a component of DFO, certainly controlled by it. The sub-committee's own 2004–06 Strategic Plan acknowledged as much, identifying "the need for autonomy from DFO as a high priority. There is a public misconception that the YSC is just a branch of DFO and the YSC would like to remedy this. As well, the YSC is financially tied to DFO and is unable to administrate [sic] its own budget."[125] The first five-year review of the *UFA* raised the independence issue, alluding to a meeting from which YSSC was excluded since participants were unwilling to have a DFO employee present.[126]

That concerns about independence from DFO are not limited to those who deal with the sub-committee is clear from meeting minutes. Among other things, the minutes record members' resistance to the prospect of being audited by DFO auditors and their "concern that the jurisdiction of the YSC could be hampered by DFO interpreting what the YSC's mandate is." In another instance, the minutes noted that "the Chair expressed concerns with DFO 'running the YSC' and about 'taking direction from DFO staff.'"[127] A prominent theme emerging from the 2004 Strategic Plan and meeting minutes was dissatisfaction with funding arrangements, both the overall level of financial support and the mechanisms for delivering it.

None of this, however, necessarily implied a subservient attitude on the sub-committee's part. The sub-committee did not lack strong independent-minded members, some of whom served for extended periods, and, of course, only two of the members were DFO nominees. A DFO employee who regularly dealt with it commented that the YSSC's understanding of its role was far wider than DFO thought appropriate – to the point at which it was "largely unchecked" in interpreting its mandate. An example was the sub-committee's interest, which among other things led to a formal recommendation to the territorial government, in the possible commercial development of coal bed methane. The sub-committee took on this issue as a potential threat to salmon habitat, whereas DFO did not view it as falling within the sub-committee's remit. At the same time, the YSSC did not generally adopt a confrontational stance towards DFO. It would, for example, write the minister with "advice" rather than issue formal recommendations. One person associated with the YSSC in its early days commented that its recommendations were less effective than they might have been because they were often vaguely worded, thus affording the minister too much "wiggle room."

The independence of staff – or lack of it – was an ongoing concern. One DFO employee who provided support to the sub-committee candidly stated: "on some issues, the advice to the committee would be different if we didn't work for the department." Another DFO employee with sub-committee responsibilities spoke of "us," meaning DFO, and "them," meaning the sub-committee, commenting that the job was "as a point of contact [between DFO and the YSSC] rather than working for the Salmon Committee." This person added: "there's a real lack of understanding on both sides [DFO and the YSSC] with respect to the independence of staff." Outside observers had less difficulty assessing the situation: for one YFWMB member with extensive experience of the sub-committee, "the executive secretary is the sand in the grease, slowly grinding down the machinery."

The *Ten-Year Implementation Review* marked a turning point for the sub-committee, though the changes did not all occur immediately. "The Salmon Sub-committee," said the review, "reports that the public perceives it as merely 'another branch of DFO' because it is closely tied to DFO in terms of both funding and the provision of staff support and facilities." The sub-committee told the review working group that it wanted an independent budget, an office not on DFO premises, and "at least one staff member of its own."[128]

By 2010, the sub-committee's aspirations had been mostly realized. An executive director, who was not a DFO employee, was hired; bookkeeping and other administrative requirements were provided by either part-time staff or consultants; DFO staff continued to provide technical-scientific information. The executive secretary served as a liaison with the department, but day-to-day operations were left to the executive director. With the sub-committee's concurrence, the executive director moved to tighten up financial procedures, lessening DFO's concern about the need for oversight. A new multi-year funding arrangement provided administrative flexibility and reduced cash flow problems. The sub-committee moved out of the DFO building into the YFWMB's office suite. Overall, sub-committee members' concerns over independence from DFO faded substantially, in part because newer members' experiences with DFO were quite different from those that had irked members in previous times.

Finances

The YSSC's annual budget is modest: $259,000 in 2016–17, all from DFO. Salaries of DFO staff who support the YSSC do not appear in its accounts. The 2016 fiscal year marked the first year of a five-year contribution agreement, replacing a process whereby the contribution agreement had to be renewed annually. As noted in the discussion of Nunavut Wildlife Management Board funding, DIAND agreed several years ago to board demands that it replace contribution agreements with more flexible funding mechanisms. DFO's position, however, is that the *UFA* requires it to adhere to Treasury Board guidelines in funding the YSSC, leaving no option other than a contribution agreement. Among the drawbacks of contribution agreements from the sub-committee's perspective is the requirement that unspent funds be returned at year end.[129] Sub-committee complaints about the "carryover" issue date from the earliest days, although the issue is more symbolic than substantive since the YSSC has made few if any requests to retain unspent funds.

In earlier times, although the sub-committee had no concerns about DFO micromanaging its finances, it did encounter problems due to delays in actually receiving its money. In one discussion of budgetary matters, for example, members were informed that they could only receive partial reimbursement for meeting expenses until funds had been transferred to the sub-committee, and the possibility was raised that they would have to pay out of pocket for travel to an important conference, "to be reimbursed when funding is received."[130] Overall adequacy of funding was also seen by the sub-committee as problematic, with meeting minutes on occasion mentioning cancellation of meetings or of members' planned attendance at meetings or conferences for lack of funding. It is fair to add that, on at least one occasion when funding ran short before the end of the fiscal year, DFO bailed the sub-committee out with a non-repayable loan.

For its part, DFO was less than entirely satisfied with aspects of the sub-committee's finances. A 2005 departmental audit detailed unorthodox procedures, most notably a long-standing practice whereby funds for sub-committee members' travel expenses and honoraria went into the personal bank account of the YSSC's executive secretary, who would cut cheques from this account to sub-committee members. While the audit turned up no evidence of personal gain on the executive secretary's part, it was adamant that such an unacceptable process could not continue. Significantly, the audit traced the problem back to the "very close ties" between YSSC and DFO. "The manner in which the YSC has been managed over the years" not only encouraged the perception of the sub-committee as "an arm of DFO" but it meant that "the Committee has no infrastructure in place to manage its own affairs, therefore it relies on DFO for all of its needs."[131]

More recently, the sub-committee appears less concerned about the adequacy and timing of funding from DFO, with 90 percent of the allocated money delivered on a regular schedule. Generally, DFO does not provide funding beyond the activities covered by the contribution agreement. If the sub-committee wants to develop a special project it must find the funds from other governmental organizations, such as the Yukon River Panel or charitable foundations such as the Pacific Salmon Foundation. A current example is YSSC's partnership with the Yukon River Drainage Fisheries Association in Alaska to deliver the long-running Yukon River Educational Exchange, which facilitates cross-border visits by Alaskans and Yukoners.

An unusual episode is said to have been a factor in DFO's recent willingness to provide the sub-committee with financial arrangements more to its liking. In December 2014, faced with bills it was unable to pay because DFO payments had not been received, the sub-committee approached the YFWMB for a $20,000 loan. Board minutes indicated: "The YSSC is unable to function properly."[132] The sub-committee proposed to use the loan to pay its creditors and then to use the money to establish a bank line of credit in order to avoid similar situations in future. The board agreed to the request and the sub-committee found itself on more solid financial footing, with both a line of credit established and a more reliable payment process from DFO.

Transformation

The Yukon Salmon Sub-Committee has undergone significant transformation since its early days and continues to evolve in response to changes in both the biophysical environment and the political context of salmon management. A strategic planning exercise in 2017 sought to position the sub-committee to respond to these changes in a variety of ways, including recourse to traditional knowledge, improved relations with co-management partners (especially First Nations), and education and outreach. Significantly, the sub-committee recognizes the foundational role of the *UFA* for its work. Before embarking on a new strategic plan, it brought in Dave Joe, a former chief CYI negotiator on the *UFA*, to give an extensive presentation on the *UFA* and subsequent land claim agreements, looking at nuts-and-bolts mechanisms as well as general principles.[133]

The sub-committee continues to face the daunting – and culturally and economically important – challenge not just of maintaining salmon stocks but of increasing them through management of harvest levels and restoration and enhancement of habitat. In this the sub-committee faces politically contentious issues in terms of both the international dimension of salmon management and the status of First Nations subsistence harvesting, which is protected by the *UFA*. An important constraint on the sub-committee's ability to function effectively has been largely removed in that the YSSC has achieved a degree of independence from DFO that it and, more important, other key players see as appropriate. The sub-committee remains strongly committed to incorporating traditional knowledge into its work, but, like so many other claims boards, struggles with how to do so in a meaningful way. So too, the sub-committee continues to work at developing and maintaining strong, trust-based relations with First Nations. A recent comment that many First Nations governments have come to feel that "they now have a seat at the table" as the sub-committee proceeds with its work, suggests some success in this direction. A long-time observer of wildlife management in Yukon maintains that, as a result of the *UFA*, the board and the RRCs First Nations have moved beyond simply "a seat at the table" and, in a number of instances, are leading processes in areas such as conservation.

First Nations Influence through the YFWMB, the YSSC, and the RRCs

It is easy to conclude that the fish and wildlife co-management system created by the *UFA* – the Yukon Fish and Wildlife Management Board, the Renewable Resources Councils, and the Yukon Salmon Sub-Committee – significantly influences policy and practice. With only minor exceptions, none of these bodies wields decision-making power, but their recommendations carry substantial weight by virtue of their members' expertise and commitment and the thorough and thoughtful deliberations behind their recommendations, rooted in close relations with First Nations as well as with organizations and businesses engaged in fish and wildlife harvesting. To be sure, the territorial government (and Ottawa, with respect to most sub-committee recommendations), as the final decision maker, doesn't always agree with board and RRC recommendations. Tensions can exist between the board and the YG, exemplified in the board's concerns that the territorial government's recent imposition of a two-year cycle for the consideration of YFWMB recommendations for changes to *Wildlife Act* regulations accepted by the minister have circumscribed the board's authority and influence. Territorial officials suggest that the board is reading too much into an essentially administrative change. It is fair to add that not all of the territorial bureaucracy is as supportive of board and RRC activity as is the Department of Environment.

Both YG officials and board members themselves suggest that the "primary instrument" language of the *UFA* leads some on the board to believe that it has more than an advisory-advocacy role, that its co-management mandate extends to setting policy. Doubtless this is true to some extent, but for the most part the board recognizes that, by being an informed, engaged advocate and by providing good advice, it does significantly affect policy and policy implementation regarding fish and wildlife and their habitat.

It's one thing to conclude that the YFWMB, the RRCs, and the YSSC are, in terms of their remits, effective and influential. What of the central question animating this book: Have the claims-mandated boards provided Northern Indigenous peoples with substantial influence over policy and administration relating to wildlife and the environment? Here the answer is a qualified, nuanced yes.

When asked directly if they thought that the YFWMB had been successful in substantially enhancing First Nations influence, First Nations citizens, including current and former board members, former *UFA* negotiators, and CYFN officials, clearly agreed that it had been, though several registered disappointment at the board's limited recourse to traditional knowledge. One former First Nations board member commented, "we want to manage people, not fish and wildlife," which meant bringing First Nations and non-Indigenous people and their worldviews together. A senior CYFN official offered a more expansive view of this process:

> The [*UFA*] boards like the Fish and Wildlife Management Board are valuable additions to territorial government because they mean our citizens engaging with and working cooperatively with non-natives to participate in decision making ... [Boards represent] very strong empowerment for the whole territory and have proven to be a very useful instrument for promoting social harmony in the territory.

Similarly, a former First Nation claims negotiator agreed that the YFWMB and other *UFA* boards have made for substantially enhanced involvement in land and resource issues but suggested that a more significant outcome is how the boards "have really empowered the non-native community ... They realize that the UFA boards mean a tremendous opportunity to influence policy development." The key, this person maintains, is that in order to take advantage of the opportunities presented by the boards, non-Indigenous people have had to learn about and engage with First Nations rights and the "social contract" that the *UFA* entails. Along these lines, for a former Yukon environment minister the YFWMB "has had remarkable success at bridging cultural differences and at dealing with difficult problems." Another person, with long experience dealing with the board, speaks of its "profound evolution" in terms of developing the trust, respect, and understanding between Indigenous and non-Indigenous Yukoners that the *UFA* sought to achieve.

The *UFA* boards and the YFWMB in particular have enhanced First Nations influence in crucial wildlife and environment decisions in three ways. The first is direct: through the involvement of First Nations members in advisory boards with real clout. The second, though indirect, may be no less important: legitimation in very practical ways of extensive First Nations participation in public governance processes. This entails respect for and application of First Nations perspectives and knowledge on the part of governance institutions in a jurisdiction in which First Nations constitute a quarter or less of the population and that, until fairly recently, saw significant elements of the non-Indigenous population resisting recognition of First Nations rights. Third, the existence of the YFWMB and the RRCs have required non-Indigenous Yukoners to learn about and engage with First Nations rights and approaches to wildlife management.

It is important to ask whether these gains have come at too high a price. Paul Nadasdy has mounted a cogent argument that the undoubted benefits of Yukon First Nations engagement with Euro-Canadian governance processes, including the co-management boards, have severely undermined fundamental aspects of First Nations culture and society. This and similar contentions from other analysts are considered in Chapter 9.

One episode cited by Nadasdy does warrant mention at this juncture: the YFWMB's decision in 2000 to sanction catch-and-release fishing. This was a deeply meaningful issue for Yukon First Nations in that "the vast majority of Yukon Indian people" find the practice of catch-and-release highly offensive because it shows disrespect for the fish, thereby threatening severe damage to the relationship between fish and humans. When Nadasdy asked a First Nation board member why, if the practice was so abhorrent, he went along with the decision, he was told it was a pragmatic, political decision, premised on the need to maintain good relations with Yukon's non-Indigenous majority and the likelihood that banning catch-and-release fishing "would have ignited a political firestorm."[134] The outcome of this issue demonstrates the limits to First Nations influence through the board, especially given the strong cultural elements involved.

Finally, the board's self-imposed policy of not making recommendations to First Nations governments, despite being permitted to do so by the *UFA*, indicates that a fair distance remains before the vision of the *UFA* and the board's role in it are fully realized. A former YG deputy environment minister commented:

> The entire premise underlying the careful weave of the UFA, final agreements and self-government agreements is that there is an intricate interconnection among public and First Nation governments. They have their own worlds of jurisdiction, but they all come together in the institutions of co-management

set up under the UFA, like the YFWMB and the RRCs ... If one of the UFA bodies believes it is not to advise First Nation governments on matters on their lands, especially on matters in critical environmental areas like species conservation, this goes against the original premise of the co-management regime.

Those at the board refer to its "uneasy" relation with First Nations fish and wildlife staff as a key reason that it is unwilling to propose recommendations to First Nations governments. In the board's view, First Nations are not prepared to give up control over fish and wildlife on their lands either to the board or to the RRCs, though it is hopeful that, over time, relations will improve. That this is more than a vain hope is suggested by the successful experiences of several Yukon First Nations in developing multi-year fish and wildlife work plans in concert with local RRCs and the YG Department of Environment. At the same time, the announced plans in 2018 by the Ross River Dena Council to require non-Kaska to obtain permits from it in order to hunt on its traditional territory, rather than working with the board and the YG to control what it sees as overhunting, confirms that First Nations trust in the co-management regime is far from complete.[135]

chapter 5

The Mackenzie Valley Environmental Impact Review Board and the Mackenzie Valley Land and Water Board

This chapter and the next look at two claims boards that differ greatly on several dimensions from the wildlife management boards examined in the preceding chapters. The Mackenzie Valley Land and Water Board and the Mackenzie Valley Environmental Impact Review Board rank among the largest and most active claims boards. They should not, however, be taken as representative of other environmental regulatory boards. Their structures and operations are distinctive, often unique. To take but one example, in Yukon and in Nunavut water licences are issued by claims boards but, unlike the Mackenzie Valley's land and water boards, land use permits are issued by other, non-claims, agencies. As well, the complex webs of political and administrative relationships within which they operate can be quite unlike those surrounding other boards, such as the Nunavut Impact Review Board, the Yukon Environmental and Socioeconomic Assessment Board, and the Environmental Impact Screening Committee in the Inuvialuit region, even though the substantive issues they face are generally similar.

Clearly, the key difference between the wildlife management and the environmental regulation boards, from which others flow, is the great distinction between their mandates, though to be sure they do share common ground. For the most part, the issues before wildlife management boards entail harvest levels and quotas, harvesting methods, habitat protection and remediation, research into fish and animals, and the like. By contrast, the environmental boards face questions about the environmental viability, broadly defined, of projects, often very large projects such as roads, oil and gas wells, pipelines, and diamond mines as well as the measures necessary to mitigate possible adverse environmental effects.

Most of the projects requiring environmental oversight, and virtually all of those entailing significant board attention, involve proposals for roads or resource development ventures. Still, the range of issues that come before the environmental boards can be remarkably wide, encompassing projects that normally might not be seen as potentially involving harm to the environment. In recent years, among the matters reviewed by territorial environmental boards have been military exercises, use of hovercraft on the tundra, filming a commercial on an uninhabited island, the route of a luxury cruise ship, the travels of an amateur Inuk prospector, the excavation by Parks Canada of the ships of the Franklin expedition, and the recreation of a Thule dwelling.

Both wildlife and environmental regulation boards deal with issues of direct concern to Indigenous people but in very different ways. As one DIAND official in a Northern regional office forcefully, if indelicately, put it, "Ottawa doesn't give a shit about wildlife." By this he meant that the health of various Northern wildlife populations and the opportunities for Northern Indigenous people to harvest them are far down among the federal government's priorities. By contrast, proposals to exploit oil and gas resources; to build roads and pipelines; to mine diamonds, gold, or uranium; and so on carry enormous potential for economic development and revenue generation and are thus of huge interest to Ottawa. Accordingly, the federal government keeps far closer tabs on the activities of environmental regulation boards. Among other things, this means far more extensive scrutiny of their recommendations and more aggressive responses to them. A telling indication of Ottawa's greater concern with the environmental regulation boards was the initial exclusion by DIAND's NWT Regional Office of wildlife management boards when it established the "Board Forum," an organization established to improve communications between DIAND and claims boards (and among boards) and to enhance collective board effectiveness.

The issues before the environmental regulation boards are typically more technical and complex than those faced by wildlife management boards. Relatedly, the procedures boards must follow in conducting environmental assessment and in licensing and permitting processes, which are set out in extensive detail in the boards' enabling legislation and regulations, entail a far more formal, legalistic approach than those that characterize the wildlife management boards. All this, of course, requires large staffs and budgets for the environmental regulation boards.

Finally, given the scale of the projects they review, and thus both their economic potential and their possible environmental effects, the environmental regulation boards are more likely to find themselves caught up in high-stakes political conflicts between industry, government, and Indigenous communities than are wildlife management boards. To be sure, bitter, far-reaching conflicts also occur with respect to wildlife management; for example, instances of renewable resource boards banning or severely limiting caribou hunting readily qualify as high-stakes political conflicts.

Through an examination of the structure and operation of the two Mackenzie Valley boards, and a number of key episodes in their development, these chapters provide material for analysis of the central issues in the evaluation of claims boards in terms of treaty federalism. The environmental regulatory regime centred on the MVLWB and the MVEIRB represents an important test for the proposition that Indigenous people exercise significant influence through claims boards. This chapter is primarily devoted to setting out the origins, structures, operating procedures, budgetary arrangements, and the like for the two boards as well as their relations with the federal government and the Government of the Northwest Territories. In so doing it is concerned with the boards' effectiveness in protecting the people and the environment of the Mackenzie Valley. Establishing that they are effective is, of course, a necessary but not sufficient condition for concluding that claims boards do entail substantial influence in resource management decisions for Indigenous people. This chapter also examines how local communities and Indigenous people, through their governments and organizations, participate in environmental regulation as well as the heavily politicized relations between the boards, the federal government, the resource extraction industry, and Indigenous organizations. The following chapter offers an account of the saga of the Ottawa-led regulatory restructuring in the form of the highly controversial 2014 amendments to the *Mackenzie Valley Resource Management Act* and considers the question of Indigenous influence through the boards.

The two chapters deal extensively with the boards' relationships with DIAND. Since 2014, the GNWT has played a far more significant role in the boards' activities than it did previously, but DIAND remains preeminent in terms of board funding and appointments as well as in other areas. This attention to DIAND is necessary not only in order to give as complete a picture of the boards as possible but also because the nature of DIAND's links to the boards impinge directly on the central question underpinning this book. If the federal government substantially controls the boards or constrains them, then the scope for Indigenous influence over the environmental issues before the boards is correspondingly decreased.

A word on terminology: strictly speaking, the MVEIRB is primarily engaged in environmental assessment and thus is not, as is the MVLWB, a *regulatory* board. However, this and the following chapter consider that both boards together with the land use planning boards and the regional land and water boards constitute an integrated system of land and water management and hence uses the term "regulatory" with reference to the MVEIRB.

The chapter begins with an overview of the regulatory process for resource development projects in the Mackenzie Valley followed by a brief account of the origin and principal features of the *Mackenzie Valley Resource Management Act*. The next section recounts the sometimes rocky early days of the new *MVRMA* regime. Two long sections chronicle and analyze the MVEIRB and the MVLWB with particular attention to their formative years and the ups and downs of their relations with the federal government and subsequently with the GNWT. A final section considers a number of ongoing issues with the two boards.

Given the chapter's extensive detail, especially regarding the growing pains of the MVLWB and the MVEIRB, it is easy to lose sight of a fundamentally important characteristic of the Mackenzie Valley boards. Although the boards continue to evolve – they have been in existence barely two decades – and although their relations with industry, with communities and with governments, public and Indigenous, can at times be difficult, these boards have developed into highly effective institutions of governance whose efforts at protecting the environment are widely acknowledged as successful.

The *Mackenzie Valley Resource Management Act*

Julia Christensen and Miriam Grant interpret the passage of the *MVRMA* as the culmination of developments in the NWT from the 1960s to the 1990s that contributed to the emergence of a postcolonial political regime: the physical transfer of the territorial government from Ottawa to Yellowknife, the establishment of "responsible government," the political mobilization of Indigenous people, the Berger Inquiry into the proposed Mackenzie Valley Pipeline, and the negotiation of comprehensive land claims.[1] Under the Gwich'in and Sahtu claims and the subsequent *Tlicho Agreement* the federal government was required to create boards to do environmental impact screening and assessment as well as licensing and permitting. Despite strong pressure, especially from the Gwich'in, who launched legal action to force Ottawa to live up to this commitment, several years passed between finalization of the claims and passage of the *MVRMA* in 1998. The act established a network of boards designed as an integrated resource management system for the Mackenzie Valley, defined as the entire Northwest Territories south of the Inuvialuit Settlement Region in the Mackenzie Delta-Beaufort Region, where boards established by the *Inuvialuit Final Agreement* hold sway, and excepting Wood Buffalo National Park.

Proposed developments in all Canadian jurisdictions are subject to environmental assessment and regulatory processes, but it is fundamentally important to recognize that the environmental regulatory regime in the NWT, like those in Nunavut and Yukon, is "different by design."[2] Unlike systems of environmental regulation elsewhere in the country, the *MVRMA* regime draws its very essence from the provisions and the principles of Indigenous-state treaties: comprehensive land claims agreements.

The outline of what would become the *MVRMA* and the system of boards it established was developed during the negotiation of the Mackenzie Valley-wide Dene-Métis claim during the 1980s. Although an agreement-in-principle (AIP) was signed in 1988, fundamental disagreements over its provisions, most notably its "extinguishment" stipulations, led to regional splits within the Dene Nation and the collapse of the claim in 1990. In short order, the federal government opened negotiations with the Gwich'in and the Sahtu Dene and Métis on regional claims. Finalized agreements, modelled on the failed Dene-Métis claim, were reached within a few years. According to one of the Dene negotiators, the parts of the claim setting out the nature and powers of the boards played no role in its rejection; not everyone in the Dene-Métis camp may have been enthusiastic, but the proposed board regime was generally seen as an acceptable compromise. Thus the *MVRMA* boards, mandated by the Gwich'in and Sahtu claims, closely followed the structures and principles set out in the Dene-Métis claim, with the notable exception of the regional land and water boards. Under the Dene-Métis AIP, a single land and water board was to have jurisdiction over the entire Mackenzie Valley.

Key elements of the *MVRMA* regime were distinctive and original, going well beyond environmental regulatory provisions of the *James Bay and Northern Quebec Agreement* and the *Inuvialuit Final Agreement*, at the time the only completed comprehensive claims. As an account of the origins of the MVEIRB noted, the environmental regulation processes in the failed Dene-Métis AIP, which were carried over into the *MVRMA*, were "groundbreaking in that the federal government agreed to share its authority over the environmental assessment process with Aboriginal people."[3] Indeed, the Dene-Métis rejected the model of environmental regulation in the Inuvialuit claim, largely because it lacked the clout they sought, though as one Dene negotiator wryly put it, "the Dene wouldn't think they had anything to learn from the Inuvialuit."

Not the least of the unusual features of the *MVRMA* was the process of its creation, and not simply that it was five years in the making. Complex bills are often subject to extensive consultation and undergo multiple redrafts – thirty-five in this case[4] – but it is unheard of that major federal legislation should be, in effect, redrafted in public. One of the DIAND officials involved recalls: "our federal brothers and sisters were aghast that we'd have draft bills posted on the walls during public meetings." While Gwich'in and Sahtu representatives pronounced themselves pleased with how consultations had proceeded, Indigenous leaders from the Dehcho and Akaitcho regions were bitterly critical of what they described as an entirely inadequate consultation process.

This discontent paled, however, in comparison with their attacks on the actual legislation. Accepting the right of the Gwich'in and Sahtu regions to buy into the regime via their claims, and thus the federal government's obligation to establish boards in accordance with the claims, they vehemently rejected the notion that the act should apply to their territories. In the words of Mike Nadli, grand chief of the Dehcho First Nations:

> The state is trying to do an end run and pass this legislation affecting our territory without having any agreement with our peoples ... We have never given our consent, implied or actual, to the legislation ... The proposed Mackenzie Valley resource management legislation is a violation of the treaties ... In effect, this legislation is a coward's way of dealing with the issues related to lands and territories of the Deh Cho.[5]

Another Dehcho leader stated forthrightly: "If this bill is passed my people's rights, aboriginal treaty rights, will be extinguished. That I cannot accept."[6] Several years after the act came into operation, this attitude had not softened. Dehcho First Nations grand chief Herb Norwegian likened the *MVRMA* to colonialism and apartheid, alleging: "we're being treated as little panhandlers in our own territory."[7] "My community," an Akaitcho leader told an MVEIRB-sponsored workshop, "does not acknowledge this board [MVEIRB] or the act it's under."[8] Although this principled objection to the board and the act persists, at a pragmatic level some accommodation has been reached, as evidenced by this same leader's presentation on socioeconomic impact analysis to a board-sponsored workshop in 2006 and her community's forthright demands the following year that the board reject an application for uranium prospecting in its traditional territory.[9]

Objections from the so-called unsettled areas did not dissuade the Liberal government and the bill was passed, receiving Royal Assent in June 1998, with most parts proclaimed – brought into force – in December of that year. The *MVRMA* replaced the *Canadian Environmental Assessment Act*, then the operative federal statute elsewhere in Canada, and ended the dominant role of the Department of Indian Affairs and Northern Development in environmental assessment and permitting processes.

The *MVRMA* regime differs markedly from the system it replaced. Among its most notable features:

- Consultation, assessment, and licensing functions, which previously had been largely carried out by DIAND bureaucrats, were transferred to independent boards half of whose members were nominees of Indigenous governments and whose staff are employed by the boards rather than by DIAND, as was the case with the Northwest Territories Water Board, which the boards replaced.
- Environmental assessment and regulation processes became far more open and transparent – in addition to vast amounts of information on individual applications being made public, ministers now had to justify, in writing and in public, instances of recommendations they rejected or modified.
- The views of local communities and Indigenous governments on proposed developments were accorded far more weight in assessment and licensing.
- The definition of "environment" was expanded to include cultural and socioeconomic considerations.[10]
- Traditional Indigenous knowledge was more explicitly incorporated – indeed, mandated – into assessment and licensing processes.
- Unique provisions were included in Part 6 of the act, for ongoing cumulative environmental impact monitoring and for periodic, independent "environmental audits," to examine in detail both the state of the environment in the Mackenzie Valley and the effectiveness of the processes devised to implement the act.

That the *MVRMA* regime brought in these and other new features is not to say that all are working as well as envisaged or hoped. Including social and cultural elements in environmental regulation, especially in terms of implementation and enforcement, for example, has proven contentious and difficult. So too, while traditional knowledge is certainly recognized and integrated into regulatory processes, critics contend that it remains undervalued and underused.

And while the environmental audits have consistently produced astute, balanced, and generally positive assessments of the regulatory process, the act contains no requirement for governments or boards to respond to their analyses and recommendations. Apparently some governments and boards did develop internal documents in response to the audits, but these were never made public. The 2015 audit commented: "Many recommendations from the first Audit were carried over to the second. Many of the key recommendations of the second Audit remain unresolved."[11] A significant advance was registered in the 2015 audit with the inclusion of written responses from DIAND, the GNWT, and boards. One long-time board observer argues that such follow-up falls to the "responsible authority" designated by the federal minister, but since this was never done, the minister is obliged to take the lead. The DIAND minister has never accepted this argument.

Overview of the Mackenzie Valley Resource Management Process

The *MVRMA* envisaged three types of boards: boards to formulate land use plans that would, among other things, prescribe permissible uses and standards for developments in the areas covered by claims; boards to do preliminary screening, permitting, and licensing of development projects; and one board to conduct detailed environmental assessments of large or problematic proposals. From the outset, land use planning – or, more accurately, its absence – was the weak link in the system. Land use plans are crucial for setting the basic framework for screening and assessing proposed developments and other uses of land; without them, the other regulatory boards are forced to make what are essentially ad hoc land use planning decisions as they deal with specific applications. For an extended period, only one land use plan was in place, in the Gwich'in settlement region, and that only after protracted delays and conflicts. More recently land use plans have been finalized in the Sahtu and Tlicho regions.[12] Most initial screening and all final permitting and licensing of proposed projects is done by land and water boards. A number of government departments and agencies may also screen projects, though they usually rely on the land and water boards to do so. As described below, this is done by the MVLWB plus three regional land and water boards: the Gwich'in Land and Water Board, the Sahtu Land and Water Board, and the Wek'èezhìi Land and Water Board. The MVEIRB performs environmental assessments of proposed projects with potentially significant adverse environmental effects; its jurisdiction extends to the entire Mackenzie Valley.

The following is a simplified account of the permitting process in the Mackenzie Valley, highlighting the roles of the boards featured in this chapter.[13] Under the framework established by the *MVRMA*, most developments require licences or permits or other authorizations certifying that their environmental effects are acceptable, either by virtue of their limited impact or because of plans for mitigation or remediation, and imposing conditions for proceeding. Not surprisingly, major projects such as roads, mines, or pipelines require regulatory approval, but so too do relatively minor undertakings, such as highway culverts or small gravel pits. The "environment" is taken to mean not only the natural, biophysical world – the land and water and the flora and fauna inhabiting it – but also, albeit in limited ways, cultural and socioeconomic concerns. The federal and territorial governments as well as First Nations must obtain licences and permits or other authorizations on the same basis as companies and individuals. Municipal government projects within municipal boundaries face a somewhat less stringent process. Notably, the process previously in place under the *Canadian Environmental Assessment Act* did not extend to governments.

As discussed at length in the following chapter, in 2014 the *MVRMA* was extensively amended when the federal government devolved most administrative control over non-renewable resources, but not ownership of Crown land, to the GNWT. Significantly, the legislation did not directly empower the GNWT to exercise *MVRMA* functions previously performed by Ottawa; rather, it delegated certain responsibilities and decision-making powers to the territorial government with a commitment to review the situation five or more years down the road. Accordingly, although in most instances it is now territorial ministers who make final decisions in *MVRMA* processes, many of the specific decisions and general processes discussed in this chapter relating to the Mackenzie Valley boards' first decade and a half are framed in terms of "Ottawa," "DIAND," or "the federal government."

The *MVRMA* and its processes are complex and, for the uninitiated, confusing. I have a PhD in political science and am broadly familiar with governmental processes, yet only after many explanations over many years from those involved have I acquired even a rudimentary understanding of environmental regulation in the Mackenzie Valley and the roles played by the *MVRMA* boards. How those without a good knowledge of government processes and jargon, especially Indigenous people with limited English-language facility, can navigate the act and the board processes is an important question. Boards are certainly concerned about this and make extensive efforts to address it, with staff routinely working with communities and with elders, especially prior to hearings, to explain the process.

The process begins with the proponent of a proposed development or activity completing a formal application that is screened for its potential effects on the environment. In many cases, this is also the final step of the process. The

Gwich'in, Sahtu, and Wek'èezhìi land and water boards have jurisdiction over projects situated in their regions. The MVLWB has jurisdiction elsewhere in the Mackenzie Valley – the areas where land claims have not been finalized – and also over projects with "transboundary" implications: those affecting either more than one claim area or a neighbouring territory or province. In 2017–18 some sixty applications underwent preliminary screenings: thirty-four by the MVLWB, twenty-one by the regional land and water boards, three by the federal government (DIAND and Parks Canada), and two by the GNWT (Department of Environment and Natural Resources).[14] None were referred for environmental assessment.

In terms of land use permits and water licences, this chapter is primarily concerned with the MVLWB. With occasional minor deviations, the processes and the decision-making principles of the three regional land and water boards closely follow those of the MVLWB. Land and water board staff determine whether the application is complete. Applications lacking necessary information are sent back to the proponents for revision. Once an application is complete, a project judged to have little or no environmental impact can be approved at this stage by the land and water board. The scope of the project determines the level of licence or permit required. Large projects, variously defined, require Type A water licences or land use permits, lesser projects Type B licences and permits.[15] On projects requiring Type B licences or permits, and on projects covered by Type A land use permits, land and water boards are empowered to make final decisions. This is a very significant power. Projects requiring a Type A water licence, which entail potentially more substantial effects, and projects needing a Type B water licence that have been subject to a public hearing must be approved by the territorial minister of environment and natural resources. Until the 2014 amendments to the act, the federal DIAND minister exercised this authority. For projects wholly or in part on "federal lands," the authority still rests with the DIAND minister.[16] Though the minister may consult informally with other departments on a board's licence recommendation, their formal approval is not required. This contrasts with the process for recommendations from the MVEIRB, where the GNWT lands minister takes the lead but responds on behalf of other ministers.

In all cases, land and water boards can impose conditions, possibly quite stringent and extensive, when they issue licences or permits. Land and water boards must hold public hearings on most applications for Type A water licences and, if they believe circumstances warrant, may hold hearings on any other licence or permit application. If, ten days before the hearing is to take place, no person or organization has indicated an intention to participate, the hearing may be cancelled. Only a very few applications generate public hearings; typically, for example, the MVLWB holds no more than two or three a year.

If the screening board believes that a project requires a fuller review, it refers it to the MVEIRB for an environmental assessment (EA). This could be on the basis of potentially significant adverse effects on the environment or, in a provision that deeply aggravates industry, a conclusion that the project might cause "public concern." The MVEIRB, which receives copies of all applications, can also take it upon itself to conduct an EA; this happens infrequently. Federal and territorial government departments and agencies, as well as municipal governments, as constituted by GNWT legislation, can also make referrals, as can the Indigenous governments with settled claims – the Gwich'in Tribal Council, the Sahtu Secretariat, and the Tlicho Government. First Nations without settled claims, however, lack this power, a sore point only somewhat mitigated by the willingness of governments to send projects to EA if Indigenous communities have concerns. The MVEIRB has called for an end to the *MVRMA*'s prohibition against First Nations and band councils referring developments to EA unless they are formally incorporated as a local government, as defined in GNWT legislation. Few are so defined, "even though in some communities they perform all of the functions of a local government." As the board notes, this issue "undermines the general acceptance of the MVRMA in the unsettled land claim areas."[17] In 2005, the Dehcho First Nations and the federal government signed a "Settlement Agreement" designed to resolve some of the issues arising from Dehcho objections to the *MVRMA* and to the composition of the Joint Review Panel for the mammoth Mackenzie Gas Project. In it Ottawa committed to referring to EA any development application that an affected First Nation in the Dehcho believed might have an adverse impact on the environment.[18] This provision has been used sparingly.

Only a small proportion of applications are referred to the MVEIRB for an EA. In the half decade ending in 2015, for example, of 250 applications screened, mostly by the land and water boards, only ten went on to the EA stage – 4 percent.[19] This rate is effectively the same as in the early years of the *MVRMA* regime; when applications screened by all boards and agencies are considered, the ratio is even lower. From 1998 to 2005, barely 3 percent of projects screened were referred to EA.[20] The Review Board has no discretion to decline a referral for an EA, though it can and does seek clarification if concerns about "cumulative effects" underlie the referral.[21] The board occasionally receives a request from the public or from a non-governmental organization to do an EA on a proposed project. These requests are typically declined.

Environmental assessments unfold in four phases: scoping, analysis, hearings, and decision. Scoping involves developing formal terms of reference for the EA, in response to the question: "What are the potential impacts that should be studied and focused on during the EA?"[22] A board staffer describes the analysis phase as follows: "The proponent submits a Developers' Assessment Report (DAR) and the Board conducts an adequacy review to make sure it fulfills the Terms of Reference. A DAR predicts how a project will affect the land and environment. The Board and Parties may then submit information requests and more information can be shared during scientific and cultural 'technical sessions.'"[23] In almost all EAs, hearings follow, at which board members and staff as well as interested parties, which can include government agencies, NGOs, and Indigenous governments and organizations, can question the project proponent and suggest ways of avoiding or mitigating potential impacts. All materials and data submitted to the board, often hundreds of documents, are posted to the board's website. As this summary suggests, an EA can be a complex, drawn-out process. Even aside from suspensions of activity requested by proponents, EAs typically take over a year to complete.

Recently, the MVEIRB has taken steps to add a new component to the EA process: formally assessing the cultural impact of proposed developments. From the outset the board did this informally, following the *MVRMA*'s requirement that the board pay attention to cultural issues. "Impact on the environment," as defined in section 111 (1) of the act, included "any effect on the social and cultural environment or on heritage resources," while section 115 (1) (b) specified that one of the board's guiding principles is "the protection of the social, cultural and economic well-being of residents and communities in the Mackenzie Valley." In that cultural impact assessment is closely tied in with traditional knowledge, a full discussion must await Chapter 8. By early 2018, the board had begun to incorporate community cultural impact sessions into its EA process, though formal guidelines were still being developed.

Once it has completed an EA, the MVEIRB makes a report of environmental assessment (REA) to government explaining why it has chosen one of the options open to it. Reports are highly detailed; two recent reports each exceeded 450 pages. Most go to the GNWT minister of lands, though in instances where proposals could affect federal lands, the EA report goes to the DIAND minister. In certain highly unusual situations, a REA goes to a "designated regulatory agency," of which there are currently two: the National Energy Board and the Canadian Nuclear Safety Commission. Only rarely has this occurred (no REA has ever gone to the Canadian Nuclear Safety Commission). The REA is posted on the board website as soon as it is sent to the minister. The board can recommend approval of the project either with no "measures" to mitigate adverse environmental effects or with specific mitigating measures. It can recommend outright rejection if it believes the project entails "significant adverse impact on the environment" that cannot be adequately mitigated.

In cases where the board believes a proposed development "is likely ... to have a significant adverse impact on the environment" it can recommend approval subject to mitigating measures or it can order an environmental impact review (EIR), a substantially more complex and extensive process than an EA. The board cannot reject a proposal on the basis of public concern; however, if it concludes that a proposal "is likely ... to be a cause of significant public concern," it *must* order an EIR.[24] A long-standing complaint from industry is that the *MVRMA* does not define "public concern" or "significant public concern," resulting in uncertainty and unpredictability and, at the screening stage, needless referral of projects to EA.

While some MVEIRB members must be involved in an EIR, the board can appoint non-members to serve on the review panel. Notably, for EIRs predominantly or wholly in the Gwich'in Settlement Area, the Gwich'in are entitled to nominate half the panel members, excluding the chair; for projects partially on Gwich'in lands, the entitlement is one nomination.[25] Similar provisions are found in the Sahtu claim and the *Tlicho Agreement*.

In nearly two decades, only two projects have been sent to EIR. One was the Mackenzie Gas Project, in which the MVEIRB was one of several agencies participating in a complex process involving, among other things, a joint review panel, to conduct the EIR.[26]

If only a single instance of a process exists, it can hardly be considered "typical"; however, the other EIR, on the De Beers Gahcho Kué diamond mine northeast of Yellowknife, is illustrative of how an EIR might unfold. At that, it involved two elements – a court case and a long developer-initiated hiatus – that would not likely be duplicated in subsequent EIRs. De Beers applied to the MVLWB for a Type A water licence and a Type A land use permit in November 2005; less than a month later, Environment Canada referred the applications to the MVEIRB for an EA. In June 2006, citing likely "significant public concern," the board ordered an EIR. The mining industry in general and De Beers in particular were highly exercised over this decision, over which the federal minister had no control. In November 2006, De Beers launched a legal challenge, arguing that the board had made procedural errors and overstepped its authority in ordering the EIR. The Supreme Court of the Northwest Territories ruled in April 2007 that, in all respects, the board acted appropriately and legally in reaching its decision.[27] This was an important judgment, affirming as it did the board's jurisdiction and its capacity to develop its own procedures; in so doing it deterred further legal challenges. In May, the board appointed a seven-person panel to conduct the EIR; four panel members were also board members, including panel chair Gabrielle Mackenzie-Scott, who had been board chair when it ordered the EIR. The panel reported to the minister in July 2013, who approved it three months later, in October 2013. Thus from the panel's appointment to its report took six years, though the process was adjourned, at De Beers's request, for over two and a half years. Permitting and licensing followed quickly. The mine began producing diamonds in September 2016.

One federal official, who had been involved in the development and early implementation of the *MVRMA*, recalled that he and others in DIAND had expected EAs to be relatively brief and straightforward, with EIRs unfolding in much the way that EAs came to operate. A GNWT bureaucrat involved with the start-up and first years of the *MVRMA* suggested that, because board members at both the MVEIRB and the MVLWB lacked training and experience, the boards' lawyer – John Donihee served for many years as counsel to both boards – became quite influential. A long-time board official argued strongly to me that Donihee never attempted to influence the outcome of board processes but recognized that he could be aggressive in ensuring that the boards were in a position to make decisions and have them respected.

The figures on the relative infrequency of EAs and EIRs should not be taken as evidence that the regime is lax. As the first independently conducted NWT Environmental Audit pointed out, under the *MVRMA* more projects were being subjected to more searching environmental review, and more smaller projects were being reviewed, than was the case prior to the act's passage.[28]

The GNWT minister of lands takes the lead in reviewing and assessing the MVEIRB's EA report and responds on behalf of other "responsible ministers," including in some instances federal ministers, whose departments may be involved. (For EAs on proposals wholly or partially on federal lands, the DIAND minister assumes this role.) Once the minister approves the recommendations, on occasion a protracted process, the appropriate land and water board (or occasionally another government entity) issues the permit or licence, unless of course the recommendation was that the project should not proceed.

For projects wholly or partially on Tlicho lands – a block of roughly 39,000 square kilometres, roughly 19 percent of Mǫwhì Gogha Dè Nįįtłèè, the Tlicho traditional use area – the Tlicho Government, along with the GNWT, is a decision maker. If federal lands are involved, the decision is a joint responsibility of the Tlicho Government and DIAND. The Tlicho Government's options in dealing with an EA are somewhat different from those of the GNWT. Whereas the GNWT may, after considering the EA, order a project to EIR, the Tlicho Government lacks that power. However, unlike the GNWT, the Tlicho Government can simply reject a proposal on the basis of an EA. These differences are far less significant than the very substantial authority possessed by the Tlicho Government in responding to EAs affecting its lands.

Although the principle of consultation with Indigenous peoples was incorporated into the *MVRMA*, a number of court judgments made after the act was passed significantly raised the bar on the Crown's duty to consult. The Review Board emphasizes that it is not an agent of the Crown, responsible for conducting consultations.[29] Accordingly, another step has been added to the process. Thus the GNWT (formerly DIAND) contacts potentially affected Indigenous governments and groups following receipt of a report of an EA. The following communication, relating to an EA on a proposed road, is typical of the GNWT's approach to such consultation:

> The Responsible Ministers (RMs) for the GNWT with jurisdiction related to the Project rely on the EA to assist in fulfilling the duty to consult and, where appropriate, accommodate with respect to potential adverse impacts of the Project on asserted or established Aboriginal and/or Treaty rights.
>
> By way of this letter, the GNWT is consulting the Katl'odeeche First Nation (KFN) to consider the concerns that KFN may have with the REA regarding potential adverse impacts of the Project on KFN's asserted or established Aboriginal and/or Treaty rights.[30]

Though the MVEIRB acts only in an advisory capacity – unlike the land and water boards, it has no authority to make a final decision on any matter before it – it exercises far more real life power than is customary for purely advisory agencies. For example, the minister has no capacity whatsoever to intervene in an EA to short circuit or speed it up but must wait until the board has issued a report before taking any action. This is important since many phases of project development in the North are highly time-sensitive. By way of illustration, delivery of essential equipment and supplies to remote sites may only be possible while winter roads are passable. Material not on site by April won't arrive until at least the following December or January. Much as a minister might wish a project expedited through a quick EA, perhaps in response to developer pressure, he or she cannot force the pace of an EA. The 2014 amendments to the *MVRMA* did impose time limits on various facets of the board's work, but the board was already meeting the deadlines in most instances.

More significantly, a minister faced with an unpalatable EA report cannot simply ignore or overturn it and substitute new recommendations and measures. The minister may modify a measure proposed by the board, so long as it does not change the intent of the measure, and then only after consultation with the board. This option has been formalized into what is termed the "consult-to-modify" process, which comes into play frequently. "Modify," however, entails only minor wording changes, not basic revision. As the board put it in a recent response to a series of revisions proposed by the GNWT to recommendations in an REA, "once the Review Board finds that a significant impact will result from a proposed development, mitigation must occur before the project can proceed."[31] A minister wanting to modify a measure proposed in an EA report in a manner that would fundamentally alter its intent, wanting to disregard a measure entirely, or wanting to approve a project that the board had rejected outright has two options. The minister can ask the board to reconsider its recommendation, which is unlikely to produce a fundamental change, or may order, and wait for the completion of, an EIR – hardly an attractive possibility. In short, the minister's practical options in responding to an EA report from the board are very much constrained, and it is the board, rather than the minister, that establishes the context and the issues for consultation and negotiation.

Once the minister has signed off, the file goes to the MVLWB, or one of the regional land and water boards, to issue the appropriate licence or permit. The boards deny very few licences or permits, though they do have various grounds for so doing, such as insufficient consultation by the applicant or inability to demonstrate the capacity to provide the requisite security deposit. More significantly, boards do have considerable leeway in crafting terms and conditions, which can be extensive and onerous. The minister has the authority to refuse to sign a board's Type A licence but never has, although, on rare occasions, ministers have sent licences back to the board for further consideration. As one participant in the process put it, "often the minister has to swallow hard and say yes."

From the outset the *MVRMA* gave the federal government authority, following consultation with the territorial government and the First Nations with settled claims, to make regulations on a range of procedural matters, including timelines. However, Ottawa made only limited use of this power so that the process had few hard deadlines and none at all for EAs or EIRs. The 2014 amendments to the act brought in a number of deadlines, mostly affecting EA and EIR processes.

Under *MVRMA* regulations, a land and water board has only ten days in which to return an application for a land use permit to its proponent as incomplete. Although no legislated timeline exists to assess the completeness of an application for a water licence, staff try to meet the same ten-day standard. Once the land and water board accepts an application as complete, in most cases it has forty-two days in which to render a decision: issue a permit or licence, with appropriate terms and conditions; conduct a hearing; refer the project to EA; or refuse the application because it does not conform to an approved land use plan or for various other reasons provided in the act. This relatively short period constrains the boards' capacity to solicit and receive comments from potentially affected communities and First Nations and to conduct a preliminary screening.

For applications requiring Type A water licences, including renewals and amendments, or Type B licences – applications that entail public hearings – the MVLWB has nine months to produce a draft licence. The minister has forty-five days, with the possibility of a forty-five-day extension, to render a decision; if no decision is rendered in that period, the licence is deemed to have been approved. Should the minister reject a draft licence, written reasons must be provided. These deadlines are not as firm as they might appear. In all instances, the minister has discretion to extend deadlines by short periods, and if that proves insufficient, on the minister's recommendation, the cabinet can authorize further extensions any number of times.

EAs that include hearings, as virtually all do, must be completed within sixteen months, and the minister has five months, which includes any consult-to-modify processes, to make a decision. If no hearing was held, the deadlines are nine months and three months. Should the MVEIRB order an EIR, it must develop terms of reference within three months. An EIR panel has eighteen months to report and the minister six months to reach a decision. As with land and water board deadlines, minister-approved extensions are possible for EAs and EIRs. With the delegation of authority to the GNWT the territorial minister of lands has the capacity to grant the initial short time extensions, provided that no federal lands are involved; however, longer and repeated extensions may only be granted by the federal cabinet. In the first years of the GNWT having prime responsibility for *MVRMA* regulatory processes, no extensions were requested by either the MVLWB or the MVEIRB.

On occasion, EAs can fall into abeyance for long periods without being cancelled. An illustration is the Tyhee NWT Corporation's proposal for a gold mine, which was referred to EA in 2005 but was still, though apparently moribund, on the books in 2019. Outright cancellation of an EA is highly unusual, though it has happened. In 2014, for example, the DIAND minister notified the board that the mineral claims underpinning two applications had lapsed, rendering their applications ineligible, and asked it to cancel and close the two EAs (the board had made EA reports to the minister on the applications in 2007 and 2008).[32]

Early Days: Adapting to the Sea-Change

Especially in the early days, the relationship between the two Mackenzie Valley-wide boards and DIAND was fraught with difficulty. The worst of the boards' clashes with Ottawa are long past, though some residue remains.

A long-time DIAND official argues that major changes in the environmental regulatory system were already in train before the passage of the *MVRMA*, pointing to the environmental assessment of the Ekati diamond mine, northeast of Yellowknife in the mid-1990s:

> The previous major mine was the Lupin gold mine, which was approved in 1981. Ekati went through a full Canadian Environmental Assessment [Act] process run by the CEA agency. This was a huge shift in the regulatory regime for the north ... from the normal DIAND-led negotiated terms and conditions in leases and land use permits ... The process brought a gravitas of formality to the hearing process and especially the normally quiet water board process ... [When a lawyer came to represent one of the Indigenous groups] it was unheard of to have a lawyer at a water board process and from then on it was the norm.[33]

Some early problems were rooted in the reluctance of some DIAND officials, particularly in the Yellowknife office, to accept the sea-change that the *MVRMA* represented. According to staff and members of both Mackenzie Valley boards, from the outset a good many DIAND officials in Ottawa and Yellowknife worked diligently to support the boards and the *MVRMA* regime, but others were simply unprepared to accept the loss of control that the emergence of the boards represented. Some in DIAND were motivated by principled concerns over board competence and worries about how the minister could be held accountable for decisions effectively taken outside his control. As one pointed out, when things go wrong, it's the minister who becomes the target of criticism. Others, however, loath to give up the power and influence they had long enjoyed, were simply protecting their turf. Indeed, one interpretation of the delay in finalizing the *MVRMA* was DIAND foot-dragging designed to minimize the loss of power the act entailed and to put it off as long as possible.

Looking back, one board member recalled: "It was always a fight with DIAND; the more responsibility we took from them the more panicked they got ... At the beginning, DIAND treated the board like a band council, not like an independent board." According to a board staff member interviewed late in 2000, the DIAND middle managers who used to do what the boards now did under the *MVRMA* were "very upset and threatened ... [because] they're no longer the full support to decision making." Another board official noted the problem but understood it somewhat differently: "Government created these boards, but finds that they're like kids: you prepare them to live on their own but find it very hard to let go of them ... [Accordingly, DIAND was] unprepared for the changes that the MVRMA brought about and used financial levers to control board actions. Many in DIAND sought to understand and work with the board, but others feared for how board decisions would reflect on the minister."

For their part, some in DIAND acknowledged that elements in the department were having difficulty accepting the *MVRMA* regime; others expressed grave reservations about the boards' competence and their immature attitudes. One DIAND official offered a scathing assessment of the boards' early days: "It's a case of the blind leading the blind; both the members and the staff are incompetent ... [Board members are] novices advised by idiots." Another federal bureaucrat focused on the confrontational attitude of board staff, arguing that, for some, "it's Heart of Darkness time ... They've 'gone native' and can't get beyond thumbing their noses at the feds ... [Their attitude can often be] we're going to show you how long our arms can be in our arm's-length relationship ... There's a knee-jerk feistiness at some boards against DIAND." A more neutral observer, a veteran GNWT bureaucrat with extensive experience in environmental regulation, took a similar view: "Mackenzie Valley board staff almost seem indoctrinated not to like or trust DIAND ... This is frustrating for DIAND which does have a lot of expertise to offer." Both federal officials quoted above acknowledged that DIAND's long and not always benign history in the North – one termed the department "arrogant" – was a factor underlying the boards' antipathy towards the federal government.

A long-time DIAND official noted another basis for conflict. Local DIAND staff tended to have training in geography or forestry, and their outlook reflected having worked through difficult on-the-ground operational issues, especially during the oil and gas boom of the 1970s and later the diamond rush of the

1990s. Their experience came in the form of "practical hard knocks solutions operationally ... with a view to economic development and activities on the ground. As one inspector would always say, 'it [the land] is open for use and there will be residual evidence of that use; if you want it to be pristine, change my uniform, give me a pull-away tie and a booth at the border to greet people to Canada's largest park.'" By contrast, the boards hired bright young people with degrees from newly created environment programs who were "book-smart [but] with no practical sense of activities on the ground in the North." Their "environment-first philosophy" not surprisingly created friction with the DIAND field staff.

Yet another DIAND bureaucrat noted that the friction between Ottawa and the boards was exacerbated by "legal excesses," claiming "the MVEIRB won't do anything without asking their lawyer what to do." As this official and others noted, as soon as disagreements arose, each side called in its legal people. Involving lawyers, who tend to be process-oriented, concerned with formality, and given to zero-sum thinking, often led to hardened positions rendering compromise more difficult. Not surprisingly, given the complexity of the *MVRMA* and its major departures from established practice, disagreement was rife over the interpretation of key provisions. A board official, interviewed in the early years of the *MVRMA* regime, commented: "the federal government often says [about boards and their processes] 'that's not what we intended' – they're quite unhappy with how the boards interpret the act, which is very unclear in important areas."

Excess legalism may have added to the strains in the relationship, but more fundamental were funding issues. Much of the problem stemmed from DIAND's initial allocations, which were based on woefully inaccurate projections as to the boards' workloads and thus their financial needs. One of the senior officials responsible for explaining the bill to the Commons committee reviewing it in 1997 estimated that the *entire* cost of *all MVRMA* boards for the first decade of their existence would be $4 million.[34] Well before the ten-year mark was reached both the MVLWB and the MVEIRB were each spending nearly that much annually. A long-time DIAND bureaucrat with extensive experience of Northern governance correctly noted shortly after the act came into force that the underfunding of the boards – a function of "the huge pressure in the [federal fiscal] system to bring in a bare bones budget to keep implementation costs down" – together with efforts at reducing funding for the DIAND functions taken over by the boards was "a recipe for disaster." Moreover, this official observed that it was not simply a case of inadequate funding levels leading to conflict. The lack of stability and long-term predictability inherent in the funding processes also led to difficulty: "it's difficult [for the boards] to put in place logical systems of staff and management if you don't know your long-term budget."

An Indigenous claims negotiator traces some of these problems to a serious flaw in the process: "Negotiations over the boards was a painful and uncertain process for both sides at the table; nobody had a clear idea of what needed to be done in terms of the boards ... [This reflected the fact that] there were no operational people at the table."

As detailed below, much of the early hostility dissipated as disputes were either settled or faded in significance. Perhaps growing pains were inevitable given the magnitude of the changes to the environmental regulation regime in the NWT. Of course, irritants and disagreements, some of substantial import, persist between the boards and DIAND. "There's always mistrust," one long-time observer suggested, "because of DIAND's dual role of fostering resource development and supporting boards." Others are less circumspect, referring not to DIAND's "dual role" but to its inherent conflict of interest in its dealings with the Mackenzie Valley boards. Now that the GNWT has become the primary decision maker under the *MVRMA*, the conflict of interest problem has largely been shifted to the territorial level.

Beyond DIAND, the distinctive nature of claims boards is often unappreciated in the federal government. Line departments as well as central agencies are often oblivious to the constitutional status of the settled claims, treating the claims boards as they would any other federal agency. Indigenous governments and land claim organizations are constantly emphasizing, usually to little effect, that the modern treaties were signed with the Crown and therefore that treaty implementation is the responsibility of the entire Government of Canada, not simply DIAND. A telling indication of what might be termed "the Ottawa mindset" in this regard is found in a report of the auditor general of Canada. Chapter 6 of the auditor general's 2005 report focused on environmental regulation in the Mackenzie Valley and the relationship of DIAND to the *MVRMA* boards. Prefacing its analysis on the observation that the investment climate for non-renewable resources in the NWT is "uncertain," the report took DIAND to task for failing to manage the boards and board process properly. According to the report, the department's initial decision "to leave the boards to administer the process on their own in order to ensure that the Aboriginal peoples of the NWT understood that the federal government was sincere in relinquishing control" had led to problems and should be revisited.[35] Virtually all the auditor general's recommendations, which DIAND accepted without reservation, called for the department to be more dirigiste with the boards.[36] Though passing reference was made to the basis of the *MVRMA* in the land claims, the report effectively ignored the nature and import of the claims. This was more than slightly ironic, given that in a report published eighteen months earlier, the auditor general castigated DIAND for fulfilling the letter but not the spirit and intent of Northern comprehensive claims.[37]

The Mackenzie Valley Environmental Impact Review Board

Over the course of its nearly two decade-long existence, the Mackenzie Valley Environmental Impact Review Board has emerged as one of the most active and influential of the claims boards engaged in environmental regulation. Its members and staff have developed imaginative and innovative approaches and procedures; it has been, to take but one illustration, a leader in incorporating traditional knowledge into its work. At the same time, it has encountered its share and more of serious conflicts with the federal government, over funding, mandate, independence, and substantive recommendations. It has also found itself the target of significant criticism from both industry and First Nations. And it has experienced episodes of debilitating internal strife.

At full strength, the MVEIRB has nine members, four nominated by the federal and territorial governments and one each from the Gwich'in Tribal Council, the Sahtu Secretariat, the Tlicho Government, and the Dehcho First Nations. Ottawa makes the actual appointments; this remains the case despite the devolution of extensive authority over land and resources from the federal government to the territorial government. Although no claim has been finalized in the Dehcho, the 2001 *Deh Cho First Nations Interim Measures Agreement* between Ottawa, the GNWT, and the DFN provides for a DFN nominee. No similar provision exists in the Akaitcho area in the southeast NWT; accordingly, First Nations in that region have no formal role in the appointment process.

As is the case with all *MVRMA* boards, the minister may appoint alternate members "to act in the event of the absence or incapacity" of members.[38] No alternate members have ever been appointed, likely because appointing regular members is difficult enough. Nor would having alternate members available solve the perennial vacancy problem since a vacancy would not be considered a member's "absence."

Members are expected to act independently, "in the public interest," rather than as delegates of the parties that nominated them. At the same time, the co-management nature of the board is underlined by its quorum provisions. The board quorum is five members but must include two members nominated by Indigenous organizations and two members nominated by the territorial or federal governments (excluding the chair).

When the *MVRMA* was passed in 1998, it authorized the federal minister to impose policy directives on the MVLWB but not on MVEIRB. The 2014 amendments to the act extended this power to the Review Board. In only three instances has the minister sent policy directives to the MVLWB, on relatively minor matters; as of early 2019, no policy directives had been issued to the Review Board. Significantly, in the 2014 changes, the power to set policy directives was not extended to the GNWT.

The act requires the DIAND minister to appoint as chair a person nominated by a majority of board members, unless the minister does not find the person "acceptable." If the board fails to nominate a "person acceptable to the federal Minister within a reasonable time,"[39] the minister has free rein to appoint any person. Similar provisions apply to other Mackenzie Valley boards, save the Wek'èezhìi Land and Water Board. As discussed below, in one controversial episode, the minister did reject the board's nominee and appointed his preferred candidate. The vice-chair is selected by the board from among its own members and takes over as acting or interim chair should the chair be absent or incapacitated or if the chair's position becomes vacant.

As of early 2019 the MVEIRB had fourteen full-time employees, down from seventeen a year earlier, plus a private practice lawyer. Initially, and for some time, the lawyer attended all board meetings; in recent years, as the board and its members have matured and gained confidence, they rely on their counsel primarily for processes such as report writing so that he no longer attends all meetings. Staff levels have sometimes been substantially lower. From early on, staff positions were benchmarked in terms of the salary and benefits against comparable positions in the federal public service in order to maintain morale and forestall turnover. MVEIRB staff do not conduct original research or studies into possible environmental effects of proposed projects nor do the consultants they hire. Board staff review and analyze data and reports produced by industry, by government, and by Indigenous communities and governments.

As employees of independent boards, staff lack formal rights to transfer to vacant federal or territorial positions; however, given their expertise and experience, it is not unusual for board staff to move into federal or territorial jobs. Staff are not unionized but are protected by policies very similar to those in federal and territorial collective agreements on matters such as attendance and leaves, staffing and discipline. Executive directors, akin to deputy ministers, serve at the pleasure of their boards and may be dismissed by them, as was the highly regarded executive director of the MVLWB in 2007.

The MVEIRB's budget in 2016–17 was roughly $3.02 million, of which $2.84 million came in core funding through the implementation contract for the Gwich'in land claim,[40] with the balance a carry-over from the previous year. Under the new funding regime announced in late 2017, discussed later in this chapter, the board's core funding was increased by 21 percent to about $3.44 million. As with other Mackenzie Valley boards, annual increments are determined by a complex formula.

A decade earlier, the board's budget was higher than in 2016–17: roughly $3.4 million (technically it was some $6.4 million, but just over $3 million was essentially a flow-through, covering the board's one-third share of the costs of the Joint Review Panel conducting the Mackenzie Gas Project EIR).[41] The board's workload in 2006–07, it must be noted, was significantly higher than in 2016–17. Since the board has no own-source revenue, and implementation funding was lower, the additional money – several hundred thousand dollars – came, as it did every year, in supplementary funding acquired, in the words of one board staff person, by "scratching and scrounging with DIAND."

Scratching and scrounging didn't always work. Towards the end of the 2012–13 fiscal year, the board was facing a financial crunch as a result of having an unusually large number of complex EAs on its plate. Although in previous similar situations Ottawa had always come through with additional money, the board's repeated requests for supplementary funding to cover expenses arising from its heavy workload were denied. Thus the board found it necessary to lay off almost half its staff and cut back on travel and training.[42] It did not, however, delay completion of the environmental assessments under way, as some board figures retrospectively thought might have been a more appropriate response. DIAND's motivation in denying funding remains unclear, though one interviewee knowledgeable about the situation suggested that Ottawa officialdom was displeased by what it saw as the unreasonable honoraria claimed by the board chair and members and their free-spending ways on travel and other perks. Following significant belt-tightening and changes in board membership, the board rebuilt its staff capacity, though not all laid-off staff were rehired and some of the positions they had occupied were eliminated or modified.

Review Board finances were also adversely affected, as were those of other boards (though not to the same extent), by the end of the Joint Review Panel on the Mackenzie Gas Project in 2009. Substantial funds in support of the Joint Review Panel had been funnelled through the board, some of which, quite properly, were directed to board administration.

Budgeting at the MVEIRB is at best an imprecise exercise because the workload, in terms of the number and scope of the EAs it will be called on to perform, cannot be predicted with any accuracy. Thus the board builds flexibility into its budget so as to be able to carry out whatever EAs come its way. In 2017 the

The MVEIRB and the MVLWB

board negotiated a ten-year core funding agreement with DIAND, which included a 21 percent increase to the board's funding base. Contingency funding is also available from DIAND should the board be faced with an unusually heavy workload.

As mandated by the *MVRMA*, the board offices are located in Yellowknife, a short walk from the Mackenzie Valley Land and Water Board offices, across the street from the DIAND Regional Office and an elevator ride from the GNWT's Department of Lands. The board typically meets once or twice a month for one or two days, more frequently in preparation for or following a hearing. Meetings take place mostly in Yellowknife but on occasion are held in communities where it has other business. Several times a year, the board holds public hearings or community visits in connection with EAs. In an effort to enhance awareness of the board and its work, in recent years staff have also routinely visited sites of proposed developments and engaged local communities about developments early in the EA process.

The board maintains a comprehensive website that, along with the public registry, provides guidelines, interpretation bulletins, explanations of board procedures, annual reports, newsletters, and transcripts of public hearings. The public registry is a user-friendly, searchable database containing the full text of all documents presented to the board in the course of its EAs, together with the board's EA reports and the formal ministerial responses to them.

Like the *MVRMA* land and water boards but unlike most wildlife management boards and land use planning boards in the NWT and elsewhere, the Review Board has the "powers, rights and privileges of a superior court with respect to the attendance and examination of witnesses and the production and inspection of documents."[43] In other words, the Mackenzie Valley boards have the power to subpoena documents and persons and to require witnesses to testify under oath. The MVEIRB has never had recourse to these powers, though on occasion it has had to insist that government departments reluctant to appear at hearings did appear to answer questions. Simply having the authority to issue subpoenas has, in the board's experience, proven sufficient to secure the information it requires, while putting witnesses under oath would entail a degree of formality the board is reluctant to impose on its processes. The board is subject to federal freedom of information (FOI) legislation, though in light of the extensive documentation available through their public registries, few FOI requests are made.

Workload is highly variable, so that no year is "typical." In 2005–06, for example, the board had twelve EAs under way; eight were new referrals and four had been initiated the previous year. The four carry-overs were all completed;

on two the responsible ministers signed off on the board's reports during the year and the other two were awaiting ministerial approval at year end.[44] The board had some involvement in the Joint Review Panel for the Mackenzie Gas Project but otherwise had no EIRs under way. A decade later the board had six EAs under way; two were new referrals, one of which was withdrawn by the proponent. One of the four carry-over EAs was completed and referred to the GNWT minister for a decision. Another carry-over had been suspended two years earlier when the developer was unable to provide requested information; no work was done on this EA in 2015–16, but it was still technically on the books. No EIRs were under way.[45]

Early Tribulations

In May 1996, more than two years before the Mackenzie Valley Environmental Impact Review Board itself came into existence, the Mackenzie Valley Environmental Impact Review Working Group was established, composed of "notional nominees" to the board plus officials from the federal and territorial governments and from the Gwich'in Tribal Council and the Sahtu Secretariat.[46] The working group developed procedures, budget plans, and oversaw staffing but did not engage in actual EA work. Three members of the Working Group were appointed to the board, though two resigned within eighteen months.

As is common with newly created agencies, what transpired in its early days established the pattern for the board's subsequent development. Looking back some years later, a GNWT official involved in the design and implementation of the *MVRMA* offered the opinion that the initial board staff set the tone for how the board went about its business. The GNWT had wanted to have reciprocal arrangements between itself, the boards, and DIAND so that board staff could transfer benefits, pensions, and the like should they leave government to work for a board, but DIAND refused, in part because it was upset at losing authority to the boards. The result was that most board staff members were relatively junior and inexperienced (a federal official at the time commented that there were "not enough grey hairs" at the boards). To demonstrate their worth to a sceptical DIAND, they chose to show what they could do and to advocate for certain approaches and goals. A culture of aggressiveness and excessive activism developed that continued to shape board processes years later. According to this person, the original idea behind the *MVRMA* was that environmental assessment would be quick and that most projects would go on to an EIR; instead the EA process became what was expected to happen in an EIR.

According to a board member from the early days, some in DIAND, piqued at the loss of authority the boards represented, adopted a "let-them-fail" attitude, which was manifested in a lack of training and support. Another early board member recalled feeling "hopelessly outgunned" in dealing with Ottawa and with major developers.

In the first EA it completed, the board found itself embroiled in a treacherous political dispute not of its making, a harbinger of the uncalm future ahead. A long-established small sawmill owner in Hay River applied to cut timber on Crown land in Dehcho territory. Under the recently proclaimed *MVRMA*, a preliminary screening by the MVLWB was required. The settlement of Fort Resolution, prompted by the local Deninu K'ue First Nation (DKFN), referred the application to an EA. The actual EA was relatively straightforward, though it did demonstrate to both Mackenzie Valley boards that they would encounter issues, forestry in this instance, on which they had little or no in-house expertise. The outcome, however, was anything but routine. When the MVEIRB gave the project the green light and the federal and territorial ministers concurred, the DKFN refused to accept the board's authority, arguing that it ignored both treaty rights and a recently signed interim measures agreement. Though it did not follow through on threatened road blockades or other unspecified "direct action,"[47] DKFN did launch a court challenge disputing the legitimacy of the DIAND minister and the board to decide on land use in its territory. The issue was never joined in court; the First Nation and DIAND agreed that the earlier ministerial approval would be overturned.[48] As one of the DKFN leaders acknowledged, the dispute was not one of environmental concern; rather, it was "a political issue."[49]

Not surprisingly, the MVEIRB's early days were marked by minor friction with the Mackenzie Valley Land and Water Board over roles and responsibilities.[50] Indeed, this was only one aspect of intermittent discord among the various *MVRMA* boards. As one analyst put it, "what initially appears to be a simple mechanism to facilitate EA practice has on occasion been transformed into a much broader conflict about the mandate and authority of the different boards, capacity issues, different perceptions about how best to implement the Act, and the need of all participants in the assessment process to be empowered."[51]

Of far greater consequence, the board began butting heads with DIAND. On the operational front, the board's first major EA report, on the Ranger Oil/Canadian Forest Oil/Chevron application for gas wells and a pipeline tie-in near Fort Liard, occasioned great consternation in Ottawa.[52] Significantly, perhaps, when DIAND and the National Energy Board conducted the preliminary screening of the project, they concluded that it did not warrant an EA. The

MVEIRB decided, on its own motion, that an EA was required. The DIAND minister's response, on behalf of the "responsible" federal ministers, rejected or varied most of the report's recommendations. Ottawa officialdom saw the EA report as well-meaning but uninformed and naive, with recommendations that were either vague or beyond the board's mandate, for example that the GNWT upgrade the highway adjacent to the affected area.[53] Though the minister's response was not nearly as tough as some bureaucrats had wanted, it set an antagonistic tone that soured relationships for some time. Still, through exchange of documents and face-to-face meetings, accommodation was reached on all measures, leading to a ministerial sign-off barely a month after the report was issued, an especially impressive accomplishment given that this included the Christmas holidays. The board conducted a forthright "lessons-learned" study of the whole exercise, leading to various procedural changes but no fundamental reorientation of its approach to environmental assessment.[54]

Another major contretemps occurred in early 2001 over BHP Billiton's application for the water licence necessary to expand its existing diamond mine at Lac de Gras to include three additional kimberlite pipes, the diamond-bearing geological formations. The board's report on the EA contained some sixty-two "recommendations," many of which, according to the board, took the form of "notes to regulatory authorities ... to consider certain issues" when the permit was developed.[55] A curt letter from the DIAND minister two months later gave notice that the government wished to consult the board on modifying two of its recommendations, but that, "with respect to the remaining 60 recommendations, the Board did not make a finding of significant adverse impacts regarding each of the matters addressed. Consequently, it is not open to the responsible Ministers to adopt these Board recommendations."[56] In other words, in DIAND's view, sixty of the sixty-two recommendations were outside the board's mandate. One federal bureaucrat commented: "Many of them [the sixty recommendations] were good ideas but there was no legislative authority for them; this put the minister in a horrible position ... You can't make friends that way." But that was not the worst of it.

The two recommendations that, according to DIAND, the board did link to adverse effects were unrelated to the biophysical environment. One called for the development of a plan to mitigate the social and economic effects on BHP Billiton employees when the mine eventually closed. On this, DIAND signalled general acceptance but endorsed the GNWT view that no plan had to be in place until three years before the mine was to close. The other recommendation was guaranteed to raise federal hackles. The board argued that "the fiscal arrangement between the federal government and the territorial government with respect to the BHP development [was] having a significant adverse impact on the GNWT's ability to diversify its economy in order to avoid a boom-bust cycle."[57] It thus recommended that Ottawa revisit its formula financing agreement with the GNWT to provide it with sufficient funds "to support, and where necessary, expand its role in the management and mitigation of effects associated with development."[58] Even couched in formal language, DIAND's response was frosty: "Since the federal-territorial fiscal arrangement is not the development under review, Indian and Northern Affairs Canada concludes this measure to be improper in the context of this assessment.[59]

Nor did revision of the formula financing agreement fall under DIAND's remit. Control of the agreement rests with the powerful Department of Finance, which views it in a highly proprietary way. DIAND simply lacked the clout to affect it.

For its part, BHP Billiton, citing the time, twenty-seven months and counting, and the inadequacies in the process, voiced a common industry concern with the *MVRMA*:

> The current situation provides a timely example of the many concerns that the industry has with the efficiency and effectiveness of the present regulatory process in the North. We believe that if the present regime continues ... Northern competitiveness for mineral investment will be seriously diminished.[60]

Administratively, the board chafed under what it saw as micromanagement from federal bureaucrats. One MVEIRB member cited DIAND's refusal to authorize a staff position for an economist to assist with the board's socio-economic impact mandate as an example of the close scrutiny it had to endure, and, more significantly, as an indication of the board's lack of independence. Another board member spoke of having to justify to DIAND the board's need for a staffer to work primarily on traditional knowledge issues.

A more serious confrontation, on finances, occurred towards the end of the MVEIRB's first year. The board found itself running out of money because of a higher than anticipated workload, compounded by what one participant termed "a shoestring budget." Several written requests for additional funding received no response (one board member suggested that the delay reflected disagreement between the regional office of DIAND and Ottawa headquarters over who should take responsibility for the additional funding). In frustration, the board wrote the DIAND minister, threatening to resign en masse, lay off the staff, and close the office. This action got the minister's attention and the funding situation was quickly resolved, but DIAND officials saw the board's gambit as unwarranted and unprofessional; said one, "we wouldn't let them close their doors ... they could come to us if they needed money." Relations between the board and DIAND, especially at the staff level, predictably deteriorated. The board, for example, interpreted Ottawa's imposition of a financial management review by an outside consultant as punishment for its actions, given the absence of evidence or suspicion of misspending let alone fraud or duplicity.

In the wake of this episode, DIAND officials proposed to manage the financial constraints the board faced by reducing its staff and having DIAND provide it with analysis and interpretation on the model of the NWT Water Board, which relied for technical information and advice primarily on a technical advisory committee composed of DIAND officials. This idea, predictably, was entirely unacceptable to the board.

The impression should not be left that the board was at constant loggerheads with DIAND and federal officialdom in this period. EAs were scoped, planned, and completed in reasonable time and, in many cases, without significant friction over board recommendations or proposed mitigative measures. As in any relationship, though, one bad experience is remembered more than several positive ones.

The Burlingame Controversy and the Wray Dismissal

The appointment of a new chair early in 2002 marked the onset of a whole new set of tensions between the Mackenzie Valley Environmental Impact Review Board and DIAND. Late in 2001, Todd Burlingame, a geologist with extensive Northern experience, was appointed to the board by DIAND minister Robert Nault to fill a vacant federal seat. By this point the MVEIRB, in accordance with *MVRMA* procedures, had put forward to Ottawa its recommendation that founding chair Gordon Lennie, a Sahtu Secretariat nominee, be reappointed. Nault rejected the board's advice and appointed Burlingame as chair in February 2002. It was widely thought that Burlingame's appointment had been engineered by the NWT's Liberal MP, Ethel Blondin-Andrew, who was known to take a hands-on approach to government appointments. Serious friction soon developed within the board, and in the summer and fall of 2003 a very public fracas rocked it to its foundations.

Doubtless personality conflicts contributed to the discord, but the root cause was more fundamental. Some board members and staff had come to regard Burlingame's appointment as a thinly disguised attempt by Ottawa to undercut the board's independence and to ensure its acquiescence in federal plans to expedite approval of the imminent application for the Mackenzie Gas Project. The leading figure in this group was Gordon Wray, an outspoken former GNWT cabinet minister who also chaired the NWT Water Board. The members of the group saw Burlingame as uncommunicative and high-handed in dealing with staff.[61] Worse, they believed he had secret arrangements with Ottawa aimed at giving DIAND effective control of the board.

Matters came to a head following a board meeting in July 2003, at which Burlingame secured board approval for a "Partnership Protocol" between the MVEIRB and the NWT Region of DIAND. Wray had been away on vacation when the meeting took place. On his return he convinced the board that the protocol was no innocuous administrative housekeeping, as some apparently believed, but that it carried far-reaching implications and, moreover, that it contravened the spirit and the letter of the Gwich'in and Sahtu claims by failing to include them, or the GNWT for that matter, in the proposed process for dispute resolution. At Wray's urging, the board overturned its earlier decision and disavowed the protocol.

The backroom intrigue and finger pointing escalated, culminating in a board meeting of October 8 at which a motion of non-confidence in Burlingame was passed, as was a series of motions severely limiting his activities on behalf of the board. He was, for example, directed to have no dealings with staff other than through the executive director, and he had his travel and spending authority curtailed. At the end of the meeting, Burlingame, who was not present for the discussion and the votes on various motions, returned to the room with a letter, dated October 8, from Nault dismissing Wray from the board.

An earlier letter from Nault to Burlingame, dated October 3 but not seen by the board until October 8, conveyed the minister's "understanding that at recent Board meetings the actions of Mr Gordon Wray have been disruptive and contrary to recent efforts by the Board and my department to resolve long-standing issues."[62] On October 7, Burlingame had written board members indicating that the minister was thinking of removing Wray from the board and asking for their comments in writing the next day. Board members refused to respond, citing lack of time and proper process (under the act the minister must consult with the board prior to removing a member).[63]

If the process by which Wray was sacked may have stood on uncertain legal grounds, the outcome was clear: the board was in disarray. Dissident board member Frank Pope publicly described the episode as "a travesty of justice," adding "we [the board] were of the opinion he [Burlingame] was working in the best interests of [DIAND] and not of the people of the Northwest Territories. He took his direction and orders directly from [DIAND]"[64] For his part,

Burlingame responded that the non-confidence motion had no legal effect and proposed to carry on with board business despite lacking a quorum.[65]

Some years later, a senior official at DIAND headquarters recalled "many long nights" spent dealing with the Wray-Burlingame contretemps, adding that these deliberations were not shared with the regional office since once the regional office was informed, "it would be out on the street immediately."

Despite howls of protest from the GNWT and Indigenous leaders and pointed questions from editorial writers,[66] Nault stood firm, refusing to rescind or explain his actions. With the appointment of two new board members with what surely rates as record-breaking speed he managed to bring the situation back to a semblance of normality by the end of October when all board members were again participating in meetings. Early in the new year, Pope resigned from the board. Burlingame's term as chair expired in February 2005 and he did not seek another term, though, as will be seen, he would in short order find himself at the centre of another claims board controversy. The dust from the Burlingame-Wray brouhaha had largely settled in a few months, but the implications for board independence are substantial.

Repairing Relations

Reflecting concern as to the fate of its recommendations, the MVEIRB launched an innovative effort to track and categorize government action – or inaction – on mitigation measures in EA reports that had been approved by Ottawa. This was a far more complex undertaking than might first appear, with significant definitional and methodological difficulties abounding. At the same time, it was an essential step in ensuring that the board's recommendations were being implemented and in identifying areas where more attention was needed to ensure compliance with the measures that the board and government agreed were required to protect the people and the environment.[67]

These initiatives certainly advanced the board's efforts at fostering a reputation for innovation and professionalism and doubtless contributed to the assessment in the first NWT Environmental Audit that the MVEIRB was to be commended "for taking a leadership role in developing tools to ensure the effectiveness of the system."[68] Equally noteworthy, however, was the long-term improvement in the board's routine relations with DIAND over its EA reports. The highly conflictual tenor of the early days gave way to a more mutually respectful relationship. In part this reflected improvements, noted by the authors of the first NWT Environmental Audit, in the quality of the MVEIRB's EA processes and its reports.[69] In part, the passage of time led to a maturation of the relationship, as played out through the institutionalization of the "consult-to-modify" process. The exchange of formal documents supplemented by informal personal exchanges at the staff level became standard practice in instances in which Ottawa was unprepared to sign off completely on a board recommendation and associated "measures." Resort to the "consult-to-modify" option by no means eliminated all disagreements, nor was it always quick – one EA report from the board, on proposed geotechnical work by Imperial Oil in the Dehcho, languished unresolved for four and a half years.

A particularly significant milestone was Ottawa's acceptance, albeit more than two years after the initial board EA report was issued, of the board's recommendation that a proposed diamond exploration project at Drybones Bay on Great Slave Lake be rejected. Not only was this the first application to be rejected outright by the MVEIRB, the decision was based solely on the basis of potential cultural impact, ascertained largely through assessment of traditional knowledge.[70]

None of this is to suggest that all irritants between the board and DIAND were resolved. The board did not hesitate to criticize DIAND on matters ranging from its disappointment over the delay in making board appointments, which led two experienced board members to withdraw their consent to be reappointed,[71] to the untoward consequences of long delays in resolving disagreements over mitigation measures in EA reports.[72] Additionally, the board steadfastly resisted Ottawa's suggestion that the process of responding to and approving MVEIRB EA reports could be expedited were the board prepared to share draft reports with DIAND staff. For the board, such a procedure would have represented an unacceptable loss of independence.

Another point of contention was the board's continuing frustration at its inability to tap directly into what it termed "probably the most knowledgeable group of people regarding the situation on the ground" – DIAND's inspection and enforcement staff – noting "generally the Board does not have direct access to government experts at the federal or territorial level."[73] This despite section 22 of the *MVRMA*, which authorizes the MVEIRB, as well as the land and water boards, to "obtain from any department or agency of the federal or territorial government any information in the possession of the department or agency that the board requires for the performance of its functions." Communications with inspectors is still something of an issue, but the board has adopted a new approach to monitoring the implementation and effectiveness of its measures. By way of illustration, the 2016 REA on the Jay extenstion of the Ekati diamond mine northeast of Yellowknife included requirements that the developer, Dominion Diamond Ekati Corporation, report annually to the board on a wide range of matters relating to environmental protection, wildlife management, socioeconomic concerns, cultural impacts, and use of traditional knowledge.[74] These reports are posted on the board website. The REA also required governments and regulatory authorities to report annually on the effectiveness of various mitigation measures. The GNWT has been making reports to the board; the Wek'èezhìi Land and Water Board has not. And, of course, disputes over funding levels and processes continued.

Improvements in the oftentimes rocky relations with the Mackenzie Valley boards (as will be seen, the MVEIRB was hardly alone in its querulous dealings with Ottawa) were not solely the result of changes at the boards. DIAND was also taking steps to provide support to the boards without coming across as heavy-handed. One initiative was a "NWT Practitioners' Technical Workshop" jointly sponsored by the MVEIRB, the MVLWB, and DIAND. Organized and facilitated by a respected team of consultants, the workshop, held in Yellowknife in September 2001, reached some useful conclusions about a range of technical issues arising in preliminary screening and in environmental assessment under the *MVRMA*.[75] Rather more important, however, was the progress made in terms of personal relationships. Members and staff of boards, officials from DIAND and other federal agencies and departments, GNWT bureaucrats, and representatives of Indigenous organizations met and exchanged views and experiences in a neutral setting. By no means were all personal and professional hostilities set aside, but a foundation was laid for improved interpersonal relations among key players in the process.

Good personal relations are important in any political-bureaucratic setting, but they are especially crucial in the North. Northern societies are very small so that personal links loom especially large and are ever-present. It would not be unusual for officials who met in a Yellowknife government boardroom in the morning to run into one another at the grocery store or the post office on the way home from work or to see each other at the curling rink or at a school concert in the evening. When hearings or other gatherings take place in small communities, participants and observers from all governments and agencies typically stay at the same hotel and eat at the same restaurant. One long-time observer of the board process observes: "Southern business and bureaucracy doesn't fully appreciate how socially connected everyone is with everyone else ... The social connections present certain challenges in terms of conflict of interest, confidentiality, apprehension of bias and so on, but it gives business a great opportunity to get its message across."

Related to the positive momentum from the September workshop was an important institutional initiative within the NWT Regional Office of DIAND. A small Board Relations Secretariat (BRS) was created, in the words of one

DIAND official, "to repair relations with the boards." Its central remit was to facilitate communications between various branches of the department and the boards, especially, but not exclusively, the *MVRMA* boards, and to support the boards in their work.[76] (At one stage during the early implementation of the *MVRMA*, an ad hoc unit had been cobbled together to facilitate interaction with the emerging boards, but, lacking permanent funding, it was wound up after a few months.) An indication of DIAND's desire to make this initiative work was its inclusion of senior board staff in the process of hiring for the BRS.

An illustration of the contribution the BRS was able to make is a meeting it brokered between local DIAND lands staff and their counterparts at the MVLWB. Prior to the meeting, "they wouldn't talk to each other" and literally did not know who each other was, but subsequently they opened regular and useful communications.

Among the tasks taken on by the BRS was management of the appointment process, coordination and facilitation of board budget requests, and provision of a "one window" approach to tracking down documents that had, in the words of one board staff person, "disappeared down some black hole at DIAND." Particularly valuable was the creation, under BRS auspices, of a "Board Forum," a regular gathering of members and staff from boards and senior DIAND and GNWT officials and the National Energy Board. The activities of the Board Forum proved an important element of the department's response to a critical 2005 report from the auditor general on board-DIAND relations in the NWT. Significantly, nothing akin to the Board Forum, or the BRS for that matter, has ever existed in Nunavut or Yukon, though a pan-territorial board forum was established in 2015. Initially the Board Forum met twice a year but in recent years has met annually, providing for exchange of ideas and experiences not only on technical issues but also on basic policy and financial concerns. At the outset, participation was limited to environmental regulatory boards, but the "chairs caucus" at the Board Forum took it upon itself to invite representatives of the wildlife management boards. The Board Forum, supported by the BRS, has undertaken communal projects useful to all – for example, by sponsoring the development of training manuals and online courses for board members.

Inevitably, the Board Forum became something of a two-edged sword for DIAND. Like the BRS, it has unquestionably contributed to better communications in the board sector and to more effective board operations. But it has also encouraged among boards a synergy not always to the government's liking. It was, for example, at a Board Forum meeting that the idea was hatched of a letter from board chairs to the heads of the relevant Indigenous organizations urging them to push the DIAND minister to deal with the increasingly intolerable delays in making board appointments.

In 2015, the Northern Projects Management Office within the Canadian Northern Economic Development Agency, which is charged with improving environmental review processes for proposed major resource development and infrastructure projects in northern Canada, established the Pan-Territorial Assessment and Regulatory Boards Forum. Among other things, it holds annual workshops bringing together members and staff of environmental regulatory boards – land use planning and wildlife management boards are not included – from the three territories to exchange information and ideas and to develop cross-territorial relationships. Board staff indicate that these gatherings and the organizational links they foster have proven valuable. Given the nature of its mandate and the diversity of the boards involved, the pan-territorial boards forum has not taken on the political character of the NWT Board Forum.

It will be some time before a clear pattern is evident as to the MVEIRB's relations with the GNWT now that most REAs go to the territorial minister of lands. In the five years since devolution the board has produced only three REAs, one of which went to Ottawa because it involved federal lands. Early indications, however, are that relations will be better between the board and the GNWT than they were with DIAND. Doubtless, the minister and the lands department staff will not always see eye to eye with the board on the substance of EAs, but two of the prime sources of antagonism between the MVEIRB and DIAND, and indeed between DIAND and other *MVRMA* boards, over the years – funding and delays in appointments – remain Ottawa's responsibility.

In other respects, it is evident that significant changes in board-government relations have occurred as a consequence of devolution, though one knowledge-able participant has commented that the regulatory process in the NWT "is still tied to Ottawa at the hip." "The big improvement," according to one board official, "has been the ability of the GNWT to give timely decisions." With DIAND, the decision process would involve back and forth between the region and headquarters and would often have low priority in terms of coming to the minister's attention. With the GNWT the process is more straightforward, not least because the Department of Lands is in the same building as the board. The smaller-scale and more personalized character of interaction among officials has improved communications. One senior board official cited the new-found ability to call GNWT deputy ministers and assistant deputy ministers directly about board issues, which was simply not possible with DIAND. As well, a GNWT official pointed out that, while staff in Ottawa, who lacked direct experience of the NWT, sometimes confused one ongoing EA with another, this would not happen in the GNWT.

More generally, the different outlooks between DIAND headquarters and the NWT regional office, and indeed the tensions between them, have no equivalent within the GNWT. Although too much should not be read into single, isolated observations, the contrast between headquarters and the DIAND Yellowknife office was nicely captured in two comments made in interviews conducted at roughly the same time. "MVEIRB pushes government in ways that other boards don't" was the assessment of the Ottawa-based official, while the Yellowknife staffer commented "the Review Board gets all the tough ones."

With potential developments of strong and direct interest to the GNWT, its politicians are much more attuned to board processes. Moreover, GNWT ministers routinely interact with bureaucrats at all levels to an extent unknown in Ottawa. At the same time, now that they are the decision makers, territorial ministers and their officials must exercise a new caution in their dealings with developers. Ministers were explicitly warned by staff that they should have "no more dinners with mine proponents." As well, the days of GNWT ministers appearing personally as advocates at board hearings are over.

MVEIRB Initiatives

Even in the darkest days, of course, all was not conflict and dissension. As it gained experience, the Mackenzie Valley Environmental Impact Review Board continued to refine its EA procedures and to work on improving communications with governments, industry, and Indigenous communities. A small but significant illustration is the distinction the board began to make in its reports between "measures," specific mitigation actions it specified as requirements for regulatory approval, and "suggestions," proposed mitigation favoured but not required by the board.

In terms of enhancing the opportunities for local communities and Indigenous organizations, an important advance was the shift in the board's hearing procedures. In the early days, some EAs were conducted by way of "paper hearings," in which the board reviewed documents submitted by affected parties but did not offer them the opportunity to appear in person before the board. This approach is still open to the board under section 24 of the *Mackenzie Valley Resource Management Act*, but for some time it has rarely been invoked. Given the capacity pressures on communities and First Nations, as well as the preference of many Indigenous people, especially elders, for oral over written communications, this was a noteworthy change.

With the planning and implementation of EAs becoming routine for members and staff alike, the board was able to devote significant energy and resources to a range of special projects. These ventures were designed to give effect to the distinctive features of the board's mandate under the *MVRMA* and to place it at the forefront of EA practice. At the same time, the board was developing a series of guidelines and explanatory bulletins for development proponents and possible participants aimed at demystifying the process and assisting those finding themselves affected by an EA. Board staff are active in presenting papers about the board's work at conferences in Canada and abroad.

One major project was a concerted effort to imbue board operations with traditional Indigenous knowledge (TK). The *MVRMA* specifies that the MVEIRB is to treat TK on the same basis as "Western" science but offers no guidance as to how this nebulous objective is to be realized.[77] Chapter 8 explores in some detail the board's efforts in this direction; at this juncture, only the highlights need be sketched out. A staff position dedicated to TK issues was established in 2001 and a major conference titled "Traditional Knowledge in Environmental Impact Assessment" was held in Yellowknife late in 2002. Ideas from this conference and from extensive consultations were distilled into "Guidelines for Incorporating Traditional Knowledge in Environmental Impact Assessment," which was issued by the board in July 2005.

A related endeavour was a series of workshops for translators to assist them in the difficult tasks of translating technical terms from the EA process into Indigenous languages and of rendering complex Indigenous concepts about wildlife and the natural world into English. This was an important initiative in that the board routinely provides simultaneous translation of hearings and other meetings into Indigenous languages. It also publishes a limited range of documents in Indigenous languages, for example, a plain-language guide to environmental impact assessment that is available in Chipewyan, South Slavey, North Slavey, Tlicho, and Gwich'in.

Another major undertaking was the development of detailed guidelines for the conduct of socioeconomic impact assessment, a critical but ambiguous component of the board's mandate. Like the TK initiative, this project involved extensive consultation, workshops, and multiple drafts widely circulated throughout the NWT. The final document, featuring extensive plain-language discussion of best practices relating to process, indicators, community consultation, and the like, was published late in 2006; a marginally revised edition came out in March 2007.[78]

In addition to these substantial projects, the MVEIRB began and has maintained a range of ongoing activities to augment and enhance its EA functions.

Annual two-day EA practitioners workshops brought board members and staff together with a wide range of individuals and organizations – including government, community representatives, and industry – involved in or affected by environmental assessment. These workshops developed into major events covering much more than environmental assessment and are typically offered in concert with the land and water boards, the GNWT, and DIAND. The 2018 workshop, for example, was organized around "the stages of a project lifecycle after the environmental assessment is complete, including regulatory permitting, ongoing project monitoring and compliance, and closure and reclamation."[79]

From the outset, one of the board's key objectives was the encouragement and facilitation of participation of local communities and First Nations in its processes. Like the Land and Water Board, it expended great effort to ensure that local people and their representatives were notified of EAs on projects that might affect them or the lands and wildlife of their region and that they understood the EA process and the opportunities it affords them to influence board decisions. In the interests of explaining its work and encouraging community participation in EA processes, the board developed a program of community education visits. It also began to make informal community visits, prior to holding formal public hearings, to meet local people who stand to be affected by projects undergoing EA.

The board's first strategic plan, produced in July 2004, underlined the importance of this work and the need to improve on it, setting increased participation, defined largely in terms of local communities, as one of its three central goals.[80] Elements of this goal were included in subsequent strategic plans but with less emphasis, though subsequent plans reiterated the board's strongly held view that the absence of participant funding seriously undermined the capacity of communities and organizations to participate effectively in EAs. Among other things, this exercise led to the hiring of a community liaison officer to encourage community involvement in EAs and to communicate the outcomes of the process to people at the community level. This position was eliminated several years later in a budget crunch. Not mentioned in the strategic plan but motivated by similar concerns was the board's initiative to stream live webcasts of its public hearings (initially audio only) via its website.

The Mackenzie Valley Land and Water Board

The role and significance of the Mackenzie Valley Land and Water Board must be understood in the context of the three regional claims-based land and water boards: the Gwich'in Land and Water Board, the Sahtu Land and Water Board, and the Wek'èezhìi Land and Water Board. The *Mackenzie Valley Resource Management Act* designates the regional boards as "regional panels" of the MVLWB, and the members of the regional boards are members of the MVLWB. However, the regional boards are not branch offices; rather, they are separate institutions, with their own staff. They screen, hold hearings, and make decisions on land use permit and water licence applications in their regions. The continued existence of the regional boards was in grave doubt during the term of the Harper Conservative government in Ottawa. Chapter 6 presents the saga of Bill C-15 in 2013–14, which, among other things, would have abolished the regional boards and fundamentally restructured the MVLWB. As discussed there, the regional boards survived and continue to operate.

Each of the regional boards has five members and an additional five members are appointed under section 99 (4) of the act to deal with applications from the "unsettled areas." All told then, the MVLWB has, at full strength, twenty members, including the chair who is one of the section 99 (4) members. The usual formula obtains whereby half the members are nominated by Indigenous organizations and governments and half by the federal and territorial governments, and Ottawa makes the appointments, with one notable variation. Under the *Tlicho Agreement*, the Tlicho Government makes the *appointment*, not simply the nomination, of two members of the Wek'èezhìi Land and Water Board and, by extension, of the enlarged MVLWB. The MVLWB chair is appointed by the federal minister, in the same manner as the MVEIRB chair.[81] Significantly, as of early 2019 all five section 99 (4) members were Indigenous, and four, including the chair, were women.

Projects requiring land use permits or water licences in lands wholly within the territory comprising the Gwich'in, Sahtu, and Tlicho claims are reviewed, permitted, and licensed by the regional boards. Elsewhere, in the "unsettled areas," proposed developments are subject to the jurisdiction of the MVLWB. Since for most of the period since the *MVRMA* came into force the great bulk of applications for licenses and permits has come from the unsettled areas, the board has not lacked for work. The MVLWB is also responsible for projects with "transboundary" implications, that is, that either affect more than one claim area or spill over into a neighbouring province or territory. When and if land claims are settled throughout the NWT, and regional land and water boards established in the currently unsettled areas, the MVLWB will find itself with a much reduced workload. Even in this eventuality, however, the board will remain an important player in the *MVRMA* regulatory regime.

The full board, sometimes called "the big board," meets twice a year. The agenda of the "main" section 99 (4) board is sufficiently full that members meet roughly every two weeks. The full board has set its quorum at eight, which must include a member from each regional board and one from the section 99 (4) board. Quorum for the regional boards is three, which must include one First Nation nominee and one member nominated or appointed by the federal or territorial government. Much of the MVLWB's work is carried out by panels established by the chair to review applications. Panels must have at least one member nominated by an Indigenous organization and one nominated by government. The main board – the section 99 (4) members – is expected to deal with files from the unsettled areas; however, if it is short of members, as happens from time to time, it may be necessary to add a member from one of the regional boards to fulfill the quorum requirements. This can result in logistical problems. Normally, panels have five members, but the act allows for three-member panels and for larger panels. In reviewing applications, these panels in effect become the board; their decisions do not require confirmation or authorization from the entire board. In putting panels together, at least one chair was known to "bench" board members who were not pulling their weight.

Section 106 of the *MVRMA* authorizes the MVLWB to "issue directions on general policy matters or on matters concerning the use of land or waters or the deposit of waste that, in the Board's opinion, require consistent application throughout the Mackenzie Valley" – in other words, to impose policy on the regional boards. This became a flashpoint in the initial, highly conflictual relations between the MVLWB and the regional boards – at times, according to one long-time board official, as antagonistic as those between the boards and DIAND. The regional boards adopted what this observer termed a "radically independent" stance vis-à-vis "the mother board." An early MVLWB attempt to use its section 106 power to give direction to the regional boards occasioned a powerful backlash, with the regional boards making it clear that they were not going to be told what to do by a Yellowknife-based organization. The MVLWB was forced to back off, and a working group was established to sort out differences. Over time, in large part due to turnover among board chairs and senior staff, relations thawed and lines of division became blurred or redefined. As befits the cooperative atmosphere that gradually emerged between it and the regional water boards, the MVLWB has not exercised this power. Instead, the four land and water boards work closely together to develop consistent procedures and policies.

As of early 2019, the board had a permanent staff complement of nineteen. In addition, the three regional land and water boards had nearly another twenty staff among them. Like the MVEIRB, it routinely hires consultants to provide expertise it lacks in-house. The board's long-serving lawyer, who also serves as legal counsel to the MVEIRB, actively participates in many phases of the board's work. For several years, salary and benefits for board employees lagged behind those enjoyed by staff of the MVEIRB, which had been pegged to levels in the federal public service. In 2006, employees received a substantial increase, which brought them up to par with their colleagues at the Review Board and in the federal government.

Despite their common origin in the Gwich'in and Sahtu and later Tlicho claims and in the *MVRMA*, the two Mackenzie Valley boards are funded in very different ways. Whereas core funding for the MVEIRB comes via the claims implementation agreements, supplemented by individual funding requests to DIAND, the MVLWB was initially financed through the "A-Base" (the ongoing operating budget) of DIAND's NWT Regional Office, under the department's Northern Affairs Program. This anomalous arrangement reflected the MVLWB's status as the nominal successor to the NWT Water Board, which had been funded through an A-Base allocation. Since, at least in the early years, it held fewer public hearings than the Review Board (typically only two or three a year), the MVLWB's financial needs were more predictable and so it did not usually need to seek additional funding from DIAND, though when it encountered substantial hearing costs, DIAND was prepared to underwrite them. One board figure at the time commented that, when it came to finances, "we rarely get what we want but we do get what we need ... we've never had a serious issue with money." The board did have a concern regarding timing; given the tempo of the federal government's budgetary cycle, it could be well into the fiscal year before payments arrived, forcing it to get by on a series of interim contribution agreements and requiring board staff to literally check the mail several times a day for the cheque.

As time passed, however, a more serious problem emerged: unlike the other *MVRMA* boards, MVLWB's core funding had no inflation escalator. From 2010–11 to 2016–17, core funding was fixed at $2.4 million with an additional $200,000 earmarked for the "Dehcho panel."[82] This meant not only regular last-minute emergency bailouts, causing stress and additional work, but, as one DIAND official acknowledged, it also resulted in continual staff reductions. In order to ensure that the board's regulatory capacity was maintained, human resources, financial, and information technology staff were trimmed or eliminated altogether. In 2008–09 and 2009–10, DIAND directed some $2.2 million to the board for "oil and gas capacity building." This money, which went to increasing staff complement, development of a robust public registry, mapping, and so on, was premised on the expectation that the board would soon be tasked with substantial extra responsibilities arising from the Mackenzie Gas Project.

As the prospect that the project would actually go ahead dimmed, however, this funding was reduced and eliminated entirely in the 2010–11 fiscal year.

In terms of actual regulatory decisions, the MVLWB's interactions with government differ markedly from how the Review Board relates to the GNWT (and before it to Ottawa). One key difference is that, on all applications for land use permits and water licences, save major projects requiring a Type A water licence or a Type B water licence following a public hearing, the board is empowered to make final and binding decisions. No appeals are possible, beyond judicial review on the basis of procedural or legal irregularity. Since only a small proportion of proposed projects reviewed by the board call for Type A water licences, this is a significant power.

No consult-to-modify process, akin to that available for MVEIRB EAs exists beyond the requirement that the minister respond within forty-five to ninety days; whether establishing one would be legally possible is subject to differing opinions. This has not been a problem since Ottawa never found itself at odds with the board in any significant way over Type A licences. In this regard, it is important to recognize that, although the board usually has no choice but to proceed with licensing projects once the minister has approved an EA report from the MVEIRB, save in unusual circumstances, it retains very substantial discretion in attaching conditions to the licences and permits it issues. This is a noteworthy board power.

At the same time, the DIAND minister has from the outset enjoyed an important power over the MVLWB and, since 2014, over the MVEIRB (as well as over the land use planning boards). Following consultation with the board, the minister has authority to issue binding policy directions to it. Only three such directives to the MVLWB have been enacted, none since 2004. One requires the board to observe provisions in the *Deh Cho First Nations Interim Measures Agreement* designating certain lands as "withdrawn from disposal" and thus off limits for seismic exploration. The others direct the board to consult with the Manitoba Denesuline and the Saskatchewan Athabasca Denesuline on permit and licence applications in regions of the southern NWT in which they have unresolved claims relating to harvesting rights.[83] In the case of the Wek'èezhìi Land and Water Board, the Tlicho Government has authority to issue binding policy directives. Notably, not only is this a power not available to the GNWT – for any board – but in case of conflict, the Tlicho Government's policy direction trumps that of the federal government.

The board holds public hearings on applications for Type A water licences, including applications for renewal, and on any other applications it believes warrant hearings. Hearings are principally designed to gather information and opinion relevant to setting terms and conditions for licences rather than for deciding whether a project should be referred to EA. Accordingly, for cases in which the MVEIRB has conducted an EA, the MVLWB hearings take place after the minister has approved the EA report. On occasion, the board will cancel a hearing it has scheduled if no comments are received from potential participants. Like the Review Board, the MVLWB is authorized to subpoena witnesses and documents and to take evidence under oath, but it too has not seen fit to exercise these powers.

As the board's no-nonsense "Engagement and Consultation Policy" makes clear, project proponents are required to engage in extensive and genuine interaction with local communities and to do so *before* submitting an application. Tellingly, the policy refers to "engagement" and "involvement" rather than "consultation." Would-be applicants are warned that they will be required to complete an engagement plan and an engagement record demonstrating the extent of community involvement as part of the formal application and indicating how a specific proposal was modified or prepared to reflect the regional community concerns.[84] That such warnings are not just empty words is evident from board decisions such as that on an application from Consolidated Gold Win Ventures to conduct diamond exploration drilling. The MVLWB referred the project to an EA on the basis of "potential public concern and insufficient consultation by the developer with the Yellowknives Dene First Nation."[85]

In addition to screening new land use permit and water licence applications and establishing detailed permit and licence conditions, the board has a number of related functions. It reviews applications for renewals, extensions, and amendments of existing licences and permits as well as requests for "assignment" of existing permits and licences when a new company or organization acquires ownership or control of a development. The board has wide scope in framing the terms and conditions for permits and licences, including ordering compensation to those adversely affected by approved projects. The only example to date of this function was the board's determination that the Northwest Territories Power Corporation had to pay $100,000 to the owners of a fishing lodge in compensation for lost business and other losses following construction of a power dam upriver from the lodge.[86] The board had agreed on a decision on another instance of a compensation request, also involving a lodge, but the parties settled privately before the process was completed.

An increasingly significant board function involves setting levels of security deposits for projects such as mines. These deposits, which can run into the tens of millions of dollars or more, are designed to ensure that remediation and reclamation costs are covered should proponents be unable to afford them when the projects are finished or if serious environmental damage occurs.

The board also assesses reports that project developers are required to file as licence conditions. Together with the review of reports from GNWT (formerly DIAND) inspectors, these assessments may form the basis of a decision to suspend or cancel a licence, though to date the board has not resorted to this extreme measure. Otherwise put, under the *MVRMA*, "the land and water boards have an enforcement role which extends their responsibilities beyond the mere issuance of permits."[87] As well, orders issued by inspectors to project operators relating to land use permits may be appealed to the board. Prior to the *MVRMA*, appeals were made to the minister.[88] This is not, however, a common occurrence; all told, the board has only had to deal with a literal handful of such appeals.

Though the MVLWB's workload ebbs and flows from year to year, it remains far higher than had been expected when the *MVRMA* was formulated. Even with the Wek'èezhìi Land and Water Board, which became operational in 2006, taking responsibility for some of the larger, more complex files (much of the diamond mining in the NWT occurs in traditional Tlicho territory), the MVLWB faces a substantial workload. In 2016–17, the board made 384 decisions relating to new land use permit or water licence applications, or existing permits and licences. This included thirty preliminary screenings, none of which resulted in an EA referral; no public hearings were held.[89]

The Early Years
Prior to the Mackenzie Valley Land and Water Board formally coming into existence, the Mackenzie Valley Land and Water Working Group was established to prepare for the transition from regulatory oversight by the NWT Water Board and DIAND to the *Mackenzie Valley Resource Management Act* regime. Ten of fifteen working group members were appointed to the MVLWB and two others became senior board staff. In order to promote continuity, four members of the NWT Water Board were among the initial appointments to the MVLWB. This proved a useful bridging mechanism. Nonetheless, with the formal appointments coming only a few weeks before the board became operational and with several employees hired with a similarly short lead time, members and staff found themselves scrambling to deal with the substantial workload they faced as soon as they opened for business. A year along, one board figure commented, "we've been catching up ever since [start-up]." The Gwich'in and Sahtu land and water boards had already been active for some months before the "big

board" came on stream, but this seems not to have had any significant impact on its operations.

The MVLWB may not have experienced the dramatic clashes with DIAND that characterized the early days of the MVEIRB, such as the Ranger and Beartooth EAs and the threat to close down, but in its first years its relationship with DIAND often took on an antagonistic tone. As noted above, elements of DIAND officialdom held a poor opinion of the Mackenzie Valley boards, and their staff in particular, while some MVLWB employees revelled in asserting their independence from and their distaste for DIAND. "Board staff have no hesitation in telling DIAND to bugger off" was how one of them put it. This aggressive stance was not to all board members' liking, and one of them lamented at the time: "there is major resistance among board staff to working in any way with DIAND or with staff of the NWT Water Board [who were also DIAND employees], who have extensive experience and expertise." The board's first executive director was said to have told staff that they should avoid speaking with federal government officials. Although this friction did not surface in specific high-profile episodes such as those that marked the Review Board's first years, the relationship between the board and DIAND bordered on dysfunctional.

Not only were its dealings with the federal government problematic, but the MVLWB also suffered from significant internal tensions. Some board members disagreed with the first chair's management style, their concern exacerbated by the limits her job as a full-time GNWT bureaucrat placed on her capacity to spend time in the office. Relations between members from the Gwich'in and Sahtu boards and those from the unsettled areas were, at times, testy, marked by turf wars rather than cooperation. As if this were not enough, divisions appeared between members and staff. One board member commented at the time: "[There is] fragmentation between members and technocracy ... Some staff are colonial and intimidating to many board members ... [Staff] focus on issues of process over content; a key problem is that the board should not be technical, it should be looking to do what's best for people and the environment." Another board member made a similar point with reference to the role of traditional knowledge in the board's operations: "The importance of TK is a given among board members, but not among technical staff ... The staff have expressed considerable unhappiness about the board and how it makes decisions, which in their view has been without adequate appreciation of technical staff and [with] too much concern with TK." In this atmosphere, and given the uncompetitive compensation packages, it is not surprising that staff morale was poor and turnover high.

Still and all, the board continued to process applications and did make good on one of the central objectives of the *MVRMA* – the realization of an open, transparent process for local communities, Indigenous organizations and governments, and the general public of the NWT to influence decisions relating to resource development projects and their environmental impact. Early on, the board moved to implement an important *MVRMA* requirement, adopting a wide-ranging, aggressive practice of notifying First Nations, municipalities, and government agencies about proposed developments and encouraging them to comment. Though First Nations and local communities oftentimes lack the wherewithal to take full advantage of the more consultative processes mandated by the *MVRMA*, the opportunities for genuine participation on the part of those previously excluded from decision-making processes go far beyond what was available to them under the previous environmental regulation regime.

Nor was the board impervious to criticisms it encountered from industry, government, and Indigenous organizations, as witnessed by the three-day workshop it co-hosted early in 2001 for those involved in the *MVRMA* process, aimed at improving its procedures and its relations with key "stakeholders." As well, in recognition of the widespread ignorance about the board, it mounted an extensive program of community visits to explain its work and the opportunities it represents for people to participate in environmental regulation.

By the fall of 2001, the MVLWB had overcome many of its internal problems and was enjoying markedly better relations with DIAND, leading one prominent board figure to proclaim "the war's over." The board and its staff were now seeking and receiving technical data and expert advice from both the GNWT and DIAND; interactions were becoming markedly more open and professional. The "NWT Practitioners' Technical Workshop" and associated efforts at improving relationships between the federal government and the boards, alluded to earlier, were partly responsible. So too was staff turnover, including the departure of the board's first executive director, who was widely regarded as cultivating a combative stance towards DIAND. His replacement brought to the job a pragmatic approach honed over many years as a senior GNWT bureaucrat.

Though many of the board's responsibilities and processes were new and unfamiliar, a good deal of its work followed patterns and precedents established by the NWT Water Board. It thus did not need to devise principles and guidelines de novo to the same extent as had the Review Board. The MVLWB did not content itself, however, with simply processing routine business and following the lead of the MVEIRB on TK and socioeconomic assessment. Rules of procedure and guidelines, such as those on public involvement, were developed as were mechanisms for dealings between the "big board" and the Gwich'in and Sahtu boards. As it became clear that DIAND's existing model for determining levels of security deposits was inappropriate for many of the projects the board was asked to licence, it developed its own policy on them. An informal mediation process was instituted to resolve differences among interested parties on complex technical issues prior to the public hearing stage. A wide-ranging strategic planning exercise took place. The community visits program was expanded and refined and greater attention was directed to communications through such means as newsletters and a beefed-up website. Linkages to both senior, "process" DIAND officials in the Yellowknife Regional Office and the department's field inspectors and technical experts were nurtured. A good deal of time and energy was devoted to ensuring that when the *Tlicho Agreement* came into force the transfer of responsibilities to the Wek'èezhìi Land and Water Board would be seamless, as indeed it proved to be.

An important landmark in the board's maturation came as a response to the manifold problems that enveloped a major project. In December 2003, BHP Billiton submitted an application for renewal of the Type A water licence at its Ekati diamond mine. Some twenty months elapsed before the licence, which in the end much resembled the original licence, was approved. (The untoward length of the process could not be attributed to delay at the EA stage since, as a licence renewal, no EA was required.) It was evident that the process was fraught with inefficiency and inadequacies. The board commissioned a "lessons-learned" exercise by an independent consultant. His analysis pulled no punches, citing, among other things, indications that board staff took important decisions without the knowledge or approval of the board, lack of technical expertise, and cumbersome processes.[90] The board accepted virtually all of the criticism and committed to implementing most of the consultant's recommendations for improving its processes and enhancing its capacity.[91]

Burlingame Redux

Though hardly immune from problems and controversy, as it moved into 2005, the MVLWB had largely moved beyond the initial conflicts, internal and external, which had bedeviled its early days. Then transpired a series of events bringing to mind the words of Fabian in *Twelfth Night*: "If this were played upon a stage now, I could condemn it as an improbable fiction."

Following Melody McLeod's resignation as chair in fall 2004, the board advertised for a replacement, interviewed a number of applicants, and forwarded a list of three suitable candidates to Ottawa. Astonishingly, the minister ignored the board's recommendations and appointed none other than Todd Burlingame, who had only weeks earlier completed his controversial term as MVEIRB chair.[92]

A firestorm of opposition erupted immediately, with MLAs angrily calling for the minister to rescind his decision and appoint a chair from the board's short list. Perhaps because it is easier politically to tap into Northerners' distaste for Southern Canadians placed into positions of power than to explain the murky political infighting at the Review Board, much of the criticism focused on the minister's decision to pass over qualified Northern candidates in favour of Burlingame, who had by this point moved to British Columbia. As one MLA told the CBC, "it sends a bad message out to Northerners that we really do not have any control over the Mackenzie Valley Land and Water Board."[93] NWT premier Joe Handley was incensed, both at the appointment and at having to learn about it from the media, commenting: "This cannot continue to happen. We cannot have these kinds of decisions being made for us in Ottawa and us finding out after the fact."[94] The Legislative Assembly passed without debate a motion objecting "to the appointment of a non-resident of the NWT, who is not nominated by the board members, as the chair of the Mackenzie Valley Land and Water Board."[95]

Shortly after announcing Burlingame's appointment, the hapless DIAND minister, Andy Scott, found himself roundly attacked at townhall meetings in Yellowknife and elsewhere in the NWT called to discuss Ottawa's "Northern Strategy" over his decision. Scott defended the appointment, citing Burlingame's "credentials," adding that "I wouldn't know him if I saw him" and that he had been told Burlingame would be a good choice.[96] It was widely assumed that local Liberal MP, Ethel Blondin-Andrew, was behind the appointment. Stephen Kakfwi, premier at the time of Burlingame's appointment as MVEIRB chair, had reportedly been furious about it but had refrained from commenting publicly. Now retired from the legislature and no longer speaking on behalf of the GNWT, he saw little need for diplomacy in speaking to the media. "As far as I know, the name Todd Burlingame was put forward by Ethel Blondin-Andrew, and the minister just did a favour to a Liberal crony," he charged. "She said he is the only one with the technical background to expedite the [Mackenzie Gas Project] process, which is horseshit."[97]

Barely had the initial brouhaha subsided when the board was plunged into difficulty. It had come to light that, unlike his predecessor, who had been remunerated by way of per diems, Burlingame was in effect a salaried employee of DIAND. Fearing that this might constitute a conflict of interest and open its decisions to legal challenge, the MVLWB passed a motion calling for Burlingame to step aside until the issue was resolved. "If the chair is being hired and paid by DIAND, what's the difference between that and the chair being paid by another intervenor?" asked one board member.[98] Burlingame immediately suspended all board business. At a meeting in Inuvik two weeks later, the board accepted legal advice that no conflict existed and agreed to get on with its work. Within days, however, the verbal cease-fire had broken down with board member Stephen Nielsen, one of the three candidates who had been proposed for the chairship, publicly claiming that the Inuvik meeting had been a "setup" orchestrated by Burlingame.[99]

Over the next few weeks the soap opera continued. Burlingame again suspended board business in response to members' criticism of his decision to replace board members from the unsettled areas scheduled to review applications from the Dehcho and Akaitcho regions with members from the Gwich'in Land and Water Board (GLWB). He also wrote to Scott seeking Nielsen's dismissal from the board on the grounds that members of the GLWB wanted him removed and were refusing to participate in meetings that he attended – an assertion denied by the chair of the GLWB.[100] An exasperated Premier Handley called on Scott to fix the problem, declaring "this board is not functioning."[101]

In Ottawa, Conservative MP Jim Prentice, shortly to become DIAND minister, criticized the Burlingame appointment in Question Period and released a letter from Burlingame to Scott, dated December 20, 2004 – while the board was developing its shortlist – in which Burlingame put himself forward for the chairship "if it were the desire of yourself and the minister of state for northern development [Blondin-Andrew]."[102]

Despite the apparent disarray at the MVLWB, Bob Wooley, its respected executive director, declared that all the troubles had only caused minimal disruption to the board's operations. "The work is getting done ... we're not at all impeded by what is going on ... it has not seriously impacted the way we do business."[103] Indeed, despite Burlingame once again finding himself in the public eye over consulting he had performed for the GNWT while serving as MVEIRB chair,[104] the board did manage to get on with its work through the fall of 2005 and attain a semblance of normalcy. Early in the new year, Burlingame announced his resignation with two-thirds of his term still to run. Willard Hagen, chair of the GLWB, became interim chair and was subsequently appointed chair.

Maturation at the MVLWB
As with the Mackenzie Valley Environmental Impact Review Board, the tribulations of the Burlingame episode are long past and the MVLWB and its processes

have developed and matured in various ways. Perhaps the board's most notable accomplishment has been its continuing ability to process a large number of oftentimes complex applications, entailing hundreds of decisions each year, within tight deadlines, even when it was experiencing serious internal dissension. Its success in handling substantial workloads even as its core funding was eroded by inflation, leading to staff reductions, is also noteworthy.

Whereas the Review Board has produced significant documents and policies on such intangibles as TK in environmental assessment and socioeconomic impact assessment, the MVLWB has made important contributions in terms of technical processes and standards. It has taken the lead in working with the other land and water boards and the federal and territorial governments to produce a series of guidelines on such topics as water and effluent quality management, costing of mine closure and reclamation, aquatic effects monitoring, and solid waste disposal. It has also developed a wide range of templates and policy documents for applicants, especially municipal governments, covering consultation and engagement, sewage treatment systems, water use fees, and the like.[105]

Although the four land and water boards are separate institutions, they have developed what one board official dubbed "a sharing ethos." By way of illustration, should the staff of one board not be busy, they might help out another board with a heavy workload, sometimes working from their own office, sometimes travelling to the other board office. Boards also share training opportunities, such as for information technology development. The executive directors of the four boards meet on a regular basis, as do the board chairs. As well, many of the workshops and conferences mentioned under the rubric of MVEIRB accomplishments have been joint projects with the MVLWB.

Ongoing Issues

The *Mackenzie Valley Resource Management Act* regime is and doubtless will continue to be a work in progress. The legal framework is highly complex, new technology is constantly emerging – fracking was unknown in the NWT when the act was passed – and the political situation is subject to far-reaching change, both long- and short-term. Accordingly, the number of ongoing issues is substantial, as is their range. This section briefly considers some of the more significant ones.

Funding inevitably ranks as a major concern for the boards, which perennially see themselves as underfunded, and for Ottawa, which is constantly mindful of keeping costs under control and of ensuring accountability for monies transferred to the boards. While funding issues will never be resolved to everyone's satisfaction, an important recent development should go some distance towards reducing the boards' short- and medium-funding concerns. Following a detailed review of board workloads, in August 2017 the minister announced a major injection of funds for NWT claims boards and other claims-based commissions and committees, such as Inuvialuit hunters and trappers committees and Gwich'in and Sahtu Renewable Resources Councils. All told, the commitment was for $6.2 million of new money, representing a 40 percent increase in core money.[106] The MVLWB and the MVEIRB each received $600,000 in new core funding (increases of 25 and 21 percent, respectively); Wek'èezhìi Land and Water Board funding went from $732,767 to $1,943,402, a 165 percent increase.[107] With the new arrangements in place, no boards needed emergency supplementary core funding at the end of the 2016–17 fiscal year. The expectation was that the new funding regime would provide stability and predictability for boards so that they would not require supplementary core funding for at least five years.[108] DIAND also revamped its process for providing supplementary funding to boards for unusually high workloads so that it could respond to board requests more effectively and more quickly.

Relatedly, the minister also directed departmental officials to conduct a long-overdue review of board honoraria, which had not been increased since 2002 despite repeated requests from boards and board members for higher rates. The review, though not necessarily the minister's decision, was expected by the end of 2018.[109] It would almost certainly also affect rates for boards in Nunavut and Yukon.

An enduring problem for Mackenzie Valley boards has been the unseemly delay that so often occurs in appointing replacements when positions become vacant. This issue, endemic across the three territories, is discussed in Chapter 7.

Other contentious issues involve implementation and enforcement of the terms and conditions imposed by land and water boards on water licences and land use permits arising from the wide scope of environmental assessment under the *MVRMA*. In 2007, the chairs of MVEIRB and all the land and water boards wrote to the DIAND regional director in Yellowknife alleging "only about 46% of the [MVEIRB's] measures accepted by the Minister of INAC are being implemented by regulatory authorities and that, of those, less that [sic] 50% are actually inspected for purposes of compliance or enforcement. At best, only 25% of the Review Board's measures are having any affect [sic] on the impacts they were designed to mitigate."[110]

Another set of issues entail so-called orphan measures. Measures proposed by the Review Board, and approved by the minister, may not fall clearly into the remit of any particular government agency for implementation and thus fall by the wayside. An internal DIAND study commented:

> There are sometimes "orphan measures" that are routinely left out of mitigation strategies or not enforced because there is no clear regulatory authority responsible to enforce them and no clear standards to apply. These may include air quality, some aspects of wildlife management and socio-economic well-being. These areas are covered in the land claim agreements, and the public boards established by the agreements have a mandate to set terms and conditions to meet risks of impacts in those areas, but up to now, no action is being taken.[111]

As the 2015 environmental audit noted, since inspection processes are essentially limited to biophysical aspects of development projects, "Land Use Permits and Water Licences, the primary authorizations used in the Mackenzie Valley, can only include conditions related to the use of land and water and deposit of waste. INAC and GNWT inspectors indicated that if other conditions were included in authorizations, they do not have a mandate to enforce these."[112] One long-time board official believes that industry, at least the large companies, did a better job than government of ensuring that orphan measures were implemented, out of concern about risk and possible liability issues.

The 2015 audit did hold out hope that the planned use of enforceable "development certificates," included in the 2014 amendments to the act, would largely resolve the orphan measure issue.[113] Others familiar with the board regime also see the development certificates as holding great promise. However, implementation of development certificates proved more complex than initially expected. A broadly based working group was established to develop a process, but, as of early 2019, it had yet to be put in place. Whether *MVRMA* development certificates will emulate the thorough and highly institutionalized monitoring system integral to the operation of the Nunavut Impact Review Board (NIRB) remains to be seen. NIRB is unique among Northern environmental assessment boards in that it was assigned a strong monitoring mandate in the land claim, subsequently bolstered by legislation.[114] NIRB technical staff make annual site visits to projects and routinely receive additional inspection reports from other government agencies and Inuit organizations. The project certificates NIRB issues in tandem with licences and permits require developers to submit detailed annual reports on a range of matters. These reports, posted on the board's website for public comment, may occasion reports and recommendations from the board. Actual enforcement, should it become necessary, falls to DIAND.

Even for terms and conditions falling clearly into the remit of inspectors, concerns exist as to the adequacy of inspections. Resource constraints have required inspectors to adopt a "risk management approach" so that, as the DIAND report put it, "only the sites that are deemed to present the highest environmental risk and that are affordable to inspect receive attention."[115] In 2009, the auditor general found that, of some twenty-four hundred licences and permits in the NWT, not all of which emanated from the *MVRMA* regime, only about 13 percent of affected sites had been inspected.[116] Significantly, within a few months of assuming primary responsibility for inspections, the GNWT announced that it had hired additional inspectors beyond those who had been transferred from DIAND to the GNWT under the devolution agreement and had doubled the budget for inspections.[117]

When GNWT or DIAND inspectors encounter projects not adhering to the terms and conditions required of them, they "take an 'educational enforcement' approach, working with proponents to come back into compliance, followed by progressive enforcement, if required."[118] According to a DIAND study, departmental officials and company representatives believed that compliance monitoring was appropriate and effective, but GNWT officials and representatives of Indigenous communities were critical of what they saw as inadequate implementation and lax enforcement of EA measures.[119]

A related issue has been the Review Board's inclusion of "suggestions" in its EA reports. These are not "measures," the formal terms and conditions that the board believes are necessary to prevent or mitigate the adverse effects of a proposed development, which at the end of the regulatory process would be incorporated into the licence or permit. Nor are they, in the language of the *MVRMA*, "recommendations": the board's overall judgment on a proposal – approve, approve with measures, reject, or send to EIR. "Suggestions" are just that: nonbinding suggestions to the proponent or to government about how to proceed with a development.

The Review Board's REA on the proposed Prairie Creek zinc mine in the southwest corner of the NWT illustrates the difficulties that can arise from "suggestions." The board concluded that the mine was not likely to cause significant adverse effects on the environment and thus recommended that it proceed to the regulatory phase of the project and proposed no measures to be included in the necessary licences and permits. It did, however, offer three suggestions "that would improve the monitoring and management of potential impacts from this development." The suggestions pertained to water storage, tailings management, and transportation of ore concentrate. The report framed the suggestions in the following language: on water storage, "The Review Board suggests that the Mackenzie Valley Land and Water Board consider this during the licensing phase"; on tailings management, "The Review Board suggests that the Mackenzie Valley Land and Water Board consider this during the licensing phase"; on concentrate transportation: "The Mackenzie Valley Land and Water Board and Parks Canada can best address this during the regulatory phase."[120]

The problem, as the MVLWB saw it, was not that the suggestions were unreasonable or impractical. Rather, the board had been handed rather imprecise ideas without a clear basis as to how to proceed. One of the board members put it more succinctly and colourfully: "we've been hung out to dry." In the end, after some difficulty, the board did develop specific terms and conditions operationalizing the suggestions. This episode illustrates the key issue of delineating the boundary between the functions of the MVEIRB and the MVLWB, an issue that was apparent early on. One senior board official suggests that the Review Board should be primarily concerned with assessing potential environmental impacts in terms of values, leaving the technical work of establishing terms and conditions to the MVLWB. Given the complexity of the environmental problems that arise in resource development and extraction, however, such a division is difficult to establish and maintain, though the boards continue to work on clarifying roles and responsibilities.

A major impediment to effective community and First Nations participation in EAs, and indeed in all phases of the *MVRMA* regime, has been the lack of participant funding, previously known as intervenor funding. The act makes no reference to funding for would-be participants whose resources, human and financial, are insufficient to allow them to take part in the regulatory process. Nor until very recently has DIAND or any other government agency had programs to routinely provide such funding. It is not simply that small communities cannot afford the legal and technical expertise that is sometimes needed in the complex processes surrounding large projects; indeed, the board does not usually look to local communities for technical reports but for TK and for advice based on local experience. The problem is often far more basic: staff of communities and First Nations, who receive notifications and invitations to participate, are often simply too hard pressed to be able to respond meaningfully, if at all, or to assist local people's participation in the process.

The *MVRMA* makes no provision for participant funding for environmental assessments. Participant funding had been provided to communities and organizations during the environmental assessment of the Diavik diamond mine, but this occurred just prior to the establishment of the *MVRMA* regime. On occasion, as with the EA of the Giant mine remediation project, DIAND provided participant funding on a case-by-case basis, but such instances were uncommon. Through the Interim Resources Management Assistance Fund the GNWT provides limited funding to Indigenous communities and organizations in the unsettled areas for participation in EAs, permitting and licensing processes, and other land-related matters.

For environmental impact reviews, which are at once more extensive and much rarer than EAs, DIAND may be prepared to provide financial support for intervenors or participants. The MVEIRB's *Environmental Impact Assessment Guidelines* strongly imply the availability of participant funding for EIRs,[121] though they do not explicitly promise funding, not least because the money would have to come from Ottawa. At one point DIAND clarified that it would not guarantee participant funding for an EIR but that "proposals would be considered on a case-by-case basis."[122] Participant funding was provided on the Mackenzie Gas Project, but the unique nature of this exercise renders it of uncertain value as a precedent. For the other EIR, on DeBeers Canada's proposed Gahcho Kué diamond mine, DIAND provided $210,000 in participant funding to five Indigenous governments and organizations.

The *MVRMA* boards repeatedly argued the need for participant funding. The Review Board pointed out that such funding is available for "comprehensive studies" under the *Canadian Environmental Assessment Act*, and that EAs under the *MVRMA* can be equally or more complex.[123] In pushing for participant funding, though, the board has been adamant that it should not be involved in funding potential participants lest its neutrality be compromised.

According to a DIAND insider, on several occasions departmental officials requested cabinet approval of participant funding for Mackenzie Valley boards but were rejected without a clear explanation. Late in 2018, the federal government announced a Northern Participant Funding Program, to provide $10.3 million over five years for groups and individuals in the three territories to assist their taking part "in impact assessments and regulatory decision-making processes for major projects." Indigenous individuals and groups, "Northern individuals," and incorporated not-for-profit organizations are to be eligible for funding. Panels of representatives from Indigenous, territorial, and federal governments recommend allocation of funds to Ottawa.[124] The program was up and running quickly, with funding allocations made within a few weeks of the announcement to groups involved in two Nunavut environmental assessments and engagement processes under way with Indigenous governments and organizations in Yukon and the NWT. In the early going at least, panel members were selected by program staff on the basis of recommendations from what one official termed "our co-management partners," Indigenous organizations, and territorial governments.

This chapter, in setting out the history and the mechanics of the MVLWB and the MVEIRB, looks at the ups and downs of the *MVRMA* boards in terms of both their internal dynamics and their dealings with the GNWT, Indigenous governments and organizations, and, especially, the federal government. And while it would be foolish to assume that all their troubles are in the past, it seems clear that they have moved beyond the growing pains of their early days and have matured into well-run, effective organizations.

It is beyond the scope of this book, not to mention my expertise, to assess the important question of how effective they are at protecting the environment of the Mackenzie Valley, though the independent environmental audits required by the *MVRMA* have consistently given them positive assessments. The first found the *MVRMA* regime "adequately protective of land and water," and identified most of the system's shortcomings as lying beyond the boards' responsibilities.[125] Similarly, the second audit "generally found [the Mackenzie Valley boards] to be effective in protecting the environment,"[126] and the third reached an almost identical conclusion: "Since the last Audit in 2010 the environmental regulatory system in the NWT has continued to improve. The integrated system of land and water management is generally effective in protecting the environment."[127]

As for the central question animating this book – whether these claims boards represent a significant enhancement of Indigenous peoples' influence over resource development – the following chapter attempts to provide an answer. Chapter 6 examines the highly controversial amendments to the *MVRMA* proposed by the federal government in 2013–14 and concludes by drawing on material from Chapters 5 and 6 to assess Indigenous influence. Still, an important preliminary conclusion can be ventured at this point. A prominent theme of this chapter is the maturation and improved effectiveness of both the MVLWB and the MVEIRB, a necessary but not sufficient condition for Indigenous influence.

chapter 6

The Mackenzie Valley Boards and the Regulatory Improvement Saga

Far and away the most significant and politically charged recent developments affecting the *Mackenzie Valley Resource Management Act* regime arose from the Harper government's Northern Regulatory Improvement Initiative, the capstone of which was a highly controversial set of amendments to the act. This episode carries far-reaching implications for the prime focus of this book: the influence of Indigenous people over wildlife and environmental management decisions through co-management boards. Simply put, to the extent that the federal government can fundamentally reorder the board regime over the strenuous objections of the affected Indigenous people, the prospects for real influence dim substantially.

This chapter examines the politics and process leading to the introduction of Bill C-15 in the fall of 2013; reaction to the bill, especially on the part of First Nations; and the changes wrought by the amendments as well as planned changes that did not survive the change of government in late 2015.

It had long been evident that amending the *MVRMA* was in order. Indeed, discussions and reports as to needed and desirable revisions began shortly after the act was passed in 1998. Overall, the act's regulatory regime worked well, though those involved had identified a number of areas in need of clarification or revision. Representatives of industry frequently criticized what they contended were long, costly delays and needlessly burdensome provisions both in the regulatory process and in the conditions imposed by licences and permits. Industry thus sought sweeping change. Industry demands that the process be "streamlined" found favour with the Conservatives, who commissioned a special report that led to the wide-ranging Action Plan to Improve Northern Regulatory Regimes, the centrepiece of which was a thoroughgoing revision of the *MVRMA*.

The most contentious aspects of Ottawa's attempt to restructure the regulatory system in the Mackenzie Valley reflected its sensitivity to complaints from industry about the length of the licensing and permitting process and about associated bureaucratic burdens and hurdles. A notable but hardly isolated illustration came in one of DIAND minister Jim Prentice's first major pronouncements about Northern resource development after the Conservatives assumed power in 2006. Prentice left little doubt that he found unacceptable what he termed "the 'spider's web' of suffocating northern regulation."[1] Accordingly it is worth exploring the nature and validity of industry's discontent with the *MVRMA* regime.

This chapter thus begins with an account and an analysis of industry's criticism of the *MVRMA* and the environmental regulatory boards it established. The following sections outline the context and the substance of the McCrank Report, *Road to Improvement*; the "Pollard Mission" regarding land and water board restructuring; and the boards' response to McCrank and Pollard. A long section sets out the process, the content, the parliamentary committee hearings on Bill C-15, the *Northwest Territories Devolution Act*, and the subsequent Tlicho court challenge to key aspects of the bill. A concluding section reviews material from this and the preceding chapter to address the central question of Indigenous influence through the Mackenzie Valley environmental regulatory boards.

Industry Criticisms of the *MVRMA*

From the outset, industry criticism of the regulatory system in the Mackenzie Valley was vociferous and relentless. Even as the *MVRMA* was being drafted, the NWT Chamber of Mines argued that the proposed regime "was complex, unworkable, and presented a serious deterrent to mineral exploration in the NWT." Other industry figures objected to the unnecessary lengthening of the permitting process.[2] Once the act was in place, first and foremost among industry concerns was the complexity and length of the process. Objections were also registered about what industry sometimes perceived as anti-development bias among board staff and about "needless" environmental assessment and permitting requirements. The latter included annoyance that "minor" projects such as exploratory drilling might be called up for a costly and lengthy EA and that ill-defined and possibly insincere "public concern" could trigger an EA.

Any time a company cancelled or scaled back a project, company officials, backed by leaders of organizations such as the NWT and Nunavut Chamber of Mines, could be expected to blame the regulatory system and to compare it unfavourably to processes in other jurisdictions. The chorus of industry representatives was nothing if not direct and unrelenting in attacking the *MVRMA* regime. Dave Nickerson, a former Conservative MP and member of several mining company boards, claimed: "the dysfunctional regulatory system is driving away investment in the North."[3] According to the president of the NWT Chamber of Commerce, "our regulatory process in the territories is broken and it needs to be fixed."[4] The manager of a company that pulled out of a plan to conduct a large seismic survey lamented: "We can't spend any more money in the territory ... This [EA] process has taken such a long time ... we don't have any confidence it [approval] may come."[5]

In 2007, the Mackenzie Valley Environmental Impact Review Board recommended that a proposed exploratory uranium project at Screech Lake not go ahead because of the spiritual and cultural significance of the drilling sites for local First Nations. Industry was appalled. The NWT and Nunavut Chamber of Mines, the Mining Association of Canada, and the Prospectors and Developers Association of Canada called the recommendation "deeply troubling" and requested that DIAND minister Prentice refer the recommendation back to the board for further consideration. Their letter to Prentice emphasized the limited scale of the proposed exploration and complained about the "apparent bias" in the EA process "that always favours traditional aboriginal activities, tourism and outdoor recreation over economic development initiatives." It also challenged "whether the Review Board has the authority to delve into 'spiritual' concerns and question[ed] the emphasis the Board has placed on such concerns in reaching its conclusions."[6] A few months later, the newly installed DIAND minister, Chuck Strahl, accepted the board's recommendation.

Dissatisfied as industry might have been about the regulatory regime in the Mackenzie Valley, it did tend to mute criticism of Indigenous peoples and their organizations, which is not to say that it fully understood Indigenous perspectives or was always respectful of Indigenous culture and traditions. Rather, developers and their organizations focused on the uncertainty, complexity, length, and ultimately the cost of EA and permitting processes.

Generally speaking, small and mid-sized firms were and continue to be more publicly and vehemently outspoken about the NWT regulatory regime than larger companies. To some extent this is because they lack the resources to endure delays and to some extent it is because they lack the sophistication of the large multinationals, which have learned to accommodate local concerns and regulatory processes. If need be, of course, the big players are willing to publicly raise the ante in their dealings with the boards, as evidenced by De Beers's threats to close an operating diamond mine, with the loss of hundreds of jobs, if requests for looser conditions on water contamination levels were not accepted by the Mackenzie Valley Land and Water Board. Over objections from nearby First Nations, the water licence was amended by the MVLWB along the lines sought by De Beers. A senior board figure maintains that the board applied its usual processes and standards in assessing De Beers's application, which, in effect, sought conditions that the company had initially not thought necessary, and firmly rejects the interpretation that the board "caved" in the face of a threat that the mine could not continue to operate under the licence's existing conditions. In the event, less than three months after the amended licence was approved, De Beers announced it would be shutting down the mine, citing heavy costs at the mine and a significant downturn in the diamond market.[7]

In 2015, the Wek'èezhìi Land and Water Board referred to EA a small exploration project at Whitebeach Point on the North Arm of Great Slave Lake, designed to analyze the quality and quantity of silica sand for use in fracking. In response Tom Hoefer, executive director of the NWT and Nunavut Chamber of Mines, penned an op-ed piece in *News/North NWT*, the territory's leading paper. He questioned the necessity of an EA on a "fledgling exploration project" because it "might be a cause of public concern," arguing that "decisions that unnecessarily refer early-stage exploration projects to environmental assessment" constitute a significant threat to the economic well-being of the NWT.[8] A few months later, when the proponent abandoned the project rather than undergo an EA, the op-ed's relatively measured tone was replaced by outrage from Hoefer, who labelled the outcome "ludicrous."[9] Another mining executive weighed in on this issue with an op-ed, proclaiming: "Husky [the proponent] played by the rules but our ever-increasing demands and our overly sensitive regulatory system with its 'hair trigger' to public concern pulled them into a needless and costly-for-all regulatory process."[10]

News/North NWT may have given voice on its op-ed page to industry complaints about the environmental regulatory processes in the Mackenzie Valley, but its editorial stance was hardly sympathetic. In an editorial titled "The Case for Red Tape" it called Hoefer's comments on the Husky project "a tone deaf response to the concerns of people who live in the area and care about Whitebeach Point. His assessment that environmental reviews make investors nervous about spending money in the territory may be true but it's no reason to open the floodgates to development without weighing the impact development will have."[11] Several years earlier the paper had been even less restrained in its views of industry complaints about the regulatory regime: "The chamber [of mines] largely represents outside interests who have no stake in the NWT economy, environment or people. They would prefer no environmental reviews, no hiring quotas, no benefit agreements, just give us the rocks."[12] Lest it be thought that *News/North NWT* was an uncritical cheerleader for the boards, it readily accused the MVEIRB of responsibility for significant process delays, calling it "a red tape jungle where only the most patient with the deepest pockets do not fear to tread, essentially multinational resource development companies that can withstand the organic mix of politics and science undefined by either timelines or commitment to any particular process."[13]

Industry's complaints about the *MVRMA* regime engendered more than a lack of editorial sympathy. A range of systematic analyses, from independent consultants, the boards, and DIAND itself disputed industry criticisms about delays and unfairness in the process. As a starting point, it is worth bearing in mind that, as noted in the previous chapter, consistently only 3 to 5 percent of all project applications have undergone EAs.

Unquestionably, the process takes longer and is more complicated than was the case prior to the passage of the *MVRMA*. One of the central objectives of the act, however, was improving environmental regulation through the establishment of a more transparent, participatory regime. This objective has been met at the cost of lengthening the process somewhat. Notably, however, the first NWT Environmental Audit concluded: "since the inception of the MVRMA, the Environmental Assessment process has improved significantly,"[14] adding that the *MVRMA* process was no more complex than others across Canada.[15]

The issue of complexity was addressed by DIAND assistant deputy minister Jim Moore just as the *MVRMA* was coming into force. "The number of boards involved may at first glance," he told a gathering of industry representatives, bureaucrats, and Indigenous leaders, "suggest a very complex process but in fact it is very much a single-window approach ... The intent of the legislation is to centralize four critical aspects of the regulatory process" – a single entry and issuance point for licences and permits, a single environmental assessment process, a single set of imposed mitigative measures, and a central distribution point for reports and decisions.[16]

From the outset, under the *MVRMA*, both EA and permitting could take considerable time; indeed, this remains the case today. Yet it was also true that some of the longest delays occurred as completed EA reports awaited ministerial approval and the "consult-to-modify" process unfolded. The MVEIRB pointed out that several EA reports effectively "sat on the minister's desk" for more than a year, which was longer than the EA itself required.[17] As well, the board added, some delays in the EA process were government's responsibility since the MVEIRB "frequently receive[d] requests for extending comment periods from government departments and regularly receive[d] government submissions late."[18] At the same time local communities and First Nations frequently complained that the process unfolded too quickly, making it difficult for them to respond effectively and straining their limited resources.

The second NWT Environmental Audit, released in early 2011, offers the most thorough publicly available analysis of the timeliness of land and water board and MVEIRB processes. Based on detailed data on the time taken in various phases of the permitting, licensing, and environmental assessment processes, the auditors concluded "the vast majority of MVRMA applications are processed in a timely manner," noting that the average time taken for EAs was similar to that for EAs conducted elsewhere in Canada and that "a MVRMA process, on average, takes no longer than a CEAA [*Canadian Environmental Assessment Act*] process."[19]

As the MVEIRB had done a few years earlier, the authors of the audit attributed much of the delay pertaining to EAs to government: "post-REA [report of environmental assessment] consultation and ministerial decision phase accounts for, on average[,] 50% of total elapsed EA time."[20] Although the audit recognized how complex Ottawa's internal and external consultation processes for responding to EA reports could be, it explicitly recommended legislation to impose maximum timelines for ministerial decisions on EAs.[21] It is worth bearing in mind that the audit, with its favourable assessment of the *MVRMA* regime, appeared as the Action Plan to Improve Northern Regulatory Regimes was under way and as the amendments to the act were being developed.

Another significant element of industry discontent with the act was the new requirement that licences and permits be renewed every five to seven years. Whereas previously a project proponent could negotiate a long-term lease with DIAND based on an environmental review that would be good for the life of the project, under the *MVRMA* a thirty-year project would have to go through the licensing/permitting process four or five time.

A frequent theme of industry criticism has been what it sees as the needless subjection of very small projects, such as at Screech Lake and Whitebeach Point, to complex and protracted and thus costly environmental assessments. In a brief case study of a similarly small proposal for exploratory drilling near

Drybones Bay on Great Slave Lake, two Review Board staff summarized the board's rationale for its approach to such proposals as follows: "it was clear that it is the scale of the issues, and not only the scale of the developments, that dictate the effort required and the complexity of the environmental assessments."[22]

A noteworthy refutation of industry criticisms of the *MVRMA* regime came from DIAND itself. A 2009 internal departmental analysis of, among others, the Gwich'in and Sahtu claims, concluded: "the regulatory regime, in most instances, has been operating in a timely fashion and it has not been a deterrent to resource development and investment."[23] The report went on: "interviews with representatives of resource development industry associations and non-Aboriginal companies doing business in the settled areas, demonstrate a high level of comfort with the new way of doing business."[24] It will shortly become evident that these observations, which, to repeat, came from DIAND itself, are hardly consistent with the premises underpinning the federal government's Northern Regulatory Improvement Initiative and the McCrank Report.

Although he subsequently became reluctant to comment on government plans to restructure the land and water boards, in an interview with a Northern business magazine shortly after the release of the McCrank Report, Mackenzie Valley Land and Water Board chair Willard Hagen voiced scepticism about the need for board amalgamation, commenting: "A lot of this is growing pains ... we're just coming up on 10 years for most of these boards." Hagen forcefully rejected criticisms that the MVLWB was not well staffed and that its decisions lacked timeliness and fairness: "Show me where we ever held up the process. We are now into assessing our fourth diamond mine." And he pointedly added that many of industry's complaints related to the fraught Joint Review Panel on the Mackenzie Gas Project, "which has nothing to do with us."[25]

Not everyone in the resource development industries offered simplistic bombast in assessing the regulatory process. Rick Schryer, a senior official of a junior mining company, with experience working for large diamond companies in the NWT, publicly acknowledged lack of capacity among First Nations as a key problem: "It's consultation overload ... they've got too many people banging on their doors. They don't have the people or the time and have other issues that need to be addressed." As a result of their inability to respond to the demands of regulatory participation in a timely way, or at all, "the process grinds to a halt." Similarly, delays on the part of board staff and federal bureaucrats were, in his view, largely attributable to their being understaffed and overworked.[26]

Moreover, as exemplified in some of the comments cited below during the parliamentary hearings on Bill C-15, industry representatives, typically from the larger enterprises, have come to accept the *MVRMA* regulatory process and to register positive comments about the boards and their staff. As well, industry and Indigenous organizations are increasingly coming to understand one another and to work together as they negotiate and implement impact and benefit agreements that now typically accompany resource development projects.[27]

All told, evidence and expert opinion offered at best lukewarm support for industry's complaints about long delays, stultifying complexity, and lack of predictability in the *MVRMA* regime. Still, no one involved in the process, boards included, disputed the need to overhaul the act. Indeed, considerable agreement existed as to necessary changes. However, for the boards, as for many in the NWT, amending the act called for tinkering and fine-tuning, whereas industry sought wholesale revision, as did Ottawa, especially after the 2006 federal election, which brought Stephen Harper's Conservative Party to power.

The McCrank Report

Although the process moved into high gear following the election, DIAND officials had been working for some time on what became the Northern Regulatory Initiative. The precipitating event was a 2005 report from the auditor general on "Development of Non-Renewable Resources in the Northwest Territories," which was seen in the department as highly critical. In light of subsequent developments, it may be significant that the report adopted a remarkably narrow-gauge, Ottawa-centric approach. The report, which was entirely focused on the land and water boards and the Mackenzie Valley Environmental Impact Review Board, acknowledged the boards' roots in land claims but failed to appreciate the significance of the claims. Neither in its analysis nor in its recommendations did it contemplate any role for Indigenous people or organizations in revising the act or in the department's procedures for dealing with the boards; the term "co-management" does not appear in the report. Rather, the auditor general's report identified weaknesses in the department's processes for administering the boards and related accountability regimes, emphasizing the need for DIAND to take a more dirigiste approach to the boards. No attempt was made to examine the effectiveness and efficiency of board processes.[28] For its part, the department indicated agreement with all the report's recommendations and committed to take action on them.[29]

Among DIAND's actions that led, five years later, to favourable comments from the auditor general as to the department's progress in dealing with the issues raised in the report,[30] were the creation of the Board Forum, discussed in the previous chapter, and the commissioning of a wide-ranging independent study of relations between DIAND and the boards. The study, conducted by Terriplan Consultants, a Yellowknife firm with extensive experience working with *MVRMA* boards, said almost nothing about the boards' internal operations or effectiveness. It did, however, offer some hard-hitting criticism of organizational and procedural issues at DIAND that were adversely affecting the boards. Prime among them was the anomaly of the Mackenzie Valley Land and Water Board and the (then) Northwest Territories Water Board being funded through the NWT Regional Office of the Northern Affairs Program (NAP), without an inflation escalator, whereas all other Mackenzie Valley boards were funded by the Claims and Indian Government Implementation Branch (CIG) of the Implementation Management Directorate with annual inflation increases. NAP and CIG reported to different assistant deputy ministers, and whereas NAP had significant regional presence through the regional offices in the territories, CIG was entirely a headquarters operation. Accordingly, not only had this produced "an overlap of roles and responsibilities and ... inefficiencies within the system," but "concern that different offices may be providing different views, opinions and advice to the Boards on the same matter ... There have been times when certain offices have made decisions without communicating with other offices, leading to duplication and confusion, especially regarding board funding."[31] The report quoted one board representative as saying, "INAC's left hand doesn't know what the right hand is doing."[32]

As well, the study cited other concerns. These included a lack of standard processes within DIAND for dealing with boards; a sense from boards that CIG, being headquarters-bound, was distant, inflexible, and "unaware of operational realities and challenges faced by the Boards" in terms of costs and workloads; disappointment on the boards' part that DIAND was unsupportive when boards encountered legal challenges and indeed, was sometimes "on the other side"; and frustration at the department's lack of rigorous enforcement of terms and conditions in licences and permits.[33] Department officials countered: "some Boards are operating outside of their regulatory mandate, and conducting work that is above and beyond what is necessary ... developing terms and conditions that are not realistic or defensible."[34] A few years later funding responsibility was indeed shifted from the Northern Affairs Program to Claims Implementation, though the lack of inflation adjustment for core funding continued. Otherwise the report seems to have had little impact.

Given the Conservative government's pro-development approach and the distaste expressed by leading Conservatives for the regulatory processes in the

Mackenzie Valley, it was to be expected that they moved to "fix" the system. In November 2007, DIAND minister Strahl announced the wide-ranging Northern Regulatory Improvement Initiative highlighted by the appointment of Neil McCrank as his "Special Representative" charged with reviewing regulatory processes across the three territories, but with special emphasis on the NWT.[35] McCrank was a former chair of the Alberta Energy and Utilities Board, which gave him significant familiarity with regulatory issues but which also generated considerable suspicion on the part of environmentalists and others as to possible biases. The NWT's NDP MP, Dennis Bevington, was among the critics, commenting: "we've taken on somebody that's proved he can't run a utility board that can address the needs of people ... and we're going to put him in charge of deciding how our regulatory process works in the Northwest Territories."[36] He subsequently labelled McCrank "a hack."[37]

McCrank held fifty-five days of meetings across the North and elsewhere and convened a two-day roundtable in Yellowknife of "stakeholders and interested parties" to discuss potential changes to the regulatory process. His May 2008 report to the minister was titled *Road to Improvement* as a signal that his recommendations, some of which entailed "fundamental restructuring," were not aimed at subverting the system but at changing it for the better. (A DIAND employee recalls a meeting at which the minister introduced McCrank as the person who would "fix" the NWT regulatory system, whereupon McCrank described himself as working to "improve" it.)

As expected, the lion's share of the McCrank Report, as it was universally called, was devoted to the NWT; only three of thirty-eight pages dealt with Nunavut and Yukon. Two central principles drove the analysis. First, "the people of the North want and deserve to have the ability to co-manage the development of [renewable and non-renewable] resources with government."[38] In seeking to ensure the important goal of local involvement in resource development, McCrank wrote, "a regulatory structure has been created with too many regulatory bodies that do not (and will not) have the capacity to perform their duties. This complex structure is the result of the interpretation of the comprehensive land claim agreements and the MVRMA. While the goal is laudable, the execution of the processes is such as to hinder, rather than enable, resource development."[39] Thus the far-reaching restructuring McCrank proposed was "not an attempt to diminish or reduce the influence that Indigenous people have on resource management in the North."[40] Second, the numerous criticisms levelled at it "call into question the very structure of the regulatory system."[41] In particular McCrank voiced significant concerns about the neutrality of board members, timelines, the system's consistency and predictability, inadequate coordination between boards and governments and within governments, and the lack of clear mandates, noting "serious allegations that the regulatory bodies are tempted to act outside their mandate."[42] These and other deficiencies, he argued, "can be addressed and remedied."[43]

Beyond proposing options for bringing about fundamental restructuring, McCrank set out eighteen specific recommendations relating to regulatory processes in the Mackenzie Valley. An additional four recommendations pertained to Nunavut and Yukon; the Inuvialuit Settlement Region was not within his remit. As McCrank noted, many of these recommendations had been proposed in earlier reports. The more important of these specific recommendations called for completion of land use plans, improved board capacity (but no participant funding), development of "effective timelines," legislation to clarify criteria for triggers for environmental assessments and reviews, better enforcement, and more timely appointment of board members by the DIAND minister.[44]

McCrank left no doubt in his eighteen recommendations that more than tinkering was needed. He offered two options for achieving fundamental restructuring. Four far-reaching recommendations underpinned both: completion of regional land use plans, provision of adequate funding for the MVLWB, and establishing both the MVLWB and the MVEIRB as final decision-making bodies, eliminating the need for ministerial approval of board recommendations. It was on the fate of the three regional land and water boards that the two options diverged. McCrank clearly preferred Option 1, which would see the elimination of the regional boards with their functions folded into the MVLWB.

Option 1 may have been McCrank's preferred option but it was also the more difficult, for the report explicitly stated that it would necessitate the renegotiation of the Gwich'in, Sahtu, and Tlicho claims: "Section 35 [of the *Constitution Act, 1982*] protection," he wrote, "cannot be legislated away."[45] In light of the subsequent political conflict over the constitutionality of key features of Bill C-15, McCrank's conclusion that the regional land and water boards could not be purged without amending the claims, requiring the agreement of the affected Indigenous governments, is noteworthy. McCrank had impressive legal credentials, having served for nearly a decade as deputy minister of justice in the Alberta government.

Option 2 would not, in McCrank's view, be as effective but had the advantage of probably not requiring the claims to be reopened.[46] It would see the regional boards continue "but as administrative boards only, with no quasi-judicial responsibilities."[47] It was not entirely clear what this meant beyond the regional boards becoming subservient to the MVLWB in the decision-making process. Disadvantages to Option 2 included continuing complexity and mis-allocation of funds.[48]

At the press conference at which his report was released, McCrank put forward a significant argument that did not appear in *Road to Improvement*. Recognizing that local input was essential to the process, he said that it should take place at "the right point": at the land use planning stage rather than when complex applications were being processed, which "should be handled by a professional regulatory body."[49]

The Pollard Mission

Among the Conservatives' promises in the 2008 election campaign was a com-mitment to implement the McCrank Report.[50] It took some time to put the pieces in place, but in a May 2010 speech to the NWT Chamber of Commerce, DIAND minister Strahl announced the Action Plan to Improve Northern Regulatory Regimes. The action plan would go further than the McCrank rec-ommendations to ensure "more certainty and timeliness and less regulatory overlap and duplication." The minister was at pains to emphasize that the reform process, entailing far more than consolidating the land and water boards, would "continue to build on strong partnerships with Aboriginal governments and organizations that have been established and maintained through land claims agreements." "Land and water board restructuring," he added, "will not elimin-ate the co-management approach or the shared decision making approach to resource development that is rooted in the land claim agreements."

A key element in moving the process along was the appointment of former NWT finance minister John Pollard as chief federal negotiator responsible for dealing with government, First Nations, and industry in developing a "stream-lined" system of land and water boards.[51] From the outset, Pollard maintained that in reforming the land and water boards – possibly including wholesale consolidation – it would not be necessary to reopen the Gwich'in, Sahtu, and Tlicho land claims.[52] Few in the NWT agreed, but his position reflected the opinion of the federal government's lawyers.

Although Pollard reported to the DIAND minister, his mission was a cabinet-level initiative overseen by the Prime Minister's Office. Pollard's remit extended only to the structuring of the land and water boards; it excluded the MVEIRB and such fraught procedural issues as the definition of "public concern." Among his tasks was enticing the Inuvialuit, whose claim included a separate environ-mental system, into the Mackenzie Valley regime. Nellie Cournoyea, the powerful head of the Inuvialuit political organization, the Inuvialuit Regional Corporation, and a former premier, declined to become involved, though she did indicate a willingness to reconsider based on how the revamped MVLWB worked out.

Pollard was assigned a DIAND lawyer and, through another DIAND staffer, had good access to whomever he needed to consult in Ottawa, including in other departments. He had little contact with the team of policy analysts and lawyers working on the amendments to the *MVRMA*. Pollard's was a political, not a bureaucratic task, which culminated in oral reports to the minister, one of which recommended the eleven-member structure for the MVLWB contained in Bill C-15.[53]

Among the issues that stirred controversy and undercut Pollard's credibility with Indigenous leaders was his prediction about how large and unwieldy the MVLWB would become unless regional land and water boards were eliminated. The current membership of twenty, reflecting the five members of each regional board, would, he argued, balloon to forty or more once the claims still under negotiation were settled, with each region establishing its own land and water board whose members would also sit on the "big board."[54] Indigenous leaders hotly disputed this claim, pointing out that in only two of the pending claims was there an expectation that a land and water board would be created.[55] They might have added that once all claims were settled the entire NWT would be within the jurisdiction of a regional land and water board, hugely reducing the MVLWB's workload. Nor did Pollard win much Indigenous support by pointing out, as he frequently did, that the Mackenzie Valley-wide Dene-Métis claim, which came close to finalization, included a single land and water board and that its collapse in 1990 had nothing to do with the regulatory regime it proposed.

Pollard made a good deal of the inconsistencies industry encountered in dealing with different boards. In this he was on solid ground, though one experienced board staffer argued that, while some inconsistencies did reflect idiosyncratic variations lacking any rationale, others were legitimately rooted in the differing circumstances and priorities characterizing the various regions. Still, industry, especially oil and gas companies, could point to similar applications producing different outcomes under different boards. As noted in Chapter 5, the boards had been working on improving cooperation and consistency since well before the McCrank Report, though it is fair to say that, as the McCrank and Pollard processes unfolded, they recognized their vulnerability to charges of inconsistency and devoted particular attention to improving coordination across all the *MVRMA* boards.

Unsurprisingly, Pollard encountered hostility from Indigenous leaders, some of whom reportedly refused to meet with him and others who spoke in their own languages, which he did not understand. Towards the end of his mandate, he was asked to leave before the start of a scheduled meeting with Indigenous leaders, who were aggrieved by what they said was short notice of the meeting, which had been organized by DIAND. He was invited to return later in the day, but the atmosphere was not helped by logistical issues: an inadequate sound system and a lack of translators.[56] According to one of those present at the meeting, Indigenous leaders were unanimous in their opposition to the proposal to eliminate the regional land and water boards.[57]

Pollard held over fifty meetings, roughly half with First Nations, though dissatisfaction was evident among Indigenous leaders as to the process. Ethel Blondin-Andrew, head of the Sahtu Secretariat, told a Senate committee: "Mr Pollard would appear, drop a load of information and disappear for 10 months. We were in a begging position asking for information, for details. We got none."[58] "We feel this is a flawed process on behalf of the aboriginal people," said Łíídlįį Kų́ę́ First Nation chief Jim Antoine, a former NWT premier: "We're not taken seriously. We're back in the old colonial days where a power from Ottawa is telling us what to do with no respect for our treaty rights."[59] Nor did Pollard's management style endear him to key participants. One board official recalls receiving a letter from Pollard just before Christmas outlining his recommendation that the regional land and water boards be eliminated – a letter that was held back from board staff until January lest their holidays be ruined by fears of losing their jobs.

According to Pollard, his consultations and his recognition of the importance to Indigenous people of local involvement led to his suggesting to the minister, and the minister approving, several changes to the draft legislation designed to respond to concerns he encountered. These included setting the normal panel size at three in order to facilitate, but not require, panel travel to regions; encouraging the MVLWB chair to include on a panel dealing with an application in a particular region the board member from that region; and requiring the minister to consult the MVLWB before appointing the chair.[60]

The Boards Respond

Well before the McCrank Report, the land and water boards, recognizing the validity of industry's complaints about inconsistency across boards, had initiated a number of projects aimed at better coordination and consistency. Six working groups had been formed to look at both technical and administrative issues and a chairs and executive directors committee was established to oversee the reform process.[61] The various policy guidelines that were produced, such as those on water and effluent quality and on document submission standards, went some way towards overcoming industry's criticisms of inconsistency across boards but did not dissuade the government from its plans to consolidate the regional boards into what was being called the "super-board," a term disliked and disavowed by federal officials.

In May 2011, the MVLWB, in concert with the regional boards, published a paper setting out the boards' position on regulatory reform. "Perspectives on Regulatory Improvement in the Mackenzie Valley" was not defensive in tone. Instead, it affirmed the role of the regional boards and set out a wide-ranging reform agenda, premised on the view that "the system is not broken; rather it is incomplete."[62] Noting that, because of its genesis in comprehensive land claims agreements, the regulatory regime in the Mackenzie Valley is indeed different from those elsewhere in Canada, the document pointedly notes that it "is effectively a 'negotiated' regime, making the 'spirit and intent' of the land claims a fundamental underpinning of the system."[63]

As previous analyses had done, "Perspectives" divided issues of concern into those within and those falling outside the boards' jurisdiction. The former, it was argued, were being addressed internally by the working groups and other processes. The latter – and many of their solutions – had been identified by McCrank, by the NWT environmental audits, by reports of the auditor general, and by other studies. Several of the proposed reforms in the "Perspectives" document echoed McCrank's recommendations; indeed, they were explicitly set alongside specific recommendations from *Road to Improvement*. They need not be repeated here, though some key points of difference with McCrank warrant highlighting. Where McCrank had proposed that the MVLWB be made the final decision-making body (within, of course, the context of eliminated or weakened regional boards), "Perspectives" did not address this issue.

The boards' proposals went beyond McCrank in two important areas: the need for participant funding and the proposal that the boards be given responsibility and resources for inspection and enforcement.[64] Over the years, Ottawa had refused repeated entreaties for participant funding and was unlikely to change its position at this point. Nor was the federal government enthused about turning over inspection and enforcement authority to the boards for fear of compromising the neutrality of the regulatory process, though the Nunavut Impact Review Board's long-standing inspection powers had not occasioned complaints of bias.

Bill C-15

Process

Within DIAND, policy and drafting work had been under way for some time on amendments to the *Mackenzie Valley Resource Management Act*. As early as 2006 a "Joint Examination Project" (JEP) had been established on the act with representation from the federal and territorial governments, the Gwich'in Tribal Council, the Sahtu Secretariat Incorporated, and the Tlicho Government. As notable as the composition of the working group was the lineup of those excluded: representatives from the "unsettled" areas and the boards themselves. One senior board official links DIAND's fundamentally flawed approach to the bitterness that emerged over amending the act:

> The consultation process initiated by DIAND treated the land claim organizations as just another stakeholder when they were not. They were partners with DIAND and the GNWT ... [The *MVRMA*'s unique status as an emanation of a constitutionally protected land claim means] it is only subject to change with the agreement of the land claim organizations ... The whole consultation process was doomed to fail because it was designed around this false premise and as a result the land claim organizations were upset with the process right out of the gate. Unfortunately, some good ideas and innovative thinking were "thrown out with the bathwater."

In March 2011, DIAND circulated to the GNWT, Indigenous governments and organizations, boards, industry, and NGOs a long document outlining problems with the *MVRMA* and potential legislative remedies. Based on reactions to that paper, a revised document was produced in August titled "Amending the MVRMA: Issues for Discussion," which bore the warning "For Discussion Purposes Only – Not for Public Distribution."[65] The revised paper explored a wide range of concerns and potential legislative changes, some minor and highly technical, others with far-reaching potential, such as participant funding, giving Indigenous governments the power to appoint rather than nominate board members (a power the Tlicho Government already had), and timelines. The issue of land and water board restructuring received only the briefest, non-committal treatment. A short follow-up document in November, which was not initially given to the boards, specified a limited number of issues and potential remedies to be pursued.[66] Most would be subject to "policy discussion meetings" with Indigenous governments and organizations as well as boards. Some would go directly to the drafting stage, subject to subsequent consultation. Land and water board restructuring was not mentioned under either rubric.

The November document was premised on an expectation that some *MVRMA* amendments would require revisiting the settled land claims:

> AANDC proposes to move forward with the amendments to the MVRMA that the JEP Working Group reached consensus on, with supporting amendments to the Gwich'in Comprehensive Land Claim Agreement and the Sahtu Dene and Métis Comprehensive Land Claim Agreement (as agreed by the JEP Working Group), if the organizations that composed the working group continue to support the agreed upon changes.[67]

An entirely separate process unfolding at the same time involved the negotiation and drafting of a devolution agreement with the GNWT. Territorial politicians had for decades been trying to get Ottawa to transfer control over – not, at this point, ownership of – non-renewable resources. Most other province-like powers, such as health, education, social welfare, and renewable resources, had been devolved to the GNWT from the 1970s on. Lack of acceptance by Indigenous leaders of various devolution proposals over the years had been instrumental in their failure. An agreement-in-principle was signed in 2011 with the GNWT and several, but by no means all, Indigenous governments and organizations. The final agreement was signed in June 2013.

From a legal standpoint, implementing devolution was complex, entailing amendment or repeal of a number of federal statutes. This included bringing elements of the federal *Northwest Territories Water Act* into the *MVRMA*. Thus in the spring and summer of 2013 some four separate bills were in preparation. Consultations on revisions to the *MVRMA* had been held separately from those on the legislative changes necessary for devolution. This reflected the fact that, while a limited degree of overlap existed between the two initiatives, overall they entailed very different issues. In August 2013, four sets of proposed changes were sent to Indigenous groups in a single package along with a request for comments.[68] The consultation process on the draft bill differed notably from the model followed in drafting and revising the original *MVRMA*. In the 1990s, the DIAND staff drafting and redrafting the bill that would become the *MVRMA* operated with a transparency that had raised eyebrows in Ottawa officialdom. With Bill C-15, at meetings with DIAND officials about the draft bill all copies were watermarked and numbered to prevent wider circulation. This concern with confidentiality was not unique to the *MVRMA* process; it had become standard procedure under the Harper government. It did mean that for certain aspects of the process some players were excluded since they were not prepared to be constrained by confidentiality requirements.

In that parliamentary time is one of the most valuable commodities in Ottawa, it was never in the cards that DIAND would be permitted to bring forward to Parliament four different NWT-related bills. What did come as a surprise to many, and a most unwelcome surprise at that, was that when Bill C-15, the *Northwest Territories Devolution Act*, was introduced for first reading on December 3, 2013, it included not just the changes necessary to bring about devolution but also a wide range of amendments to the *MVRMA*, including elimination of the regional land water boards and a fundamental restructuring of the MVLWB. At least one Indigenous government only learned of this bundling when the bill was introduced in Parliament, while another noted that DIAND officials in the previous four or five years had treated the devolution and *MVRMA* amendment processes as essentially unrelated.[69]

This "omnibusing," as one critic termed it, had far-reaching implications for the *MVRMA* amendments. All of the Indigenous governments with settled land claims, and thus regional land and water boards, had signed on to the devolution agreement and were strong supporters but adamantly opposed land and water board restructuring. When the Conservatives refused to split the bill, as demanded by NDP and Liberal MPs, Indigenous leaders were left affirming their support for devolution while railing against key provisions of Bill C-15 affecting the land and water boards. Indigenous governments could and did loudly proclaim their opposition to board restructuring, but the GNWT was effectively neutered by the Conservatives' ploy. Devolution ranked as perhaps its top priority, so that, whatever its true feelings, the GNWT was not prepared to jeopardize the long-sought agreement and thus meekly accepted the planned elimination of the regional land and water boards and led the cheerleading for the bill.

In speaking about the bill before the Aboriginal Affairs and Northern Development Committee, DIAND minister Bernard Valcourt said that, had it not been for the GNWT's desire to proceed with devolution on an expedited basis, he might have brought forward two bills. A DIAND official involved in the process confirms that, had it not been for the GNWT's urgent insistence on fast-tracking devolution, *MVRMA* amendment and devolution would likely have been implemented via separate bills. GNWT deputy premier Michael Miltenberger explained to the committee that the GNWT was concerned that Ottawa's 2015 target date for effecting devolution could prove uncomfortably close to the NWT election, set for October 2015 but subsequently moved back to November. The GNWT wanted to avoid delay, fearing "the process would have been stuck between elections and between governments. We were fully intent on moving this forward so it could be concluded within the life of the government."[70] Ottawa's price for agreeing was having its regulatory reform legislation passed at the same time.[71]

If the NWT cabinet was not prepared to push back on the *MVRMA* elements of Bill C-15, some NWT politicians were. In February 2014, Yellowknife MLA Bob Bromley put forward a motion to the Legislative Assembly seeking to mitigate the bill's provisions relating to the land and water boards. The NWT legislature could not, of course, amend federal legislation, so Bromley's motion sought to have the GNWT "work with our regional Aboriginal government partners to determine the desirability and feasibility of establishing and staffing regional offices as a basis for ensuring meaningful input into land and water management issues ... [and that it] make a public commitment to work with future federal governments to delay the elimination of or reinstate the regional land and water boards."[72]

Save Premier Bob McLeod, who spoke on behalf of the government, only "regular" – non-cabinet – MLAs spoke in the debate, most echoing Bromley's arguments that eliminating the regional land and water boards was a step backwards, promising as it did a sharp curtailing of local involvement in important environmental processes as well as heightening adversarial tensions in environmental assessment and permitting processes. Perhaps the most interesting contribution was that of Sahtu MLA Norman Yakela, who had been one of the Indigenous negotiators on the Sahtu Dene and Métis claim. "When we settled our land claim," he said, "we understood in the future, once all the other regions had come to a point of settling their own land claims, we would look at a territory-wide board ... We said okay, but based on our elders' guidance ... we wanted decisions to be made as close to our communities as possible on our own lands." Accordingly, regardless of the possibility of an eventual territory-wide board, the spirit and intent of the treaty, as those in the Sahtu understood it, was to assure strong local involvement in decisions affecting Sahtu lands and waters. Bill C-15 thus contravened the spirit and intent of the claim: "They [the federal government] sure fooled me as a former negotiator of the Sahtu Dene/Métis Land Claim that our guaranteed participation, our constitutional rights, can be played with in a modern treaty."[73]

The premier's response defended the proposed new *MVRMA* regime in terms both of its effectiveness and capacity to identify and consider regional concerns and of its constitutional propriety. The motion, he told the House, contained "a number of factual errors," though a close reading of his remarks suggests not factual errors but differences of interpretation.[74] With three regular MLAs joining the entire cabinet in voting against it, the motion was defeated eleven to seven.

Content

Few features of Bill C-15 relating to devolution excited much attention, save the unsurprising rejection by leaders from the Dehcho, Akaitcho, and the Dene Nation of the entire notion that Ottawa could transfer to the GNWT authority over lands and governance. These organizations adamantly maintained that neither they nor their forebears had ever agreed that Ottawa should have any such authority. The extensive amendments to the *MVRMA*, which constituted three-fifths of the 126-page bill, did generate widespread, often vehemently critical, reaction. The DIAND officials drafting the *MVRMA* amendments had been assigned three fundamental objectives: board restructuring, imposition of timelines, and provisions for cost recovery for board processes. By far the most contentious features of the bill were the provisions to eliminate the regional land and water boards and restructure the MVLWB. Bill C-15 also made a host of other changes to the *MVRMA*, some minor, some substantive; many garnered wide support and little controversy. Among the most significant proposed changes:

- Bill C-15 affirmed the provisions of the *Devolution Agreement* by which the federal minister delegated many of the powers and duties held under the *MVRMA* to the GNWT minister of lands and the minister of environment and natural resources provided that no part of a proposed development involved federal lands. It is noteworthy that this authority was delegated rather than transferred.
- Timelines were specified for many elements of the screening/EA/permitting process.[75] Significantly, time limits were imposed for ministerial responses to EA reports. Few of the new time limits were firm, however; provision was made for the minister to authorize two-month extensions with further extensions possible. Most participants indicated that they did not expect to encounter difficulty meeting the time limits. Criticism arose in that developers were accorded leeway to stop the clock in order to provide or collect information or conduct studies, but communities and Indigenous organizations were not allowed the same privilege to collect and report traditional knowledge.
- The new timelines were consistent with those in the *Canadian Environmental Assessment Act (CEAA)*.[76]

- "Development certificates" modelled on the project certificates in the pending *Nunavut Planning and Project Assessment Act* were instituted as a means of implementing and enforcing non-biophysical "orphan measures."
- The DIAND minister was given authority to issue policy direction to the MVEIRB and the land use planning boards; previously, only the MVLWB was subject to such directives.
- Maximum levels of fines were raised and provision made for recovery of EA and EIR costs from developers.
- A serious potential problem of lost quorum or aborted EAs/EIRs was avoided through a provision authorizing the federal minister to extend the about-to-expire terms of MVEIRB or EIR panel members until the EA or EIR in which they were engaged was complete.
- Decision-making power on EAs and EIRs, previously held by a variety of ministers, was consolidated in the DIAND minister.

Beyond these and other changes to the *MVRMA*, in several instances provisions of the act that had attracted criticism were untouched. Bureaucrats working on amendments were instructed that the package should be revenue neutral, which, among other things, meant no move in the direction of better participant funding. The terms "public concern" and "significant public concern," which so exercised industry, were neither changed nor defined, in keeping, one senior DIAND official pointed out, with the approach in other Canadian environmental assessment legislation, including the *Canadian Environmental Assessment Act*.[77] The federal government retained the power to appoint board members. One former GNWT official suggested that this in part reflected Ottawa's concern that the GNWT had been nominating too many "bozos" to be trusted to make good appointments. Retention of this power paralleled the situation in Yukon, where Ottawa continues to make the appointments to the Yukon Environmental and Socio-economic Assessment Board

The lightning rod for opposition to the *MVRMA* provisions of Bill C-15, especially among Indigenous governments and organizations, was the proposed elimination of the regional land and water boards and the restructuring of the MVLWB. The Gwich'in, Sahtu, and Wek'èezhìi land water boards would simply disappear. DIAND minister Valcourt, his officials, and Premier McLeod all offered vague commitments as to retaining or creating some regional structures or processes to facilitate local involvement in land and water licensing and permitting, but no clear or concrete proposal came forward. Unsurprisingly, these pledges failed to assuage criticism.

The MVLWB was to be scaled back from twenty members (with the prospect of additional members should pending land claims be settled) to eleven and was unlikely to grow further. Save the member from the Tlicho region, who would be appointed by the Tlicho Government, members would continue to be appointed by the DIAND minister: one on nomination of the Gwich'in Tribal Council, one on nomination of the Sahtu Secretariat, two on nomination of the GNWT, and two in consultation with First Nations lacking finalized claims. A reasonable presumption was that the latter two members would be Indigenous, but this was not specified. The minister would also appoint three "federal government" members and the chair. Opponents of the restructuring noted with concern a change in the language surrounding the appointment of the chair that would enhance Ottawa's power over the board. Under the existing act, the minister was expected to appoint as chair a person nominated by a majority of the board members, though notably this had not happened with Todd Burlingame. The new provision would only require the minister to seek the board's advice before appointing the chair and he or she would not have to do even that for the appointment of the first chair of the restructured board.

When an application for a licence or permit or another matter would come to the board, three members would be selected by the chair to review and decide on the matter, at least one of whom would be an Indigenous government nominee/appointee or someone who had been appointed following consultation with First Nations in the unsettled areas, and at least one of whom would be a federal or territorial nominee/appointee. If necessary, the chair could add more members to the panel dealing with an application; the bill was silent on their provenance. In a provision greeted with scepticism and alarm by Indigenous leaders, the chair was authorized to include nominees of Indigenous governments on panels dealing with matters within their settlement areas "if it [was] reasonable to do so."[78] "Reasonable to do so" struck the Indigenous leaders as well short of a guarantee.

In an attempt to placate opponents of board restructuring, Valcourt, McLeod, and other supporters of the bill held out hope of revisiting land and water board structures and related issues when the devolution agreement was reviewed by Ottawa, the GNWT, and the Indigenous parties to the agreement in five years. As opponents recognized, this was a good deal less than a guarantee of change since the agreement specified that a review of its *MVRMA*-related provisions would begin "no earlier than the fifth anniversary of the Transfer Date," that is, April 1, 2019. Moreover, negotiations to develop terms of reference for the review could only begin after the five years, and the review would only go forward if all parties agreed on the terms of reference.[79]

The Committee Hearings

As is routine for major bills, Bill C-15 was subject to committee hearings in both the House of Commons and the Senate. In the House, the Standing Committee on Aboriginal Affairs and Northern Development met six times in December 2013 and January 2014, including a day-long meeting in Yellowknife, to hear deputations. The Standing Senate Committee on Energy, Environment and Natural Resources held eight meetings on Bill C-15 from December to March.[80] Virtually all those who appeared before the Senate committee, many by videoconference, also made presentations to the Commons committee, making the same points, often using precisely the same language, to both committees. A number of witnesses, primarily those at the Yellowknife meeting, only appeared before the House committee. The Senate hearings, as is typically the case, were substantially less adversarial and politicized than those in the House committee, in part because, whereas Dennis Bevington, the NDP MP representing the NWT, consistently and aggressively challenged the government on the *MVRMA* amendments, no one from the NDP sat on the Senate committee.

In one sense the committee hearings were a pointless exercise in that no amendments were made to the part of the bill affecting the *MVRMA*. The NDP and the Liberals did propose a number of amendments but all were defeated by the Conservative majority; one minor amendment relating to devolution was made to the bill. In another sense, however, the hearings gave voice to deeply held views among virtually all Indigenous leaders that key elements of Bill C-15, and the process leading up to them, represented a serious breach of fundamentally important aspects of their constitutionally protected land claims and their trust-based relations with the federal government. As such the C-15 proposals and their fate stand out as important indicators of the influence – or lack of influence – of Indigenous peoples through a claims-based co-management regime. The intensity of Indigenous opposition to Bill C-15 that characterized the hearings doubtless also affected the Liberals' commitment to modifying it should they come to power.

The leaders of the three Mackenzie Valley Indigenous governments with settled claims – Grand Chief Eddie Erasmus of the Tlicho Government; Ethel Blondin-Andrew, chair of the Sahtu Secretariat; and Robert Alexie Jr., president of the Gwich'in Tribal Council – all appeared before both the House and Senate committees.[81] As well, representatives of the Dehcho First Nations, the NWT Treaty 8 Tribal Corporation, the Dene Nation, and the Katł'odeeche First Nation appeared before the House committee. This latter group opposed Bill C-15's proposed amendments to the *MVRMA*, some with considerable vehemence, but their more fundamental concern was with the concept and the reality of devolution, which they saw as illegitimate in light of their existing treaties with the Crown. The North Slave Métis Alliance also appeared before the House committee, primarily to argue that the devolution agreement "runs roughshod over our members' aboriginal rights" in that the alliance was excluded from the devolution process.[82] Harry Deneron, chief of the Acho Dene Koe First Nation, was the sole Indigenous leader in support of the *MVRMA* amendments, telling the committee "the super-board I have no problem with" and indicating basic satisfaction with the *MVRMA* regime.[83]

The full-day meeting of the Commons committee in Yellowknife was the defining episode in the committee hearing process. Presentations, followed by questioning, were made by NWT premier McLeod, Indigenous leaders, industry spokespeople, representatives of environmental NGOs, organized labour, and the Northwest Territories Association of Communities as well as Neil McCrank and John Pollard. Several deputants thanked the MPs for making the long trip north to gather information and opinion, though some frustration was expressed at the limited time available to them and at the committee's scheduling, which did not permit travel to the communities where regional board offices would be closed. Nor did it escape attention that simultaneous translation was offered between English and French but not for any of the territory's Indigenous languages.

Premier McLeod was the first witness. His presentation was, as had been his op-eds and numerous speeches, almost entirely about the desirability and importance of devolution. He recognized concerns about changes to the *MVRMA* regime but said that they should not delay devolution, adding that he expected, over time, the GNWT would take full responsibility for environmental regulatory processes and do so in a manner acceptable to its Indigenous partners.[84]

Subsequent presentations by Indigenous leaders from areas with settled claims, who stood to lose their land and water boards, were not so sanguine. After reiterating their support for devolution, they directed most of their comments to board restructuring. Three sets of arguments predominated. The first held that, while provisions of their claims did contemplate a single land and water board for the entire Mackenzie Valley, the Bill C-15 amendments to abolish the regional boards directly contravened the spirit and intent of the treaties. A second insisted that there was no evidence that doing away with the regional land and water boards would enhance effectiveness and efficiency and, indeed, that amalgamating boards was likely to render the system less effective and efficient. A third argument predicted a drastic reduction in the ability of local people to bring their expertise and their values into the regulatory system with potentially disastrous consequences for the environment and for their ways of life. Grand Chief Erasmus was especially eloquent:

> [Bill C-15 is] a bill that seeks to destroy what we had agreed to in our Tlicho agreement ... Tlicho's equal voice in those decisions about the use of land or water was at the heart of a promise enshrined in the Tlicho agreement ... Our voice is being silenced. We cannot and will not let this happen. We cannot let down our elders who told us that protecting our way of life was the most important thing ... Canada has returned to the old colonial way of thinking, that they know what is best for us. They are silencing our voice ... We need to be equal in decisions about the use of land and water in Wek'eezhii. There is no other way we can ensure that our way of life is protected. To the Tlicho there is nothing more important than this.[85]

Several witnesses, Indigenous and non-Indigenous, warned that proceeding with the "superboard" would generate acrimony and mistrust rendering environmental assessment and licensing more confrontational and more subject to delay and causing other problems for developers. Blondin-Andrew spoke ominously about potential Sahtu actions, including litigation and unspecified "other means," should the Bill C-15 amendments be implemented:

> If the MVRMA cannot protect the lands and waters of the Sahtu settlement area, the Sahtu will be forced to employ other means to protect its interests and maintain the integrity of the land claim agreement, including litigation. While such measures would likely result in protracted timelines and higher costs, the Sahtu may have no other option.[86]

Although they did not directly reference the arguments of Indigenous witnesses relating to their rights under the historic and modern treaties, representatives of the NWT Federation of Labour and two environmental groups, Alternatives North and Ecology North, were highly critical of Bill C-15's amendments to the *MVRMA*. The labour spokespeople told the committee: "creating one mega-board will only allow greater outside political interference in the development decision-making and will adversely affect working people in the Northwest Territories." They also stressed the difficulties local people would have in putting forward their views on proposed developments to a Yellowknife-based board as well as the negative economic consequences at the community level of shutting down the regional boards.[87] The witnesses from Alternatives

North voiced similar concerns about the ability of people to participate in regulatory proceedings affecting their regions and noted the close working relationship that existed between the regional land and water boards and the regional land use planning boards, which would be adversely affected were the regional land and water boards to be eliminated.[88] The written brief from Alternatives North and Ecology North made an additional point not raised in the committee meeting: the irony of a devolution bill characterized by multiple enhancements to the power of the federal minister at the expense of the GNWT and the boards.[89] The chair and senior staff of the MVLWB appeared before the committee but offered neither personal nor corporate views on the proposed board restructuring; rather, they suggested several important but technical changes to procedures affecting the board.[90]

Industry was represented at the Yellowknife meeting by officials of the NWT and Nunavut Chamber of Mines and of the NWT Chamber of Commerce; others appeared at a subsequent meeting. For the most part, their presentations were predictable: the Bill C-15 amendments to the *MVRMA* were "a step in the right direction" but further reform was needed. Tom Hoefer of the NWT and Nunavut Chamber of Mines cited continuing industry concerns over, among other things, "the unwarranted referral of the small exploration projects" to environmental assessment and the imprecision of the key term "public concern," the imbalance in the regulatory regime between the economy and the environment, lack of clarity on processes involving Indigenous consultation, and the proposed cost-recovery provisions.[91] The NWT Chamber of Commerce reiterated or expanded upon the points set out by Hoefer.[92]

Less expected from industry was a modicum of support for the regional land and water boards. Overall, both the Chamber of Mines and the Chamber of Commerce favoured board amalgamation. However, Hoefer not only acknowledged that "we recognize that the aboriginal community is validly concerned by the loss of the existing regional panels," he also noted that "a number of industry members, especially those who have developed close working relationships with the regional boards, have likewise expressed reservations."[93] Similar sentiments were expressed at the subsequent committee meeting by Rick Meyers, vice-president of the Mining Association of Canada: "In recent years we've seen an increase in the maturity and professionalism in board management and the processes that they administer. Our members have established productive working relationships with the regional panels. I particularly want to point out the Wek'eezhii board here. We want to emphasize the importance of those relationships, going forward."[94] So too, former NWT cabinet minister Brendan Bell, president of Dominion Diamond Corporation, a major player in both the Diavik and Ekati diamond mines, was effusive in his praise of the regional boards: "Our experience in dealing with the local boards, especially the Wek'eezhii Land and Water Board, a regional board, has been very positive. I think there's been some incredible capacity that has been developed there, and that needs to be maintained."[95] Both Meyers and Bell emphasized the need to maintain and support local involvement in regulatory processes. According to Bell, "the most important element here is local control – those who are most invested in the outcomes here are making the decisions."[96]

Implementation Plans and the Tlicho Court Challenge

Bill C-15 passed third reading in the Commons on February 2, 2014, whereupon it went to the Senate for formal review. The committee held several meetings beyond those held during "pre-study" before reporting the bill back to the Senate without amendment. Bill C-15 received third reading on March 3, with Royal Assent following three weeks later. That did not mean, however, that the bill immediately became law. As is typically the case with complex legislation requiring substantial administrative preparation, many elements of the bill did not come into force immediately. In some instances, such as the main components of devolution, specific dates were mandated on which certain sections of the bill would become operative. Other sections would come into force "on a day to be fixed by order of the Governor in Council [the cabinet]." This procedure, termed "proclamation," is often employed when it is uncertain when the necessary administrative machinery will be ready. Giving cabinet discretion as to when various parts of a bill would actually become law meant, however, not only useful flexibility but also the possibility that some sections would never be proclaimed. Governments are under no legal obligation to bring into force sections of acts that have not been proclaimed. Sections 136 and 137 of Bill C-15, which would have consolidated the land and water boards, were among those to be proclaimed by the cabinet; the target date was April 1, 2015.

With consolidation looming, staff of the land and water boards were deeply engaged in planning for the new regime. The restructuring elements of the act did not specify how staff and administration were to operate, offering considerable leeway for designing the new system. A plan was developed with a single, centralized board but with decentralized staff in regional offices. Applications would not be assessed on a regional basis as before but on a functional basis, with oil and gas files handled in one office, mines in another, and so on. Overall, no jobs were expected to be lost, though some job descriptions would change and some staff might have to relocate. Though regional offices were to be maintained, stress and uncertainty was high among staff who did not know if their jobs were safe or in which community those jobs would be, but very few staff left during this period.

By the time Bill C-15 passed, it was generally, though not universally, accepted that, under a strict legal reading of the claims, Ottawa had the authority to do away with the regional land and water boards, consolidating them into a larger, though not necessarily Mackenzie Valley-wide, board. Section 24.4.6 of the Gwich'in claim reads:

(a) Where, by legislation, any other Land and Water Board is established having jurisdiction in an area which includes the settlement area, it shall assume the powers and responsibilities of the Land and Water Board in 24.4.1 and shall become the Land and Water Board for the purposes of this agreement.

(b) Legislation may provide for regional panels of the Land and Water Board in (a).

(c) The Gwich'in Tribal Council shall be consulted with respect to any such legislation.[97]

The Sahtu claim had almost identical language; wording of the *Tlicho Agreement* was slightly different but, federal lawyers maintained, had similar effect. As detailed above, Indigenous leaders and their legal advisors argued vociferously that abolishing the regional boards would constitute a clear and serious abrogation of the spirit and intent of their claims. In May 2014, the Tlicho Government launched a legal action in the Supreme Court of the NWT against the provisions of Bill C-15 relating to elimination of the Wek'èezhìi Land and Water Board and, by extension, the other regional boards. The action sought a temporary injunction preventing the federal government from proclaiming the operative sections of the act pending resolution of the constitutional status of board consolidation.

The Tlicho Government advanced several arguments, first and foremost, that "the [Bill C-15] amendments violate the Tlicho Agreement. Specifically, it argues the amendments violate the Tlicho Government's right to effective and guaranteed participation in the [*MVRMA*] co-management regime." It further contended that Ottawa's consultation process about the amendments was flawed in that it had already "firmly committed to its decision to overhaul the land and water regulatory regime." Failure to grant the injunction the Tlicho sought would lead, it asserted, to "irreparable harm." Finally, the Tlicho case argued the need for an injunction on the grounds that, should the restructuring ultimately be found unconstitutional, "the validity of decisions made by the newly structured MVLWB in the intervening period [would] be cast into doubt."[98]

For its part, Canada maintained that it did consult the Tlicho properly and that the wording of the *Tlicho Agreement* expressly sanctioned the elimination of the Wekʼeezhìi Land and Water Board and the transfer of its functions to a larger board. Ottawa also brought technical arguments to bear, most significantly that the court lacked the legal authority to issue an injunction preventing the cabinet from passing an order-in-council proclaiming sections of the bill in force and that doing so "would constitute an inappropriate intrusion by the Court into the executive's sphere of authority."

In February 2015, barely weeks before the relevant sections of the act would have come into force, Justice Karan Shaner of the NWT Supreme Court issued the injunction sought by the Tlicho Government. She made it clear that she was not ruling on the Tlicho's claims about Bill C-15's constitutionality or about the consultation process, but that she accepted that an important constitutional question was at issue and that it deserved full consideration. As well, she agreed with the Tlicho that "irreparable harm" would occur if the amalgamation went ahead prior to the resolution of the central constitutional questions, noting that the risk to the federal government in such a case was low whereas for the Tlicho the risk was high.[99]

The federal government immediately appealed, but the appeal had not been heard when the October 2015 election brought to power the Liberals, who directed that the appeal be put in abeyance. The new Liberal DIAND minister, Carolyn Bennett, responded to a question about the "superboard," saying: "Under a renewed spirit of respect and cooperation, we committed in the [election] campaign to undo the unilateral changes imposed by the previous government. We continue to work in partnership on a nation to nation basis with First Nations as well as the territorial government, and other stakeholders to move forward on the Mackenzie Valley Resource Management Act."[100] With the formal withdrawal of the appeal, the continuation of the regional land and water boards was confirmed. In November 2018 the federal government introduced a bill (C-88) to Parliament, which, among other things, repealed the section of the 2014 legislation that would have permitted, by regulation, consolidation of the boards. In June 2019, the bill was passed, eliminating the possibility that the regional land and water boards could be amalgamated into the MVLWB by cabinet decree.

Less than a month after assuming responsibility for decisions on most EAs, water licences, and land use permits, the GNWT minister of environment and natural resources signed the first water licence. Ironically, the first EA report completed after devolution went to the DIAND minister since the project involved federal lands. The first post-devolution EA for which the GNWT was responsible, on an amendment to De Beers's Snap Lake mine, went to the territorial minister in early September and was approved before the end of October.

Indigenous Influence?

What may we conclude from this and the previous chapter about the influence of the Mackenzie Valley Environmental Impact Review Board and the Mackenzie Valley Land and Water Board, and through them the influence of Indigenous people, on important environmental regulatory decisions in the NWT? When asked about this, one long-time board official had no hesitation in affirming that the co-management boards have hugely enhanced Indigenous influence over wildlife and land decisions and policies, noting, for example, that the MVLWB is "a powerful board chaired by an Aboriginal woman, taking very seriously the views and experiences of elders into account in reaching decisions."

Clearly, Indigenous people are extensively involved in board processes, as board members and as participants at hearings and as sources of written and oral information on proposed projects. Only a relatively few senior or technical board staff are Indigenous, but non-Indigenous staff are typically sympathetic to Indigenous interests and perspectives, not least because hiring is entirely in the boards' hands. Still, in most instances, the ultimate power to decide on major resource development issues rests not with the boards – and certainly not with Indigenous people – but with government, until recently DIAND, now primarily the GNWT.

It is nonetheless evident that, in important respects, the boards wield real power through the expertise – technical/scientific as well as traditional Indigenous knowledge – they bring to bear on large complex resource development proposals; in their capacity to establish the frameworks for negotiation of government approval of problematic projects; in their capacity to force government's hand, at least partially, through the requirement that their processes be completed before ministerial approval is granted; and, in some instances, through their authority to issue final, binding decisions.

The vehemence of industry criticism of the boards and the determination of the federal government to force fundamental restructuring of the land and water boards through Bill C-15 in the face of fierce opposition confirm the boards' status as powerful players in NWT governance. But do the Mackenzie Valley boards base their operations and decisions on the perspectives of

Indigenous people in a serious and systematic way? As in other facets of the *Mackenzie Valley Resource Management Act* regime, while the possibilities for improvement are substantial, overall the conclusion seems warranted that the boards strive to involve Indigenous people in their processes and to take their opinions and beliefs fully into account in making decisions. To be sure, lack of capacity at the community and First Nations level, exacerbated until very recently by the absence of participant funding, constrains Indigenous involvement and influence. Moreover, even post-devolution, Ottawa retains significant power over the boards in terms of appointments and funding as well as in the capacity to amend the *MVRMA*. Some academics maintain that Indigenous influence in co-management processes, such as those established by the *MVRMA*, is severely limited by comparison with what Indigenous people have had to give up in agreeing to abide by government-controlled processes. This argument is examined in the final chapter. At this juncture, an observation of the first NWT Environmental Audit seems apropos: the regulatory process in the NWT is "unique" in Canada by virtue of "the degree of community involvement, the proactive nature of this involvement and the influence that communities can have in the decision-making process."[101] In the NWT, since virtually all communities are overwhelmingly Indigenous, Yellowknife and Hay River being the principal exceptions, "community" is largely equivalent to Indigenous.

Assessing Indigenous influence in and through the MVEIRB and the MVLWB is necessarily imprecise and impressionistic. This is not to say, however, that substantial evidence cannot be adduced in support of the proposition that Indigenous peoples of the NWT do indeed possess significant influence on environmental regulation through the boards. Especially persuasive here are the powers of the Tlicho Government. Not only does the Tlicho Government appoint, rather than nominate, board members, it exercises decision-making authority at least equivalent to that of the GNWT when it comes to approving or rejecting environmental assessments on Tlicho lands. As well, it has the power to issue binding policy directives to the Wek'èezhìi Land and Water Board, a power denied the GNWT.

Community and Indigenous influence on the process, and on eventual resource management decisions, is, to an important extent, a function of the degree to which traditional knowledge is incorporated into the operations and the decision making of the Mackenzie Valley boards. A detailed analysis of this key topic must await Chapter 8, but a preliminary conclusion can be offered at this point. Many participants in the *MVRMA* process, especially Indigenous participants, voice significant reservations as to how extensively TK is used by the boards. Yet a significant body of work maintains that recourse to TK has substantially enhanced Indigenous people's influence in resource management. A close study of TK in the MVEIRB, significantly titled "These Days, We Feel We Have a Say," concludes: "the greater authority given to [TK] has ... been one of the major factors in shifting power in [resource management] to Aboriginal organizations ... The incorporation of indigenous knowledge under the MVRMA represents greater local decision-making capacity with regard to resource management."[102]

Chapter 5 cites instances of proposed projects either rejected outright or approved subject to stringent conditions arising from taking TK into account during environmental assessments. A small but telling TK episode involved Gabrielle Mackenzie-Scott, a Dene member (and later chair) of the MVEIRB, during a public hearing on a proposed diamond drilling project:

> A Dene woman stepped forward, pleading with the board to protect the area because her baby teeth were buried there. "A lot of people would have found that to be strange, but I could relate to the woman," says Mackenzie-Scott. "She was about my age and I too had the experience of having my baby teeth buried in a ceremony. This was an important moment in life for both me and my mother. I know where my baby teeth are buried. Many people have sacred places like this."[103]

However, an emerging literature maintains that the concerns and experiences of Indigenous women are not accorded sufficient weight in Northern environmental regulatory processes. "Studies and reports documenting the perspectives of Indigenous women towards EA processes," one recent analysis concluded, "have suggested that EAs often do not adequately consider the gendered impacts of proposed projects ... Despite its importance ... the traditional knowledge of women is often ignored in formal decision-making processes involving resource development in the north."[104]

With political power and influence typically zero-sum affairs, the effectiveness of the Mackenzie Valley boards is hugely affected by their relations with government, initially DIAND, now primarily the GNWT. Board independence, in terms of funding arrangements, appointments, and the like are examined in Chapter 7, but some comments specific to the Mackenzie Valley boards are warranted here. A good starting point is the recognition that DIAND, let alone the entire federal government, has never behaved as anything like a unified monolith with an internally consistent stance towards the boards. From the outset, some federal officials were enthusiastic and supportive of the boards; others were, and continued to be, sceptical if not outright hostile. One of the initial MVEIRB members complained that, "at the beginning, DIAND treated the board like a band council, not like an independent board," while also acknowledging that in the early days the board could not have done its job without the support of the DIAND staff, who provided initial support before the board had fully staffed up with its own people. A wide spectrum of views exists within the board community as to the motives and behaviour of DIAND bureaucrats. At one pole of the continuum, efforts of the Board Relations Secretariat staff were widely acknowledged and appreciated by board members and staff, who saw the BRS as a valuable ally. Other board members and observers were rather less positive, though not all would be as critical as the board member who proclaimed: "The boards were created on the premise that the Aboriginal groups were to be partners, but DIAND treats them like stakeholders ... The feds would never treat the National Energy Board they way they do our boards, but because it's the North and [because] they don't respect the First Nations, they treat them like an arm of DIAND."[105]

At a political level, that the Harper government's attempt, which very nearly succeeded, to consolidate the land and water boards and to make other far-reaching changes to the *MVRMA* over the vociferous objections of virtually all local Indigenous people, stands as a noteworthy cautionary tale. Indigenous leaders strongly believed that the proposed changes to the act would have substantially diminished their influence, contravening the all-important "spirit and intent" of the claims. It is worth considering whether the level of Indigenous influence developed over the first two decades of the *MVRMA* regime is as precarious as this episode suggests.

As for the GNWT, many decisions once taken in Ottawa now rest with territorial ministers. Given that many, at times most, are Indigenous, it is reasonable to expect that they will be highly sensitive to the preferences of local Indigenous people, as expressed in board recommendations.

Paradoxically, a powerful indication of Indigenous influence in board decision making came in the form of a dissenting opinion from two Indigenous members of the MVEIRB in an EA report. In 2011, a board REA on Canadian Zinc Corporation's Prairie Creek Mine recommended approval of the project, without proposing formal measures to mitigate possible environmental damage. The six-page dissenting opinion concluded, among other things, that the majority report did not take sufficiently into account TK supplied by nearby Indigenous communities (or technical information from DIAND) and that it put too much credence in commitments from the proponent that were not legally binding. Overall, the two board members did not oppose approval of the mine: their position was that the board should have imposed more stringent and extensive measures on the project.[106] On the face of it, this episode suggests not Indigenous influence but, rather, lack of Indigenous influence. Its significance, however, lies in its exceptionality. Indigenous members of the MVEIRB and other *MVRMA* boards have typically been strong, forceful individuals prepared to voice strong opinions reflecting Indigenous values and interests, yet dissenting opinions, such as that on Prairie Creek, have been few and far between. Indeed, no other Review Board EA has included a dissent. This is not to suggest that divisions along Indigenous/non-Indigenous lines are unknown at the boards but, rather, that Indigenous board members are sufficiently satisfied with outcomes and so do not find dissenting opinions necessary.

Indigenous influence of a different sort is occasionally mentioned by participants in and close observers of the *MVRMA* regulatory regime. Both Indigenous and non-Indigenous interviewees said that, especially in the "unsettled" areas, Indigenous organizations and communities refer projects to environmental assessment, or threaten to do so, not out of genuine environmental concerns but to advance their political agendas. One Indigenous board member commented that Indigenous groups "call up projects [for EA] because they can; it's all about politics." In the case of the sawmill in Hay River alluded to in Chapter 5, the Indigenous leaders who challenged the mill's permit application publicly acknowledged that they did so for political rather than for environmental reasons. According to a Yellowknife-based federal bureaucrat, "assertions [about projects under the *MVRMA*] are being made to leverage negotiations." A former GNWT official cited an instance of a contract being taken away from one First Nation-owned company and given to another, lest "concerns," which would require an EA, be raised against a pending project by the second First Nation.

In a speech to a conference of oil and gas producers, Kenya Norwegian, chief of Łíídlįį Kų́ę́ First Nation in Fort Simpson, forthrightly set out the prospects for developers who failed to accept Dehcho conditions for projects. Referring to a recent settlement agreement between the Dehcho First Nations and Ottawa under which the federal government committed to refer to EA any project that concerned a Dehcho First Nation:

> Whether or not this change in the EA process will affect northern investment
> can only be answered by industry. Companies that 1) do not respect the right
> of Deh Cho communities to protect their lands and 2) refuse to negotiate
> project agreements will find themselves put into what can be a long and
> costly EA process. Conversely, companies that do respect the communities

and are willing to negotiate fair project agreements will not be impacted by this change and will likely be able to avoid the EA process.[107]

Nothing like a systematic inventory of NWT Indigenous leaders' views on the *MVRMA* regime exists, but a good many leaders, accepting that the co-management boards represent a compromise, indicated in interviews that they believe they have fulfilled their objectives. One senior negotiator on a finalized claim maintains that a key element behind the creation of the co-management boards was the desire of Indigenous leaders to ensure that local, Northern knowledge would be used as the basis for land and wildlife decisions by Northern people rather than by people from the South who didn't understand or have the same involvement with the land. Looking particularly at the environmental regulatory boards, he commented, "the spirit and intent [of co-management] is there."

Significantly, it is not only Indigenous leaders and organizations with settled claims and thus formal involvement in *MVRMA* processes who judge the boards a success. Consider the observations about the *MVRMA* regime expressed by the Katl'odeeche First Nation in a brief to the parliamentary committee on Bill C-15. KFN has long been among the more intransigent First Nations in the Dehcho region in terms of insisting on its treaty rights and opposing many elements of the DIAND-GNWT governance regime, and yet its views on the *MVRMA* are essentially positive:

> One of the main purposes of the MVRMA was to establish an integrated co-management system for the assessment and regulation of resource development projects in the Mackenzie Valley, consistent with concluded and pending regional land claims agreements and in accord with federal government constitutional obligations to include First Nations in resource management decisions associated with their traditional territories. It is KFN's belief that the structure established under the current MVRMA ... has fulfilled that purpose for those Aboriginal claimant groups that have settled claims, and that it has the adaptive capacity to address the requirements of those groups with pending claims, including KFN.
>
> From KFN's perspective, the current environment assessment (EA) and regulatory processes established through the MVRMA have allowed resource development projects to proceed while providing reasonable balance between environmental protection, respecting of First Nation rights, and territorial economic benefits.[108]

PART 3

A REVIEW OF THE KEY ISSUES

chapter 7

Issues of Board Independence

Formal independence from government, supplemented by strong informal norms reinforcing independence, is a standard design feature of regulatory boards and advisory agencies in Canada. Unsurprisingly then, the co-management boards established under the Northern comprehensive land claims are premised on independence from government. Yet if board independence in any context can be problematic, co-management boards and their members are, almost by definition, subject to endemic challenges to their independence.

This chapter explores issues of independence experienced by Northern claims-mandated co-management boards, with special emphasis on the tension between the imperatives of independence and the boards' co-management character. It begins by considering the appointment process and issues relating to the independence of members once appointed, including pressures on boards from governments, Indigenous as well as public. Staffing and support are discussed in the next section, followed by an examination of the boards' financial dependence on government and the implications for independence. Concerns about direct control, including the prospect that governments will fundamentally alter boards, or even abolish them altogether, are addressed in the following section. A final section offers an overall assessment of board independence.

Independence and Co-management

The explanation for how boards with independent members can be co-management boards is rooted in a pervasive co-management ethos. Both the boards themselves and what are sometimes styled their "co-management partners" recognize that the boards represent a political compromise by which the perspectives and the aims of government and Indigenous peoples are to be accommodated. By way of illustration, the website of the Mackenzie Valley Land and Water Board, which has a similar role in environmental regulation as various federal and provincial agencies, states:

> In sharp contrast to the provinces, the regulatory regimes in the NWT came about as a direct result of the negotiation of comprehensive land claim agreements and are based on two principles: a) Integration and Coordination; and b) Co-management of resources between governments and Aboriginal groups.[1]

The Nunavut Wildlife Management Board (NWMB) puts it this way:

> The Board is an independent administrative tribunal ... The NWMB acts as the primary decision-making agency within a co-management system of wildlife management. Co-management refers to a system of partnerships in which the partners – Inuit and Government – work co-operatively to assist the Board to make particular decisions, to conduct and commission research, and to provide approvals, advice, recommendations and information.[2]

The board also refers to its role in the decision-making process as "co-jurisdictional" with the territorial and federal governments.[3]

Michael d'Eça, the long-time lawyer for the NWMB, makes the intriguing argument that it is *because* of the independence of the board and its members that co-management works:

> The independence of IPG [institution of public government] members translates into credibility, and having credibility results in respect and cooperation. If both Government and Inuit know that an IPG is not a spokesperson or a representative of the other, then when that IPG makes a decision, everyone knows that it reached the decision without interference or undue influence from its co-management partners. It cannot be accused of simply being a mouthpiece for one or the other ... Although co-management thrives upon partnerships, and upon cooperation and shared management, decision-making takes place solely within the co-management agency – thus ensuring the agency's independence and credibility.[4]

This interpretation also provides an explanation for the similarity between the operation of "independent" boards and of true co-management boards, such as the Inuvialuit wildlife boards, in which members are explicitly designated in the claim as representatives of their nominating organizations.

Board Members: Appointment and Behaviour

Central to the boards' co-management character is the nomination and appointment process. Indigenous nominees or appointees are almost invariably Indigenous, but not all public government nominees are non-Indigenous. One long-time negotiator for Indigenous organizations voiced surprise at the character of government-nominated members once the boards became operational: "the [Indigenous] leadership would never have dreamed that government would appoint natives to the boards." Indeed, nominees of the Nunavut and NWT governments are often Indigenous, as on occasion are those of the federal government. The upshot is that, as the data in Table 2.4 show, on many boards Indigenous members are in the majority.

Since it impinges directly on questions of independence, it is important to recall that in most cases, while the territorial and Indigenous governments *nominate* members, it is the federal government that actually *appoints* members. In Yukon, the territorial government rather than the federal government appoints board members, some of whom are federal nominees, except for the Yukon Environmental and Socio-economic Assessment Board, whose members are federal appointees. For the most part, Ottawa accepts the nominations from the other parties, but from time to time it rejects nominees. Nominations are not made public, nor does the federal government give reasons for turning down nominees. On occasion complaints surface about Ottawa's rejection of nominees, but overall it is not possible to know how frequently nominees are rejected or on what basis.

Elements of co-management are often evident beyond the nomination or appointment of board members. A number of boards have, in effect, co-management provisions in their quorum requirements. By way of illustration, quorum of the nine-member Mackenzie Valley Environmental Impact Review Board is five, but two of the five must be nominees/appointees of Indigenous governments and two must be public government nominees or appointees. Further, when the board establishes a panel to conduct an environmental impact review, members of the panel, save the chair, must come in equal numbers from nominees or appointees of Indigenous and public governments.

Issues of Board Independence

National and provincial governments rarely attempt to direct the behaviour of members they have appointed to advisory and regulatory boards, but they typically appoint people whose views they find compatible. This truism applies no less to Northern claims boards. Thus the implicit presumption is that the Indigenous nominees and appointees of Indigenous governments will bring Indigenous sensibilities to their work and will defend and promote Indigenous interests in board activities. It is common for Indigenous organizations to solicit applications from land claim beneficiaries to fill board positions, sometimes explicitly seeking members to "represent" Indigenous organizations or interests.[5] With public governments, the expectation is not that nominees and appointees will toe some official line but that, in their board work, they will recognize the validity and importance of government interests.

This is not to imply that the boards are riven by rigid divisions between Indigenous and non-Indigenous members. To be sure, Indigenous board members may raise issues or express views that non-Indigenous members are unlikely to put forward. In actual decision making, however, boards strive for consensus and to a remarkable degree achieve it. Otherwise put, Northern co-management boards rarely experience clear Indigenous/non-Indigenous divisions.

A distinctive Northern wrinkle in all this reflects the small, tightly knit nature of territorial society. The entire population of the three territories is barely more than a hundred thousand, and, more significantly, each territory's political, bureaucratic, and business elites are small and closely intertwined. Accordingly, the possibilities of conflict of interest, a next-door neighbour to compromised independence, are extensive.[6] This is a perennial condition of territorial governance more generally but it is widely recognized and, for the most part, handled effectively. Still, in the Northern context, the observation of a senior DIAND official, who had been deeply involved in claims negotiations, is noteworthy: "in the early days [of board operations] no one – in government or the Indigenous organizations – really understood what independence of boards and board members meant." Boards take seriously the need for independence. For example, as noted in Chapter 3, new members of the NWMB swear to perform their duties "faithfully, truly, *impartially* and honestly."[7]

From time to time, Indigenous leaders or governments refer to "their" members on co-management boards, and Indigenous board members occasionally refer to themselves as "representatives" of the Indigenous organization that nominated or appointed them. Rarely if ever, however, is it the case that Indigenous board members are given or take direction from their nominating governments. One long-serving DIAND official, with extensive experience of co-management boards, commented: "The great success of the boards is the lack of politicization of the members. They really are there to serve the public and not to shill for whoever appointed them ... They don't bang the table in support of [say] the Gwich'in Tribal Council, though they may bang the table for the Gwich'in people." An Indigenous leader, noting that many boards and board members exhibit strong independence, "much to the chagrin of all three orders of government," declared: "it's a political nightmare to meddle with [board members]." According to a non-Indigenous advisor to more than one Indigenous organization during claims negotiations, who continued to work closely with various co-management boards, "many native leaders certainly expected that they would have control over their appointees"; however, with fixed terms for board members and provisions that they can only be removed for cause contributed to members seeing themselves as independent decision makers who are neither controlled by their nominating parties nor amenable to such control.

Of course independence is not just an issue for Indigenous board members. The person just quoted pointed to an important element of board dynamics that became evident as board operations began, a development Indigenous leaders had not expected: "the government appointees [to boards] were not hard-line bureaucrats pushing the government's line; they were very independent." Still and all, although public governments and Indigenous organizations rarely if ever try to influence their nominees/appointees on claims boards, members of boards and others familiar with them acknowledge that some members see themselves as representing particular interests and organizations.

Vacancies and Patronage

Appointments to boards are important but so too is the lack of appointments – vacancies on boards. Aside from reducing the range of experience and perspective among board members and increasing the workload of sitting members, vacancies can impede boards' ability to conduct business. If one or two positions on a board are vacant and one or two members are ill, absent, or unavailable because of conflict of interest, the board may lose quorum and be unable to meet. Worse, at times, due to vacancies, even if all board members turn up for a meeting this may not be enough to reach quorum. This is more than a theoretical possibility. Several boards have been hamstrung and unable to meet because they were short of members due to vacancies.

Vacancies occur to some extent because of federal rejection of Indigenous or territorial government nominees, but a more fundamental problem is pervasive delays in making appointments. Vacancies sometimes last for years; the position on the Nunavut Wildlife Management Board designated for the Canadian Wildlife Service lay unfilled for more than four years. In the case of the Mackenzie Valley Environmental Impact Review Board, six years passed without a Gwich'in-nominated member. According to Robert Alexie Jr., former president of the Gwich'in Tribal Council, "we have nominated about five people over five years [to the MVEIRB], and all five have been rejected by Canada for whatever reason. They don't give us a reason."[8]

The 2005 NWT environmental audit concluded that what it termed a "complicated and protracted nomination and appointment process" for board appointments had developed into a serious problem. Though all parties were responsible for delays in the nomination process, the federal government was singled out for special criticism for the complexity, and thus the sluggishness, of its appointment process. The review cited an internal DIAND study that noted:

> As it stands today ... [the process] involves each nomination package passing
> through a minimum of 24 pairs of hands in five different government operat-
> ing units before Ministerial approval is finalized. In total, the current process
> requires more than fifty discrete activities and steps. Appointments that do
> not follow the "standard" process invariably pass through additional steps
> and hands.[9]

The audit noted that as a result of the delays in making appointments, three of the six *Mackenzie Valley Resource Management Act* boards had experienced periods when they lacked sufficient members to constitute a quorum, one for nearly a year. Given the integrated regulatory process, this meant that the work of other boards beyond the one lacking quorum could be hampered. By way of illustration, in one instance the Gwich'in Land and Water Board was unable to issue a permit since the Gwich'in Land Use Planning Board could not, for want of a quorum, approve an exception to its land use plan.[10]

Imperial Oil, the lead proponent of the Mackenzie Gas Project, publicly complained about the untoward length of the permitting process attributable to delays in bringing board membership up to full strength.[11] In 2011, *News/ North NWT* reported that only two of thirteen regulatory boards were operating with a full complement of members and at least one was unable to meet because it lacked quorum.[12] An editorial placed the blame squarely on DIAND minister John Duncan for "taking his precious time, and wasting ours, to act on nominations."[13]

Similar complaints have been made in Nunavut about boards being unable to perform their duties for months at a time because delays in making appointments left them short of a quorum.[14] In this instance, a federal official said the vacancies reflected a lack of nominations from Nunavut Tunngavik Incorporated and the Government of Nunavut. Moreover, according to the official, the boards could still operate and render decisions without having quorum, a proposition the executive director of the Nunavut Water Board rejected.[15]

Various reports have examined the vacancy problem, noting its disruptive effects on board functioning and pointing the finger mainly at Ottawa as responsible for delays in making appointments. In 2007, consultants looking at the relationship between DIAND and Northern boards identified delays in appointment as a significant problem, commenting: "a solution is needed to speed up the review process at the Minister's Office; however, interviewees noted that it is difficult to know how to provide assistance at this level, as it is not clear what help is needed."[16] A report from the auditor general the same year concluded that delays in appointments to Inuvialuit boards resulted not from lack of timely recommendations from departmental officials but from holdups at the cabinet level.[17] A few years later, a Commons committee, in a wide-ranging study of co-management boards, called for a streamlining of the appointment process to resolve the problem of vacancies. Among its recommendations were paying closer attention to staggering appointments and extending existing appointments until new members were available or existing members were reappointed.[18]

Complaints about delays in making board appointments, notable while the Liberals held sway in Ottawa, became more strident still during the Harper Conservatives' tenure. Little changed when the Liberals returned to power in 2015. As evidenced by the data in Table 2.4, significant vacancies, caused by delays, continue to bedevil the appointment process. In 2017, Michael Neyelle, chair of the Sahtu Renewable Resources Board, went public complaining that his seven-member board had five vacancies and thus could not meet for lack of quorum.[19]

Especially galling for those affected by delays in appointment is the fact that all parties know precisely when a particular member's term will expire. Government bureaucrats who manage the process try to be proactive in anticipating the need for replacement or renewal of board members, but oftentimes they find that their preparatory work has disappeared into the political black hole that is the minister's office. At the same time, a former senior GNWT bureaucrat who was extensively involved in the appointment process maintained that in situations Ottawa saw as urgent – boards lacking quorum to deal with significant issues or needing a full complement of members to begin a major project – it was capable of making appointments "with the speed of light."

Delays in making appointments not only cause administrative problems. They also raise questions about the federal government's motives in rejecting nominees: whether Ottawa is subtly impinging on board independence by refusing to appoint board members not to its liking. At the same time, as a wise person once observed, in politics there is often less than meets the eye. Ottawa's delay in making appointments may reflect not attempts to undercut board independence so much as its cumbersome processes and the low priority often accorded claims boards, plus garden-variety partisan considerations, which were rumoured to be in play with the Gwich'in nominees to the MVEIRB. Moreover, often it is the "federal" positions on boards that remain vacant for extended periods.

Two further problems bedevilling the appointment process – patronage and lack of competence – may not directly impinge on board independence but certainly affect board operations. Though not common, instances of straight-up partisan patronage have occasionally marked board appointments. One former board chair commented: "you don't want people appointed to boards because they're being paid off for supporting a political party, but that has happened and it's caused problems." Especially given the small, extensively intertwined elites in the North, "patronage" involves more than politicians nominating or appointing their friends and supporters, who may be quite capable of serving effectively. It entails placing friends or supporters on boards because they are friends or supporters rather than because they possess the requisite competencies for the job. Those familiar with the boards generally agree that all three orders of government have engaged in patronage in their nominations and appointments, though the consensus is that the practice is now less common than in the past. Candidate screening and assessment remain opaque, but recruitment has become significantly more transparent, with federal and territorial governments periodically running ads in Northern newspapers soliciting candidates for board positions, and many Indigenous organizations doing likewise. Bureaucrats involved in candidate recruitment indicate that these ads attract substantial numbers of strong candidates and that the merit principle is followed in choosing among them.

Still, competence – or, more accurately, lack of competence – remains an issue for boards. Executive directors and chairs bemoan members who lack the capacity to understand or assess the complex materials before boards or who are unwilling to devote the necessary time and energy to engage effectively in board work.

Unquestionably, for some Indigenous governments and organizations finding good board members can be a challenge, considering that talent pools may be small but the demand for people to fill governmental positions (extending far beyond claims boards) is heavy. This problem is particularly evident in Nunavut. To be clear, this is not a backhanded way of suggesting that Indigenous elders and hunters who may have limited formal education lack the competence to serve on boards. What they may lack in terms of official credentials is often more than compensated for by their extensive first-hand experience and their ability to bring traditional knowledge to bear in board deliberations. Complicating the question of competence is the adequacy of board per diems and honoraria, which are widely thought to be too low to attract and retain good members.

Public Servants as Board Members

The question of independence arises very directly in the case of members employed by the federal or territorial governments that nominated or appointed them. Positions on some wildlife management boards are effectively designated for employees of specific governmental organizations. For other boards the practice may not be so explicit but public servants are nonetheless appointed as members. For still other boards, such as the Nunavut Planning Commission, the claim or the enabling legislation prohibits public servants from sitting as board members.

Only a small minority of board members are public servants, and such appointments seem to be declining in frequency. However, public servants' positions can become problematic in certain situations, though typically those appointed are aware of the need for independence, both real and perceived. Still, instances have occurred in which public servants serving on boards acted at their departments' behest.[20] A senior territorial government official, who noted that "governments like to have control of boards," was not aware of any overt attempts to give direction to board members who were government staff but argued that their position inevitably affects their behaviour. "The degree of independence of board members," this person added, "depends on whether one is a government employee ... Non-government employees don't feel a need to be mindful of the government position."

According to a former GNWT deputy minister, the territorial ethics counsellor once ruled that a GNWT employee serving as a member of a claims board was in a conflict of interest situation. The employee was removed from the board, despite being widely acknowledged as a strong appointee.[21] The GNWT subsequently developed a policy covering appointment of GNWT staff to claims boards and other "external" boards and committees. The policy recognizes that it may be appropriate and valuable to have GNWT staff on claims boards but that their responsibilities as GNWT employees remain operative. The policy does not seem to take account of the requirement that, other than for some *Inuvialuit Final Agreement* boards, members of claims boards are to act independently, in the public interest. It does not address this issue and consistently refers to such appointees as "representatives" of the GNWT.[22]

An interesting dynamic arises when, as occasionally happens, an Indigenous government or organization wants to nominate or appoint a GNWT employee to a claims board. In such cases, according to a senior GNWT official:

> The GNWT cannot tell an Indigenous government who they can and cannot appoint as their representatives; but it is made clear to employees that an appointment to represent a third party qualifies as "outside activity" under our Code of Conduct and that their DM [deputy minister] approval is required. In cases where a DM concludes that an employee could not easily represent the GNWT in their day job while representing another government outside their day job without the perception of conflict, DM approval to participate would be denied.

More common than the appointment of public servants to claims boards is the appointment of former public servants. Such members do not face the same issues of independence that may confront board members who are government employees. While former public servants are familiar with the activities and stances of their former departments, this by no means implies that they necessarily favour their former employers' positions. Indeed, it is not unknown for them to criticize government, including their former departments, vigorously. At a board meeting I attended, for example, a former public servant took the lead in vociferously arguing ("let's hold their feet to the fire") for strong action against his former department on an issue.

Chair Appointments

Board chairs can exercise substantial influence, selecting members to sit on panels, directing staff, and generally leading both internal board activities and dealing with external players such as governments. Accordingly, formal processes and informal practices for determining board chairs can impinge directly on issues of board independence. As mentioned in Chapter 6, the provisions in Bill C-15, which would have strengthened Ottawa's hand in appointing the chair of the MVLWB, generated concerns among Indigenous leaders about loss of independence on the board's part.

Chairs of some boards are appointed by the federal minister "on nomination" by the board, implying that the minister could reject a nomination but not impose a chair on the board against its wishes. In some instances the chair is chosen by the board from among its members. In yet other cases, the federal government has effectively unfettered power to appoint the chair.

As with most board appointment processes, selection of board chairs occurs behind closed doors. From time to time, though, conflicts over chair appointments, sometimes with significant potential to affect board independence, come into the open. Perhaps the most notable cases involved Todd Burlingame's appointment first as chair of the MVEIRB and subsequently as chair of the MVLWB, discussed in Chapter 5. At this remove, it is impossible to determine whether in appointing Burlingame to chair two important co-management boards the federal government was attempting to undermine the boards' independence. Certainly some saw it that way. What is not in doubt is the potential that these episodes reveal for government to use its appointment power to secure the outcomes it wants from co-management boards.

Staff and Support

All claims boards constantly interact with government. This occurs both through exchange of documents and at formal meetings as well as in informal back channel interaction, primarily at the staff level. Even when relationships are close and built on mutual trust – and, as documented earlier, trust can sometimes be in short supply – the boards remain separate and distinct from government. In particular they have their own staff whose mandate is to serve the boards rather than government. While the boards cannot match government's research and policy capacity, and indeed carry out little if any original research on their own, their staff have the expertise to evaluate technical reports and government policy analyses. When boards need expertise not available in-house, they engage consultants or other professionals. This could entail a single contract to conduct research or provide services such as IT support, or it could mean engaging private practice lawyers for long terms. Some boards have relied on the same lawyers for decades.

In a few instances, claims boards are supported by government staff. Significantly perhaps, the *Inuvialuit Final Agreement*, the first comprehensive claim finalized in the territorial North, specifies that staff support for several co-management boards is to be provided by government: the GNWT for the

Wildlife Management Advisory Council (NWT), the Yukon Government for the Wildlife Management Advisory Council (North Slope), and the federal government for the Environmental Impact Review Board and the Arbitration Board.[23] The reality for board independence, however, is less concerning than might be thought since much of the staff support for these boards comes from the Joint Secretariat, which, save in financial terms, is independent of both federal and territorial governments.

Reliance on staff support from government can prove problematic for board independence, both real and perceived, as is evident in Chapter 4's discussion of the Department of Fisheries and Oceans relations with the Yukon Salmon Sub-Committee.

An intriguing argument as to the implications for board independence when staff are government employees comes from a person with long experience of the Yukon Water Board. This person maintains that it is easier for board staff who are government employees to resist pressure because they enjoy greater security, by virtue of formal human relations procedures and union protection, than staff of small stand-alone agencies.

Finances

To what extent does the "golden rule of politics" – he/she who has the gold rules – apply to claims boards? Virtually all board funding comes from the federal government. For the most part, formal, highly detailed implementation contracts or plans, negotiated in concert with the claims, specify Ottawa's financial obligations to the boards. It might therefore be thought that board finances would be assured and accordingly that funding concerns would not threaten board independence. For several reasons, however, board funding is often more precarious than this would suggest.

First, funding levels in the implementation contracts were usually established before the boards were up and running, so that a good deal of guesswork went into determining prospective board budgets. Real-life financial needs often turned out to be greater than anticipated. Moreover, the implementation contracts were usually negotiated by people other than those who had negotiated the claim. Second, the implementation contracts were for a set period, usually a decade, and negotiations for new contracts have often proven protracted and difficult (claims board funding is only one of a great many components of the contracts, which can run to hundreds of pages). The most troubled contract renegotiation involved the Nunavut claim: when the original contract expired in 2003 several fruitless years of negotiation ensued. Even so notable a figure as

Thomas Berger was unable to bring about agreement. To this day a new contract has yet to be signed, though many of the key issues, including board funding, were resolved in 2015 when Nunavut Tunngavik Incorporated, the Inuit land claim organization, accepted a $255 million settlement in its billion-dollar suit against Canada for non-implementation of the Nunavut claim.

Third, for the environmental regulatory boards and, to a lesser extent, the land use planning boards, the implementation contracts principally covered core operating costs. Public hearings and other legally required formal processes can be costly and, more significantly, it may be all but impossible for boards to predict how many public hearings they will have to mount in a given period and how extensive, which is to say expensive, they will be. Such boards must thus routinely submit supplementary funding requests to cover the costs of public hearings that could not have been anticipated when initial budgets were prepared. Generally speaking, Ottawa provides the funding required for hearings, though sometimes at a lower level than requested and often with delays that generate cash flow problems for boards. At other times, however, supplementary funding is not forthcoming; two such instances are cited below. Finally, both core and supplementary funding are contingent on Ottawa's approval of board budgets and associated workplans. While boards appreciate that public money must be carefully managed, they maintain that it is not appropriate for federal bureaucrats to second guess the operations of institutions established to implement constitutionally protected treaties. Particularly objectionable from the boards' standpoint was that, for extended periods, Ottawa's preferred funding mechanism was the single-year contribution agreement, which did not permit year-end carryover of unspent money. Over time, boards were able to secure more flexible arrangements, so that most are now funded on a multi-year basis permitting carryovers.

Complaints about political intervention in board funding allocations have not been common, and, with the more solid financial footing NWT boards now enjoy, as outlined in Chapter 5, the scope for such activity has diminished. Still, the lament of Yellowknife-based DIAND officials towards the end of the first decade of the *MVRMA* regime are worth noting: "every year we resort to bandages in funding boards." These bureaucrats maintained that, overall, enough money was in the system for all boards but that some went to boards that didn't need it, leaving others short, and that attempts to take it away from those that didn't need it were often vetoed for political reasons. "There is," they concluded, "so much political interference."[24]

A major source of grievance is that, while financial scrutiny and budgetary approval are formally DIAND responsibilities, it is widely thought that DIAND officials are unwilling to stand up to Ottawa's powerful Treasury Board Secretariat on behalf of the boards and thus subject them to inappropriate standards and processes. One official of an Indigenous organization who had extensive experience of claims boards put it simply: "DIAND is terrified of Treasury Board." Northern co-management boards are hardly the only governmental institutions whose funding problems reflect a lack of familiarity and understanding of their work and circumstances on the part of government financial staff whose prime focus is cost containment. Nonetheless, especially given the distinctive, and unusually costly, character of government operations in the territorial North, it is an ongoing reality.

In the early days of the Mackenzie Valley boards, following a major confrontation between the MVEIRB and Ottawa over funding, one board figure remarked: "There's still a strong tendency for DIAND to try to control and manage board expenditures ... The board thinks this is a fundamental issue of independence ... DIAND controls boards by limiting their budgets." Subsequent interviews with board officials in the three territories suggest that overt federal attempts to control boards through their budgets are rare but that low-level interference with board finances, often in the form of unnecessarily complex processes and delays, is common. For the most part, board and federal officials agree that boards get the money they need but not the money they want. At that, not all boards would agree that they get the funds they need. By way of illustration, one board official observed that her board did have enough money for its core activities, such as public hearings, but little if any funding for other important endeavours such as outreach and training for board members and staff.

On occasion, however, boards have had requests for funding of core activities rejected. Ottawa's refusal to help the MVEIRB deal with a major funding crunch in 2013, leading to extensive staff layoffs, is related in Chapter 5. Although it had significant operational ramifications, this does not seem to be an instance of government attempting to undermine board independence, other than, perhaps, in terms of curbing what DIAND saw as the board's free-spending ways.

A more direct and dramatic challenge to board independence based on federal control of funding affected the Nunavut Planning Commission (NPC). The details are complex, with opinions widely divided as to the motivations of key players and the validity of their positions. The essential facts are as follows. After many years of work, in 2012 the commission produced a draft land use plan for Nunavut. Two years of consultations in Nunavut, Nunavik (Northern Quebec), Saskatchewan, and Manitoba followed. Along the way, Ottawa took the unusual step of commissioning an independent review of the draft plan, which pronounced the document "reasonable."[25] The commission scheduled a final set of public hearings for November 2014 in Iqaluit and requested some $1.7 million from DIAND to cover the cost. In June 2014, the NPC issued a press release, pronouncing itself "astonished by the refusal of Aboriginal Affairs and Northern Development Canada (AANDC) representatives to fund the Public Hearings" on the draft plan and postponed the hearings indefinitely.[26] Following a fruitless and increasingly confrontational series of exchanges between the commission and the department, the NPC brought a lawsuit against Ottawa in the Federal Court. Among the commission's allegations was that DIAND used its funding power to compromise the NPC's "independent integrity" and that problems relating to an Ottawa-imposed deadline for completing the plan "came about by way of political interference by federal ministers in the reappointment of the NPC chair, at the time."[27]

In 2015, the commission received significant new base funding as part of the settlement of the NTI suit against Canada mentioned above and dropped its suit, but it continued to ask for supplementary funding to hold the long-postponed public hearings, which eventually began in March 2017. Relations between the commission and the federal government improved little in 2015, at least until the election of the Trudeau Liberals in October (with former NPC chair Hunter Tootoo winning the Nunavut seat for the Liberals).

Linked to the question of funding public hearings for the draft land use plan was conflict over the NPC's handling of the massive Mary River (Baffinland) iron ore project on northern Baffin Island. According to the commission, one reason it needed supplementary funding for the planning hearings was that it had spent much of its core funding in reviewing the complex situation around Baffinland. Subsequently, in April 2015, the NPC decided that a major change proposed by Baffinland to its plans did not conform to the existing North Baffin Regional Land Use Plan. Without an amendment to the land use plan, Baffinland's proposed changes could not move forward in the regulatory process, but the commission stated that it lacked the funding to consider an amendment in a timely fashion. This did not sit well with the federal and territorial governments, both of which saw Baffinland as essential to economic development in Nunavut. Nunavut premier Peter Taptuna bitterly criticized the NPC for holding up a critically important job creation opportunity in pursuit of funding from Ottawa and suggested that Ottawa audit the commission to determine whether its claims of underfunding were justified. The federal government did just that, ordering an audit by a private-sector firm to assess whether the commission was properly funded. Commission chair Tootoo responded that the NPC had nothing to hide and that it annually provided detailed workplans and audited statements to Ottawa. Taptuna wrote to the federal minister requesting that he use his authority under the claim to pass Baffinland's application directly to the Nunavut Impact Review Board, bypassing the NPC. In explaining to reporters why he hadn't copied the commission on his letter to the minister, he said that he didn't want to be seen as interfering with the process.[28]

The audit, which was never made public, was not delivered until the new government took over. While it did turn up potential conflicts of interest involving consultants working for the board, apparently nothing in it suggested that the NPC was crying wolf over its funding situation.[29] As for the larger significance of this episode, it is difficult to avoid the conclusion that the audit was at least in part designed to intimidate the commission and to impose government priorities on its activities – in other words, to undermine its independence.

Overall, however, this appears to be an isolated episode. To be sure, the history of Northern claims boards is replete with requests, pleas, and demands from boards for enhanced funding, mostly made in private but occasionally brought to public attention.[30] While Ottawa's responses have ranged between full acceptance of board applications for additional money to partial acceptance to (rarely) complete rejection, little evidence supports the interpretation that the underlying motivation was reducing board independence.

As mentioned in Chapter 4, Paul Nadasdy argues that the Yukon Government has frequently used its control of Renewable Resources Council budgets to limit council activity. Yukon officials contend that only reasonable accountability standards are being applied in order to ensure that Ottawa's funding of RRCs is not compromised. Whether, to use a well-known Canadian phrase, this constitutes "reasonable limits" on RRC independence is an important question.

Unilateral Government Assaults on Boards

Although the boards come out of commitments in settled comprehensive claims, many were formally established through federal legislation. This would seem to imply that a subsequent act of Parliament could fundamentally revamp a board or do away with it altogether. For some time, the widely held view was that, since the claims require co-management boards for specified functions, were a board to be abolished, a very similar board would have to be created to replace it. It was further presumed that the three parties to a claim – the federal and territorial governments and the Indigenous government/organization –

would have to agree to amend the claim before any fundamental board restructuring could occur.

The Conservative government of Stephen Harper did not subscribe to this interpretation and attempted to impose extensive changes on co-management boards in the Northwest Territories and Yukon over the strenuous objections of Indigenous governments and organizations. More existential threats to board independence could hardly be imagined. As it turned out, the changes proposed by the Conservatives either did not occur, though not for want of trying, or were subsequently reversed. Nonetheless, they offer important lessons for board independence.

The bitter contretemps over Bill C-15, which, among other things, would have abolished the three regional land and water boards in the NWT and fundamentally restructured the Mackenzie Valley Land and Water Board is recounted in Chapter 6. A similarly caustic conflict erupted in Yukon over provisions to implement the Conservatives' regulatory action plan. Here the issue centred on amendments to another federal statute, the *Yukon Environmental and Socioeconomic Assessment Act*, the legal basis for the Yukon Environmental and Socio-economic Assessment Board, the main environmental regulator in the territory. A review of the act and the board that had taken five years had produced a number of proposed revisions agreed to by all parties but left other matters unresolved. When Bill S-6, which sought to amend *YESAA* (as well as amend legislation dealing with Nunavut boards), was given first reading in June 2014, it contained provisions that deeply angered Yukon First Nations. According to the Council of Yukon First Nations, some far-reaching elements of the bill "were never discussed during the Five-Year Review and in some cases, go against agreements reached by the CYFN, Canada and Yukon during that review."[31]

Yukon First Nations vociferously objected to provisions of the bill giving Ottawa authority to issue binding policy directions to the board, which, together with a new ability to delegate powers to the territorial government, "permit[s] political interference ... [and] undermines the independence of the Board and Designated Offices."[32] They also took serious issue with the bill's shortened environmental assessment timelines and its elimination of the need for assessment of renewals or amendments to existing licences and permits. The First Nations perspective was evident in the title of a widely circulated CYFN pamphlet: "Changes to YESAA Threaten Our Land, Our Economy, Our Yukon." First Nations leaders' anti-Bill S-6 rhetoric rivalled that heard in the NWT: "We are deeply troubled," said one, "that Canada is proposing to give the minister the authority to unilaterally issue binding policy direction to the board. The board's independence is a fundamental principle that Canada, Yukon and First Nations agreed to and was intended to avoid the influence of any one party." Another maintained: "our agreements are under attack constantly and basically they want to go back to where we don't have any say in what happens in the Yukon."[33]

Within days of Bill S-6 passing into law, Liberal Indigenous affairs critic Carolyn Bennett committed on behalf of her party that, should it form government, it would rescind the parts of the new act that First Nations found objectionable.[34] When the Liberals won the October election, Bennett became minister, whereupon three First Nations dropped the legal challenge to the act they had mounted. In June 2016, Bill C-17, *An Act to amend the Yukon Environmental and Socio-economic Assessment Act and to make a consequential amendment to another Act,* was introduced to make good on Bennett's promise. A few months later a territorial election saw the Yukon Liberal Party, whose platform emphasized a cooperative approach to First Nations issues, vanquish the Yukon Party, which had supported Bill S-6. Bill C-17 received Royal Assent at the end of 2017.

Board Independence

In concluding, it needs to be emphasized that not all challenges to board independence come from Ottawa or, under devolved regimes, territorial capitals. Indigenous organizations and governments may also threaten board independence. An illustrative case involved an application for a water licence for a proposed gold mine in western Nunavut that had been delayed for some time by the Nunavut Water Board. Pressing for quick approval in order to create jobs and economic development were the Kitikmeot Inuit Association as well as Inuit-dominated business organizations. When board staff issued a long, detailed critique of the proponent's most recent revision of its application, the board summarily fired its long-serving and highly respected executive director, whereupon the board's entire technical staff and its director of corporate services resigned in protest, citing blatant political interference.[35]

Effective co-management, as envisaged in the settled Northern comprehensive land claims agreements, requires cooperation built on trust. Paradoxically, as Michael d'Eça has argued, robust independence of claims boards and their members is essential to successful co-management.

This chapter explores a range of structural and operational features of Northern claims-based co-management boards, setting out instances of actual or potential challenges to board or member independence. That potential threats to independence sometimes become actual assaults should not be taken to imply that they occur more than infrequently. Although nothing like systematic data exist, if indeed they could even be collected, it is almost certainly the case that breaches, or attempted breaches, of board independence are rare. However, if governments generally respect board independence, possible threats to independence need to be identified, not least because, as this chapter demonstrates, when potential threats come to fruition, the consequences, including serious harm to the spirit of co-management, can be substantial.

chapter 8

Traditional Knowledge in Claims-Mandated Co-management Boards

According to Fikret Berkes and Thomas Henley, "one of the major mechanisms for creating an equitable [co-management] relationship [between Indigenous peoples and the state] lies with the recognition of indigenous knowledge as a legitimate source of information and values."[1] Indeed, the role of traditional knowledge and Inuit Qaujimajatuqangit in the work of Northern claims boards has come up a number of times in previous chapters. This chapter considers two related sets of issues pertaining to TK/IQ in claims boards.[2] Both are centrally important in the determination of Indigenous influence on the boards.

First, the chapter examines boards' efforts at acquiring TK and using it in their decision-making processes. "Proponents of traditional knowledge," Stephen Ellis has written, "maintain that it can offer contributions to environmental decision making from a broader scope of environmental values, practices and knowledge."[3] At the same time, critics, including Ellis, maintain that Western science is dominant, often overwhelmingly so, in claims boards' processes and decision making and that TK is thus not taken seriously.

Discussions of TK often emphasize differences between TK and Western science in terms of fundamental intellectual orientation, methodology, and substantive findings. Some analysts suggest that the two knowledge paradigms need not necessarily be in conflict and indeed can, with good will and open-mindedness, complement one another.[4] A related argument holds that the two knowledge systems are not as different as they are sometimes said to be and that the differences that do exist can be overstated.[5]

The question of how TK is balanced with or melded with Western science is critically important in assessing Indigenous influence. Research into wildlife co-management institutions in Northern Canada not rooted in land claims indicates that TK plays at best a minor role in the operation and decisions of boards such as the Beverly and Qamanirjuaq Caribou Management Board (BQCMB) and the Ruby Range Sheep Steering Committee.[6] Claims boards, however, are very different from bodies such as the BQCMB in that their existence and authority derive from comprehensive land claims agreements and also in that, typically, they are legally required to give serious consideration to TK. Yet this by no means assures that claims boards give full and proper weight to TK in their decisions.

The chapter's second prime concern involves the extent to which board processes are compatible with or antithetical to Indigenous culture. The chapter explores an arguably more intractable potential incompatibility than that between TK and Western science – that between TK and the values and procedures of Western-style governance.

Governance is very much a function of the rules, formal and informal, and the organizational culture of the institutions of governance. In turn, rules, institutions, and cultures are deeply rooted in world views and values. In politics and government, *how* an institution gathers information, processes ideas, reaches decisions, and formulates and implements policies may be just as important, if not more so, than the actual decisions it makes and the policies it develops. And, of course, the "how" profoundly affects the "what." Thus Indigenous influence on the boards depends a good deal on them operating according to Indigenous principles and values. In turn, this leads to what has been termed "a deeper question, which has hardly been raised at all ... whether the historical values and practices of Dene or Inuit society, as these have survived the massive changes of the last century, are at all compatible with modern governing procedures, mass societies and public bureaucracies?"[7]

The chapter begins with a discussion of the nature of TK and its significance for claims boards. This is followed by an account of a public hearing held by the Mackenzie Valley Environmental Impact Review Board, at which questions relating to TK and to the compatibility of board processes with Indigenous culture were prominent. Next is a section that looks at how boards incorporate TK into their decision making and the extent to which they do it. The next section explores the TK policies and practices of two of the boards examined in detail in earlier chapters, the Nunavut Wildlife Management Board and the MVEIRB. It asks whether fundamental incompatibilities exist between Indigenous world views and the values, implicit as well as explicit, of the Western rational-bureaucratic model of public administration, which suffuses claims boards. This question focuses attention on a key issue: Do the norms and operating procedures that structure the boards' activities represent a barrier to thoroughgoing, genuine Indigenous influence on board processes? A concluding section follows.

Traditional Knowledge: Nature and Significance

Attempting to develop a clear operational definition of traditional knowledge brings to mind what Louis Armstrong reputedly replied to a woman asking him to explain jazz: "lady, if you have to ask, you'll never understand." One observer wisely commented: "Defining Traditional Knowledge is the responsibility of First Nations and Inuit. It may not be possible, or advisable for one definition to be adopted universally."[8] Henry Huntington identifies a fundamental flaw in academic treatments of TK that also bedevils claims boards: "the use of a single concept, often called 'traditional knowledge,' implying that there is such an entity, that it is singular, and that it can be defined. It further suggests that the knowledge is held in a particular way and that there is thus a proper way to study it and depict it."[9] The literature on TK is vast, a good deal of it having been generated by writers focusing on the Canadian North. Within the literature disagreement is endemic not only as to definitions but also as to specific elements of TK in particular settings.

Still, it is useful to have at least a very broadly framed conceptualization. Berkes's oft-quoted formulation well captures the central elements of TK:

> A cumulative body of knowledge, practice and belief, evolving by adaptive processes and handed down through generations by cultural transmission about the relationship of living beings (including humans) with one another and with their environment.[10]

One characteristic of TK does elicit widespread agreement: TK is inherently political. According to Caroline Butler, "the use of Indigenous knowledge is a political act – it is a claim of Aboriginality, an assertion of land and resource rights, and a demand for management power."[11] Stephen Ellis asserts that "aboriginal groups have supported and promoted discussion around traditional knowledge in the interests of aboriginal empowerment,"[12] while for Berkes "indigenous knowledge is *political* because it threatens to change power relations between indigenous groups and the dominant society."[13]

If attention to TK offers the possibility of political gains on the part of Indigenous peoples, Leanne Simpson, among others, points to the profound harm caused by misunderstanding and misuse of TK on the part of non-Indigenous scholars and policy makers. It impedes decolonization and worse, "coercing our knowledge to the rules of the colonial power structure serves only to further denigrate and attack the nature of Indigenous Knowledge."[14]

Any number of analysts have developed schemas contrasting TK with Western science, often to elucidate the difficulties inherent in integrating the two knowledge systems into governmental processes. In Marc Stevenson's formulation, which captures the key differences, TK is, compared with Western science:

- intuitive and holistic, as opposed to analytical, reductionist and law-seeking;
- qualitative, as opposed to quantitative;
- moral, as opposed to supposedly value-free;
- subjective and experiential, as opposed to objective and positivist;
- inclusive, as opposed to decisive;
- inconclusive and internally differentiating, as opposed to conclusive and externally differentiating;
- slow to create, as opposed to fast and selective;
- broad in time and narrow in geographic focus, as opposed to narrow in time and broad in geographic focus;
- open to spiritual explanation, as opposed to mechanistic explanation.[15]

Epistemological and methodological difficulties abound in understanding TK and in relating it to Western modes of thought.[16] Marie Battiste and Sákéj Henderson flatly state that "Indigenous knowledge must be understood from an Indigenous perspective using Indigenous language; it cannot be understood from the perspective of Eurocentric knowledge and discourse."[17] As a Kluane woman quoted by Paul Nadasdy put it, "it's not really 'knowledge' at all; it's more a way of life."[18] Another Yukon First Nations woman explained: "TK is fundamental to the identity of our people; it is us."

Among the issues identified in the literature are the centrality of language, carrying as it does very different conceptual frameworks and ways of thinking and knowing; scepticism as to the validity of comprehensive, all-encompassing ideas about TK, leading some to prefer to think in terms of "local knowledge"; and misconceptions about what is "traditional" about TK.[19]

"What is traditional about traditional ecological knowledge," Battiste and Henderson write, "is not its antiquity, but the way it is acquired and used."[20]

The word "traditional" carries misleading connotations, suggesting customs and beliefs "frozen at a particular point in time (usually the distant past),"[21] with limited relevance to current-day realities. This is one reason why, in Nunavut, the recently developed phrase "Inuit Qaujimajatuqangit" – "the combining of the traditional knowledge, experience and values of Inuit society, along with the present Inuit knowledge, experience and values that prepare the way for future knowledge, experience and values"[22] – has come to be preferred over "traditional knowledge." Nonetheless, outside Nunavut, "traditional knowledge" seems the term of choice in both governmental and Indigenous circles; accordingly, it will be used in this chapter.

The terms "traditional knowledge" and "traditional ecological knowledge" (TEK) are often used interchangeably. Recognizing that dividing what is a unified conceptual framework into discrete categories is very much a Western approach, I distinguish for purposes of this chapter between TK and TEK, with TK a far more broadly encompassing concept than TEK.[23] It is surely correct that "the heritage of an indigenous people is not merely a collection of objects, stories and ceremonies, but a complete knowledge system with its own concepts of epistemology, philosophy, and scientific and logical validity."[24] Frank Duerden and Richard Hunt capture a common understanding of TEK, as opposed to TK: "TEK is quintessentially geographic information."[25] It is thus important to recognize, as does Frances Abele, that TK comprises at least three interrelated components: (1) a distinctive political and social perspective, rooted in shared history; (2) local knowledge; and (3) ethical and cosmological knowledge.[26]

This formulation underlines an important point, which is not always adequately addressed in treatments, especially governmental treatments, of TK. Traditional Indigenous knowledge and values about the natural environment, including detailed understandings of the land and the behaviour of animals in addition to ethical codes governing the proper relations of humans to the land and the animals ("traditional ecological knowledge"), are clearly crucial elements of TK. However, TK is a far broader concept than TEK, rendered in this way, encompassing as it does analyses and prescriptions for all manner of social interaction among people as well as deeply spiritual and philosophical precepts, often implicit and unspoken. "Dene TEK," according to Martha Johnson, "consists of a spiritually based moral code or ethic that governs the interaction between the human, natural and spiritual worlds."[27]

Even claims boards with strong commitments to basing their decisions in TK rely heavily on "Western science," whose practitioners can be sceptical of TK because of its spiritual element. Johnson argues that Western scientists fail to recognize "that the spiritual explanation [for environmental phenomena] conceals conservation strategies and does not necessarily detract from the reality of a situation and the making of appropriate decisions about the wise use of resources. It merely indicates that the system exists within an entirely different cultural experience and set of values."[28] Stevenson suggests that concerns over the spiritual aspects of TK are based on a misunderstanding of the nature of spirituality, which incorrectly equates it with religion: "'spiritual teachings' in definitions of TK refer not just or even predominantly to a higher power, but to the respect and reverence Aboriginal people have for the land and the living resources upon which they depend."[29]

A prominent theme in the TK literature highlights the different conceptual frameworks, methodologies, and underlying values of TK and Western science. Indeed, in a paper significantly titled "Uses and Abuses of 'Traditional Knowledge': Perspectives from the Yukon Territory," Julie Cruikshank argues: "in much of the resource management literature there seems to be a growing consensus that indigenous knowledge exists as a distinct kind of epistemology that can be systematized and incorporated into Western management regimes."[30] Although a good deal of literature examines the use of TK in environmental assessment processes and in co-management regimes in the Canadian North, it primarily focuses on the natural environment and human interaction with it. Social relations, integral elements of TK, receive rather less attention.

The Cameron Hills Hearings: Indigenous Culture Meets Board Processes

Doubtless every application or issue that comes before a claims board is in some measure unique. As well, boards' formal procedures and informal practices vary substantially. Accordingly, the following account of a public hearing held in February 2004 in Hay River, Northwest Territories, by the Mackenzie Valley Environmental Impact Review Board is not held out as in any way "typical." For understanding both board receptivity of TK and the congruence – or lack thereof – of board processes and Indigenous culture, it is nonetheless instructive.

Paramount Resources Ltd., a mid-sized Calgary-based company, wished to substantially expand its seismic drilling and, ultimately, its extraction activities in the Cameron Hills just north of the Alberta-NWT border, southwest of Great Slave Lake. It applied to the Mackenzie Valley Land and Water Board in April 2003 for the requisite permits and licences. The MVLWB conducted a preliminary screening of the project, which included consultations with twenty-one organizations (governmental, Indigenous, and local communities). In May of that year, citing "the potential for public concern and significant environmental impacts related to cumulative effects," the MVLWB referred the proposal to the MVEIRB for environmental assessment, which began almost immediately.

This process entailed extensive gathering of technical data, along with communications with Paramount and with government departments as well as with the communities and First Nations organizations close to the potentially affected area. Most of this proceeded by way of compilation and exchange of documents. However, as part of its review of the project, the MVEIRB held a public hearing in Hay River, the nearest substantial centre to the area in question. Notices of the meeting were sent to various federal and territorial government departments, to potentially affected individual First Nations, and to other Indigenous organizations. The media were also alerted and publicity was directed to the general public. The day before the public hearings began, board members and staff, joined by members and staff of the MVLWB, held an informal community meeting in Kakisa, the closest First Nations community to the Cameron Hills.

Elements of informality were evident in the Hay River hearings. As is typical in the North, almost no one wore jackets and ties, but jeans were much in evidence. Participants mingled freely for coffee and cookies during breaks. Overall, however, the process could hardly be called informal.

To walk into the good-sized hotel meeting room where the hearing took place was to encounter an imposing setting with an unmistakable aura of formality and bureaucratic officialdom. Tables for the official participants, piled high with documents, all but completely filled the room. Six board members, supported by four staff, a consultant, and the board lawyer, sat at a table in one corner of the room, facing the participants. At another table, the Paramount contingent consisted of nine people. Other tables held nine officials representing four federal departments and the ten staff sent by three Government of the Northwest Territories departments. Yet another group of tables was set aside for Indigenous organizations. Four individual First Nations were represented at the hearing, as were two more broadly based Indigenous organizations and one community resource management board. Not all attended in person; several were represented by a single consultant. Five members and two staff of the MVLWB, who attended as observers, occupied yet another table. A handful of chairs for the public were set out along one wall. All told, this was an intimidating, unwelcoming environment for anyone not used to such settings.

The hearing began, as is customary in the North, with one of the Indigenous board members offering a prayer in his language. Brief welcoming and introductory remarks by the board chair stressed that the hearing was not designed to be adversarial and that "the purpose of questioning is to seek clarification of points made in these presentations, and not to engage in debate or adversarial cross-examination."[31]

Virtually all of the presentations, as well as the questioning, took place in English with simultaneous translation available into Slavey. One Indigenous leader spoke in Slavey, which was translated into English. Elders brought to the hearings by one Indigenous group spoke in English but indicated that they would have been more comfortable and could have spoken more effectively in Chipewyan, but no translation was available. One First Nation prefaced its submission with a fifty-minute video about traditional usage of the land and animals in the area in question. Presenters and questioners were given all the time they required; no one was rushed.

Paramount made the first formal presentation; over the next two days each organization, governmental or Indigenous, that had previously registered was given the opportunity to make a formal statement. Most, but not all, did so. Questioning followed each presentation. Board members were afforded the first chance to ask questions but generally preferred to listen to exchanges among the other participants. Every registered organization was invited to comment on or question the organization that had just made its presentation. Once all registered participants had had their say, board staff could ask questions, which they did on occasion to clarify technical points or to crystallize points of agreement or disagreement. Finally, the "public" was called upon to voice any comments or questions. For most of the hearing, the "public" consisted of a solitary University of Toronto political scientist, who declined to put forward any opinions or questions. Occasionally, one or two genuine members of the public would wander into the hearing room, but few stayed for any length of time and none spoke.

Most of the exchanges were civil and many were technical, but some had a confrontational edge to them and were highly political in nature. At one point, for example, a Paramount representative referred to the local First Nations as "neighbours"; this incited an Indigenous leader to take the Paramount "newcomers" to task and to stipulate that the First Nations were not Paramount's neighbours but their "landlords." He also objected to Paramount's conceptual approach, based as it was on such non-Indigenous concepts as "wildlife" and "remoteness." Even more telling, for purposes of this chapter, was a sharp clash between Paramount and the First Nations representatives about "traditional usage" of lands that stood to be most affected by the exploration and drilling. According to Paramount, since the First Nations could not produce lists of persons who had hunted or trapped in this area for the past few years, this meant that the land was not actually in use. The elders and the consultant explained

TK in Claims-Mandated Co-management Boards

that harvesting had occurred in the area in years past and might well again, depending on the animals' migration patterns and on the harvest in nearby regions and that, accordingly, they still used and occupied the land. Paramount officials aggressively and repeatedly challenged this view, and the elders who put it forward, to the visible annoyance of at least one Indigenous board member. One First Nations representative explicitly commented in his closing statement that some of Paramount's questions were disrespectful.

That the board held an informal community meeting and two days of formal public hearings should not obscure the dominance of documentary evidence in the Cameron Hills process. By the time the public registry was closed in March 2004 as the board prepared to make its decision, some 234 separate documents had been logged, all of which were available for public inspection. Some were no more than one-page faxes proposing or confirming arrangements for meetings, document exchanges, and the like, but many were extensive technical documents or detailed position papers. Virtually all were in English.

In June 2004, the board issued an eighty-four-page report presenting its analysis and recommendations to the federal minister of Indian affairs and Northern development. The board concluded that the project should be allowed to proceed, subject to a number of conditions ranging from air quality monitoring to measures for mitigating fish habitat to negotiation of a socioeconomic agreement between Paramount and affected communities.[32] The minister was not prepared to accept all the recommendations; thus ensued "consult-to-modify" negotiations between the minister and the board. Agreement was reached in March 2005 and the board's amended conditions were forwarded to the appropriate agencies for implementation.

Claims Boards' Efforts at Using TK and IQ

Few would disagree that claims boards make genuine efforts to use traditional knowledge in reaching decisions on environmental regulation and wildlife management. The real question is: How effective are those efforts? Following general discussion of issues that arise for claims boards attempting to incorporate TK into their decision-making processes, this section primarily looks at TK use at the Mackenzie Valley Environmental Impact Review Board and the Nunavut Wildlife Management Board.

Writers such as Johnson and Ellis contend that Western scientists and those who privilege their views are biased against TK, seeing it as unsystematic anecdotes and folklore: "Notions outside the realm of science and Euro-Canadian values are often considered unworthy of serious discussion in environmental decision-making processes ... When traditional knowledge is not substantiated by scientific methods, results and conclusions, it is commonly ignored or discarded."[33] Unquestionably, Western science is not easily melded with TK and some scientists are sceptical if not outright hostile to TK. Leonard Tsuji and Elise Ho argue that "TEK and western science should be viewed as two separate but complementary sources of information and wisdom,"[34] and scientists seem increasingly to be coming to appreciate the value and validity of TK, though establishing this in a systematic, empirical manner is not possible. Episodes such as that recounted in Chapter 3, in which Department of Fisheries and Oceans scientists dramatically revised their estimate of the number of bowhead whales in the waters off Nunavut to accord with what Inuit TK had indicated, have had an impact. As well, Indigenous members of claims boards often push hard to take TK seriously.

To be sure, problems and barriers exist. One, identified by Peter Usher and others, has been that neither the claims nor supplementary legislation, such as the *Mackenzie Valley Resource Management Act*, offer any guidance whatsoever as to how boards are to implement TK in their work. "This suggests," he argues, "an insufficient understanding on the part of policy-makers of what TK actually is, and hence the implications and practicalities of incorporating it into formal decision-making processes."[35] This was evident in the lament of one board executive director, interviewed in 2003, who pointed out that, despite serious commitment to TK, "we keep sending people to workshops but we really haven't gotten anywhere; we're still a long way from figuring out just what TK is or how to use it." Similarly, a GNWT assistant deputy minister admitted difficulty in coming to grips with TK: "you listen to what they [Indigenous people] say, especially the elders, and try to understand it."

Although made in the context of pre-*Umbrella Final Agreement* Yukon land use planning institutions, the observation of Frank Duerden and his colleagues doubtless remains at least occasionally valid for claims boards. "The tendency continues," they wrote, "for bureaucrats to assume that the very presence of First Nations representatives on planning boards and committees is a good surrogate for hard, systematically organised local environmental knowledge."[36]

Stevenson identifies another major impediment for Euro-Canadian institutions, such as claims boards, in coming to grips with TK:

The importance of context for understanding and communicating knowledge in northern aboriginal society cannot be overstated. As meaning for many aboriginal people is derived as much from the context of communication itself as from the information communicated, it is important to understand the differences between what is being communicated and the situation in which the communication takes place. For many aboriginal people, experience is knowledge and knowledge is experience. Thus, knowledge has to be constructed for each individual, and is not easily shared among individuals unless there is a mutual understanding and appreciation of that experience. This is why, for example, it is difficult for northern aboriginal people to communicate to outsiders what traditional knowledge is, and why it is equally hard for non-aboriginals to understand and appreciate how that knowledge can be used in environmental assessment and management. This is also perhaps why aboriginal people have been reluctant generally to share their experiential observations with outsiders.[37]

Effective communication is often hampered by barriers of language and methods of communicating. Three experienced MVEIRB staff observe:

Elders often convey their knowledge not only in their own language but through implicit conclusions described by story telling. Non-Aboriginal members of the Review Board, and others, thus received only a second hand translation and in a way that makes it difficult for them to easily recognize the pertinent points.

Traditional knowledge is generally delivered in a holistic way, not compartmentalized. For Elders it is often inconceivable to talk about one specific development or one specific type of animal only. This can be a poor fit with EIAs [environmental impact assessments], which organize issues and often hearings along specific subject lines.[38]

Just as elders can have difficulty conveying their knowledge, scientists' application of TK can entail misconceptions and misunderstandings. The need for translation sometimes makes for overly simplistic or inaccurate renderings of TK:[39]

Even among those western scientists who do acknowledge the value of TEK, they generally apply scientific categories and methods to collect, verify, and validate it. Too often information is translated directly into English, without making the effort to examine whether or not scientific terminology accurately reflects the indigenous concepts being described.[40]

Yet even careful efforts at accurate translation may not be enough. As Natasha Thorpe writes in the context of IQ about caribou in Nunavut, "Considerable evidence demonstrates that the process of defining or codifying knowledge changes it in a fundamental way."[41]

Mackenzie Valley Environmental Impact Review Board

A few years into their work it had become evident to MVEIRB members, especially Indigenous members, that, despite their commitment to incorporating TK into board practices, more effort was needed to develop practical measures for doing so. This was more than an inchoate aspiration, it was a requirement under the *MVRMA*, section 115, which states: "in exercising its powers, the Review Board shall consider any traditional knowledge and scientific information that is made available to it." However, the act offered no guidance as to how the TK requirement should be implemented nor did it provide a definition of traditional knowledge. A further complication was the act's provision in section 11 defining environmental impact not simply in terms of effects on the physical environment but also as "any effect on the social and cultural environment or on heritage resources." In attempting to come to grips with these challenges, the board hired a TK coordinator, one of whose duties was to organize a workshop to consider how to bring TK into its environmental assessment processes.

Originally conceived as a small gathering, the November 2002 meeting generated such wide interest across the NWT that it became necessary to hire the largest meeting room in Yellowknife to accommodate all those who wished to attend.[42] Most of the nearly one hundred delegates or observers were Indigenous, many representing Indigenous organizations. Officials from governmental agencies, including claims boards, were also present in significant numbers. The latter, mainly non-Indigenous, primarily came to listen; discussions and comments mostly involved Indigenous participants, some of whom spoke in Slavey or Tlicho, which was translated for those unable to understand. Few issues were resolved and few practical procedures devised for incorporating TK into Northern environmental assessment. Still, the meeting provided an opportunity for Indigenous leaders and elders to set out their views as to the nature and importance of TK. As well, it identified many points, both of principle and practice, which the board would need to address in developing its approach to TK. Two conclusions were evident from the meeting. First, the board was serious in trying to determine how to incorporate TK into its work. Second, this would be a daunting task, fraught with difficulty.

One obvious source of difficulty was language. Again and again, Indigenous participants at the workshop stressed the inextricable intertwining of language and TK. "Expressing some aspects of TK in English is practically impossible," said one. Another argued: "We're faced with the problem of [having to deal with] non-Dene people and non-Dene systems to make ourselves understood ... If you want to understand us [and TK] you [non-Dene] must learn our language." And yet, then, as now, virtually all MVEIRB proceedings were in English as were all key documents; some proceedings, but few documents, were translated into one or more Dene languages. Translation, when available, is often a poor substitute for understanding the unique conceptual apparatus every language carries. An especially problematic concern with TK is rendering subtle Indigenous concepts into English and technical English terms into Indigenous languages. In recognition of this concern, the board sponsored a three-day translators workshop devoted to working out concepts and terminology that would at least partially bridge the linguistic gap between English and the Indigenous languages for purposes of environmental assessments or impact reviews. Subsequent workshops, organized by the MVEIRB in concert with the land and water boards, continued efforts to facilitate exchanges involving TK concepts and scientific terminology.

The workshop fed into a related board initiative – the development of written guidelines for using TK in environmental assessment. The very process of developing the guidelines, as described by the board's lead staff person on the project, underlines the impediments, conceptual and political, facing boards attempting to incorporate TK into their decision making. Three key challenges were fears that the board intended through the guideline to regulate TK, concerns over the adequacy of public involvement in developing the guidelines, and issues relating to confidentiality and research ethics involving TK.[43]

Early drafts, entitled *Traditional Knowledge Guidelines*, did not sit well with Indigenous people consulted during the process in that they "assigned the Review Board with the authority to verify and authenticate traditional knowledge presented to it."[44] However, it became clear from the feedback received that this authority should rest in the hands of the community and not the Review Board. Related issues arose from the board's initially limited consultation as to the nature and purpose of the guidelines, which generated misconceptions and distrust in Indigenous communities. More robust community consultation led to revisions to the draft guidelines emphasizing the importance of community and regional TK policies and guidelines and clarifying that the board guidelines would not infringe upon Indigenous rights. As well, the title of the document was changed to *Guidelines for Incorporating Traditional Knowledge into the Environmental Impact Assessment Process*.[45] A final challenge was the most basic: the need to respect Indigenous desire to keep certain elements of TK confidential while fulfilling the board's legal requirement that it be transparent in its procedures, especially as they relate to information. An important aspect of this issue for the board was assuring that project proponents obtained informed consent from Indigenous communities for research into and use of TK.[46]

The final version of the *Guidelines* was published in July 2005, two years after the first draft. According to the paper cited above, the board intended to review the *Guidelines* regularly and, "if revisions are required, the Review Board hope[d] to accommodate the need quickly."[47] As of early 2019, no revisions of the 2005 document had been published, though it is fair to add that the board has been actively developing guidelines for a cultural impact assessment initiative, which has substantial TK elements.

Various considerations and recommendations from the TK guidelines, as well as comments from the Yellowknife workshop, are considered in a following section. At this point discussion is confined to the basic conceptualization of TK in the *Guidelines*. The preamble sets out the board's understanding of the role of TK in its work:

> In order to ensure that aboriginal cultures, values and knowledge play an appropriate role in its decisions, the Review Board is committed to fully consider any traditional knowledge brought forward in its proceedings.[48]

Arguing that TK is an evolving concept that admits of no easy formulation, the *Guidelines* do not offer a precise definition. However, three "particularly important elements" of TK are outlined: first, "Knowledge about the environment," essentially factual knowledge about the natural environment (in the terms set out above, TEK); second, "Knowledge about use and management of the environment," which includes "cultural practices and social activities, land use patterns, archeological sites, harvesting practices, and harvesting levels, both past and present." In light of the subsequent discussion, use of the term "management" is noteworthy. The third component is the most interesting and the most problematic. "Values about the environment" involves preferences as well as moral and ethical positions about the environment and are in large measure determined by Indigenous spirituality.[49] As discussed more extensively below, the *Guidelines* illustrates the inherent incompatibilities between the Indigenous worldview of TK and the Euro-Canadian legal-bureaucratic model of governance within which the board functions.

The *Guidelines* are just that – guidelines. What of the MVEIRB's record of actually incorporating TK into environmental assessments? Unsurprisingly, pluses and minuses can be identified. As mentioned in Chapter 6, the board once recommended that a proposed exploratory uranium project not go ahead because of the spiritual and cultural significance of the drilling sites to local First Nations. A paper by board staff cites an instance in which "the Review Board rejected the proponent's analysis of wildlife impacts based on relatively short term scientific observation. Instead the Review Board relied on the long term traditional knowledge base, which spans centuries of oral history."[50] On the other side of the ledger, the sole instance of a dissenting opinion in a board environmental assessment report, also mentioned in Chapter 6, arose in large part because Indigenous board members concluded that TK had not been sufficiently considered, while critics such as Ellis contend that board recourse to TK is flawed and inadequate.[51]

The authors (all board staff) of a study looking at TK in board environmental assessments conclude that their three case studies "demonstrate the clear influence on project design to avoid impacts, and the relevance of TK to so many stages of EIA. These case studies demonstrate that the challenges of using TK in EIA are surmountable, and the benefits of using TK in EIA are considerable."[52] While the case studies do support a positive assessment of the board's commitment to TK, features of them raise difficult issues. In all three cases, local Indigenous organizations commissioned or carried out their own TK studies, which they presumably had to pay for themselves. Not all communities or Indigenous organizations have the wherewithal to self-fund such studies. As well, two of the three TK studies were submitted to the board "under confidential cover," while in the third case, the local First Nation and the developer signed a confidentiality agreement "in order to protect sensitive TK information from being made public and possibly misused."[53] Under the board's TK guidelines, such confidentiality agreements are to be exceptional.[54] The question thus arises as to the role of TK in board processes when confidentiality is not possible.

Shortly after completing the TK guidelines, the board embarked on a project to develop both a conceptual approach to what it termed "cultural impact assessment" and practical ways to incorporate it into its environmental assessments. A May 2009 status report indicated that the initiative was well under way and set out a timeline that projected publication of a final version of a cultural impact assessment guidelines document in early 2010.[55] The project stalled for several years, in part because it became clear that the diversity of cultures across the Mackenzie Valley added substantial complexity to the process of developing guidelines and in part because the board's interest in cultural impact assessment waned.

Subsequently, with changeover of members, the board made it a high priority. Processes for incorporating cultural impact into environmental assessment were still being developed at the time of writing, though one approach, employed in Nahanni Butte and Fort Simpson in July 2017 as part of an EA on a proposed road, proved successful in the board's view.[56] The board had recognized two gaps that it wanted to address: the technical sessions held prior to public hearings "primarily have focused on scientific information and not TK ... There was limited opportunity for traditional and local knowledge holders to provide comment to the Review Board on potential cultural impacts between the community scoping sessions and the Community Public Hearings." A TK specialist was hired to facilitate technical sessions in the two communities. These were "similar to typical 'technical sessions' hosted by the Board for all EAs, but ... [with a] focus exclusively on cultural impacts [and] focus on the community members, not on 'parties' to the EA." The facilitator and board staff went door to door in the communities explaining the process and encouraging participation. "This contributed to strong attendance in general, including amongst elders and council members ... [and was] very worthwhile and effective [for the board] for gathering evidence on cultural values, impacts and traditional knowledge."

Based on this experience, as well as a belief that culture and TK vary too widely for a "one-size-fits-all" approach, as of 2018, the board was looking to employ locally knowledgeable TK consultants, rather than developing in-house staff TK capacity, to enhance its access to and use of TK. All told, reaching anything like a precise evaluation of the MVEIRB's use of TK is not possible, but overall it is clear that the board takes TK seriously, does incorporate TK into its decision making, and is developing new and apparently effective methods of gathering and evaluating TK.

Nunavut Wildlife Management Board

As set out prominently on its website, the NWMB defines its mission as "conserving wildlife through the application of Inuit Qaujimajatuqangit and scientific knowledge." Most involved with the board agree that it has seriously attempted to incorporate IQ into its work, but, at the same time, many, including board members and staff, recognize that the board has struggled to realize its vision.

For the NWMB, IQ entails far more than factual knowledge. Its definition recognizes the ethical, indeed cosmological, elements of IQ:

IQ consists of Traditional Ecological Knowledge (TEK), as well as Inuit beliefs about how the world works, and the values necessary to behave in an ethical manner in human interactions with animals and the environment. TEK is specific factual knowledge – obtained through Inuit experience – about various parts of the environment, including plants, animals, weather and other physical elements.[57]

A visit to the board's website makes immediately evident its commitment to IQ. In light of the importance of language for TK/IQ, it is noteworthy that all documents – annual reports, board minutes, research studies – are available in Inuktitut, though to be sure written minutes of meetings, annual reports, and the like reflect Western bureaucratic rather than IQ principles. Enjoying a prominent position on the board's home page are links to major studies commissioned or conducted by the board with extensive IQ elements: the Bowhead Knowledge Report, the Southeast Baffin Beluga Study, and the mammoth Nunavut Wildlife Harvest Study.

For several years the NWMB sought to develop a formal set of policies regarding IQ but made little progress. As early as 2001, the board put a funding request to Ottawa, seeking $11 million to establish an Inuit Qaujimajatuqangit wildlife fund, structured in a similar fashion to the Research Trust, set up as a charity with payouts coming from interest not from capital. The proposed fund would "pay for the systematic research, collection, recording, validating, organizing and presenting of IQ related to the conservation and protection of wildlife and wildlife habitat" as well as a full-time IQ coordinator at the board.[58] The request was denied.

At its September 2005 meeting in Igloolik, the NWMB committed to developing formal guidelines for the incorporation of IQ into its work.[59] Despite the board's obvious and persistent desire to base its decisions and processes in IQ, no guidelines have yet been produced, a clear indication of the difficulty of formalizing TK/IQ in claims boards activities. Subsequent consultants reports developed a much scaled down IQ program, focused on creating a database: collecting, digitizing, and making available to the board, its co-management partners, and the public existing literature on IQ relevant to wildlife and wildlife habitat in Nunavut.[60] This project is proceeding. In 2011, the board decided to appoint a full-time IQ coordinator, but it was not until mid-2013 that the position was filled and it has been vacant for extended periods. Generally speaking, the board has preferred to bring IQ perspectives to bear through the experience of board members and the extensive involvement of Inuit at the community level, for example through the local Hunters and Trappers Organizations, which have close links with the board. In turn, this entails practices designed to encourage and facilitate participation in board activities by those, especially elders, with intimate knowledge of the land and the animals. A notable illustration has been the board's practice of involving elders and HTO representatives in public hearings on polar bear quotas, as described in Chapter 3.

Recently the board established the Inuit Qaujimajatuqangit Research Fund using money from the undersubscribed Research Studies Fund. An IQ workshop, held in early 2014, developed plans for an extensive IQ database to assist the board and others in incorporating IQ into both research and decisions on wildlife and habitat.

Among the prominent board efforts at generating IQ for use in its decision making have been the major studies it undertook and the more limited studies it supports. Both the bowhead study and a less extensive, board-sponsored beluga study were very much IQ-focused.[61] The harvest study incorporated IQ into its methods and analysis, but it also employed techniques and approaches of Western science, for example in its attempts to tote up comprehensive numbers of animals harvested. All three studies incorporated extensive use of Inuit researchers employing IQ methods and interpretations and provided the basis for important board decisions on harvest levels and quotas. When the board considers research funding, either from the Research Trust or from the NWMB Studies Fund, the commitment to IQ and the means proposed to gather it are among the criteria in assessing applications. The Inuit Qaujimajatuqangit Research Fund was explicitly designed to encourage IQ studies.

A telling indication of the value of IQ and its potential to shape board decision making involved the numbers of bowhead whales that underpinned total allowable harvest decisions. As discussed in Chapter 3, although IQ proved more accurate than Western science, this did not lead to increased quotas. It was only when the DFO scientists revised their estimate of bowhead stocks that the board was able to significantly raise the TAH with the confidence that the DFO minister would not reject its decision.

Although it is evident that, while the NWMB has successfully integrated IQ and Western science into the empirical knowledge base upon which its decisions rest, important elements of its structure and operation remain essentially rooted in the Western bureaucratic paradigm. A board self-assessment suggests as much, maintaining that the board

> has brought together the best of the Inuit way and the best of the Anglo-European way; it has brought together traditional knowledge and modern science; it has brought together a knowledge of the land and animals, based on thousands of years of experience, and a knowledge of the workings of modern government and its bureaucracy.[62]

The following section considers ways in which the bureaucratic imperatives of the "Anglo-European way" limit the capacity of boards such as the MVEIRB and the NWMB to thoroughly imbue its operations with TK/IQ.

Culture Clash: TK/IQ and Claims Boards' Euro-Canadian Governance Processes

That incompatibilities should exist between Northern Indigenous TK and the precepts underpinning the Euro-Canadian legal-bureaucratic model will not surprise anyone familiar with the clash of cultures endemic to Indigenous-state relations in Canada. An extensive literature, for example, highlights the often-times fundamental incongruence between ideas about and processes of justice among Indigenous people and Canadians of European heritage. Still, an enumeration of how the two worldviews differ is essential to understanding why, even for claims boards with extensive Indigenous membership and that value TEK, incorporating TK into their operations is problematic. David Natcher and Susan Davis's research in Yukon lead them to comment that "the language of devolution and local control permeates local-state interaction, the new institutions that have been created via the land claims process have little resemblance to indigenous forms of governance and management ... [with related] difficulties of applying indigenous cultural ideals into a management process that is derived from nonindigenous values and principles."[63]

Governmental institutions in Canada, claims boards included, are very much cast in the mould of classic Weberian bureaucracy. Among its essential features: it is hierarchical, with a notable concentration of power at the top; it operates according to extensive, written, formal, impersonal rules and procedures; authority is based on office-holding rather than on personal attributes; it is based on extensive compartmentalization of functions and division of labour; it is premised on a sharp division between the public and private spheres; employment and promotion within it depend on merit, defined according to formal criteria; "facts" and knowledge are to be ascertained and verified by rigorous, often adversarial, challenging of assertions; decisions are reached through "rational" evaluation of the empirical evidence so gathered; and as much information as possible should be made available to all those potentially affected by its actions. (Since the emphasis in this chapter is on the bureaucratic rather than the political sphere of governance, such principles as majoritarian decision making and delegation of far-reaching powers to elected representatives are not considered. Even here the conventional Western distinction between the political and the bureaucratic is incongruent with Indigenous approaches to governance.)

Bearing in mind that some are of greater relevance to claims boards than others, the following subsections consider the consistency of these characteristics with the values and practices of traditional Northern Indigenous cultures in the operation of the MVEIRB and the NWMB.

Hierarchical with Power Concentrated at the Top

A phrase frequently applied to Western bureaucracies, which well captures their fundamental nature, is "command and control." The classic Weberian bureaucracy is characterized by a clearly specified hierarchy of positions, with explicitly defined reporting relationships. All members of the organization know who has authority to issue orders to them, just as they know to whom they can issue orders. The higher one's position in the hierarchy, the greater one's power. As well, the powerful positions at the top of the hierarchy are few in number; indeed, typically a single person sits atop the entire organization, with authority over all others, although the few officials in the next rung or two down from the top also wield extensive power. Recent trends in organizational engineering that have produced "flatter" governmental organizations (with fewer levels) have not fundamentally altered either their hierarchical design or the concentration of power at the top.

Northern Indigenous cultures are by no means all of a piece; however, by and large they tend to be egalitarian and non-hierarchical, though powerful "camp bosses" were certainly prominent in parts of the North. Typically, "leaders [in Inuit society] didn't exercise their authority by giving orders or acting superior but rather by giving advice or using their knowledge and experience to guide the group."[64] Moreover, in many traditional Northern societies those who did exercise authority were circumscribed in their spheres of influence. The person who led the hunt carried no special authority in matters spiritual, while the person entrusted with dealing with others, such as non-Indigenous traders or government figures, would not necessarily have had influence when it came to hunting or to healing.

Extensive, Written, Impersonal Rules and Procedures

The hallmark of the Western bureaucracy is extensive reliance on precise, written rules and formal, oftentimes rigid procedures. Officials' discretion is fettered in this way, in part to avoid favouritism or prejudice. Rules are formulated so as to anticipate as many contingencies as possible and to produce similar outcomes in similar situations. Accordingly, they take on enormous complexity, in turn requiring specialized training to understand them as well as intimate familiarity with bureaucratic culture to cope with them.

Nothing could better illustrate these features than the *Mackenzie Valley Resource Management Act*, with its two hundred pages of complex procedures set out in dense legal and technical prose, plus dozens of pages of regulations. Lawyers and experienced bureaucrats may be able to navigate the act, but others – well-educated non-Indigenous, let alone Dene elders with limited English-language skills – find it little short of baffling and impenetrable. Even a much-simplified schematic diagram displaying the basic steps in the permitting process fills an entire page.

TK, by contrast, emphasizes simplicity and flexibility. One of the principles of IQ, for example, as spelled out in Nunavut's *Wildlife Act*, is *Qanuqtuurunnarniq/ Kaujimatukanut*, "the ability to be creative and flexible and to improvise with whatever is at hand to achieve a purpose or solve a problem."[65]

The MVEIRB must constantly be concerned with leaving itself open to legal challenges on procedural grounds and thus must conduct its business far more formally than the NWMB, which faces few such concerns. The MVEIRB does attempt to operate as informally as possible, as evidenced in two of its rules of procedure:

30 In conducting its proceedings, the Review Board is not bound by the strict rules of evidence.

31 To the extent consistent with its duty of procedural fairness, the Review Board will emphasize flexibility and informality in its proceedings and in the manner in which it receives information or documents.[66]

A perusal of the other ninety-four rules, let alone the pertinent sections of the act and the regulations, suggests, however, that the board's capacity to be flexible and informal is significantly circumscribed by the legal framework within which it operates.

Legal imperatives do not loom so large for the Nunavut Wildlife Management Board. In 1999, the board published an eleven-page document setting out procedures for public hearings. One of the rules in that document echoed the MVEIRB's aspiration: "The NWMB shall, consistent with the broad application of the principles of natural justice and procedural fairness, emphasize flexibility and informality in the conduct of a hearing."[67]

The rules in the 1999 document were developed before the NWMB had actually held a public hearing; it had visited many communities and held informal community consultations but did not designate them as "public hearings." Subsequently, after the board had conducted public hearings, that document was replaced by a far shorter set of procedures posted on its website. It is fair to say, however, that while the revised rules do not include all the provisions of the 1999 rules, such as the emphasis on "flexibility and informality," the board generally follows the principles captured in the earlier document.

In the 1999 rules, the board gave itself scope for bringing *Qanuqtuurunnarniq/ Kaujimatukanut* to its hearings: "The NWMB may waive or amend any of these Rules, if the Board considers it to be in the interests of fairness. Where any matter arises that is not envisioned by these Rules, the Board shall do whatever it considers necessary, to enable it to deal with the issue in a just manner."[68] The current rules simply note the board's commitment to procedural fairness, adding that "the Board reserves the right to modify the Rules for any particular in-person, electronic or written hearing."[69] That the earlier commitment "to deal with the issue in a just manner" is no longer explicitly stated does not mean that it has been abandoned.

The MVEIRB has a rule that points in a similar direction, though it is framed in more legalistic language and appears less all-encompassing than that of the NWMB: "The Review Board may, in any proceeding, dispense with, vary or supplement these Rules by way of a direction or procedure."[70]

The emphasis on documents and written rules raises questions about the place of oral communications in claims boards operations. Traditional Northern Indigenous cultures are oral and often convey ideas or information through stories or metaphors; at the Yellowknife TK workshop, one Indigenous participant explained TK as "listening to the river." Most boards, including the MVEIRB and the NWMB, employ hearings, where oral evidence is presented and discussed, though oftentimes oral presentations amount to little more than reading of documents. And while information and opinion gathered orally are certainly taken seriously, documents are often more extensive and more prominent in board proceedings

The NWMB explicitly placed audio recordings on the same footing as written submissions in its hearing rules, thereby offering elders and others who may have limited facility with written English or Inuktitut the opportunity to present their views to the board. In over two decades, however, no individual or group has availed itself of this option.

Practices that facilitate, or inhibit, communications between those with TK and claims boards highlight the central role of language. TK is first and foremost a set of cultural constructs and, as is well known, culture is inextricably bound up with language. In the Canadian North, the inescapable reality is that rules and procedures are set out in English, even if they are subsequently translated into Indigenous languages, as is the case with Nunavut boards. Clearly, this puts a premium on facility in English and emphasizes capacity to draft and interpret English documents. By extension, those without strong English language skills, particularly in written English, are disadvantaged. Perhaps even more important are the implicit assumptions and conceptualizations inherent in formulating ideas and information in English rather than in Indigenous languages. Mention was made earlier of the difficulty – some would say impossibility – of conveying important aspects of TK in non-Indigenous languages.

Still, translation is important, and it is noteworthy that the NWMB requires translation of all short (less than ten pages) documents presented to it at hearings (less than five minutes for recordings), while longer documents or recordings must be accompanied by a translated summary. Presentations from individuals do not require translation. Meetings of some boards, as illustrated by the Hay River hearings, are conducted largely or entirely in English. Others, especially in Nunavut, where Inuktitut often predominates in board meetings, use Indigenous languages extensively. The NWMB's *Governance Manual*, echoing the provisions in the claim, specifies that the board "is required to conduct its meetings in Inuktitut and, as required by legislation or policy, in Canada's official languages."[71] Nonetheless, with most non-Inuit board members and staff lacking anything but the most rudimentary Inuktitut skills, communications frequently occur via translation rather than in the form of genuinely bilingual exchanges, where all or most participants speak and understand both languages. And even experienced, professional translators may have lapses: one NWMB meeting I attended was punctuated by complaints from an Inuktitut-speaking board member of unsatisfactory translations.

A rather different, but nonetheless significant illustration of the incompatibility of the formal procedures central to Weberian bureaucracy is to be found in the accountability regimes imposed by the NWMB on local Hunters and Trappers Organizations. Since each HTO receives annual funding from the NWMB, it expects an accounting of how the money was spent, just as Ottawa expects the board to account for the funds it distributes to the HTOs. By normal governmental standards, the reporting requirements are not at all onerous. Still, the upshot is that small local Inuit organizations primarily concerned with wildlife find themselves being transformed into bureaucratically constrained organizations. The uneasy relationship between Inuit primarily interested in caribou, seal, and char, and the expectations of the modern bureaucratic state, was evident in Chapter 3's account of the administrative disarray that often characterized HTOs and that led to the creation of the Nunavut Inuit Wildlife Secretariat.

Authority Based on Office-Holding

In the Weberian schema underpinning Euro-Canadian bureaucracies, authority is vested in the office, not in the person holding the office. On leaving the office, an official loses authority, which is transferred to the new office-holder. Northern Indigenous societies accord influence to people based on their personal attributes rather than on their formal position. An important special case of this characteristic is the respect accorded elders on the basis of the wisdom they have acquired through life experiences.

Compartmentalization and Division of Labour

Like many Indigenous cultures, Northern Indigenous societies are holistic. They do not compartmentalize life or the world around them into discrete realms – economic, political, spiritual, and so on. Phenomena cannot be understood in isolation but only in a very broad context including the physical environment and the spiritual dimension. This contrasts markedly with the Western tendency to conceptualize human relations, as well as relations between humans and the natural environment, in terms of discrete spheres of activity. A telling illustration is the widespread insistence on "separation of church and state." At a micro level, the division of labour and task specialization characteristic of Euro-Canadian bureaucracies also runs directly contrary to Indigenous ways, though some division of labour, most notably between men and women, characterized traditional Northern Indigenous societies. The division of responsibilities and expertise typically found in government bureaucracies, which might include a polar bear biologist, a caribou specialist, an air quality expert, and others with narrow specializations, is decidedly foreign to Indigenous people who perforce must know about all manner of animals and their environment.[72]

This deep-rooted philosophical divide appears in another important way: though the demarcation may be constantly in flux, Western societies assume a clear distinction between the private and the public. Many aspects of life – educational techniques and standards, financial transactions and other economic activities, and so on – are deemed to be in the public domain and thus appropriate subjects for government intervention. Many others, however – relations with friends and relatives, personal habits, and the like – are seen as essentially private matters in which the state normally plays no role. The public-private divide has evident applications in bureaucratic organizations: the worklife of the government official is entirely separate from his or her personal life. Traditional Northern Indigenous societies knew no division into public and private realms; this way of characterizing the world and human relations is foreign to how Indigenous people understood the world and their place in it.

One particular element of the disjuncture between holistic Indigenous worldviews and compartmentalized Western concepts of the world and humanity's place in it has special relevance to claims boards, especially those concerned with "managing" wildlife. Western thought sees human beings as separate from and indeed superior to nature, and thus capable of mastering and managing its components, including wildlife. For Northern Indigenous peoples, humans are part of nature but with no claim to enhanced status over its other elements. Accordingly, the notion that people could "manage" wildlife is alien to Indigenous understandings.

In short, the very notion of a governmental agency, no matter who serves on it and how much TK/IQ they bring to their work, "managing" wildlife involves a fundamental contradiction between Northern Indigenous worldviews and the Western bureaucratic paradigm.

Merit

The Weberian bureaucratic model accords a central place to the "merit principle," whereby officials in an organization are hired and promoted on the basis of merit rather than through favouritism or by virtue of ascriptive characteristics such as ethnicity or gender. At an abstract level, Northern Indigenous societies were typically also merit-based, with, for example, the best hunter recognized as the appropriate choice to lead the hunt. At an operational level, though, a marked divergence is evident. In modern Canadian governments, merit is largely defined in terms of formal credentials, primarily educational achievements and experience in similar organizational environments. Practical experience outside of institutional settings counts for little, yet it is precisely such qualifications that are most valued in Indigenous cultures. The credentialism that characterizes government bureaucracies means that someone with a university biology degree is presumed to possess the expertise needed in developing and implementing government policy, whereas an Indigenous elder who has spent decades on the land but lacks formal scientific training is not seen in the same light. The Indigenous perspective, of course, is precisely the opposite.

While the NWMB's current hearing rules do not make special provision for elders, it is evident to anyone observing a board meeting or hearing that the 1999 rule regarding elders remains a key operating principle:

> Recognizing the role of Elders in Inuit society, the NWMB shall provide reasonable opportunity for Elders to speak at a hearing. The Board shall make every

reasonable effort to accommodate Elders, with respect to seating, order of appearance, and opportunity to raise matters and to comment on and respond to matters raised at the hearing.[73]

Adversarial Challenging of Assertions and "Rational" Evaluation of Evidence

Northern Indigenous societies tend to be non-confrontational, with decisions typically reached by consensus after prolonged discussion. Disagreements are expressed in respectful, oftentimes elliptical fashion. The wisdom of elders is accepted without question. The contrast with the aggressive, adversarial approach to expressing disagreement or challenging assertions in Western bureaucratic and legal processes is stark.

Even nominally non-conflictual bureaucratic settings can take on characteristics incompatible with Northern Indigenous practices. Meetings frequently unfold with participants attacking and defending one another's positions, questioning alleged facts and interrupting one another. These are generally not acceptable behaviours in Northern Indigenous cultures.

By design the Western legal system is highly adversarial, built on the assumption that "the truth" will come out through the cut and thrust of debate and challenging of evidence. Assertions are not accepted at face value but are subject to demands for "proof" according to specified rules of evidence that permit, indeed often encourage, aggressive cross-examination of witnesses and impugning their truthfulness and integrity. While not all those who negotiated the land claims or who developed and drafted the legislation to implement the claims were lawyers, many were, and they clearly brought the conceptual apparatus of their profession to bear. And although efforts were made to deal with the problem of excessive legalism and formality, board processes, especially those of regulatory boards like the MVEIRB, are shot through with exactly those characteristics. Still, one Yukon First Nations leader, who was involved in negotiating the *Umbrella Final Agreement* and subsequently dealt extensively with its boards, commented that the formal, legalistic, adversarial aspects of some board processes are generally not a concern. Instead, he thought it important for First Nations to be able to take on state institutions on their own terms: "we wanted to couple Western management systems with our traditional beliefs to help resolve issues"

In a board hearing, lawyers representing a licence applicant would presume it their right, as indeed it is in the legal framework underpinning regulatory board processes, to vigorously cross-examine an elder on a TK-based assertion. Such practices, however, may not just be discordant with Indigenous customs, they may be profoundly offensive. As one Indigenous participant at the Yellow-knife workshop put it, "questioning TK is attacking the integrity of the elders ... which is the most disrespectful thing you can do."

The MVEIRB is clearly sensitive to concerns of this nature, yet it is constrained by its mandate and legislation. An intriguing illustration emerges from a comparison of the final and penultimate versions of the board's TK *Guidelines*. The November 2004 draft stipulated that "traditional knowledge submissions do not have to follow the strict rules of evidence as long as the nature of the evidence is relevant to the EIA [environmental impact assessment] process." This statement was immediately followed by the admonition that "the information must be supported and proven by the parties sharing the information." In the final version, this provision was entirely dropped, whereas the following statement survived intact from the draft to the final version: "Traditional knowledge evidence provided to the Review Board during a formal hearing shall be subject to verification in the same manner as all other evidence."[74] As noted earlier, though, the board does not accept that it is bound by "the strict rules of evidence."

Maximum Public Release of Information

Indigenous communities are often prepared to share their TK with scientists, governments, or anyone else who is interested in it, but this is by no means universally the case. Indigenous peoples may not wish to provide information to governments or to industry for fear that it will be used in ways contrary to their interests and wishes, for example, in attempts to bolster the case for developments such as mines or oil and gas exploration that might harm the land or interfere with its use. Even more problematic are elements of TK that are simply not to be shared with outsiders. Deeply held ethical codes may proscribe any discussion of certain matters with anyone not of the community.

Though Western governments certainly have their secrets, key elements of modern government activity are subject to pervasive requirements of transparency and public access to information. This is very much the case for Northern co-management and regulatory boards. Like other regulatory agencies, the MVEIRB maintains a public registry of documents submitted to it in the course of environmental assessments and reviews. Board procedures require that all documents, both routine administrative correspondence and substantive reports, requests, and comments, be made public via its registry save in unusual circumstances. Full text of all documents on the registry is available via the internet.

The board is aware of the potential conflict between the desire not to make public certain elements of TK and the procedural need for openness. Its TK *Guidelines* provide for the possibility of exempting on request particular information from inclusion in the public record. The presumption, however, is that TK will be made public:

> The Review Board's acceptance and use of traditional knowledge will be sensitive to the nature and source of the information and it will respect any arrangements made for its collection ... Public access to information that influences a Review Board decision is an important part of a fair process, and the Review Board will carefully consider any requests before granting confidential status to information."[75]

All three case studies cited by MVEIRB staff in their paper on the board and TK involved confidentiality provisions around the TK presented to the board or to project proponents. Ultimately, decisions on such matters rest with the board. In order to agree to an exemption, the board "must be convinced that significant harm may result from the release of such information, and the onus for showing harm rests with the party seeking to secure confidential status on the information."[76] Giving up control of TK in this manner may not be satisfactory to Indigenous communities or organizations, which may thus decline to provide it, presumably to the detriment of their interests in the assessment/review process. And such a procedure cannot address issues arising when the TK touches matters that are to be kept in the community. In addition, board records are subject to freedom of information requests by way of the federal *Access to Information Act* and the *Privacy Act*.

Boards and TK: A Half-Full Snowmobile Gas Tank

It is evident that both the Mackenzie Valley Environmental Impact Review Board and the Nunavut Wildlife Management Board have made sincere, sustained efforts at bringing traditional knowledge into their operations. Evident as well is the advantage the NWMB enjoys in this enterprise by virtue of the nature of its mandate. Wildlife conservation and harvesting and related matters such as wildlife research can be seen as modern-day extensions of traditional Inuit pursuits, though of course the "management" framework and other aspects of the board's activities are decidedly non-traditional. By contrast, licensing and assessing the environmental impact of diamond mines and pipelines are far removed from traditional Dene activities. The Dene have always made judgments about what kinds of activities were appropriate in different places at different times, but these judgments did not entail parts per billion of particular chemicals, provisions for storing or neutralizing dangerous substances, the likelihood of infrastructure such as pipelines adversely affecting wildlife, and the like.

Still, for both boards, though the collection of data reflects, to varying degrees, TK methods, and TEK itself is taken seriously into account in decision making, the conceptual framework within which they operate significantly limits the influence of TK.

A strong parallel exists with respect to progress on imbuing the GN with IQ, an admittedly far greater challenge. The GN's own IQ Task Force makes the point forcefully:

> At present there is a chasm – a cultural divide – separating the Inuit Culture on the one side from the Nunavut Government's institutional culture on the other side ... We cannot develop an Inuit government by taking the IQ principles, extracting them from their cultural context (life on the land) and forcing them into a new context (life within the Government of Nunavut). Because the Inuit culture is much broader than the government, we must incorporate the government into the culture.
>
> This becomes quite clear once we understand that public governments – all public governments – have their own cultural characteristics. When we try to incorporate Inuit IQ into the existing Nunavut Government we create a "culture clash." And, as is usual in all culture clashes, the dominant culture dominates. The Inuit culture is forced to take on the shape of the dominant, rather than the other way round.[77]

Ellis's analysis of how the environmental regulation boards used TK in the Mackenzie Valley reached a similar conclusion: "Initiatives to incorporate traditional knowledge into environmental decision making can be effective only if they strive to address this problem by adapting conventional environmental decision making to aboriginal ways of knowing and doing, rather than the conventional converse."[78]

Clearly, the structure and operation, indeed the very essence, of boards like the MVEIRB and the NWMB are fundamentally rooted in Euro-Canadian governance processes, with their Weberian bureaucratic character and their legalistic, evidence-testing paradigm. Accordingly, they cannot conduct themselves within the all-encompassing philosophical/ethical framework that TK entails. However, these boards have made important strides towards incorporating TEK ideas and methods into key elements of their work. As well, evidence exists that board use of TK does serve to empower Indigenous people and to enhance local influence in environmental decision making.[79] Finally, in terms of boards' recourse to TK, Tsuji and Ho cogently observe that "respect for another system of knowledge is much different than trying to be a practitioner of it."[80]

Much, of course, depends on the quality and extent of TK available to boards. As Huntington notes, "the inclusion of traditional knowledge holders on co-management boards is a welcome development, but even when represented in equal numbers, they are likely to lack the institutional support available to other members of the co-management bodies. In this view, traditional knowledge risks being treated as a source of data to be used in a scientific paradigm, rather than as a coherent system of understanding in its own right."[81] Most boards lack the mandate and wherewithal to gather TK on their own and therefore must rely on what is presented to them. For boards involved in environmental regulation, this primarily means studies conducted by or for project proponents, though Indigenous governments and communities occasionally prepare and present their own TK studies. Carly Dokis is highly critical of the quality of TK studies done in the Sahtu region of the Northwest Territories to support applications for project licences and permits, arguing that the studies typically fail to adequately incorporate the experiences and perspectives of the local people into the analysis:

> Community participants in the studies have very little say in the composition or accuracy of the final report, and, indeed, often do not see it prior to or even after its submission ... The final reports do not typically address the cultural or moral relationships between many Sahtu Dene and their land. They include very few, if any, stories about local relationships with the land and very rarely address the ways in which the land and land-based activities are essential to the physical, social, and moral well-being of the Sahtu Dene. Thus, they offer a categorical inventory of certain items or activities rather than genuinely incorporating Sahtu Dene perspectives on and knowledge of the land.[82]

For Dokis, it follows that, for Indigenous people, "participation in a traditional knowledge study is indeed a form of co-optation, an appropriation not only of knowledge, but also of consent."[83]

If indeed it is widely the case that TK studies presented to claims boards by development proponents are characterized by the failings that Dokis decries –

she also says that some are very short and superficial – this is a serious problem. Yet while this chapter emphasizes the inherent limits on recourse to TK in board decision making, surely boards have the ability and the duty to insist that TK studies submitted to them adequately convey Indigenous experiences and values. Moreover, it is clear that the MVLWB and the MVEIRB, and doubtless other boards, are unwilling to accept weak TK studies and inadequate community participation in proponents' applications.

In sum, as far as claims boards are concerned, the snowmobile's gas tank may be seen as half-full or half-empty. Both the MVEIRB and the NWMB have made substantial, sustained, and ultimately successful efforts to incorporate TK into their information gathering and decision making. At the same time, this chapter also shows that the nature of the modern bureaucratic state, of which they are integral parts, puts firm limits on just how far such efforts can go.

chapter 9

Indigenous Influence through Claims Boards?

The central question animating this book – do Indigenous peoples exercise substantial influence over wildlife and environmental decisions through the co-management boards established under the Northern comprehensive land claims? – was never far below the surface in the preceding chapters. Still, the oftentimes extensive details about the boards and their operations, necessary as they were, did not always speak directly to the question. This concluding chapter is largely given over to considering Indigenous influence through the boards.

Before the emergence of co-management regimes, the state management system, which afforded Indigenous people such minimal influence, was by no means the sole mechanism for regulation of wildlife harvesting and related activities across the Canadian North. Harvey Feit demonstrates that, in the past, Northern Indigenous people engaged in significant "self-management" of wildlife resources entirely outside the state system, sometimes as "local resistance to state forms of management," and further, that self-management continues in the co-management era.[1] Accordingly, the question is not whether Indigenous influence is greater in the land claims boards reviewed in this book than it was in the self-management processes that have co-existed with state management for many years. By definition, it could not be. Rather, the question is whether, within the state system, that influence has increased with the advent of land claims boards. For while the boards are unquestionably part of the state system, a central rationale for their creation was the enhancement of Indigenous influence over key wildlife and environmental decisions.

The chapter unfolds as follows. Following some brief reflections on claims boards as manifestations of treaty federalism is an assessment of the evidence pertaining to the central question of Indigenous influence through the boards, which, logically, has two equally important elements. First, it is necessary to establish that the boards themselves exercise significant influence over important wildlife and environment decisions. The boards could be entirely controlled by Indigenous people, but, if they are essentially powerless, this would mean little. Second, to the extent that the boards are influential players, as I argue they are, it needs to be demonstrated that Indigenous approaches and priorities are routinely and extensively incorporated into board processes, recommendations, and decisions.

Assessment of Indigenous influence on the boards and their work entails several components: the numbers of board members and senior staff who are Indigenous; the conclusions reached in the secondary literature; the insights obtained from the research conducted for this book by way of interviews and observation of board meetings and processes; the nature and extent of community involvement in board processes; and the role of traditional knowledge in board operations and processes.

None of these components are direct measures of Indigenous influence, an imprecise concept to be sure. Some would argue that, even if it is found that Indigenous people serving on boards do have influence, this is not necessarily Indigenous influence as Indigenous board members must abandon key cultural principles in order to operate within the board regime. To some extent this is necessarily true. The argument, however, is not that Indigenous influence on and through co-management boards is in complete accord with Indigenous worldviews and culture. Rather, I (and others) maintain that, through community involvement, traditional knowledge, and the personal perspectives of board members, substantial Indigenous influence does exist.

A related issue involves possible mass/elite divisions within Indigenous communities. The concern here is that the approaches and imperatives of the Indigenous elites who negotiated the claims or hold positions on boards might not correspond to those of Indigenous community members, especially since the elites must conduct themselves according to a Euro-Canadian epistemological framework to participate in board processes. While, as outlined below, I can state with assurance that Indigenous board members and other leaders believe that they exert genuine and significant influence through the boards, it is not possible to gauge how extensively community members share this assessment. Although mass/elite differences with respect to co-management boards may exist, it is important to recognize that most Indigenous board members are deeply involved in their communities and share their priorities and perceptions.

Academic critics have challenged the entire co-management regime, arguing that it not only fails to convey adequate power to Indigenous people over crucial land and wildlife policies and practices but, worse, that it promotes the extinguishment of Indigenous culture. The penultimate section of this chapter sets out and evaluates their arguments. Particularly in this phase of the analysis, but throughout the chapter, at least implicitly, recourse is made to a distinction sometimes employed by politicians seeking re-election in the face of cranky voters. "Don't compare me with the Almighty," they ask, "compare me with the alternative." Contemplating ideal but unattainable regimes for extensive, if not complete, Indigenous control of their lands and resources can be useful, but in the world of practical, compromise-ridden politics, the focus should be on what can reasonably be expected of co-management boards. This is by no means to accept the serious flaws in the co-management system or to cease striving for improvements – entailing perhaps thoroughgoing reform – but, rather, to recognize in the broadest sense what co-management through claims boards can achieve.

The case studies devoted considerable attention to specific boards' early days and traced how they changed over time. Some boards had rougher start-ups than others, but all experienced notable maturation as they gained experience and as the governments and organizations they interacted with came to understand and appreciate their roles and value. This is not my assessment alone: many of those interviewed, as well as academic and other observers, have made similar observations. To be sure, the effectiveness of individual boards waxes and wanes, nor does anything like systematic evidence exist as to the broad range of board development over the years. Still, for the boards examined in detail in previous chapters, it is important to recognize their positive trajectories when gauging influence and effectiveness.

Not all is sweetness and light with respect to the land claims agreements of which the boards are an integral part.[2] Considerable discontent with the claims is evident in Northern Indigenous communities. Internal opposition, by times substantial opposition, to the claims existed during negotiations and ratification, and indeed some Northern Indigenous communities and groups remain unconvinced of the benefits of land claims and have either abandoned negotiations or refuse to participate in them. Acknowledging this, it is not possible to determine how widespread and deep is dissatisfaction in Indigenous communities with their settled claims. Doubtless this varies a good deal. Hard data do exist on the ratification votes held on the final negotiated versions of prospective claims settlements. The federal government requires that a tentative claim be approved by 50 percent plus one of all eligible voters; in other words, abstentions count as "no's." In some instances support was clear cut. In the Nunavut ratification vote, for example, 69 percent of eligible voters approved the claim; with 81 percent of those eligible voting, this meant 85 percent of those who cast ballots opted for "yes." Support for the *Tlicho Agreement* was even stronger: 84 percent of eligible voters (91 percent of those who voted). Other votes were much closer; in the ratification votes held in Yukon by both the Kwanlin Dün First Nation and the Carcross-Tagish First Nation barely 53 percent of eligible voters (meaning, given turnout rates, support for the claims among those who voted was in the range of 60 to 65 percent) – and in the case of Carcross-Tagish, this was a second vote, the first having rejected the proposed agreement.

Has dissatisfaction with settled claims increased or diminished since the ratification vote? Again, systematic data that could provide an answer are simply not available, either generally or for particular claims. As well, we have no way of determining the extent to which discontent, which unquestionably exists, reflects rejection of board principles and operations, which are important but only partial elements of claims, or of other aspects of the claims, such as surrender of traditional lands.

Northern land claims and self-government agreements are at root compromises. Indigenous negotiators understood that they would not get all the control over land and governance processes that they and their communities wanted, but they accepted deals that they believed did provide substantial benefits. Accordingly, opposition and discontent was surely to be expected but must be evaluated against the positive aspects of the claims and, within the claims, the boards. In this regard, Douglas Clark and Jocelyn Joe-Strack detect in the North a "growing recognition that even at its fullest expression, co-management is still only a part of what's required to realize the vision of self-determination that land claim agreements were intended to move society towards."[3]

Treaty Federalism?

Chapter 1 suggests that it would be useful to consider Northern claims-mandated co-management boards through a treaty federalism lens. Although intervening chapters do not explicitly bring a treaty federalism perspective to bear, they do offer extensive material relevant to the concept's value for understanding institutions and processes beyond those entailed in the historic treaties, which have thus far been the primary focus of treaty federalism scholars.

By definition, the boards are treaty-based. They owe their existence – and influence – to provisions in settled comprehensive land claims agreements, recognized in section 35 of the *Constitution Act, 1982*, and termed by the Government of Canada as "modern treaties."

But what of federalism? Are the boards truly institutions of Canadian federalism and, more important, does treating them as such advance our understanding of either the boards or Canadian federalism? To be sure, claims boards do not constitute a "fourth order of government," as an early emanation of this project somewhat disingenuously suggested.[4] Nor are they a species of Aboriginal self-government. They do, however, exist at the intersection of the three principal orders of government in the Canadian federation: federal, provincial/territorial, and Indigenous. And, although Chapter 7 shows that important limits, especially in terms of appointments and funding, constrain board independence, it is clear that claims boards enjoy significant independence from the three orders of government. Moreover, to the extent that federalism is about shared authority across jurisdictional boundaries – as indeed is co-management – boards qualify as institutions of federalism, albeit highly distinctive, unconventional institutions. Thomas Huegelin is quoted in Chapter 1 as observing that treaty federalism "is meant to be an open-ended, horizontal and renewable partnership aiming at the autonomy and reciprocity of all participants."[5] With respect to how the claims boards deal with land, environment, and wildlife issues, Huegelin's rendering of treaty federalism captures important elements of the boards.

The value of a treaty federalism perspective for the study of co-management claims boards lies in the critically important reminder it provides as to the fundamental character of the boards. It is easy, when engrossed in the myriad details of the complex issues before them, to lose sight of the primal reality that the boards are essential elements in the ongoing implementation – and maturation – of the modern treaties covering much of the North. These, after all, are constitutionally protected co-management institutions explicitly designed to serve the interests of the Indigenous peoples who have made treaty with the Canadian Crown, bringing their knowledge and perspectives to bear on land and wildlife issues of vital importance to them.

In turn, studying Northern claims boards broadens the scope of the treaty federalism approach by demonstrating that institutions and processes coming out of comprehensive claims provide important possibilities for advancing Indigenous aspirations and interests. After all, the central tenet of treaty federalism is that recognition of the nature of the treaties and, more concretely, actions rooted in their provisions are essential for progress on Indigenous-state relations in Canada. Without losing sight of the need to respect and follow the historic treaties, implementation of comprehensive land claims offers important opportunities for innovative methods of reconciling Canada's Indigenous and non-Indigenous peoples.

Does that imply that Northern-style co-management boards hold the promise of significantly advancing reconciliation in Southern Canada? Unfortunately, this important question cannot be answered by the findings of this study. Too many contextual factors differ greatly between the territorial North and the southern provinces. To name a few: the ramifications of the historic treaties; the substantially more powerful role of the federal government "North of 60"; the far smaller proportions of Indigenous people – and thus their political clout – in the provinces; and the much greater extent of "third party" interests in the provinces, combined with provincial ownership and control of Crown land. Would these and other differences prevent successful implementation of wildlife and environmental regulatory Indigenous-state co-management boards in the provinces? The prospects seem remote, but then fifty years ago so too would the prospects that co-management boards would become such prominent players in the North.

Do the Co-management Boards Have Real Power?

Overall, the evidence presented in this book is unequivocal: co-management boards established under the Northern comprehensive land claims are important, powerful players in determining both general policy and specific decisions in the realms of wildlife and environmental regulations.

It is important to recognize that this conclusion does not apply to all Northern co-management boards. The boards rooted in land claims enjoy formal legal, indeed constitutional, status far beyond that available to non-claims co-management boards such as the Beverly and Qamanirjuaq Caribou Management Board or the Ruby Range Sheep Steering Committee (the basis for a good deal of Nadasdy's criticism of co-management).[6]

Indisputable evidence supporting the boards-are-powerful position is found in the continuous, vociferous demands from industry to rein in the boards engaged in environmental regulation. Were the boards lacking in clout, industry representatives would hardly be as concerned with them as they have been from the outset of the board regime.

For the most part, the boards are advisory, putting recommendations to the federal and territorial governments and in a few instances to Indigenous governments or organizations. Some boards, however, do have final decision-making power in certain circumstances. For example, NWT land and water boards can render final decisions on Type B water licences or land use permits. Other boards have complete authority in dispensing research funds to applicants, including federal and territorial governments.

No claims board has compiled an inventory of its recommendations and government responses to them (at least that is publicly available), though some are working on doing so. Even were such inventories available, a quantitative analysis of the fate of board recommendations would be of only limited use since it would require arbitrary decisions as to the scope and importance of individual recommendations. How, for example, would one interpret government acceptance of a dozen minor recommendations versus rejection of one of major import? That said, the clear consensus among observers of and participants in the board regime, including those at boards and those in government, is that the vast majority of board recommendations are accepted or varied only in limited ways by government. To be sure, some board recommendations, some of major consequence, have been rejected by government or varied in fundamental ways. Those familiar with the process, however, assert convincingly that such instances are very much the exception.

Many board recommendations have been allowed to pass into policy because government officials have recognized the high quality of the boards' research, consultation, and deliberations and therefore accord their "advice" the respect it deserves. A good example of the significance of boards' political legitimacy is the Nunavut Wildlife Management Board's 1996 recommendation that Nunavut Inuit be permitted to harvest a bowhead whale, which the federal minister approved despite considerable domestic and international pressure.[7]

In understanding government responses to board recommendations it is necessary to recognize that, as with all government decisions, they are suffused with politics. Two public servants (one federal, one territorial), reviewing their experience with ministerial responses to land claims boards' recommendations, commented: "in practice [ministerial] rejection or modification of a decision carries with it a high political risk and is rare."[8] This view was echoed by a Yukon public servant involved with claims boards, who argued, "it's not in a minister's interest to reject board recommendations." A similar conclusion was reached from an Indigenous perspective: Norman Simmons and Gladys Netro note that, although the regional resources councils in Yukon only offer "advice" to government, it is "advice with a difference ... this is a considerable restriction on the traditional powers of a Minister of the Crown."[9] It may even be that, as Usher notes for the Beverly and Qamanirjuaq Caribou Management Board, "ministers and senior managers seem to have recognized the political advantages of letting the Board take responsibility for some difficult decisions rather than imposing their own solutions."[10]

The politics of government response to board recommendations are very much shaped by the "negative option" entailed in many board-government interactions, whereby recommendations are deemed to have been approved if government has not formally rejected or varied them within a relatively short time period. Accordingly, for land claims boards the usual political calculus, whereby advisory bodies must expend political capital in an effort to convince ministers to accept recommendations, is reversed: ministers must expend their political resources, not least by laying out their objections in writing, and must do so quickly, or the boards' recommendations come into effect by default. Significantly, this includes board recommendations that governments would have preferred not to deal with but could not ignore by virtue of the "negative option" provision.

One board executive director mentioned in an interview a recommendation that came into force when the government, apparently through oversight, failed to respond within the stipulated time period. Given the complexity of federal government decision-making processes, it is unlikely that this was the only such occurrence.

An Inuit leader deeply involved in negotiating the claim noted that Inuit wanted the boards to have final authority in the matters before them, but that wasn't acceptable to government. The negative option, he said, was "the next best thing ... a good compromise." Still, he added, at the outset: "We were very concerned that ministers could just ignore us ... It took a couple of court cases to make them [federal government departments] understand about the importance of the claim and of the IPGs."

Another aspect of board influence derives from the very public nature of board processes. Prior to the advent of the boards, governments typically made wildlife and environmental regulatory decisions internally. Even if substantial consultations were held with Indigenous communities and organizations, which was not often the case, little occurred in public. Nor was much information available to the public. By contrast, almost all elements of the claims boards regime – project applications; evidence and argument from applicants; comments from governments, communities, and other intervenors; board recommendations and government responses – appear on the public record. A federal public servant identified this change as a key factor contributing to the major improvements in governance and policy brought about by the boards: "in the past we've had some very bad decisions by ministers; there is much less of that under the boards because of the accountability involved and the public processes."

None of this is to suggest that Northern claims boards are anything like all-powerful or to deny that their work and their recommendations are on occasion ignored or overridden. Still, the landmark court cases relating to the Peel Watershed Planning Commission's recommendations on land use strongly reinforce the central role played by claims boards.

After years of study and consultation, the commission (an *Umbrella Final Agreement* board) recommended that 81 percent of the Peel watershed, a pristine region of Northern Yukon, be designated a special management area, where, among other things, mining development would be prohibited. In 2014, the Yukon Government, claiming the power to override such recommendations, announced a plan that would protect only 29 percent of the area. Local First Nations and environmental organizations launched a successful legal challenge to the government plan. In striking down the government plan, Justice R.S. Veale of the Supreme Court of Yukon based his decision to some extent on the flawed process the government followed in dealing with the Planning Commission. However, more critical in his view was the fundamental underpinning of modern treaties and, by extension, the institutions created to implement them:

> Treaties are as much about building relationships as they are about the settlement of past grievances. They are to be interpreted in a manner that upholds the honour of the Crown ... [T]he process adopted by the Government of Yukon ... [did not] enhance the goal of reconciliation. It was an ungenerous interpretation not consistent with the honour and integrity of the Crown.[11]

The Yukon Court of Appeal subsequently issued a judgment partially supporting the Yukon Government's position, but in December 2017, the Supreme Court of Canada sided with the initial judgment, quashing the government's land use plan "on the basis that Yukon exceeded the proper scope of its authority to modify the [Commission's] Final Recommended Plan under the terms of the UFA; and, based on a contextual reading of the modern treaty, returned the parties to the prescribed process [in the *UFA*]."[12]

The Supreme Court, it should be noted, was not rejecting the notion that the Yukon Government holds final authority in establishing land use plans, as the *UFA* stipulates. Rather, like the earlier Supreme Court of Yukon judgment, it strongly upheld the principle that governments must take very seriously the process and recommendations of claims-based boards and respect the spirit and intent of the treaties.

Indigenous Influence on Claims Boards

Northern claims boards may indeed be powerful players in wildlife and environmental regulatory decisions, but do Indigenous people truly influence their processes and decisions in substantial ways? Here the evidence consistently, though by no means universally, points to a positive assessment.

Surely the vehement protests of Indigenous leaders and organizations against Ottawa's attempts to alter the environmental regulatory claims board regimes in the NWT and Yukon, discussed in Chapters 6 and 7, represent telling evidence that Indigenous people believe that they exercise significant influence through the boards.

Although, at least for now, it is unique within the board regime, with no analogue in any other Northern claims-based co-management board, the power – not influence – the Tlicho Government holds as a decision maker on environmental assessment reports from the Mackenzie Valley Environmental Impact Review Board is a highly noteworthy illustration of Indigenous influence over claims boards.

Numbers

An obvious indicator of Indigenous influence is the numerical representation of Indigenous people on the boards. Here, as Tables 2.4 and 2.5 in Chapter 2 demonstrate, the evidence is crystal clear. In terms of the full range of Northern claims boards as of February 2018, Indigenous people constituted half or more of the members on twenty-one of thirty boards (calculated on the basis of serving members; i.e., ignoring vacancies). Looking at the seven boards whose entire membership from start-up is portrayed in Table 2.5, a similar picture emerges: over their entire existence, four boards have had substantially more Indigenous than non-Indigenous members, while three have had marginally more non-Indigenous members.[13] In short, Indigenous members are in the majority on many Northern claims-based co-management boards and on virtually all others – the largely inactive Inuvialuit Arbitration Board is the sole outlier – are present in substantial numbers.

This strong evidence of Indigenous influence must be tempered by the recognition that relatively few senior or technical board staff positions are held by Indigenous people. Precise numbers are not available, but on the basis of having closely followed a number of boards over two decades, I can state with confidence that only a handful of board executive directors or senior technical staff, such as biologists and environmental assessment officers, have been Indigenous. The hope and expectation is that, over time, more Indigenous people will take up these critical board positions, but progress has been slow. In the meantime, however, it is important to bear in mind, as mentioned in earlier chapters, that Indigenous board members are usually involved in senior staff hiring and that significant proportions of senior board staff are highly knowledgeable about and sympathetic to Indigenous concepts of and approaches to land and wildlife issues.

Secondary Literature

With the noteworthy exception of the critics discussed in a subsequent section, the secondary literature supports the interpretation that Indigenous influence on the boards is significant. Prior to examining the critics' views, it is worth noting that their negative assessment rests more on concerns about harmful effects on Indigenous culture than on perceptions of weak Indigenous influence. Overall, the secondary literature on claims-mandated co-management boards clearly supports the conclusion that Indigenous people exercise significant influence on land and wildlife issues through the boards.

At first blush, the findings of the only previously published major study of the politics of co-management boards, Thierry Rodon's *En partenariat avec l'État: Les expériences de cogestion des Autochonones du Canada*, might not appear to accord with an interpretation of positive influence. Rodon categorizes the Hunting, Fishing and Trapping Coordinating Committee established under the *James Bay and Northern Quebec Agreement* as unsuccessful, a clear instance of "malentendu" – lack of understanding.[14] While he acknowledges that the Inuvialuit see the *Inuvialuit Final Agreement* co-management boards as highly successful, he sees them as fostering integration of the Inuvialuit into the Canadian state. Has the *IFA* co-management regime, he asks, enhanced Inuvialuit autonomy. "The answer to this question," he observes, "depends on the perspective one adopts."[15] Similarly, Rodon concludes that, while the experience of the Nunavut Wildlife Management Board is essentially one of integration, it has had positive results for the Inuit.[16]

As argued in Chapter 1's discussion of Rodon's analytic schema, the nature of successful co-management is to seek influence through integration. Thus, provided that Indigenous people have gained significant influence through the boards, some measure of integration is to be expected and indeed welcomed as a means of exercising influence. Rodon himself recognizes that Indigenous people wield power – power ("pouvoir"), not just influence – via the boards and, in particular, through their participation in resource management decision-making processes.[17] And he ends his book on a cautiously hopeful note: "the co-management experiment is still young with unfulfilled potential."[18]

In a comprehensive analysis of the first decade of the *Inuvialuit Final Agreement*, long-time observer and participant Lindsay Staples concludes unequivocally that, since the signing of the claim, Inuvialuit involvement in wildlife management has "improved dramatically ... The participation of the Inuvialuit in the IFA management regime is both extensive and substantive, and has had a significant influence on government decision making."[19] Lloyd Binder and Bruce Hanbidge are similarly sanguine about the *IFA*, commenting that, as a result of the claim and its institutions, "there is no 'tragedy' in the Inuvialuit commons."[20]

The conclusions of these early positive assessments of the *IFA* boards have been corroborated by two recent analyses, one by academics, one by practitioners. John-Erik Kocho-Schellenberg and Fikret Berkes's study of the Fisheries Joint Management Committee (FJMC) finds that it had significant positive effects for the Inuvialuit. It further argues that the FJMC experience demonstrates that time is required for co-management bodies to mature and become effective.[21] Long-time FJMC official Burton Ayles and his colleagues, academics and officials, conclude that co-management in the Inuvialuit Settlement Region "has enabled the Inuvialuit to have a meaningful and effective voice in the management of fisheries resources in the Western Arctic."[22]

Leslie Treseder and Jamie Honda-McNeil weigh the experiences of wildlife co-management boards and find that successes outweigh failures.[23] Writing in the early days of the modern treaties, Fikret Berkes asserts that "the co-management provisions of these [land claims] agreements are quite detailed and provide for a level of user group participation in resource decision-making which is simply unparalleled in Canada and rarely achieved elsewhere."[24] Based on decades of experience as both member of and advisor to land claims boards plus a wide-ranging academic perspective, Peter Usher writes: "The co-management arrangements [of land claims boards] work well in principle and in practice for both humans and the environment."[25] Lindsay Galbraith and colleagues rate the environmental assessment process of the MVEIRB as "exemplary," in part because it goes significantly further in meaningfully involving Indigenous people in environmental regulation than most such processes in Canada and elsewhere.[26] At the same time, they also recognize shortcomings in this regard, for example, Indigenous people's mistrust of the process, a lack of capacity to participate effectively, and insufficient resources devoted to traditional knowledge. Finally, veteran advocate for Indigenous causes Thomas Berger writes:

> Areas that do have co-management boards established under land claims agreements differ distinctly from provinces in terms of community authority for decision-making. While local communities affected by large industrial developments are not consulted in most provinces, in the Northwest Territories, local communities have extensive decision-making power. They can decide whether an investment can proceed and place conditions or restrictions on the operation.[27]

The closest approximation of a survey assessing Indigenous influence on land claims boards was conducted for the initial five-year review of the Nunavut claim. Researchers asked both business leaders and representatives of local, Inuit-dominated Hunters and Trappers Organizations about Inuit influence on public policy. Nine of ten businesspeople were of the view that Inuit have effective control over some or most important decisions affecting land and water, while all fourteen HTO officials who responded said that they had more rather than less control over wildlife decisions since the claim came into effect.[28] Neither group was asked directly about the land claims boards involved in these areas, but, given the boards' status as central players in land, water, and wildlife decisions, it is reasonable to infer that respondents' answers can be taken as positive assessments of Inuit influence through the boards.

Interviews and Observation of Meetings

On the basis of dozens of interviews and informal discussions with Indigenous board members and officials of Indigenous organizations as well as observation of board meetings across the three territories, it is clear that Indigenous people knowledgeable about the boards generally believe that land claims boards entail significant Indigenous influence over land and resource matters. To be sure, some expressed a desire for a good deal more influence while others expressed significant reservations as to the boards' value for Indigenous people. Some Indigenous people and organizations, especially in the "unsettled" areas of the NWT, express vociferous criticism of the board regime, but it is not based on a weighing of boards' strengths and weaknesses, as is the analysis in this book. Rather, it reflects a fundamental rejection of the modern treaty process and a desire for governance based in Treaties 8 and 11.

The following positive quotations from Indigenous leaders and board members about the co-management regime is not held out as fully representative of opinions voiced in the interviews, but it does capture the consensus of those interviewed. A veteran Inuit leader, for example, acknowledging that the Nunavut land claims boards are for many Inuit discouragingly formal and bureaucratic, accepts this as "a necessary evil" in light of their notable successes "in bringing issues down to the people in the communities and speaking their language." An official of Nunavut Tunngavik Incorporated, the Inuit land-claim organization, observed that "bridging the two worlds of Inuit ways and Western ways is the real challenge. Bringing the Inuit way into land and wildlife decisions is the strongest argument in favour of the IPGs in the first place ... The IPGs create the opportunity for the little guy in the community to have an impact." A Gwich'in leader, who had been involved in negotiating the claim, commented: "the Gwich'in aimed at and achieved participation in the management of the land ... It is meaningful participation, even though the boards operate at arm's-length from the Gwich'in Tribal Council." According to an Indigenous board member from elsewhere in the NWT, "the [board] process is a lot better [than what went before]; Aboriginal people are directly involved in the decision-making process, especially those most directly involved." In Yukon, the *UFA* boards have become, in the opinion of a senior Council of Yukon First Nations official, "venues for us to ensure that our people have representation and significant input on land and resource decisions," adding that, while the boards may not have formal, explicit powers, "they have very significant levels of influence." Another long-time Yukon Indigenous leader maintained that the boards "have certainly made for substantial First Nation involvement in land and resources issues."

A telling episode occurred at the 2002 Yellowknife TK workshop mentioned in Chapter 5. A young Dene man angrily attacked the Mackenzie Valley Environmental Impact Review Board as unrepresentative of the local Indigenous people, proclaiming "your [MVEIRB] views don't fit with ours ... The real decision-making power should go to the communities ... The MVEIRB doesn't really work." At this, an Indigenous MVEIRB member, a respected elder with long years of Dene politics behind him, responded with equal force, defending the claims regime of which the board is a key element: "25 years ago we were nothing ... now I can make a decision and tell the government what to do ... I sit on the board to do the work our elders said we should do 25 years ago."[29]

Such exchanges raise an important question as to possible mass/elite differences in views of the co-management boards. It could be argued that

Indigenous board members and staff have a personal and professional stake in board processes, which may incline them to judge the boards favourably, whereas community members "view the boards with suspicions if not downright hostility precisely because the boards are engaged in what they see as the culturally inappropriate process of environmental management (which involves interfering in local people's personal relationships with the land and animals)."[30] Lacking systematic evidence as to whether suspicion or hostility at the community level is isolated or widespread, we must necessarily fall back on the perceptions of board members and staff. Most Indigenous board members and staff are deeply rooted in their communities and thus share community outlooks. Accordingly, their positive evaluations of the boards and of Indigenous influence on and through them is noteworthy in terms of considering possible mass/elite differences.

Community Involvement

In the course of the interviews, several Indigenous respondents noted with approval that environmental regulatory boards are required to ensure that communities within the claim areas, many of which are overwhelmingly Indigenous, as well as Indigenous organizations, are informed and consulted about proposed projects and their potential impact. Not only must communities and Indigenous organizations be accorded the opportunity to bring forward their views on such proposals to the boards reviewing them, but the proponents must respond in public to their concerns. These requirements do not, of course, bestow upon the communities the authority to reject proposals, but they enhance Indigenous influence over the process and, indeed, its outcome.

However, as discussed in Chapters 5 and 6, the potential for Indigenous influence through the claims boards is significantly constrained by endemic capacity issues. Most, if not all, communities and Indigenous organizations in all three territories lack the human and financial resources to be able to respond effectively – in many cases to respond at all – to the seemingly endless invitations from boards and other governmental agencies to put forward their views on proposed developments and policies. Accordingly, the potential for genuine, significant Indigenous influence on board processes through community involvement in board processes is often not realized. The boards' practice of holding public hearings and information sessions in communities goes some distance towards overcoming the capacity problem. Still, the lack of substantial participant funding for community and organization intervenors, which until recently Ottawa consistently refused to provide in all but a few instances, has limited prospects for strong Indigenous influence through board processes.

Traditional Knowledge

A key indicator of Indigenous influence over claims boards is the extent to which boards respect traditional knowledge and act according to it. No point would be served in revisiting in detail the discussion in the previous chapter about TK and the boards; a quick summary will suffice. In keeping with provisions of the claims and their enabling legislation, boards have made significant efforts to take TK seriously in their operations and decision making, with TK sometimes figuring prominently in shaping recommendations. Yet despite good intentions, formidable impediments limit both the boards' appreciation of TK and their application of it in their work. The oftentimes inherent incompatibility between TK approaches and the processes of the modern bureaucratic state within which the boards operate figures prominently here. So too the difficulty, compounded by language barriers, of even well-meaning non-Indigenous board members and staff to understand TK and to incorporate it into board processes and decision making is substantial. And, as the Yukon Fish and Wildlife Management Board's decision on catch-and-release fishing, recounted in Chapter 4, brings home clearly, in some instances board actions directly contravene deeply held Indigenous cultural values.

A study of the use of TK in the NWT concluded that the *Mackenzie Valley Resource Management Act* provides "legal leverage to Aboriginal people in the Territory that allows them to influence resource management decision-making." Notably, the study found

> significant differences in the legal clout attributed to Aboriginal governments and in their capacities to ensure their knowledge is meaningfully considered. Those with settled land claim areas within the Mackenzie Valley ... may have greater advantage than those [without settled claims] ... because of the legal terms of the agreements and the capacities of their associated Land Use Planning Boards, Land and Water Boards, Renewable Resources Boards and Councils, and representation on the Mackenzie Valley Environmental Impact Review Board.[31]

Overall, boards do recognize and employ TK, making for limited but still significant Indigenous influence over boards. As virtually everyone acknowledges, however, a long distance still needs to be travelled before TK becomes as central to board processes as Indigenous people want, if indeed that is even possible.

The Critics

Consideration of the role played, or not played, by TK in land claims boards offers an entry point to the most serious critiques of the boards. For anthropologists Paul Nadasdy and Marc Stevenson, the all-but-complete absence of TK, in its cosmological sense, from co-management processes bespeaks fundamental problems with the entire regime. Although their arguments apply to the entire range of land claims boards and they refer in passing to environmental licensing and review boards, their analyses are rooted in the experiences of wildlife co-management boards. Much of their evidence comes from boards that did not arise from land claims, but their critiques are sufficiently broad to bear directly on land claims boards. Another anthropologist, Carly Dokis, has voiced similar concerns based on her research in the Sahtu region of the NWT on the Joint Review Panel assessing the Mackenzie Gas Project.

Based on his study of how the Ruby Range Sheep Steering Committee, a non–claims-based co-management board, uses traditional ecological knowledge in wildlife management in the Kluane region of Yukon, Nadasdy offers a decidedly negative interpretation of the culture clash between First Nations cosmology and the apparatus of the modern state:

> Although on the surface land claims and co-management seem to be giving Aboriginal peoples increased control over their lives and land, I argue that these processes may instead be acting as subtle extensions of empire, replacing local Aboriginal ways of talking, thinking, and acting with those specifically sanctioned by the state.[32]

Nadasdy anchors his analysis in the development literature and examines how language and discourse shape perceptions and behaviour. His central conclusion is as follows: "Without denying the sincerity of those who hope for improved management and the empowerment of First Nation people through co-management, we must also acknowledge that the complex process of co-management may have a number of other unforeseen – and unintended – consequences ... Rather than empowering local aboriginal communities ... co-management may actually be *preventing* the kind of change proponents desire. Indeed, co-management may actually be serving to extend state power into the very communities that it is supposedly empowering."[33] Although they see positive possibilities through co-management, Carlsson and Berkes acknowledge that, in situations like those found in Northern Canada, where the state has taken management power from the local people, co-management may be "an attempt of state authorities to increase the legitimacy of their domination."[34]

Nadasdy rejects what has become a standard justification for co-management regimes: that co-management is more effective than state management because it can incorporate TK into decisions. He maintains that, to be of use in co-management processes, TK must be so simplified and taken out of context that it has little value in or impact on actual decision making. However, this phase of the analysis is brief and not sufficiently developed to be convincing. In particular, it does not distinguish between the mandate and approach of the Ruby Range Sheep Steering Committee – where, as Nadasdy demonstrates, TK is of little moment – and those of claims-based co-management boards, which exercise substantial, constitutionally sanctioned clout and which are legally required to take TK into account in decision making (not that this is necessarily done nearly as well as it might be).

Far more compelling is his discussion of another principal justification for co-management: that it empowers local Indigenous people. His argument largely rests on the proposition that, "by ensnaring participants in a tangle of bureaucracy and endless meetings," co-management inhibits rather than fosters "meaningful change."[35] This occurs because, to participate effectively in co-management, Indigenous people have had to adopt Western bureaucratic structures, norms, and ways of thought: "to participate ... they have had to accept the rules and assumptions of the state management game."[36] As Berkes notes, co-management can mean "a white man's institution run by white man's rules."[37] The implicit but unarticulated conclusion for Nadasdy is that, by enmeshing themselves in processes and discourses so incompatible with Indigenous worldviews and approaches, they damage their culture and reduce their capacity for self-determination.

Acknowledging that by virtue of their land claim and the co-management bodies coming out of it "Sahtu Dene involvement in resource decision making has significantly increased," Dokis maintains that it is

> limited by non-local epistemological and ontological underpinnings of governance, management, regulatory and environmental assessment institutions and practices. Indeed these have come to reinforce the power relationships between corporate proponents, Aboriginal communities and the state ... Eliciting Aboriginal participation in environmental management can be seen

as an endeavour to rule and transform, even if it is done with the aim of "hearing" what Aboriginal people have to say.[38]

Stevenson accepts this logic but is harsher in his judgment, stating, for example, that the article of the Nunavut claim establishing the Nunavut Wildlife Management Board and its objectives and processes "introduces concepts so alien to traditional Inuit values and understandings ... as to be a recipe for the destruction of Inuit culture."[39] Nor is he as charitable as Nadasdy, who sees many players in the state co-management system as sincere and well-intentioned but unmindful of its subtle effects. Stevenson tends to see what he terms "the conservation bureaucracy" as wilfully dismissive of Indigenous people's views and methods and unconcerned about co-management's deleterious effects not only for Indigenous culture but also for preserving sensitive ecosystems.[40]

Like Nadasdy, Stevenson maintains that the conceptual framework of "environmental resource management" (ERM) and the discourse it promotes "has rendered traditional Aboriginal ways of relating to their lands and resources virtually invisible in co-management ... Whatever terminology and understandings that Aboriginal participants bring to the table are quickly dismissed as being anecdotal, unscientific or incompatible with ERM and western law." His overall assessment: "Indigenous peoples' participation in state-sponsored projects of co-management has served to disempower them by creating virtually insurmountable barriers to the inclusion of their values, understandings, knowledge and institutions into these processes."[41]

Political scientist Hayden King, the only Indigenous scholar who has written about claims-based co-management boards at any length, concurs:

> Not only do the bureaucratic land use regimes of the present force Indigenous peoples into an alien system of management that limits their decision-making power; the process also encourages them to surrender their values and, indeed, their cultural perspectives on land and resource use in favour of Western or Euro-Canadian notions of development, conservation, and science.[42]

Dokis makes a similar argument, pointing out that, although the co-management boards include Indigenous members, "the rules of engagement come from elsewhere," noting:

> The boards must adhere to the terms of the land claim agreement and must follow rules that are at odds with local ideas about appropriate uses of the land and the way in which decisions ought to be made. In the end, what the

claim actually did achieve was to put Sahtu representatives on corporate and co-management boards in the position of upholding and applying federal laws concerning land management and development.[43]

Like Dokis, King accepts that the co-management board regime "allows [Indigenous] input about land use and also provides a voice in the creation of regional land use plans." On balance, however, he is sharply critical. Using the language of disempowerment and dispossession, he approvingly cites Taiaiake Alfred and Jeff Corntassel's argument that "land claim and self-government regimes are examples of 'post-modern imperialism,' whereby the state co-opts Indigenous resistance into legal discourses that reinforce Canadian sovereignty at the expense of (authentic) Indigenous alternatives."[44]

In drawing our attention to the subtle yet powerful and far-reaching implications of the ideational context of co-management, the critics provide valuable insights into essential elements of land claims boards. They are unquestionably correct that, as Stevenson puts it, "in order to advance their needs, rights and interests in co-management, aboriginal peoples have adopted the languages, approaches and institutions of ERM and British parliamentary law."[45] And, as Nadasdy argues, co-management as practised in Northern Canada is not an "alternative to" but a "variation within" the bureaucratic state.[46] However, are they correct in concluding that participation in co-management arrangements is on balance disadvantageous to Indigenous people? Do their analyses lead to alternative proposals with a reasonable likelihood of coming to fruition? In my view, the answer in both cases is no.

Though Nadasdy and Stevenson rely heavily on examples from co-management boards not based on claims, their arguments about the dominance of the Western bureaucratic paradigm are clearly applicable to land claims boards. However, their judgment that Indigenous insights and interests are not taken seriously in board decision making lacks sufficient empirical support to warrant accepting that it applies to the entire range of land claims boards. In mandate, powers, and in other ways, land claims boards differ in significant ways from boards not arising from land claims. On the basis of the admittedly sometimes ambivalent evidence presented earlier in this chapter and throughout this book, I am sceptical of sweeping generalizations that dismiss the prospect of significant Indigenous influence on land claims boards from limited evidence.

Many in Northern Indigenous communities, as in government and in non-Indigenous circles, have criticisms, both minor and fundamental, of land claims boards, but few would countenance a return to the days when Indigenous people played little, if any, role in wildlife and environmental decisions made by Ottawa and the territorial governments. Some evince disappointment that the claim regimes have not lived up to their promise. Others believe that, from the outset, the compromise that the boards represent tilted too much to government. However, few people – and none of those interviewed for this book – dispute that Indigenous influence has increased through land claims boards. That the compromise failed to satisfy those seeking something akin to Indigenous control of land and resources is clear, but, as Usher observes, "the claims agreements are the results of negotiations, hence do not represent so much what the aboriginal parties sought as much as what they (or their advisors) thought they could get government to agree to in the particular historical context in which they were negotiated."[47] Moreover, the compromises that Indigenous negotiators accepted did not just entail differing visions of wildlife management. Often wildlife management provisions were part of larger compromises involving other components of the claim.[48]

Perhaps so, Nadasdy and Stevenson might concede, but at what cost to Indigenous culture? This is an exceptionally difficult question, even for observers as experienced and knowledgeable as Nadasdy and Stevenson. Without denying the hegemonic power of the Western bureaucratic paradigm, we should not underestimate the resilience of Indigenous cultures or their adaptability. Consider, for example, how modern communication technologies both threaten Indigenous cultures and are used to foster them. Does learning the rules of the co-management game, developing bureaucratic expertise, and engaging in the discourse of state management necessarily entail a loss of culture for Indigenous people? Indigenous cultures are not static and have repeatedly demonstrated remarkable capacity to retain their central defining values in the face of changing circumstances. This observation is not to downplay the threats to Indigenous cultures from a host of developments, including loss of language and severing of links to the land, but, rather, to suggest that the health of Indigenous cultures is a complex matter.

As well, we must be careful about reading too much into the language of land claims boards, symbolically important as language may be. Cruikshank points out that "terms like 'co-management' and 'sustainable development' and 'TEK' are highly negotiable and have no analogues in Native American languages."[49] Indeed so, but three or four decades ago these terms did not exist in English either. Stevenson and others accord considerable weight to the observation that the very notion of "managing" wildlife is inconceivable and absurd in traditional Northern Indigenous cultures.[50] True enough, but, as David Natcher and his colleagues note, "co-management has more to do with managing human relationships than resources per se."[51] An Indigenous member of a wildlife management board put it this way: "We want to manage people, not fish and wildlife."

What alternatives do the critics proffer from their pessimistic analyses of co-management? Dokis calls for project proponents to treat Sahtu communities "as equal partners" rather than as impediments to development, something that "can only occur if genuine power sharing is in place and if Sahtu communities themselves are able to determine their own futures."[52] However, she does not offer any specific suggestions for achieving these goals, either in overall terms or with respect to co-management boards.

During the question period following his lecture critical of co-management boards, published as his chapter in *Canada's North: What's the Plan?*, King was asked about "fixing" the system. Making it clear that it would be "irresponsible" for Indigenous people not to participate as best they can within the existing regime, he went on to say: "We've got to reconsider substantially how we do these things. And, unfortunately I don't really think that the institutional frameworks that do exist will accommodate that. I think we really need to revise wholesale how we do things ... None of these things is going to happen overnight ... it's going to be a process."[53] As to what a wholesale revision or the process for making it would entail he didn't say. In a subsequent piece critical of co-management he describes it as "a call for us to reflect critically on these modern treaties and question if they are really the best we can come up with, to imagine alternatives to this fundamentally unjust relationship, and then to act in unique, creative ways upon those alternatives."[54] This may well be feasible for Indigenous peoples who have yet to finalize treaties, but it is difficult to imagine creative ways of fundamentally revamping existing land claims and their co-management boards.

Nadasdy proposes "the devolution of control over local land and resources to aboriginal communities themselves and this would have to include not only control over wildlife but also over all forms of development."[55] As he recognizes, this devolution would entail "a radical rethinking of the basic assumptions, values, and practices underlying contemporary processes of resource management and environmental impact assessment,"[56] though precisely how this would come to be is vague. In response to Nadasdy, Eugene Hunn and colleagues observe:

> His "solution" imagines a world in which colonial occupation and settlement
> never occurred and nations willingly concede their sovereign power. In reality,
> indigenous communities must necessarily engage an encompassing polity

that holds ultimate power. It would seem more in the interest of the survival of indigenous communities to foster a dialogue, however imperfect, with the professional scientists and resource managers entrusted by national governments with the "protection of our natural resources."[57]

In a later publication, Nadasdy does not go beyond the admonition "that anthropologists and other scholars critically examine their own involvement in processes of knowledge-integration and co-management."[58] Sound advice, but hardly a blueprint for significant structural change.

Stevenson proposes an approach based on the "two-row wampum," a symbol of two canoes travelling parallel paths in peace and friendship, creating space for Indigenous peoples and their modes of thought and knowledge systems in co-management processes. This proposal would be effected primarily through better education for non-Indigenous resource managers, enabling them "to develop a new professional literacy that equips them with an understanding about how resource management decisions reflect and affect the social, cultural and political settings in which they live and work."[59] This proposal would not be an easy undertaking but would doubtless have salutary effects on the culture, operations, and decision making of land claims boards. However, it would not fundamentally change the institutional framework within which the boards operate. Boards would remain firmly established as part of the bureaucratic state system, with ministerial override provisions firmly in place. As Usher notes, co-management is "the antithesis of the parallel canoe approach."[60] Stevenson's idea is worthwhile but falls far short of radical restructuring of the land claims board regimes, let alone their replacement with something that would return land and wildlife decisions to Indigenous peoples.

Nadasdy and Stevenson both focus their critiques on wildlife management boards and have little to say about other types of land claims boards, most notably those engaged in environmental regulation. Wildlife management regimes controlled by Indigenous people, and run on the basis of thoroughgoing TK principles and Indigenous cultural mores, with minimal state influence, are certainly conceivable. Such principles and mores can be, and indeed are, incorporated to some extent into regulatory processes for assessing and mitigating the environmental impact of major infrastructure and economic development projects such as mines, pipelines, dams, and roads as well as processes for approving or rejecting them. However, it is difficult to imagine such a regime outside the realm of state processes and conceptual frameworks. The state simply has too extensive an interest in major projects to forgo deep involvement in regulating them. And, of course, the power imbalance between Indigenous

Indigenous Influence through Claims Boards?

communities and governments on the one hand and the state on the other heavily favours the state. Nor is anything like an analogue found in traditional Indigenous experience for regulating large-scale resource extraction projects, as exists for wildlife management. Otherwise put, it seems inevitable that environmental regulation will proceed along state-sanctioned lines, with considerable scope for Indigenous influence, but not complete control. In turn, this suggests that the possibility of the state's "devolving control over local land and resources to Aboriginal communities [including] all forms of development" is remote.[61]

Political scientists employ the concept of "path dependence" in their explanations of government policy and the development of state structures.[62] In this schema, choices and decisions at key historical junctures condition and constrain subsequent policy choices and institutional developments. It is not a determinist interpretation, but it does alert us to the weight of past decisions. And weighty decisions on the part of both the state and Indigenous peoples to enter into comprehensive land claim agreements and, inter alia, to accept the boards created under those claims, powerfully condition Indigenous-state relations. Governments, believing claims to be "final" and "settled," are unlikely to welcome attempts to renegotiate critical land and resource provisions. For their part, Indigenous governments and political organizations with settled claims are concerned primarily with ensuring that the state lives up to its commitments in terms of properly implementing their claims and are equally unlikely to initiate attempts at sweeping renegotiation. While they sometimes disagree vigorously with the policies and decisions of federal and territorial governments, Northern Indigenous governments and political organizations have become highly institutionalized and in certain ways have become enmeshed in, or adjuncts of, the state. An important example is the Indigenous groups' nomination or appointment of land claims board members, with the patronage possibilities this entails. Thus, in the absence of clearly articulated strategies for replacing the land claims board regimes, which neither Nadasdy nor Stevenson offers, no serious alternative to these boards seems likely to emerge for some time.

Arguments as to the pernicious effects of co-management institutions have recently generated notable pushback. Their analysis of the Fisheries Joint Management Committee and *IFA* boards led Ayles and his colleagues to take issue with the view that "co-management can perpetuate colonial-style relations by concentrating power in administrative centres rather than in the hands of local people, and that co-management can subvert traditional knowledge and the Aboriginal worldview by incorporation into conventional – i.e., 'western based science and decision practices' – environmental and management decision making."[63] Clark and Joe-Strack mount a more concerted attack. With respect to Nadasdy's critique, they contend:

> At the time of his research in the mid-1990s, many such institutions were new, and it wasn't uncommon to see the mere existence of co-management bodies touted as evidence of their success. Times have changed since then, but unfortunately academic perspectives have not. Nadasdy's research is still cited as if current ... and scant attention is paid to the 20 years of progress since it was conducted. Indeed, the entire evolving approach of co-management is now repeatedly critiqued as neocolonialist and assimilationist ... Each of those critiques far exceeds the scope of the data they were based upon, however, by denying both the agency of Indigenous Peoples who achieved their land claims and the hard, ongoing efforts of many Northerners (Indigenous and non-) to simply make co-management work because they believe in it.[64]

To reiterate, it is not that the critics are necessarily wrong in their analyses of the operation and implications of co-management boards, though their assessments can on occasion seem extreme. Rather, what undercuts their position is their unwillingness to accept that, unpalatable as it may be to some, the compromises represented by the claims and the boards – agreed to by astute, experienced leaders – do provide significant benefits to Northern Indigenous peoples, even if they fall short of ideal but politically impracticable alternatives.

Final Thoughts

Overall, the evidence, although fragmentary, impressionistic, and sometimes decidedly equivocal, supports the proposition that Indigenous peoples can and do wield significant influence over land and wildlife decisions through the boards established under Northern comprehensive land claims. Land claims boards exercise substantial power over land and resource decisions, their apparently limited authority notwithstanding. A high proportion of board members are Indigenous, and their influence on board decisions is substantial. Boards and board members enjoy extensive independence in their operations and in their decision making, although important constraints on their independence are evident, most notably through Ottawa's appointment prerogative and its funding processes. TK plays an important role in land claims board decisions, both in wildlife management and environmental regulation; however, although boards have sincerely tried to incorporate TK into all phases of their work, the boards' essentially bureaucratic nature means that these attempts have been only partially successful.

Criticisms of individual boards and the entire board regime abound, but no one proposes a return to the days when Indigenous peoples were effectively excluded from land and resource decisions made by the federal government. Agreement is all but universal that the land claims boards offer Indigenous peoples substantially greater influence over government decisions affecting the land and wildlife than was possible, or even imaginable, under the state system. To be sure, sophisticated critiques have been mounted on land-claim (and other) boards as agents of cultural assimilation, but the critics do not offer much guidance as to how a far-reaching restructuring of the boards and their role within the Canadian state, or their wholesale replacement by a fundamentally different regime, might come about. Current political configurations suggest that the prospects for a resource management regime characterized by genuine Indigenous control displacing the land claims boards in the foreseeable future are slim.

In his analysis of the Nunavut Wildlife Management Board, Rodon asks whether Inuit have been empowered through the co-management processes of their claim. His answer speaks to the essential trade-off characterizing claims boards:

> Not if one believes that the empowerment of Aboriginal people is related to their ability to make choices within a framework that they themselves must define. The answer is affirmative if one believes, as do the governments, that empowerment is based on the ability to make choices within the context defined by the Canadian system.[65]

For better or for worse – and unquestionably "worse" does on occasion obtain – Indigenous peoples must operate within the Canadian state system. However, the state system is not imperviously fixed; it is subject to having "context" influenced, though not defined, by Indigenous peoples – witness the legal requirement that the claims boards in the Mackenzie Valley must accord substantial weight to traditional knowledge. In Rodon's terms, co-management through claims boards can involve intercultural transaction between Indigenous peoples and the state as well as integration of Indigenous peoples into the state system as they exert influence through that system.

If "the alternative" is the state management system that largely excluded Indigenous peoples and their TK, land claims boards may be judged a success in securing Indigenous influence over important land and wildlife decisions.

Yet other alternatives that go beyond a vaguely defined ideal regime ("the Almighty") do exist. Feit's assessment that the way forward "must include the continued development of forms of self-management as well as improved forms of state-level wildlife management ... [since] in a real and practical sense they are now inseparably interlinked, and in many ways they are necessary to each other" is no less valid today than when it was put forward in the late 1980s, though it is well to recall an important question he poses regarding "whether co-management will in the long term come to constitute a form of co-optation and domination, which will weaken self-management and self-governance."[66]

Land claims boards and the role they play in Northern governance continue to evolve, and it is an open question whether, in terms of Indigenous influence, change will represent progress or regress. This book demonstrates, however, that to this point the overall record of land claims boards is positive in promoting and protecting Indigenous interests and worldviews in government policies and decisions relating to wildlife and environmental regulation.

Notes

Chapter 1: A New Species in the Canadian Governmental Menagerie

1 Royal Commission on Aboriginal Peoples, *Report* (Ottawa: Supply and Services Canada, 1996), II, 194.

2 Jamie Snook, Ashlee Cunsolo, and Robyn Morris, "A Half Century in the Making: Governing Commercial Fisheries through Indigenous Marine Co-management and the Torngat Joint Fisheries Board," in Niels Vestergaard, Brooks A. Kaiser, Linda Fernandez, and Joan Nymand Larsen, eds., *Arctic Marine Resource Governance and Development* (Cham, CH: Springer, 2018), 68.

3 Settling on a precise number is a bit of a mug's game, depending on definitions. A conservative count produces thirty claims-mandated boards across the three territories. These are listed in Table 2.3 in Chapter 2. However, while the only permanent land use planning board in Yukon is the Yukon Land Use Planning Council, the Yukon *Umbrella Final Agreement* provides for the establishment of temporary regional land use planning commissions that operate on co-management principles and that may exist for extended periods. As of early 2019, three had been established. As well, one might include the ten regional resources councils in Yukon as co-management boards established under the *UFA*. A recent federal government press release announced improved funding to thirty-three "treaty-based co-management boards and committees" in the NWT. This number included six Inuvialuit hunters and trappers committees and eight Gwich'in and Sahtu regional resources councils as well as the Joint Secretariat, which provides research and administrative support to various Inuvialuit boards. Nineteen of the thirty-three appear to constitute co-management boards as understood in this book. Indigenous and Northern Affairs Canada, "Government of Canada Renews Partnership with 33 Treaty-Based Co-management Boards and Committees in the Northwest Territories," news release, August 24, 2017.

4 Thierry Rodon, *En partenariat avec l'État: Les expériences de cogestion des Autochonones du Canada* (Québec: Les Presses de l'Université Laval, 2003). See also his "Co-management and Self-Determination in Nunavut," *Polar Geography* 22 (April 1998): 119–35; Hayden King, "Give It Up: Land Use and Resource Management in the Canadian North – Illusions of Indigenous Power and Inclusion," in Thomas Berger, Steven A. Kennett, and Hayden

King, *Canada's North: What's the Plan?* (Ottawa: Conference Board of Canada, 2010), 75–107; "Co-managing the Future?" *Northern Public Affairs* 1 (Special Issue 2013): 27–31; "New Treaties, Same Old Dispossession: A Critical Assessment of Land and Resource Management Regimes in the North," in Martin Papillon and André Juneau, eds., *Canada: The State of the Federation 2013: Aboriginal Multilevel Governance* (Montreal and Kingston: Institute of Intergovernmental Relations and McGill-Queen's University Press, 2015), 83–98; Graham White, "Treaty Federalism in Northern Canada: Aboriginal-Government Land Claims Boards," *Publius: The Journal of Federalism* 32 (Summer 2002): 89–114; "Strengthening Indigenous Peoples' Influence: 'Claims Boards' in Northern Canada," *Indigenous Affairs* 4 (December 2004): 26–29; "Cultures in Collision: Traditional Knowledge and Euro-Canadian Governance Processes in Northern Land-Claim Boards," *Arctic* 59 (December 2006): 401–14; "'Not the Almighty': Evaluating Aboriginal Influence in Land-Claim Boards," *Arctic* 61, Suppl. 1 (2008): 71–85; "Aboriginal People and Environmental Regulation: Land Claims Co-management Boards in the Territorial North," in Debora VanNijnatten, ed., *Canadian Environmental Policy and Politics*, 4th ed. (Toronto: Oxford University Press, 2015), 162–80; "Issues of Independence in Northern Aboriginal-State Co-management Boards," *Canadian Public Administration* 61 (December 2018): 550–71.

5 See, for example, Paul Nadasdy, "The Anti-Politics of TEK: The Institutionalization of Co-management Discourse and Practice," *Anthropologica* 47 (2005): 215–32; Stella Spak, "The Position of Indigenous Knowledge in Canadian Co-management Organizations," *Anthropologica* 47 (2005): 233–46; Marc Stevenson, "The Possibility of Difference: Rethinking Co-management," *Human Organization* 65 (Summer 2006): 167–80.

6 Russel Lawrence Barsh and James Youngblood Henderson, *The Road: Indian Tribes and Political Liberty* (Berkeley: University of California Press, 1980), 270.

7 Andrew Bear Robe, "Treaty Federalism," *Constitutional Forum* 4 (Fall 1992): 6, 8.

8 Royal Commission on Aboriginal Peoples, *Report*, II, 194.

9 Gina Cosentino, "Treaty Federalism: Challenging Disciplinary Boundaries and Bridging Praxis, Theory, Research and Critical Pedagogy in Canadian Political Science," in Camille Nelson and Charmaine Nelson, eds., *Racism Eh? A Critical Interdisciplinary Anthology of Race and Racism in Canada* (Concord, ON: Captus Press, 2004), 138.

10 Richard Simeon and Katherine Swinton, "Introduction: Rethinking Federalism in a Changing World," in Karen Knop, Sylvia Ostry, Richard Simeon, and Katherine Swinton, eds., *Rethinking Federalism: Citizens, Markets and Governments in a Changing World* (Vancouver: UBC Press, 1994), 3.

11 James [Sákéj] Henderson, "Empowering Treaty Federalism," *Saskatchewan Law Review* 58 (1991): 253.

12 Kiera Ladner, "Treaty Federalism: An Indigenous Vision of Canadian Federalisms," in François Rocher and Miriam Smith, eds., *New Trends in Canadian Federalism*, 2nd ed. (Toronto: University of Toronto Press, 2003), 190, 189.

13 Thomas Huegelin, "Exploring Concepts of Treaty Federalism: A Comparative Perspective," paper prepared for the Royal Commission on Aboriginal Peoples, 1994, 4.

14 Fikret Berkes, Peter George, and Richard Preston, "Co-management: The Evolution of Theory and Practice of the Joint Management of Living Resources," *Alternatives* 18 (September 1991): 12.

15 Ibid., 14.

16 David C. Natcher, Susan Davis, and Clifford G. Hickey, "Co-Management: Managing Relationships, Not Resources," *Human Organization* 64 (Fall 2005): 241.

17   Peter J. Usher, "Devolution of Power in the Northwest Territories: Implications for Wildlife," in *Native People and Renewable Resource Management: The 1986 Symposium of the Alberta Society of Professional Biologists* (Edmonton: Alberta Society of Professional Biologists, 1986), 69–80.

18   Claudia Notzke, "A New Perspective in Aboriginal Natural Resource Management: Co-management," *Geoforum* 26 (May 1995): 190.

19   Tracy Campbell, "Co-management of Aboriginal Resources," *Information North* 22 (March 1996): 2. For an overview of the range of non-claims co-management arrangements involving Canadian Indigenous people, see Notzke, "New Perspective."

20   David C. Natcher, "Co-Management: An Aboriginal Response to Frontier Development," *The Northern Review* 23 (Summer 2001): 150.

21   Fikret Berkes, "Co-Management and the James Bay Agreement," in Evelyn Pinkerton, ed., *Co-operative Management of Local Fisheries: New Directions for Improved Management and Community Development* (Vancouver: UBC Press, 1989), 190.

22   Department of Indian Affairs and Northern Development, *The Western Arctic Claim: The Inuvialuit Final Agreement* (Ottawa, 1984), s. 12 (50) and s. 14 (46).

23   This statement is based on personal observation of the meetings of an *IFA* board, the Wildlife Management Advisory Council (NWT), the Nunavut Wildlife Management Board, and the Yukon Fish and Wildlife Management Board. The resources these boards have call upon and the detailed procedures they follow differ a good deal, but the interaction of members and the perspectives they bring to bear are similar.

24   Lars Carlsson and Fikret Berkes, "Co-management: Concepts and Methodological Implications," *Journal of Environmental Management* 75 (2005): 66.

25   Ibid., 65.

26   Ibid., 67.

27   Natcher et al., "Co-Management," 241.

28   Rodon, *En partenariat avec l'État*, 20.

29   In an earlier article, he proposed three; the notion of "malentendu" only appears in the book.

30   Rodon, *En partenariat avec l'État*, 144 (my translation).

31   Rodon, "Co-management," 122–23.

32   Rodon, *En partenariat avec l'État*, 145 (my translation).

33   Ibid., 146 (my translation).

34   Ibid. (my translation).

35   Marc Stevenson, "Decolonizing Co-management in Northern Canada," *Cultural Survival Quarterly* 28 (March 2004): 68. See also Paul Nadasdy, "Reevaluating the Co-Management Success Story," *Arctic* 56 (December 2003): 367–80, and "The Anti-Politics of TEK"; and Carly A. Dokis, *Where the Rivers Meet: Pipelines, Participatory Management, and Aboriginal-State Relations in the Northwest Territories* (Vancouver: UBC Press, 2015).

36   Quoted in Rodon, "Co-management," 123.

37   Jim Bell, "A Board without Power," *Nunatsiaq News*, June 10, 2005.

38   King, "New Treaties," 85.

Chapter 2: Northern Governments, Land Claims, and Land Claims Boards

1   For more detailed accounts of the territories and their governments, see the chapters in Bryan M. Evans and Charles W. Smith, eds., *Transforming Provincial Politics: The Political Economy of Canada's Provinces and Territories in the Neoliberal Era* (Toronto: University of Toronto Press, 2015).

2   By way of illustration, most formal constitutional amendments require agreement from Parliament and from the legislatures of at least seven provinces; territorial legislatures have no role in this process.

3   Jim Bell, "Martin Commits to Nunavut Devolution by 2008," *Nunatsiaq News,* December 17, 2004.

4   Statistics Canada, Population and Demography, https://www150.statcan.gc.ca/n1/en/subjects/population_and_demography.

5   Graham White, "Traditional Aboriginal Values in a Westminster Parliament: The Legislative Assembly of Nunavut," *Journal of Legislative Studies* 12 (March 2006): 8–31.

6   Jack Hicks and Graham White, *Made in Nunavut: An Experiment in Decentralized Government* (Vancouver: UBC Press, 2015).

7   For a discussion of elections in Yukon and the other territories, see Graham White "The Territories," in Jared J. Wesley, ed., *Big Worlds: Politics and Elections in the Canadian Provinces and Territories* (Toronto: University of Toronto Press, 2016), 184–205.

8   Jerald Sabin, "A Federation within a Federation? Devolution and Indigenous Government in the Northwest Territories," *IRPP Study* 66, Institute for Research on Public Policy, November 2017.

9   The Dene Nation is an NWT-wide organization but is perennially cash-strapped and lacking political clout.

10 Christa Scholtz, *Negotiating Claims: The Emergence of Indigenous Land Claim Negotiation Policies in Australia, Canada, New Zealand and the United States* (New York: Routledge, 2006).

11 For an overview of the claims negotiation process, see Christopher Alcantara, *Negotiating the Deal: Comprehensive Land Claims Agreements in Canada* (Toronto: University of Toronto Press, 2013), ch. 1.

12 For a fascinating glimpse of the land selection process accompanying the Nunavut claim, see Robert McPherson, *New Owners in Their Own Land: Minerals and Inuit Land Claims* (Calgary: University of Calgary Press, 2003), ch. 7.

13 Although the intent was clear, the actual commitment was to recommend to Parliament legislation to create Nunavut "as a government measure" since it would be improper for the government to make a promise on behalf of Parliament. Minister of Indian Affairs and Northern Development and Tungavik Federation of Nunavut, *Agreement between the Inuit of the Nunavut Settlement Area and Her Majesty the Queen in Right of Canada* (hereafter *NLCA*) (Ottawa: 1993), art. 4.1.1.

14 Thomas R. Berger, *Nunavut Land Claims Agreement Implementation Contract Negotiations for the Second Planning Period 2003–2013: Conciliator's Interim Report* (Iqaluit, August 2005), https://www.tunngavik.com/publication_categories/thomas-berger-conciliation-reports/.

15 See NTI, "Settlement Agreement Signed in NTI Lawsuit," media release, May 4, 2015.

16 Senate of Canada, Standing Committee on Energy, the Environment and Natural Resources, *Proceedings*, December 10, 2001.

17 Quoted in McPherson, *New Owners*, 195.

18 Personal communication, November 17, 2009. Quoted with permission.

19 Quoted in McPherson, *New Owners*, 148.

20 Because the *Inuvialuit Final Agreement* extends into Yukon, two wildlife management advisory councils exist: Wildlife Management Advisory Council (NWT) and Wildlife Management Advisory Council (North Slope). The latter has jurisdiction over wildlife issues in the part of Yukon subject to the *IFA*.

21 Bob Mitchell, as quoted in the "Submission of the Government of the Northwest Territories to the Comprehensive Claims Policy Review Task Force," Yellowknife, September 24, 1985, 12.

22 The Nunavut *Wildlife Act,* passed in 2003, reaffirmed the establishment of the board but made no reference to its composition or funding and added little to its mandate and responsibilities. Most of the act's provisions relating to the board simply restate wording in the claim.

23 The Wek'èezhìi Land and Water Board, a component of the *Tlicho Agreement*, also operates under the act but came into being after the act was in place.

24 An interim Gwich'in land use planning board, authorized by the claim, which had been in place for some time, was replaced by the MVRMA board.

25 As of early 2019, the Nunavut Surface Rights Tribunal had never adjudicated a case. Those associated with it, however, make a convincing case that its substantial power to issue binding decisions and its lack of track record, making prediction of likely outcomes highly uncertain, provide powerful incentives for those engaged in surface rights disputes to settle their differences informally.

26 John Donihee, "Implementing Co-management Legislation in the Mackenzie Valley," paper presented at the Canadian Bar Association conference, "Aboriginal Governance, 2001 and Beyond," Yellowknife, NWT, 2001, 33.

27 SENES Consultants Limited, *Northwest Territories Environmental Audit 2005: Main Report* (Yellowknife: Indian and Northern Affairs Canada, December 2005), 4–8.

28 *Surface Rights Board Act*, S.N.W.T. 2014 c. 17, s. 11 (4).

29 This count excludes the Gwich'in Arbitration Panel, which at the time was completely bereft of members.

30 Madeleine Redfern, "Supporting Civil Development," in Louis McComber and Shannon Partridge, eds., *Arnait Nipingit: Voices of Inuit Women in Leadership* (Iqaluit: Nunavut Arctic College, 2010), 106.

31 *Umbrella Final Agreement between The Government of Canada, The Council for Yukon Indians and The Government of the Yukon*, May 29th 1993, s. 16.7.17.

32 *NLCA*, art. 11.4.8.

33 A distinctive feature of the *IFA* is the provision in section 18 relating to the composition of the Arbitration Board established to sort out disagreements over the meaning or application of the claim. Three of the members of this eleven-member board are to be appointed by "industry," defined as "the five largest commercial and industrial entities in the Inuvialuit Settlement Region with regard to assets," with the proviso that no more than two of the five may be controlled by the Inuvialuit.

34 N. Louise Vertes, David M.H. Connelly, and Bruce A.S. Knott, *5 Year Review 1993 to 1998 Implementation of the Nunavut Land Claims Settlement: An Independent Review* (Yellowknife: Ile Royal Enterprises, 2000), 5–39.

35 *Umbrella Final Agreement*, s. 11.4.3.

36 Save the Fisheries Joint Management Committee, the chair of which is appointed by the members.

37 *NLCA*, art. 5.2.1 (d).

38 Ibid., 38.1.2.

39 Indian and Northern Affairs Canada, *The Western Arctic Claim: The Inuvialuit Final Agreement* (Ottawa: Minister of Indian Affairs and Northern Development, 1984), s. 11 (4).

40 Mike W. Bryant, "Six-Figure Honoraria," *News/North*, November 15, 2004, A3; Jim Bell, "A Board without Power" (editorial), *Nunatsiaq News*, June 10, 2005, 12.

41 PricewaterhouseCoopers, *Second Independent Five Year Review of Implementation of the Nunavut Land Claims Agreement: Final Report* (May 2006), 40.

42 Donihee, "Implementing Co-management Legislation," 40.

43 "Minister Nault Announces New Rates for Chairs and Members Serving on Territorial Institutions of Public Government." INAC News Release and Backgrounder, January 7, 2002.

44 Andrew Webster, "Update on Funding to Treaty-Based Boards and Committees," presentation to NWT Board Forum, November 2017, 7–9.

45 Yukon Environmental and Socio-economic Assessment Board website, http://www.yesab.ca/about-yesab/organizational-chart/.

46 *Umbrella Final Agreement*, s. 16.7.10.

47 See Joint Secretariat website, https://jointsecretariat.ca/about-the-js/board-members-and-staff/.

48 Yukon Environmental and Socio-economic Assessment Board, Annual Report 2017–2018 (Whitehorse, 2018), 6.

49 Decisions as to the location of the main offices of Nunavut IPGs seem to have turned in part on the general penchant for spreading the economic benefits of stable, well-paid public-sector jobs broadly across the territory and in part on the preferences of the first chairs.

50 Indigenous and Northern Affairs Canada, "Government of Canada Renews Partnership with 33 Treaty-Based Co-management Boards and Committees in the Northwest Territories," news release, August 24, 2017.

Chapter 3: The Nunavut Wildlife Management Board

1 As of early 2019, neither the Nunavut Surface Rights Tribunal nor the Nunavut Arbitration Board have had any cases referred to them, though for very different reasons. Under the claim, the Arbitration Board could only act if all three parties agreed to arbitration, and for many years the federal government vetoed all requests to refer issues to arbitration. In 2015, however, as part of the settlement of the long-standing Nunavut Tunngavik Incorporated lawsuit against it (see below), Ottawa agreed to use the Arbitration Board for dispute resolution. No cases have come before the Surface Rights Tribunal, in part because of a lack of disputes and claims and in part because its sweeping powers and the complete absence of precedents provide strong incentives for parties to settle disputes before they reach the tribunal. A few disputes have come close to formal recourse to the tribunal.

2 N. Louise Vertes, David M.H. Connelly, and Bruce A.S. Knott, *5 Year Review, 1993 to 1998: Implementation of the Nunavut Land Claims Agreement* (Yellowknife: Ile Royal Enterprises, 1999), 6–4.

3 PricewaterhouseCoopers, *Second Independent Five Year Review of Implementation of the Nunavut Land Claims Agreement: Final Report* (May 2006), 2–4. No third review was conducted.

4 Nunavut Wildlife Management Board (hereafter NWMB), "Submission of the Nunavut Wildlife Management Board to the Five Year Independent Review of the Nunavut Land Claims and the Implementation Contract" (Iqaluit, September 3, 1999), 3, 4.

5 Terry Fenge, "Political Development and Environmental Management in Northern Canada: The Case of the Nunavut Agreement," *Études/Inuit/Studies* 16 (1992): 128.

6 Ibid., 129–30.

7 Ibid., 131.

8 Minister of Indian Affairs and Northern Development and Tungavik Federation of Nunavut, *Agreement between the Inuit of the Nunavut Settlement Area and Her Majesty the Queen in Right of Canada* (hereafter *NLCA*) (Ottawa, 1993), 1.

Notes to pages 48–57

9 Ibid., art. 5.1.2.

10 Ibid.

11 The 2003 Nunavut *Wildlife Act* contains a brief section outlining the responsibilities of the NWMB, virtually all of which simply reiterate the provisions of the claim.

12 Quoted in Robert McPherson, *New Owners in Their Own Lands: Minerals and Inuit Land Claims* (Calgary: University of Calgary Press, 2003), 146.

13 Government of Nunavut, Department of Culture, Elders and Youth, *First Annual Report of the Inuit Qaujimajattuqanginnut Task Force* (Iqaluit, 2002), 4. See also Ailsa Henderson, *Nunavut: Rethinking Political Culture* (Vancouver: UBC Press, 2007), ch. 9; and Frank James Tester and Peter Irniq, "*Inuit Qaujimajatuqangit*: Social History, Politics and the Practice of Resistance," *Arctic* 61 (2008): 48–61.

14 NWMB, *Governance Manual* (Iqaluit, March 2012), 2.

15 Ibid., 32.

16 Thierry Rodon, "Co-management and Self-Determination in Nunavut," *Polar Geography* 22 (April 1998): 128.

17 Ibid., 125.

18 Ibid., 126–27. See also P.R. Richard and D.G. Pike, "Small Whale Co-management in the Eastern Canadian Arctic: A Case History and Analysis," *Arctic* 46, 2 (June 1993): 138–43.

19 Quoted in Thierry Rodon, *En partenariat avec l'État: Les expériences de cogestion des Autochonones du Canada* (Québec: Les Presses de l'Université Laval, 2003), 234.

20 Peter J. Usher, *A Strategic Plan for the Nunavut Wildlife Management Board* (Iqaluit, May 1996).

21 Nunavut Tunngavik Incorporated, *Taking Stock: A Review of the First Five Years of Implementing the Nunavut Land Claims Agreement* (Iqaluit, December 1999), 132.

22 Article 5.2.2 provides that if a federal appointee is not a public servant, an official of the appointing minister's department has the right to attend all board meetings as a non-voting observer.

23 This is a cruder measure than counting the years actually served by Inuit and non-Inuit, but such a calculation would not likely produce a substantially different finding. The data do not include members appointed by Makivik, who have all been Inuit.

24 See ads for Chairperson/Chief Executive Officer in the *Nunatsiaq News*, August 6, 2008; March 22, 2013; March 4, 2016; and December 22, 2017, indicating that "fluency in Inuktitut and English is essential" and further specifying that preference will be given to "Inuit beneficiaries under the NLCA."

25 This statement is based on the author's observation of four NWMB meetings between 2005 and 2014. Indeed, at the 2014 board meeting in Rankin Inlet, one of the members addressed the author, by that point officially a "senior," as "young fellow."

26 Nunavut Wildlife Management Board, *Minutes*, Regular Meeting (hereafter NWMB, *Minutes*, RM) 6, January 31–February 2, 1995, 10. Minutes are available at the NWMB website: https://www.nwmb.com/en/public-hearings-a-meetings/meetings.

27 The board's recognition of Noble's value is reflected in its creation, at his retirement, of a scholarship named in his honour.

28 NWMB, *Connect and Collaborate: The Nunavut Wildlife Management Board's 5-Year Strategic Plan, 2018–2023* (Iqaluit, 2018), 38, 29.

29 NWMB, *Minutes*, RM 11, May 14–17, 1996, 6.

30 NWMB, *Minutes*, Conference Call (hereafter NWMB *Minutes*, CC) 21, June 24, 1996, 1–2.

31 PricewaterhouseCoopers, *Second Independent Five Year Review*, 19.

32 Certain extensive supporting documents do not need to be translated, but they must be accompanied by an Inuktitut summary. Documents presented to the board from individual members of the public are also exempt from translation requirements; however, the board takes responsibility for translating them. NWMB, *Governance Manual*, 27–28.

33 *Statutes of Canada 1993*, c. 29, 10 (2).

34 The Nunavut Settlement Area includes virtually all of the Territory of Nunavut. Some un-inhabited islands in James Bay and Ungava Bay are part of Nunavut but are not included in the settlement area.

35 See *NLCA*, art. 5.6.

36 PricewaterhouseCoopers, *Second Independent Five Year Review*, 44.

37 Although the Second Five Year Review described the community-based management system as "successful" (ibid.), significant problems bedevilled the program, leading to its abandonment. See Derek R. Armitage, "Community-Based Narwhal Management in Nunavut, Canada: Change, Uncertainty, and Adaptation," *Society and Natural Resources* 18 (2005): 715–31.

38 PricewaterhouseCoopers, *Second Independent Five Year Review*, 44.

39 NWMB, *Minutes*, RM 30, September 18–20, 2001, 20–21.

40 *Statutes of Canada 2002*, c. 29, s. 27 (2) (c).

41 NWMB, *Minutes*, RM 39, October 4–7, 2004, 3–4; *Minutes*, RM 45, March 28–30, 2006, 6.

42 NWMB, *Minutes*, RM 22, May 16–20, 1999, 30; *Minutes*, RM 23, August 24–26, 1999, 26.

43 NWMB, "NWMB PRESS RELEASE: Board's Position on the Protection of Caribou and Sensitive Caribou Habitat," March 16, 2016. Though clearly a response to the Kivalliq situation, the press release was worded so as to apply to all calving grounds.

44 The account of the NWMB decision-making process in this section reflects provisions of pt. 3 of art. 5 of the *NLCA*. Some nuances are overlooked. For a detailed description of the process, see NWMB, *Governance Manual*, 30–34.

45 "Happy New Year: Nunavut Bans Caribou Hunting on Baffin," *Nunatsiaq News*, December 20, 2014. See also Government of Nunavut, "Minister Initiates Interim Moratorium on Baffin Island Caribou Harvest," news release, December 19, 2014.

46 See PricewaterhouseCoopers, *Second Independent Five Year Review*, 38.

47 NWMB, *Governance Manual*, 34.

48 Indian and Northern Affairs Canada, *A Contract Relating to the Implementation of the Nunavut Final Agreement* (Ottawa: Supply and Services Canada, 1993), schedule 4, pt. 1, 5.

49 Thomas R. Berger, *Nunavut Land Claims Agreement Implementation Contract Negotiations for the Second Planning Period 2003–2013, Conciliator's Interim Report* (Vancouver, August 31, 2005), 28, https://www.tunngavik.com/publication_categories/thomas-berger -conciliation-reports/.

50 Thomas R. Berger, *Nunavut Land Claims Agreement Implementation Contract Negotiations for the Second Planning Period 2003–2013, Conciliator's Final Report, March 1, 2006, "The Nunavut Project,"* 3, https://www.tunngavik.com/publication_categories/thomas-berger-conciliation-reports/. For the parties' funding proposals, see Berger, *Conciliator's Interim Report*, 17.

51 "Statement of Claim Nunavut Court of Justice, between the Inuit of Nunavut as Represented by Nunavut Tunngavik Incorporated and the Queen in Right of Canada as Represented by the Attorney General of Canada," Ottawa, December 6, 2006, 3, 11–13.

52 Nunavut Tunngavik Incorporated, Government of Nunavut and Government of Canada, *Moving Forward in Nunavut: An Agreement Relating to Settlement of Litigation and Certain*

Notes to pages 65–72

Implementation Matters (Iqaluit and Ottawa, March 2015), https://www.tunngavik.com/publications/agreement-relating-to-settlement-of-litigation-and-certain-implementation-matters/.

53 NWMB, *Financial Statements March 2017*, 3.
54 NWMB, *Minutes*, RM 1, January 25–28, 1994, 4.
55 Ibid., CC 28, March 24, 1997, 4.
56 Ibid., CC 29, April 4, 1997, 3.
57 Ibid., CC 30, April 7, 1997, 2.
58 NWMB, "Submission to the Five Year Independent Review," 13.
59 Vertes et al., *5 Year Review*, 5–44.
60 Quoted in Dwane Wilkin, "Wildlife Board Survives Funding Flap, Learns Lesson," *Nunatsiaq News*, April 18, 1997.
61 NWMB, *Minutes*, RM 25, March 14–17, 2000, 15.
62 Ibid., CC 104, January 17, 2007, 4.
63 Ibid., RM 21, March 23–26, 1999, 17.
64 Ibid., RM 45, March 28–30, 2006, 12.
65 Ibid., RM 35, June 3–5, 2003, 15.
66 Ibid., CC 50, June 14, 2000, 5.
67 The Torngat Secretariat, which provides administrative and technical support to co-management boards dealing with fisheries, wildlife, and habitat established under the *Labrador Inuit Land Claims Agreement*, commissions and conducts a wide range of research. The research is designed to feed into the boards' interests, but it is the secretariat rather than the boards themselves animating the research.
68 NWMB, *Report for the Period January 1994 to March 1996* (Iqaluit, 1996), 37.
69 The Trust's financial statements are included in the board's annual reports.
70 NWMB, *The Nunavut Wildlife Harvest Study* (Iqaluit: NWMB, 2004), 12.
71 *NLCA*, art. 5.1.2.
72 As displayed on the NWMB's home page – https://www.nwmb.com/en/.
73 NWMB, *Connect and Collaborate*, 4.
74 Martha Dowsley and George Wenzel, "'The Time of the Most Polar Bears': A Co-management Conflict in Nunavut," *Arctic* 61, 2 (June 2008): 178.
75 All quotations in this paragraph taken from author's notes of the Rankin Inlet meeting.
76 Dominique Henri, "Managing Nature, Producing Cultures: Inuit Participation, Science and Policy in Wildlife Governance in Nunavut Territory, Canada" (D. Phil. thesis, University of Oxford, 2012), 245.
77 NWMB, *Connect and Collaborate*, 20, 34.
78 *NLCA*, art. 5.7.13.
79 Joan Scottie, "That Is Where My Spirit Lives," in Louis McComber and Shannon Partridge, eds., *Arnait Nipingit: Voices of Inuit Women in Leadership and Governance* (Iqaluit: Nunavut Arctic College, 2010), 119.
80 Joanna Kafarowski, "'Everyone Should Have a Voice, Everyone's Equal': Gender, Decision-Making and Environmental Policy in the Canadian Arctic," *Canadian Woman Studies* 24 (Summer/Fall 2005): 14.
81 Thomas K. Suluk and Sherrie L. Blakney, "Land Claims and Resistance to the Management of Harvester Activities in Nunavut," *Arctic* 61 supp. (2008): 67.
82 NWMB, *Minutes*, RM 19, August 25–27, 1998, 6.
83 Ibid., RM 22, May 16–20, 1999, 33.

84 Ibid., RM 40, December 7–9, 2004.

85 Ibid., RM 24, November 23–25, 1999, 33–34.

86 Aarluk Consulting Inc., *Inuit Participation in Wildlife Management in Nunavut* (Iqaluit, October 2004), 27.

87 The minutes of Regular Meeting 43 in Igloolik in September 2005 make only passing reference to "a brief review [by the NIWS executive director] of the status of the Nunavut Inuit Wildlife Secretariat" (9). I was present at this meeting, at which a good deal of time was devoted to the executive director's exposition of his plans, which included nine or ten staff who would not just provide financial and administrative support to RWOs and HTOs but would also engage extensively in wildlife management and policy development. One board participant described the prospective organization as "scary" during the public meeting and later privately called it "empire building."

88 NWMB, *Minutes*, RM 52, September 19–20, 2007, 13.

89 Ibid., RM 61, October 1, 2009, 6.

90 Canadian Northern Economic Development Agency, "Improving Governance with Nunavut's Hunters and Trappers Organizations," news release, February 11, 2019.

91 *NCLA*, Schedule 5–4 (emphasis added).

92 NWMB, *Minutes*, RM 14, February 22–27, 1997, 2.

93 Ibid., CC 4, April 7, 1994, 4.

94 Ibid., CC 83, February 11, 2005, 1.

95 Ibid., RM 1, January 25–28, 1994, 3.

96 Author's notes of NWMB meetings.

97 Author's notes; quotation is taken from the simultaneous interpretation of the comment that was made in Inuktitut.

98 Author's notes.

99 NWMB, "Submission," 20. The board submission notes that the minister subsequently apologized, citing an internal departmental failing. A decade later, however, another DFO minister did precisely the same thing, giving the board one day to provide advice on a turbot quota issue. To add injury to insult, the department reconsidered and set up a meeting with the board to discuss the matter but made the decision two weeks before the scheduled meeting. The Federal Court of Canada ruled that the minister and the department had acted contrary to the claim, but it declined to set aside the minister's decision, which had been adverse to Nunavut fishing interests. See Michael d'Eça, "Review and Analysis of the January 7th Federal Court Decision Concerning the Dispute between the NWMB and DFO," January 22, 2009.

100 NWMB, *Minutes*, CC 78, June 14, 2004, 2–3.

101 Ibid., CC 97, April 25, 2006, 2–3.

102 NTI, Briefing Note ("NTI Request NWMB Modify or Remove the Total Allowable Harvest Level for Eastern Arctic Bowhead Whale, as per 5.6.16 of the Nunavut Land Claims Agreement"), November 5, 2007. Copy in author's possession.

103 Department of Fisheries and Oceans, "Submission to the Nunavut Wildlife Management Board on Sustainable Removals of Eastern Bowhead Whales," December 6, 2007. Copy in author's possession.

104 Lisa Gregoire, "Nunavut Groups Applaud Decision to Change Shrimp Policy," *Nunatsiaq News*, July 7, 2016.

105 For a detailed account of the legal issues and the political manoeuvring, see Michael d'Eça, "Inuit Qaujimajatuqangit and the Development of Canada's Northern Groundfish Fishery,"

Notes to pages 80–86

in Joseph Eliot Magnet and Dwight A. Dorey, eds., *Legal Aspects of Aboriginal Business Development* (Markham, ON: LexisNexis Butterworths, 2005).

106 Thomas Rohner, "Nunavut Fish Quota Increase Is Long Overdue, Says NTI," *Nunatsiaq News*, February 10, 2017. Early in 2019, Ottawa announced a substantial temporary increase in the turbot quota, virtually all of which went to Nunavut fishers. See Beth Brown, "Nunavut Fishers Get More Turbot Quota from Ottawa," *Nunatsiaq News*, January 29, 2019.

107 Quoted in Andrea Olive, *Land, Stewardship and Legitimacy: Endangered Species Policy in Canada and the United States* (Toronto: University of Toronto Press, 2014), 183.

108 In 2005, federal environment minister Stéphane Dion recommended that Peary Caribou, a subspecies of caribou with a limited High Arctic range, be listed as endangered under *SARA*, without having consulted the board. The board and NTI reacted strongly against this move, the latter threatening legal action. The federal government subsequently reversed its decision, acknowledging that it had not properly engaged the NWMB in the process. See Greg Younger-Lewis, "NTI Threatens Lawsuit over Caribou Decision," *Nunatsiaq News* May 27, 2005; and John Thompson, "Feds Back Off Peary Caribou Listing," *Nunatsiaq News*, July 29, 2005.

109 NWMB, "An Analysis of the Roles and Responsibilities of the Nunavut Wildlife Management Board: A Category II Executive Board," February 14, 2002, n2.

110 Nunavut Implementation Panel, "Minutes of Meeting December 13–14, 1995," 11.

111 Inexplicably, per diems for other Nunavut IPGs were set by the DIAND minister.

112 NWMB, "Analysis of the Roles and Responsibilities," 22.

113 Ibid.

114 *Nunavut Tunngavik Inc. v. Canada* 2004 FC 85, January 26, 2004.

115 Berger, *Conciliator's Interim Report*, 26.

116 "The NWMB has a very significant portfolio of activities that is at least as large as, if not larger than that of other Boards in Nunavut ... We have not seen any evidence that these board members should be paid less than other board members, and consequently, *we believe that the obligation of this article* [5.2.20 on "fair and reasonable remuneration"] *was not being met*." PricewaterhouseCoopers, *Second Independent Five Year Review*, 40–44 (emphasis in original).

117 NWMB, *Connect and Collaborate*, 23.

118 NWMB, *Minutes*, RM 42, June 7–10, 2005, 7.

119 Ibid., CC 34, September 4, 1997, 1–2.

120 NWMB, *Connect and Collaborate*, 5.

121 Rodon, "Co-management and Self-Determination," 130.

122 NWMB, *Minutes*, CC 6, October 3, 1994, 1.

123 Jim Bell, "Wildlife Board Wants DFO to Drop Bowhead Charges," *Nunatsiaq News*, May 3, 1996.

124 Todd Phillips, "Kovic Clashes with Kusugak over Bowhead Whale Issue," *Nunatsiaq News*, June 7, 1996.

125 Helle Høge argues that the first hunt revealed significant differences between Inuit political leaders' approach to traditional hunting practices and the views of people in the communities and thus of the role of the claim in maintaining those traditions, while noting that the subsequent hunt was more community driven. See Helle Høge, "Bowhead Whale Hunting in Nunavut: A Symbol of Self-Government," in Jens Dahl, Jack Hicks, and Peter Jull, eds., *Nunavut: Inuit Regain Control of Their Lands and Their Lives* (Copenhagen: International Work Group for Indigenous Affairs, 2000), 196–204.

126 DFO, "Submission to the Nunavut Wildlife Management Board: Sustainable Removals of Eastern Arctic Bowhead Whales," February 25, 2008, 1.

127 CBC News, "Land-Claim Body Wants Nunavut Whale Quota Increased," March 7, 2008, https://www.cbc.ca/news/canada/north/land-claim-body-wants-nunavut-whale-quota-increased-1.729678.

128 Most Inuit hunters use snow machines when hunting polar bears; non-Inuit hunting polar bears may only use dog teams and must be guided by experienced Inuit.

129 Quoted in Sean McKibbon, "NTI Asserts Inuit Right to Choose Hunting Method," *Nunatsiaq News*, April 7, 2000.

130 Quoted in Darrell Greer, "Headed for the Courts," *News/North*, April 3, 2000.

131 *Kadlak v. Nunavut (Minister of Sustainable Development)* [2001] Nu. J. No. 1.

132 Quoted in Darrell Greer, "Minister Rejects Bear Hunt," *News/North*, February 12, 2001.

133 Ibid.

134 Scientific estimates as to changes in polar bear numbers vary a good deal across subpopulations, as does the frequency with which surveys of bears are conducted. Overall, the consensus is that numbers have increased substantially since the signing of the international treaty on polar bears in 1973, from between five and ten thousand worldwide to somewhere in the range of twenty to twenty-five thousand. See George W. Wenzel, "Subsistence and Conservation Hunting: A Nunavut Case Study," in Milton M.R. Freeman and Lee Foote, eds., *Inuit, Polar Bears and Sustainable Use: Local, National, and International Perspectives* (Edmonton: CCI Press, 2009), 51.

135 Jeremy J. Schmidt and Martha Dowsley, "Hunting with Polar Bears: Problems with the Passive Properties of the Commons," *Human Ecology* 38 (June 2010): 382.

136 Dowsley and Wenzel, "Time of the Most Polar Bears," 185.

137 For an insightful analysis of traditional and current Inuit views about polar bears and polar bear management, see Henri, "Managing Nature," ch. 6.

138 These institutions cannot prohibit hunting but can impose restrictions on the export of hides or other animal parts, effectively scuppering conservation hunting.

139 For a brief account of this decision, see Alan Diduck, Nigel Bankes, Douglas Clark, and Derek Armitage, "Unpacking Social Learning in Social-Ecological Systems: Case Studies of Polar Bear and Narwhal Management in Northern Canada," in Fikret Berkes, Rob Huebert, Helen Fast, Micheline Manseau, and Alan Diduck, eds., *Breaking Ice: Renewable Resource and Ocean Management in the Canadian North* (Calgary: University of Calgary Press, 2005), 277–82.

140 See Henri, "Managing Nature," 212–20.

141 The following account, and the quotations from participants, are taken from the author's notes. Some comments were made in Inuktitut; quotations are from the simultaneous translation.

142 The scientists indicated that this difference was not statistically significant. It was evident that neither board members nor the community representatives understood the difference between substantive and statistical significance.

143 The WHB subpopulation includes bears that spend time in Manitoba. Manitoba does not permit hunting of polar bears, so in effect the TAH was thirty-two bears. However, "defence kills," where bears are killed in order to protect human life or property, count against the TAH.

144 Moshi Kotierk, "Public and Inuit Interests, Western Hudson Polar Bears and Wildlife Management: Results of a Public Opinion Poll in Western Hudson Bay Communities,"

Notes to pages 91–94

Government of Nunavut, Department of Environment, May 2012, 18–23. The survey comprised 106 persons, ninety-three of whom were Inuit and seventy-two of whom described themselves as hunters.

145 This scepticism and hostility is linked to widespread and deeply held Inuit objections to the methods scientists use to study polar bears, primarily "catch-and-release" techniques in which bears are tranquilized, samples taken, and (sometimes) radio collars attached. Inuit maintain that such techniques are not only disrespectful but that they also adversely affect bears' disposition and produce an unpalatable taste in the meat. Such concerns surfaced repeatedly at the Rankin Inlet meeting, including from the GN deputy minister of the environment.

146 Steve Ducharme, "Nunavut Government Irks Arviat MLA, Hikes WHB Polar Bear Quota by Only 4," *Nunatsiaq News*, October 30, 2015. This story pointed out that once again the children of Arviat would not be outside at Halloween.

147 Henri, "Managing Nature," 214.

148 Ibid., 233.

149 Ibid., 235.

150 Ibid., 238.

151 Quoted in ibid., 197.

152 Dowsley and Wenzel, "Time of the Most Polar Bears,'" 185.

153 Rodon, *En partenariat avec l'État*, 247.

154 See, for example, Steve Ducharme, "Kivalliq Hunters Demanding Increase to Polar Bear Quota," *Nunatsiaq News*, September 22, 2017; "Nunavut Wildlife Board Revisits Kivalliq Polar Bear Quota," *Nunatsiaq News*, January 19, 2018.

155 Sarah Rogers, "Anger and Grief Hit Nunavut Community following Polar Bear Attack," *Nunatsiaq News*, July 7, 2018.

156 Sarah Rogers, "Polar Bear Attack Sparks Anger over Nunavut's Wildlife Management," *Nunatsiaq News*, September 7, 2018.

157 CBC News, "5 Polar Bears Shot without Tags near Arviat: Bears Not Harvested," August 2, 2018, https://www.cbc.ca/news/canada/north/five-polar-bears-killed-1.4770684.

158 Sarah Rogers, "Red Tape Hampers Response to Polar Bear Encounters: MLAs," *Nunatsiaq News*, November 2, 2018.

159 Government of Nunavut, "Submission to the Nunavut Wildlife Management Board: Nunavut Polar Bear Management Plan," for NWMB In-person Hearing, November 2018, https://www.nwmb.com/en/public-hearings-a-meetings/public-hearings-1/2018/nwmb-in-person-public-hearing-to-consider-the-government-of-nunavut-proposal-on-the-revised-nunavut-polar-bear-co-management-plan-2/proposal-for-decision-4.

Chapter 4: The Yukon Fish and Wildlife Management Board

1 Minister of Supply and Services Canada, *Umbrella Final Agreement between the Government of Canada, the Council for Yukon Indians and the Government of the Yukon* (hereafter *UFA*) (Ottawa, 1993), 16.7.1.

2 Ibid., 8.

3 Ibid., 16.1.1.

4 Section 16.7.2 of the *UFA* simply says: "The Board shall be composed of six nominees of Yukon First Nations and six nominees of Government." It is the *Umbrella Final Agreement Implementation Plan* (Ottawa: Minister of Supply and Services, 1993), 104, that specifies Ottawa's involvement.

5 Yukon Fish and Wildlife Management Board (hereafter YFWMB), *Minutes of Meeting*, June 10–11, 2014, 15. Minutes are available at the YFWMB office.
6 According to the board's procedures, if a member misses three consecutive meetings, the party that nominated the member receives a formal notice.
7 YFWMB, *Fifth Annual Report, 1999–2000*, 5. Board annual reports from 2010–11 on are available on the YFWMB website, www.yfwmb.ca; previous annual reports are available at the Yukon Archives.
8 The board's annual report for 2003–04, for example, listed an executive director, office manager, office assistant, researcher/community liaison officer, access management coordinator, harvest monitoring coordinator, and three local river stewards. YFWMB, *Ninth Annual Report, 2003–04*, 5.
9 *UFA*, 16.7.7.2.
10 YFWMB, *Minutes of Meeting*, March 11, 1988, 1. Similar comments were made by others at the meeting.
11 Letter from board chair Hector MacKenzie to David Porter, Minister of Renewable Resources, May 17, 1988, appended to Yukon Wildlife Management Board [henceforth YWMB], *Minutes of Meeting*, May 17, 1988, 1.
12 YWMB, *Minutes of Meeting*, April 27–29, 1988, 6.
13 Ibid.
14 YWMB, *Minutes of Meeting*, July 26, 1988, 1.
15 MacKenzie to Porter, May 17, 1988, 2.
16 YFWMB, *Minutes of Meeting*, March 13–15, 1995, 1.
17 Ibid. Gingell later became a member of the board.
18 YFWMB, *Minutes of Meeting*, March 13–15, 1996, 5.
19 Ibid., 6.
20 Ibid., 4.
21 Ibid., 17.
22 YFWMB *Minutes of Meeting*, June 12–14, 1995, 3.
23 YFWMB, *1995–1996 Annual Report*, 8.
24 Ibid., 9.
25 The operating procedures are listed in ibid., 29–36; the section on lawyers is on page 36. Significantly, the aversion to legalism is common to both First Nations and non-First Nations board members. Non-First Nations members tend to come from backgrounds, particularly in the private sector, where lawyers are more likely to be viewed as impediments to, rather than as facilitators of, effectiveness, while First Nations regularly express a preference for non-litigious approaches and consensus based on meaningful dialogue and transparency.
26 YFWMB, *Minutes of Meeting*, April 18, 1995, 1.
27 Ibid., March 13–15, 1995, 12–13.
28 Ibid., April 18, 1995, 25.
29 Ibid., 3. That CYI had reason for concern is clear from the meeting minutes, which quoted the minister as saying "he was anxious to develop a good relationship with the Board and that he would like to attend at least a portion of all meetings." See YFWMB, *Minutes of Meeting*, March 13–15, 1995, 4.
30 YFWMB, *Minutes of Meeting*, April 18, 1995, 4.
31 Ibid., 31.
32 Ibid., 10, 21.

Notes to pages 102–8

33 Ibid., 7, 22–23.

34 The board's activities in these and other issues are summarized in YFWMB, *1995–1996 Annual Report*.

35 Ibid., 11–16.

36 YFWMB, *Third Annual Report, 1997–1998*, 4.

37 YFWMB, *Second Annual Report, 1996–1997*, 5–6.

38 YFWMB, *Third Annual Report 1997–1998*, 5–6.

39 Implementation Review Working Group, *Five-Year Review of the Umbrella Final Agreement Implementation Plan and Yukon First Nation Final Agreement Implementation Plans for the First Four Yukon First Nations* (Ottawa: Public Works and Government Services Canada, 2000), 38.

40 Ibid., 18.

41 YFWMB, *Seventh Annual Report, 2001–2002*, 3.

42 YFWMB, *2016–17 Annual Report*, 15.

43 Implementation Review Working Group, *Yukon First Nation Final and Self-Government Agreement Implementation Reviews*, October 3, 2007 (hereafter *Ten-Year Review*), 107, https://www.planyukon.ca/index.php/documents-and-downloads/yukon-land-use-planning-council/discussion-papers/clುppreview/ch11challange/appended-documents/786-chapter-11-implementation-review-2007/file.

44 *Amendment Agreement in Respect of the Umbrella Final Agreement Implementation Plan*, February 2015, 3, https://www.rcaanc-cirnac.gc.ca/eng/1431459713139/1542811351833.

45 See Doug Urquhart, ed., *Two Eyes: One Vision: Conference Summary* (Whitehorse: YFWMB, 1998).

46 David Loeks, *Off-Road Vehicle Use and Issues in the Yukon* (Whitehorse: Yukon Fish and Wildlife Management Board, 2000).

47 YFWMB, *Protecting Wildlife Habitat in the Yukon* (Whitehorse, 2000).

48 This account reflects the process as set out on the board's website, http://yfwmb.ca/regulations/regulation-change-process/.

49 "Regulations," sometimes called "delegated legislation," are detailed government directives made under the authority of specific acts. They carry the full force of law but can be created, amended, or rescinded by cabinet, or in some instances by individual ministers, quickly without the need for review or approval by the legislature. They are restricted to matters falling within the purview of the authorizing act. Many have only minor administrative import, but some have extensive policy implications.

50 In the 2015–16 regulation cycle, the board considered proposed regulations on, among other things, use of drones in hunting, closing certain lakes to fishing for particular species, the use of motorized vehicles to transport harvested bison in certain game management subzones, special permits for school bison hunts, and modernizing standards for archery equipment. YFWMB, *Annual Report 21, 2015–2016*, 8–17.

51 Examples of all of these possibilities may be found in the board's 2015–16 annual report, which summarizes its recommendations from the 2015–16 regulation cycle. See YFWMB, *Annual Report 21, 2015–2016*, 8–17.

52 This observation is based on accounts of the outcome of recommendations in the board's annual reports and discussions with board and government officials.

53 YFWMB, *1995–96 Annual Report*, 20.

54 YFWMB regulation change process, http://yfwmb.ca/regulations/regulation-change-process/.

55 This section and especially the final paragraph draw heavily on the author's attendance at board meetings in February 2013 and December 2016. Clearly, this is a very small sample and other meetings doubtless unfolded in less harmonious fashion.

56 A recent board document noted: "Graham presents a deeply valuable source of corporate memory for the Board, having been involved in the Board's work for the majority of its existence." YFWMB, *Yukon Fish and Wildlife Management Board Report – Yukon Forum Review* (Whitehorse, March 6, 2019), 16.

57 A telling instance of respect among members occurred at a meeting I observed. Despite the presence of a quorum, the chair delayed beginning a meeting scheduled to begin at 9:00 a.m. for fifteen minutes awaiting the arrival of a board member who was known to be in town. Members present clearly saw this as reasonable and appropriate.

58 *UFA*, 16.7.1.

59 Ibid., 2.12.2.12.

60 Ibid., 16.7.4 (emphasis added). This subsection is especially curious since s. 2.12.2.1 contains the same provision.

61 Material in this paragraph, including the quotations, is taken from YFWMB, *Ninth Annual Report, 2003–2004*, 12.

62 Chuck Tobin, "Committee Struck on Captive Wildlife," *Whitehorse Star*, June 18, 2003; Stephanie Waddell, "Plan Will Help Game Farm Sale, Owner Believes," *Whitehorse Star*, July 16, 2003; "Minister and Board at an Impasse," CBC News, July 17, 2003.

63 YFWMB, *Ninth Annual Report, 2003–2004*, 3.

64 YFWMB, *Annual Report, 2005–2006*, 8.

65 YFWMB, *Annual Report 2006–2007*, 9.

66 Ibid.

67 YFWMB, *Annual Report, 2007–2008*, 3.

68 YFWMB, *Yukon Fish and Wildlife – A 20:20 Vision: Yukon Wide Survey* (Whitehorse, February 2009), 1.

69 Ibid. See also DataPath Systems, *Yukon Fish and Wildlife: A 20:20 Vision – Comment Analysis: Final Report* (Whitehorse, April 2009).

70 YFWMB, *Annual Report 14, 2008–2009*, 2.

71 YFWMB, *Minutes of Meeting*, February 9–11, 2016, 10.

72 Bob Dickson, Chair YFWMB, to Jean-Marie David, Clerk of the House of Commons Standing Committee on Aboriginal Affairs, April 16, 2015. This letter also expressed the board's disappointment that it had not been accorded an opportunity to appear before the committee when it held hearings in Whitehorse.

73 *UFA*, 13.5.3.1.

74 For example, the "knowledge and experience of Yukon Indian people" is to be applied to land use planning (*UFA*, 11.1.1.4) and the development assessment process (i.e., environmental assessment; *UFA*, 1.2.1.1.2) and in achieving conservation (*UFA*, 16.1.1.7).

75 *UFA*, 16.1.1.7.

76 Urquhart, *Two Eyes: One Vision*.

77 Paul Nadasdy, *Sovereignty's Entailments: First Nation State Development in the Yukon* (Toronto: University of Toronto Press, 2017), 292–96.

78 Information in this paragraph draws heavily on the trust's "Call for Proposals," http://yfwet.ca/projects/call-for-proposal/.

79 Information in this and the following paragraph is drawn from the trust's annual reports, http://yfwet.ca/about-the-trust/.

80 *Yukon Forum Newsletter*, December 14, 2018, 2.

81 YFWMB, "Yukon Forum Review," 17.

82 Ibid., 19–24.

83 Yukon Government Public Engagement website, Review of the Yukon Fish and Management Board, https://engageyukon.ca/en/2019/review-yukon-fish-and-wildlife-management-board.

84 Dawson District Renewable Resources Council, *Renewable Resources Council Training Handbook* (Dawson City, 2004 [?]), 1. This is surely one of the most unusual and effective training manuals ever produced. Its 110 pages contain extensive plain-language explanations of the *UFA*, especially Chapter 16 on fish and wildlife, as well as much common-sense practical advice for RRC members about bureaucratic norms and processes and about shaping and adapting to group dynamics. What makes it so unique and effective is the presentation of information and advice: the entire handbook consists of tongue-in-cheek, often hilarious, line drawings of a wise but cynical raven and his wolf sidekick explaining what RRCs are about and how to make them work. The artist, well-known cartoonist and long-time YFWMB member Doug Urquhart, worked closely with the Dawson RRC on the handbook. The Yukon Government published an RRC manual – Government of Yukon, *Renewable Resources Council Manual: Orientation and Education* (Whitehorse, 2014) – that contains much factual information but little practical advice and pales in usefulness to the Dawson RRC manual.

85 *UFA*, 16.6.0. The Ta'an Kwäch'än Council and the Kwanlin Dün First Nation have separate final agreements but a single RRC. The Kwanlin Dün Final Agreement Implementation Plan provides for an "Ibex RRC," but it has never been established, likely because of the near-total overlap of the two First Nations' designated traditional territories.

86 *UFA*, 16.6.9.

87 Tony Penikett, *Reconciliation: First Nations Treaty Making in British Columbia* (Vancouver: Douglas and McIntyre, 2006), 114–15.

88 David C. Natcher, "Gender and Resource Co-Management in Northern Canada," *Arctic* 66 (June 2013): 218–21, calculated from data in Table 1.

89 Kiri Staples and David C. Natcher, "Gender, Decision Making and Natural Resource Co-management in Yukon," *Arctic* 68 (September, 2015): 356–66, calculated from data in Table 2. In Natcher's 2012 study, in the five RRCs included in the Staples-Natcher analysis only four of twenty-eight members (14 percent) were women.

90 *UFA*, 16.6.1.

91 Daryn Leas, "Joint Boards and Committees: Do they Provide a Meaningful Role for Yukon First Nations in the Management of Lands and Resources in Their Traditional Territories?" paper presented to Sami representatives, Moscow, 2005, 16.

92 Quoted in Kelly A. Hayes, "Walking Together: An Evaluation of Renewable Resource Co-management in the Yukon Territory" (MA project, Faculty of Environmental Design, University of Calgary, 2000), 112.

93 Penikett, *Reconciliation,* 113.

94 YFWMB, *Minutes of Meeting,* April 26–28, 2016, 2–5.

95 *UFA*, 16.11.3.

96 See, for example, Na-Cho Nyäk Dun Fish and Wildlife Planning Team, *Community-Based Fish and Wildlife Work Plan for the Na-Cho Nyäk Dun Traditional Territory* (Whitehorse: Environment Yukon, 2014). This twenty-four-page document, developed by the First Nation, the local RRC, and the YG's Fish and Wildlife Branch, covered a range of issues

and set out several dozen "proposed activities" over a five-year period, indicating which entity (First Nation, RRC, YG) would be responsible.

97 Hayes, "Walking Together," 102.

98 Quoted in ibid., 124.

99 This was the funding level for the first four RRCs created when four First Nations finalized their claims and self-government agreements shortly after the *UFA* came into force. As other RRCs came on stream as more First Nations finalized their claims and self-government agreements, their base funding level was set so as to match what the first RRCs were receiving.

100 Implementation Review Working Group, *Five-Year Review,* 46–47.

101 Ibid., 47.

102 Implementation Review Group, *Ten-Year Review,* 107.

103 Nadasdy, *Sovereignty's Entitlements,* 286.

104 Ibid., 290.

105 Ibid.

106 Implementation Review Working Group, *Ten-Year Review,* 113–14.

107 YFWMB, *Fourth Annual Report, 1998–99,* 8.

108 Dawson District Renewable Resources Council, *Renewable Resources Council Training Handbook,* 70.

109 YFWMB, *First Annual Review, 1995–1996,* 15.

110 Implementation Review Group, *Ten-Year Review,* 116.

111 Quoted in Hayes, "Walking Together," 123. "YTG," for Yukon Territorial Government, was the acronym used at the time. The reference to DIAND reflects the fact that when this study was conducted, the federal government had yet to devolve responsibility for forestry to Yukon.

112 Implementation Review Working Group, *Ten-Year Review,* 98–99. The "FA 16.6.4.3 process" refers to the final agreement requirement that YG and First Nations attempt to reach consensus on RRC appointments.

113 Nadasdy, *Sovereignty's Entailments,* 111 and 112. Nadasdy presents an extraordinarily nuanced and ethnographically sophisticated argument; this quotation offers only a crude summary of his analysis.

114 Nadasdy, *Sovereignty's Entailments,* 108.

115 Nadasdy recounts a meeting of elders from Kluane First Nation and White River First Nation, an adjacent First Nation that does not have a settled land claim, which produced an agreement as to use of the overlap area. The agreement likely does not have any legal status. See Nadasdy, *Sovereignty's Entailments,* 213–15.

116 Ibid., 112.

117 David C. Natcher, Susan Davis, and Clifford G. Hickey, "Co-Management: Managing Relationships, Not Resources," *Human Organization* 64 (Fall 2005): 241.

118 Ibid., 245.

119 Ibid., 248.

120 At my request, this person read the Natcher et al. article and agreed that it rang true for the first few years of the RRC's existence, but that it no longer does.

121 *UFA,* 16.7.17.

122 Implementation Review Working Group, *Ten-Year Review,* 116–17.

123 Staff of the Inuvialuit Water Board are also federal employees, but although it operates much like a claims board, and is a member of the NWT Board Forum, it has no basis in a land claim.

124 It is worth pointing out that DFO's early, controlling approach to the Yukon Salmon Sub-Committee contrasts markedly with its far more supportive, cooperative dealings with the Fisheries Joint Management Board, a co-management board established under the *Inuvialuit Final Agreement*. See Burton Ayles, Redmond Clarke, Kristin Hynes, Robert Bell, and John Noksana, "Co-management of Fisheries Resources in the Western Canadian Arctic," in Claude M. Rocan, ed., *Building Bridges: Case Studies in Collaborative Management in Canada* (Ottawa: Invenire, 2018), 135–76.

125 Yukon Salmon Committee (hereafter YSC), *Strategic Plan 2004–06* (Whitehorse, November 2004), 7.

126 Implementation Review Working Group, *Five-Year Review,* 42.

127 YSC, *Minutes of Meeting 52, May 17–19, 2005, Whitehorse Yukon,* 13, 20, the sub-committee minutes are available at the sub-committee office.

128 Implementation Review Group, *Ten-Year Review,* 118.

129 Contribution agreements do permit carryover of funds under stringent conditions: funding can be extended only for continued application to a designated use and only if the need is identified several months before the end of the fiscal year.

130 YSC, *Minutes of Meeting 51, April 5–7, 2005, Dawson City, Yukon,* 9.

131 Fisheries and Oceans Canada, "Audit and Evaluation of the Contribution to the Yukon Salmon Sub-Committee," May 6, 2005, 5–7.

132 YFWMB, *Minutes of Meeting,* December 14, 2014, 3.

133 Yukon Salmon Sub-Committee, *Meeting Minutes,* November 3, 2016, 5–6.

134 Nadasdy, *Sovereignty's Entailments,* 292–96.

135 "Yukon First Nation causes stir with plan to issue their own hunting permits," CBC News, June 25, 2018; https://www.cbc.ca/news/canada/north/yukon-hunting-ross-river-dena-council-1.4721409. It is likely not coincidental that the Ross River Dena Council has no settled claim or final agreement and thus no RRC.

Chapter 5: The MVEIRB and the MVLWB

1 Julia Christensen and Miriam Grant, "How Political Change Paved the Way for Indigenous Knowledge: The Mackenzie Valley Resource Management Act," *Arctic* 60 (June 2007): 115–17.

2 Mackenzie Valley Land and Water Board, "Perspectives on Regulatory Improvement in the Mackenzie Valley," May 18, 2011, i.

3 MVEIRB, "The History of the Mackenzie Valley Environmental Review Board," February 2007, 3.

4 House of Commons Standing Committee on Aboriginal Affairs and Northern Development, *Evidence* (hereafter Standing Committee, *Evidence*), November 18, 1997 (testimony by Will Dunlop, director, Resource Policy Directorate, Northern Affairs Program, DIAND), 2.

5 Ibid., 23–24.

6 Ibid., December 3, 1997 (testimony of Tim Lennie), 2.

7 Quoted in Derek Neary, "Kakisa, Paramount at Odds," *Nunavut News/North,* June 14, 2004.

8 Author's notes from the MVEIRB conference "Traditional Knowledge in Environmental Impact Assessment," Yellowknife, November 2002.

9 See MVEIRB, transcript of Community Hearing Lutsel K'e January 16–17, 2007, EA0607-003 UR ENERGY SCREECH LAKE (2006), http://mail.tscript.com/trans/mac/jan_16_07/index.htm.

10 The CEAA process did include reference to socioeconomic effects but "only with socio-economic and cultural impacts as they arise from the changes to the biophysical environment. Direct social impacts are therefore excluded." See Alan Ehrlich, "Comparative Overview of EIA across Selected Jurisdictions," Mackenzie Valley Environmental Impact Review Board, November, 2001, 20.

11 Arcadis, *2015 Northwest Territories Environmental Audit*, March 2016, 63, https://www.assembly.gov.nt.ca/sites/default/files/td_2015_nwt_environmental_audit_27-june-16.pdf.

12 The Gwich'in and Sahtu claims provide for land use planning boards; under the *Tlicho Agreement* land use planning is done by the Tlicho Government. In the southern NWT, where claims have not been settled, interim measures agreements make provision for land use planning. In 2005, the Dehcho Land Use Planning Committee produced a draft land use plan, but both the federal and territorial governments rejected it.

13 The outline of the permitting and assessment processes in the following paragraphs is very much a simplification of a highly complex process. Exceptions and qualifications apply in some specific cases. For a somewhat more detailed, plain-language account of the process, see Planit North, "Resource Co-management Workshop," Kátł'odeeche Community Complex, Hay River Reserve, NWT, January 25–26, 2017, 5–13.

14 MVEIRB, "List of Preliminary Screenings 2017–18 Fiscal Year," July 18, 2018, http://reviewboard.ca/about/media/news/archives/2018.

15 For projects on Tlicho or Déline lands (Déline is a small self-governing community in the Sahtu), which do not require Type A or Type B permits or licences, Type C permits or licences may be required.

16 All Crown land in the NWT and the other territories, which constitutes the vast bulk of land, is owned by the federal rather than the territorial government, but most is not designated "federal lands." The most common instances of federal lands are national parks or park reserves and contaminated sites.

17 MVEIRB, "EIA Made in the North: The Mackenzie Valley Environmental Impact Review Board's Submission to the 2005 NWT Environmental Audit," April 2005, 30.

18 *Settlement Agreement between Her Majesty the Queen in Right of Canada, as Represented by the Minister of Indian Affairs and Northern Development and Grand Chief Herb Norwegian on His Own Behalf and on Behalf of the Deh Cho First Nations*, 2005, s 12.1.

19 Arcadis, *2015 Northwest Territories Environmental Audit*, 1.

20 SENES Consultants Limited, *Northwest Territories Environmental Audit 2005: Main Report* (Yellowknife: Indian and Northern Affairs Canada, December 2005), 5–3.

21 "Cumulative effects" refers to situations in which, considered singly, individual developments may not adversely affect the environment but, together, may harm it.

22 Brett Wheeler, "Preliminary Screening and Environmental Assessment," in Planit North, "Resource Co-management," 9.

23 Ibid.

24 *Mackenzie Valley Resource Management Act* [hereafter *MVRMA*], *Statutes of Canada*, 1998, s. 128 (1).

25 DIAND, *Comprehensive Land Claim Agreement between Her Majesty the Queen in Right of Canada and the Gwich'in as Represented by the Gwich'in Tribal Council*, 1992, s. 24.3.7.

26 Because of its enormous scale and because the pipeline was to cross Yukon, the Inuvialuit Region, settled and unsettled claims areas in the Mackenzie Valley, and Alberta, the process for reviewing its environmental impact was both unique and hugely complex. Accordingly,

while the *MVRMA* boards were involved in the pipeline review (a member of the MVEIRB sat on the Joint Review Panel examining socioeconomic aspects of the project), the processes examined in this chapter do not apply in this case. The principal recommendations to government on the Mackenzie Gas Project came from the National Energy Board.

27 Supreme Court of the Northwest Territories, *De Beers v. Mackenzie Valley et al.*, 2007 S.C.N.W.T. 24 (April 2, 2007).

28 SENES Consultants, *Northwest Territories Environmental Audit 2005*, 5–4.

29 In its submission to the first NWT environmental audit, the board agreed that it was important that consultation be done well, in part to avoid legal challenges, but emphasized: "The Review Board is not vested with any fiduciary duties. This is Canada's and at times the NWT Government's responsibility." See MVEIRB, "EIA Made in the North," 34.

30 Kate Hearn, Assistant Deputy Minister, GNWT Department of Lands, to Chief Roy Fabian, Kátł'odeeche First Nation, September 2017, http://reviewboard.ca/registry?f%5B0%5D= project%253Afield_project_company%3A307. Note that the First Nation, and others potentially affected, would have had the opportunity to participate in the MVEIRB's public hearing on the project and to submit written material to the board.

31 Joanne Deneron, Chairperson, MVEIRB, to Louis Sebert, GNWT Minister of Lands, August 15, 2018, http://reviewboard.ca/node/444/documents/D-POS. This letter, and its attachments, available on the board website under "Tli cho All Season Road EA-1617–01," are good illustrations of the consult-to-modify process.

32 MVEIRB, *Annual Report 2014–15*, 12. The annual reports are available on the board's website: http://reviewboard.ca/about/annual_reports_and_strategic_plan.

33 The Canadian Environmental Assessment Agency did the environmental assessment on the proposed mine; the (pre-claim) Northwest Territories Water Board held hearings on the mine's water licence. For an account of the hearings, see Ellen Bielawski, *Rogue Diamonds: The Rush for Northern Riches on Dene Land* (Vancouver: Douglas and McIntyre, 2003), ch. 5, 10–12.

34 Standing Committee, *Evidence*, November 18, 1997 (testimony by Will Dunlop), 15.

35 Office of the Auditor General of Canada, *Report of the Auditor General of Canada to the House of Commons* (Ottawa, April 2005), s. 6.4.

36 Ibid., ch. 6, *passim*.

37 Office of the Auditor General of Canada, *Report of the Auditor General of Canada to the House of Commons* (Ottawa, November 2003), s. 8.2.

38 *MVRMA*, s. 11 (2).

39 Ibid., s. 12.

40 MVEIRB, *Annual Report 2016–17*, 18.

41 Ibid., *Annual Report 2006–07*, 37.

42 Thandiwe Vela, "Major Layoffs at Review Board," *News/North NWT*, February 11, 2013.

43 *MVRMA*, s. 25.

44 MVEIRB, *2005–06 Annual Report*, 8–11.

45 Ibid., *Annual Report 2015–16*, 11–17.

46 Standing Committee, *Evidence*, December 4, 1997 (testimony of Alestine André, Working Group member).

47 Richard Gleeson, "Deninu Kue Band May Block Road," *News/North*, November 12, 2001.

48 Paul Bickford, "Sawmill Loses Another Round," *News/North*, November 18, 2002.

49 Quoted in Dave Sullivan, "Mill Passes Environmental Review," *News/North*, October 15, 2001.

50 Derek R. Armitage, "Collaborative Environmental Assessment in the Northwest Territories, Canada," *Environmental Impact Assessment Review* 25 (2005): 246.

51 Derek R. Armitage, "Environmental Impact Assessment in Canada's Northwest Territories: Integration, Collaboration, and the Mackenzie Valley Resource Management Act," in Kevin S. Hanna, ed., *Environmental Impact Assessment: Practice and Participation* (Toronto: Oxford University Press, 2005), 198.

52 MVEIRB, *Decision, Reasons for Decision and Report of Environmental Assessment of the Ranger Oil Limited, Canadian Forest Oil Ltd., and Chevron Canada Resources Limited Integrated P-66A/N-61/K-29 Gas Wells and Pipeline Tie-in, Fort Liard NWT* (Yellowknife, December 7, 1999).

53 One DIAND official commented that even the terminology in the report was incorrect. What were described as "recommendations" should have been labelled "measures" (to mitigate adverse effects); the sole "recommendation" must be "yes," "no," or "yes" with measures to mitigate. The board subsequently revised its terminology.

54 MVEIRB, *Report of Lessons Learned from the Environmental Assessment of the Ranger et al Fort Liard Pipeline Development Proposal* (Yellowknife, August 18, 2000).

55 Ibid., *Report of Environmental Assessment on the Proposed Development of the Sable, Pigeon and Beartooth Kimberlite Pipes* (Yellowknife, February 7, 2001), 2.

56 Robert D. Nault, Minister of Indian Affairs and Northern Development, to Gordon Lennie, Chair, MVEIRB, April 12, 2001, copy in author's possession.

57 MVEIRB, *Report of Environmental Assessment on the Sable, Pigeon and Beartooth Kimberlite Pipes*, 2.

58 Ibid., 55. The territorial formula finance agreements, somewhat analogous to the equalization program for "have-not" provinces, provide the bulk of territorial government revenue through large unconditional grants.

59 Robert D. Nault, Minister of Indian Affairs and Northern Development, to Gordon Lennie, Chair, MVEIRB, April 12, 2001, enclosure, copy in author's possession.

60 J.D. Excell, President, Ekati Diamond Mine, to Hon. Robert Nault, Minister, Department of Indian Affairs and Northern Development, March 2, 2001, 3, copy in author's possession.

61 Well after Burlingame's departure, two MVEIRB staff separately said in interviews that he was responsible for a significant, positive change: insulation of staff and staff function from interference by board members.

62 Robert D. Nault, Minister of Indian Affairs and Northern Development, to Todd Burlingame, Chair, MVEIRB, October 3, 2003, copy in author's possession.

63 The minister was also required to consult with the responsible territorial minister or Indigenous group that nominated the member, but this was unnecessary in this case since Wray had been a federal nominee.

64 Quoted in Bob Weber, "Nault Muzzling Regulatory Board, Critics Say," *Globe and Mail*, October 11, 2003, A14.

65 Ibid.

66 "Integrity at Stake" (editorial), *News/North*, October 20, 2003, A7.

67 For a preliminary report on this exercise, see MVEIRB, "EIA Made in the North," 16–24.

68 SENES Consultants, *Northwest Territories Environmental Audit 2005*, 5–1.

69 Ibid., 5-1–5-6.

70 See MVEIRB, *Report of Environmental Assessment and Reasons for Decision on the New Shoshoni Ventures Preliminary Diamond Exploration in Drybones Bay* (Yellowknife, February

10, 2004); and Jim Prentice, Minister of Indian Affairs and Northern Development to Gabrielle Mackenzie-Scott, Chair, MVEIRB, April 10, 2006. See also the exchange of letters between the minister and the chair in which DIAND sought clarification and explanation of the board's reasoning and response: Andy Scott, Minister of DIAND, to Gabrielle Mackenzie-Scott, April 15, 2005 and Mackenzie-Scott to Scott, June 23, 2005. All letters are available on the MVEIRB's public registry: http://reviewboard.ca/registry?f%5B0%5D =project%253Afield_project_company%3A317.

71 MVEIRB, "Former Review Board Members Withdraw Names from Reappointment Consideration," News Release, November 30, 2006. One of the nominees was in fact subsequently reappointed to the board.

72 Gabrielle Mackenzie-Scott, Chair, MVEIRB, to Jim Prentice, Minister of DIAND, September 22, 2006, http://reviewboard.ca/node/380/documents/D-POS. This letter urged a quick decision on the long-standing EA report on Imperial's proposed Dehcho Geotechnical Program and chided Ottawa for introducing new information in the consult-to-modify process, on the grounds that this "is unfair to all the parties who participated in the original environmental assessment, as the 'Consult to Modify' process is not conducted in a similarly open and transparent manner."

73 MVEIRB, "EIA Made in the North," 12.

74 MVEIRB, *Report of Environmental Assessment and Reasons for Decision: Dominion Diamond Ekati Corp. Jay Project*, EA13–14–01, February 1, 2014, app. A.

75 See Terriplan Consultants Ltd./IER Planning, Research and Management, *Workshop Report: Preliminary Screening and Environmental Assessment under the Mackenzie Valley Resource Management Act – Developing a Collaborative Approach for the Northwest Territories* (Yellowknife, November 2001). See also, Armitage, "Collaborative Environmental Assessment."

76 Regrettably, the original plan to call this entity the Board Relations Unit came a cropper when it was realized that its acronym – BRU – would give rise to unsubtle humour ("things will go better with a BRU").

77 Section 115.1 of the *MVRMA* requires the board to "consider any traditional knowledge and scientific information that is made available to it." A similar provision in s. 60.1 applies to the land and water boards.

78 MVEIRB, *Socio-economic Impact Assessment Guidelines* (Yellowknife, 2007).

79 "Final Agenda: Mackenzie Valley Resource Management Act Workshop, Explorer Hotel, Yellowknife, February 13–4, 2018," 1.

80 MVEIRB, "MVEIRB Strategic Plan 2005/06 to 2007/08" (Yellowknife, July 30, 2004), 6, 8, 10.

81 The 2014 amendments to the act included a provision allowing the minister to appoint the first chair of the restructured MVLWB without consulting the board. As of early 2019, this provision had not been proclaimed into law and it seemed unlikely that it would be.

82 These funds, which ceased as of 2017–18, were associated with DIAND's ongoing claims and self-government negotiations with Dehcho First Nations and were designed to facilitate greater board engagement with Dehcho communities.

83 The text of these policy directions is available on the MVLWB website, https://mvlwb.com/ resources/policy-directions-minister.

84 MVLWB, "Engagement and Consultation Policy," June, 2013, 10–11, https://mvlwb.com/ resources/policy-and-guidelines.

85 MVLWB, "Referral to Environmental Assessment" (public notice), *News/North*, September 19, 2005.

86 Mavis Cli-Michaud, Chair, MVLWB, to Robert C. McLeod, Minister of Environment and Natural Resources, GNWT, August 10, 2017. This matter had been under way for many

years and involved an initial hearing, a judicial determination that a new hearing was needed, and a new hearing. The owners had initially sought $6 million, later reduced to $3.2 million, in compensation. See Melinda Trochu, "NTPC Should Pay N.W.T. Fishing Lodge Owners $100K for Damage to Business, Says Land and Water Board," CBC North, August 16, 2017, http://www.cbc.ca/news/canada/north/ nonacho-lake-fishing-lodge -compensation-award-1.4250266.

87 John Donihee, "*The Mackenzie Valley Resource Management Act*: A Review of the New Regime," in John Donihee, ed., *Resource Development and the Mackenzie Valley Resource Management Act: The New Regime* (Calgary: Canadian Institute of Resources Law, 2000), 83.

88 Ibid., 89.

89 MVLWB, "Annual Activity Report 2016–2017," 1.

90 Jacques Whitford Limited, *Final Report: Review of the Water Licence Renewal Process for the Ekati Mine, Northwest Territories* (Yellowknife, January 3, 2006).

91 The board's responses to the recommendations are included in the consultant's report.

92 Section 108 (5) of the act states, "If a majority of the members do not nominate a person acceptable to the federal Minister within a reasonable time, the Minister may appoint any person as chairperson." According to a chronology published in *News/North*, no response, indicating that the three nominees were unacceptable, or otherwise, was ever received by the board to its letter of nomination or to its written request for clarification about the minister's desire to have the board consider Burlingame as a potential chair. See "Appointment Chronology," *News/North*, April 25, 2005.

93 Quoted in "Northerners Outraged at Appointment to MVLWB," CBC North, webposted March 10, 2005, https://www.cbc.ca/news/canada/north/northerners-outraged-at -appointment-to-mvlwb-1.561415.

94 Quoted in "MLAs Angered over Appointment to MVLWB," CBC North, webposted March 11, 2005.

95 Legislative Assembly of the Northwest Territories, *Hansard*, March 10, 2005, 1975.

96 Quoted in Mike W. Bryant, "Burlingame Best Candidate: Scott," *News/North*, March 18, 2005.

97 Quoted in Mike Bryant, "Strategy for Discontent," *News/North*, March 18, 2005.

98 Quoted in Jack Danlchuk and Mike W. Bryant, "Water Panel Dunks Burlingame," *News/ North*, April 25, 2005.

99 "The Fix Was in for Burlingame, Says Water Board Member," CBC North, webposted May 5, 2005.

100 "Letters Detail Water Board Bickering," CBC North, webposted June 13, 2005.

101 Quoted in "Premier Weighs in on Land and Water Board Dispute," CBC North, webposted May 24, 2005.

102 Bob Weber, "N.W.T. Pipeline Regulator Defends Chair," *Calgary Herald*, June 18, 2005.

103 Quoted in ibid.

104 "MVLWB Head Scrutinized for Possible Conflict," CBC North, webposted October 19, 2005.

105 Guidelines and policy documents on these and other topics are available at the MVLWB website, https://mvlwb.com/resources/policy-and-guidelines.

106 Indigenous and Northern Affairs Canada, "Government of Canada Renews Partnership with 33 Treaty-Based Co-management Boards and Committees in the Northwest Territories," news release, August 24, 2017.

107 Data supplied by Implementation Branch, Treaties and Aboriginal Government, Crown-Indigenous Relations and Northern Affairs.

Notes to pages 196–203

108 Andrew Webster, Indigenous and Northern Affairs Canada, "Update on Funding for Treaty-based Boards and Committees," PowerPoint presentation to the NWT Board Forum, November 2017, 4–5.

109 Ibid., 7–9.

110 Letter from Mackenzie Valley board chairs to Trish Merrithew-Mercredi, Regional Director, INAC, December 11, 2007.

111 DIAND, Evaluation, Performance, Measurement and Review Branch, Audit and Evaluation Sector, *Final Report: Evolution of the Northern Regulation, Resources and Environmental Management Programs* (February 2012), v.

112 Arcadis, *2015 Northwest Territories Environmental Audit*, 9–10.

113 Ibid., 10.

114 Minister of Indian Affairs and Northern Development and Tungavik Federation of Nunavut, *Agreement between the Inuit of the Nunavut Settlement Area and Her Majesty the Queen in Right of Canada* (Ottawa, 1993), art. 12.7. See also *Nunavut Planning and Project Assessment Act*, S.C. 2013, c. 2, s. 135.

115 DIAND, "Final Report: Evolution," iii.

116 Office of the Auditor General of Canada, *Report of the Auditor General of Canada to the House of Commons Spring 2010*, ch. 4, "Sustaining Development in the Northwest Territories," 22.

117 CBC North Radio News, "GNWT Says It's Done a Lot to Fix Resource Management System It Inherited," transcript, September 8, 2014. Copy in author's possession.

118 Arcadis, *2015 Northwest Territories Environmental Audit*, 22.

119 DIAND, "Final Report: Evolution," 23.

120 Mackenzie Valley Environmental Impact Review Board, *Report of Environmental Assessment and Reasons for Decision EA0809–002: Canadian Zinc Corporation Prairie Creek Mine* (Yellowknife, December 8, 2011), iv.

121 MVEIRB, *Environmental Impact Assessment Guidelines*, 40–41.

122 MVEIRB, "Special Chambers Brief of the Respondent," filed with the Supreme Court of the Northwest Territories in the case of *De Beers Canada Inc v. Mackenzie Valley Environmental Impact Review Board*, hearing date November 21, 2006, 22.

123 MVEIRB, "EIA Made in the North," 5.

124 Crown-Indigenous Relations and Northern Affairs Canada, "Government of Canada Provides Funding to Facilitate Indigenous and Northerners' Participation in Major Impact Assessments in the North," news release, December 19, 2018.

125 SENES Consultants, *Northwest Territories Environmental Audit 2005*, S-2.

126 Ibid., *2010 Northwest Territories Environmental Audit*, March 2011, ES-1.

127 Arcadis, *2015 Northwest Territories Environmental Audit*, ES-1.

Chapter 6: The Mackenzie Valley Boards and the Regulatory Improvement Saga

1 Hon. Jim Prentice, "Notes for an Address to the Canadian Energy Pipeline Association Annual Dinner," Calgary, May 23, 2006, 6.

2 Mackenzie Valley Environmental Impact Review Board, "The History of Mackenzie Valley Environmental Impact Review Board," February 2007, 6.

3 Nathan Vanderklippe, "Great White North Tied Up in Red Tape" *National Post*, August 27, 2008.

4 "Debate about Environmental Reviews Heats Up in the NWT," CBC News, November 13, 2012, https://www.cbc.ca/news/canada/north/debate-about-environmental-reviews-heats-up-in-the-n-w-t-1.1282873.

5   Quoted in Pieta Wooley and Sean Percy, "WesternGeco Pulls Out," *The Hub* (Hay River), February 4, 2004.

6   Tony Andrews, Executive Director, Prospectors and Developers Association of Canada; Gordon Peeling, President and CEO, Mining Association of Canada; Mike Vaydik, General Manager, NWT and Nunavut Chamber of Mines, to Honourable Jim Prentice, Minister of Indian Affairs and Northern Development, May 25, 2007, http://reviewboard.ca/registry?f%5B0%5D=project%253Afield_project_company%3A326.

7   Guy Quenneville, "To Avoid Breaking Law, De Beers Seeks Water Licence Change," CBC North, November 29, 2014, http://www.cbc.ca/news/canada/north/to-avoid-breaking-law -de-beers-seeks-water-licence-change-1.2854514; Guy Quenneville, CBC North, September 17, 2015, "Snap Lake Diamond Mine's Water Licence Change OK'd by N.W.T. Minister," http://www.cbc.ca/news/canada/north/snap-lake-diamond-mine-s-water-licence-change -ok-d-by-n-w-t-minister-1.3232589; "N.W.T.'s Snap Lake Diamond Mine Halts Operation, De Beers Says," CBC North, December 4, 2015, http://www.cbc.ca/news/canada/ north/n-w-t-s-snap-lake-diamond-mine-to-cease-operations-immediately-1.3350770.

8   Tom Hoefer, "Mineral Exploration Regulated Out of the NWT?" *News/North NWT,* March 23, 2015.

9   Quoted in Karen K. Ho, "Husky Withdraws from Whitebeach Point" *News/North NWT,* June 22, 2015.

10   Gary Vivian, "Beware the Nail in the Economic Coffin," *News/North NWT,* July 27, 2015. The episodes cited above are by no means isolated examples of industry's complaints about the *MVRMA* regulatory system.

11   "The Case for Red Tape" (editorial), *News/North NWT,* October 19, 2015.

12   "Northern Bashing" (editorial), *News/North NWT,* May 3, 2010.

13   "Safe Development Vital" (editorial), *News/North NWT,* December 3, 2012. See also "Review Board Delays Unacceptable" (editorial), *News/North NWT,* July 30, 2012.

14   SENES Consultants Limited, *Northwest Territories Environmental Audit 2005: Main Report* (Yellowknife: Indian and Northern Affairs Canada, December 2005), 5–4.

15   Ibid., 4–1.

16   James R. Moore, Keynote Address, in John Donihee, ed., *Resource Development and the Mackenzie Valley Resource Management Act: The New Regime* (Calgary: Canadian Institute of Resources Law, 2000), 30–31. This book contains materials from a June 1999 University of Calgary conference on the *MVRMA*.

17   MVEIRB, "EIA Made in the North: The Mackenzie Valley Environmental Impact Review Board's Submission to the 2005 NWT Environmental Audit," April 2005, 10–11.

18   Ibid., 9.

19   SENES Consultants, *2010 Northwest Territories Environmental Audit*, March 2011, 3–1, 3–5, 3–8.

20   Ibid., 3–8.

21   Ibid., 3–10.

22   Mary Tapsell and Alistair MacDonald, "The 'Awakening' of SEIA in the Northwest Territories, Canada – the Mackenzie Valley Environmental Impact Review Board's Experience," paper presented to the International Association for Impact Assessment, Seoul, Korea, 2007, 12–13.

23   Indian and Northern Affairs Canada, "Impact Evaluation of Comprehensive Land Claim Agreements," February 2009, 36.

24   Ibid., 39.

25   Quoted in Darren Campbell, "Roadmap to Nowhere," *Up Here Business,* October 2008, 9.

26 Quoted in Andrew Livingstone, "The Red Tape Diaries," *Up Here Business,* November 2011, 4.

27 On impact and benefit agreements, see Ken J. Caine and Naomi Krogman, "Powerful or Just Plain Power-Full? A Power Analysis of Impact and Benefit Agreements in Canada's North," *Organization and Environment* 23, 1 (2010): 76–98; and Brad Gilmour and Bruce Mellett, "The Role of Impact and Benefit Agreements in the Resolution of Project Issues with First Nations," *Alberta Law Review* 51, 2 (2013): 385–400.

28 Office of the Auditor General of Canada, *Report of the Auditor General of Canada to the House of Commons April 2005,* ch. 6, "Indian and Northern Affairs Canada – Development of Non-Renewable Resources in the Northwest Territories."

29 Ibid., 1.

30 Office of the Auditor General of Canada, *Report of the Auditor General of Canada to the House of Commons Spring 2010,* ch. 4, "Sustaining Development in the Northwest Territories," 15.

31 Terriplan Consultants, "Examining and Improving the Relationship between INAC and Resource Management, Advisory and Environmental Assessment Boards in Northern Canada," January 2007, 13–14.

32 Ibid., 30.

33 Ibid., 22, 25, 30, 14, 30, 28.

34 Ibid., 26.

35 "Minister Strahl Announces Initiative and Appointment to Improve the Northern Regulatory System," DIAND News Release, November 7, 2007.

36 Quoted in CBC News, "Strahl Appoints Adviser to Review Northern Regulatory System," November 8, 2007, https://www.cbc.ca/news/canada/north/strahl-appoints-adviser -to-review-northern-regulatory-system-1.676794.

37 Quoted in Herb Mathison, "Federal Candidates Questioned on Commitment to the North," *News/North NWT,* October 6, 2008.

38 Neil McCrank, *Road to Improvement: The Review of the Regulatory Systems across the North* (Ottawa: Minister of Indian Affairs and Northern Development, 2008), I.

39 Ibid., 15.

40 Ibid., 13.

41 Ibid., ii.

42 Ibid., 10.

43 Ibid., 11.

44 Ibid., 40–43.

45 Ibid., 14.

46 Option 2 would require amendments to the *Mackenzie Valley Resource Management Act* but "*may* not require" amending the claims. See McCrank, *Road to Improvement,* 18 (emphasis in original).

47 Ibid., 17.

48 Ibid., 18.

49 Quoted in Guy Quenneville, "Limit Regional Boards, Says Environmental Regulatory Report," *News/North NWT,* July 21, 2008. The report did say that land use plans "will provide local input into a framework for resource management" (McCrank, *Road to Improvement,* 15) but did not make the argument that this should be the limit of local involvement.

50 Conservative Party of Canada, "Leadership Certainty for Canada's North," media release, September 20, 2008.

51 Government of Canada, "Minister Strahl Delivers a Speech on the Action Plan to Improve Northern Regulatory Regimes; Notes for an Address by The Honourable Chuck Strahl, PC, MP to the Northwest Territories Chamber of Commerce," May 3, 2010, https://www.canada.ca/en/news/archive/2010/05/minister-strahl-delivers-speech-action-plan-improve-northern-regulatory-regimes.html.

52 Jeanne Gagnon, "No Need to Reopen Land Claims: Negotiator," *News/North NWT*, May 17, 2010.

53 Senate of Canada, Standing Committee on Energy, the Environment and Natural Resources, *Evidence* (hereafter Senate Committee, *Evidence*), February 13, 2014, 47.

54 Representatives of the K'atl'odeeche First Nation and of Alternatives North (an environmental organization) both told the Commons committee reviewing Bill C-15 that Pollard had spoken of as many as fifty members on the MVLWB once all claims were settled. K'atl'odeeche First Nation, "Brief to the Standing Committee on Aboriginal Affairs and Northern Development Regarding Amendments to the Mackenzie Valley Resource Management Act Contained in Bill C-15," January 13, 2014, 2; Alternatives North and Ecology North, "Brief to the Standing Committee on Aboriginal Affairs and Northern Development Regarding Section 4 of Bill C-15," January 17, 2014, 5.

55 The brief from the K'atl'odeeche First Nation listed the groups currently in negotiations, concluding that only two were planning on land and water regulatory boards, and thus no more than ten new members for the MVLWB, noting that the federal minister was aware of these numbers. See K'atl'odeeche First Nation, "Brief," 2–3.

56 CBC News, "Federal Negotiator Kicked out of N.W.T. 'Superboard' Meeting," March 28, 2012, http://www.cbc.ca/news/canada/north/federal-negotiator-kicked-out-of-n-w-t-superboard-meeting-1.1174770.

57 Paul Bickford, "Regulatory Proposal a Hard Sell," *News/North NWT*, April 2, 2012.

58 Testimony of Ethel Blondin-Andrew, president of the Sahtu Secretariat, Senate Committee, *Evidence,* January 30, 2014, 36.

59 Quoted in CBC News, "Federal Negotiator Kicked Out."

60 Senate Committee, *Evidence*, February 13, 2014, 47–48.

61 The working groups were: Public Engagement and Board Consultation; Plan Review Process and Guidelines; Water/Effluent Quality Guidelines; Terms and Conditions; Data Resource Sharing and Standards; Application Processes. For a summary of the mandates and activities of the working groups, see Mackenzie Valley Land and Water Board, "Perspectives on Regulatory Improvement in the Mackenzie Valley," May 18, 2011, 6–7.

62 Ibid., 5.

63 Ibid., 3.

64 Ibid., 11–12

65 "Amending the *Mackenzie Valley Resource Management Act*: Issues for Consideration," August 2011. No authorship, individual, or organizational, is indicated but the person who conveyed this to me assured me it was produced by DIAND.

66 "Amendment of the *Mackenzie Valley Resource Management Act*: Aboriginal Affairs and Northern Development Canada Plan for Moving Forward with Amendments," November, 2011.

67 Ibid., 2.

68 See testimony of Wayne Walsh and Tara Shannon, both of DIAND, House of Commons Standing Committee on Aboriginal Affairs and Northern Development, *Evidence* (hereafter Commons Committee, *Evidence*), February 4, 2014, 2.

Notes to pages 220–25

69 Testimony of Bertha Rabesca Zoe, legal counsel for the Tlicho Government, and of Daryn Leas, counsel for the Sahtu Secretariat Incorporated, Commons Committee, *Evidence*, January 27, 2014, 14.

70 Ibid., 10.

71 Ibid., December 5, 2013, 5.

72 Legislative Assembly of the Northwest Territories, *Hansard*, February 20, 2014, 3782.

73 Ibid., 3788–89.

74 Ibid., 3790–92. One of the "factual errors" the premier identified was the motion's claim that "many NWT residents" opposed board amalgamation. With no systematic data available one way or another and extensive anecdotal evidence about opposition, the premier's conclusion was less than convincing. See Legislative Assembly of the Northwest Territories, *Hansard*, February 20, 2014, 3790.

75 Certain MVLWB screening/licensing processes were already subject to legislated time limits. As well, non-enforceable timelines were developed by the MVEIRB in conducting EAs.

76 Testimony of Tara Shannon, director, Resource Policy and Programs Directorate, DIAND, Commons Committee, *Evidence*, February 4, 2014, 5.

77 Ibid., 4.

78 House of Commons, Bill C-15, *Northwest Territories Devolution Act*, s. 136.

79 Government of Canada, Government of the Northwest Territories, et al., *Northwest Territories Land and Resources Devolution Agreement*, June 2013, s. 3.18.

80 For bills originating in the Commons, such as C-15, Senate review does not formally begin until the bill has received third and final reading in the House. However, the Senate often conducts "pre-study" of the subject matter of major bills while the House is engaged with them. Hence C-15 was subject to parallel sets of committee hearings.

81 C-15 made changes to the Northwest Territories Water Board, including changing its name to the Inuvialuit Water Board. However, these changes were unrelated to the proposed changes in the *MVRMA*. Moreover, the NWT/Inuvialuit Water Board is not a claims-based board. No one from the Inuvialuit Settlement Region or its governing organization, the Inuvialuit Regional Corporation, appeared before either committee.

82 Commons Committee, *Evidence*, January 27, 2014, 38.

83 Ibid. His First Nation, located in Fort Liard, in the southwest corner of the NWT, had broken with the Dehcho First Nations and signed an agreement-in-principle with Ottawa and the GNWT on a stand-alone comprehensive land claim. It was still under negotiation as of early 2019.

84 Commons Committee, *Evidence*, January 27, 2014, 1–8.

85 Ibid., 11–12.

86 Ibid., 11.

87 Ibid., 45–47.

88 Ibid., 52–54.

89 Alternatives North and Ecology North, "Brief," 7–8.

90 Commons Committee, *Evidence*, January 27, 2014, 17–19.

91 Ibid., 41–43.

92 Ibid., 43–44.

93 Ibid., 43.

94 Ibid., January 30, 2014, 4.

95 Ibid., 9.

96 Ibid.

97 Indian and Northern Affairs Canada, *Comprehensive Land Claim Agreement between Her Majesty the Queen in Right of Canada and the Gwich'in as Represented by the Gwich'in Tribal Council* (Ottawa, 1992), 24.4.6.

98 The paraphrases and quotations in this and the following paragraph are taken from *Tlicho Government v. Canada (Attorney General)*, 2015 N.W.T.S.C. 09, February 27, 2015, 6–8.

99 Ibid., 14–26.

100 Quoted in Jerald Sabin, "A Federation within a Federation? Devolution and Indigenous Government in the Northwest Territories," *IRPP Study* 66, Institute for Research on Public Policy, November 2017, 20.

101 SENES Consultants, *Northwest Territories Environmental Audit 2005*, 4–3.

102 Julia Blythe Christensen, "'These Days, We Feel We Have a Say': Indigenous Knowledge, Political Change and Resource Management in the Mackenzie Valley" (MA thesis, University of Calgary, 2005), 154–56.

103 Ed Struzik, "Guardian of Sacred Place," *Edmonton Journal,* February 24, 2008.

104 Suzanne Mills, Martha Dowsley, and David Cox, "Gender in Research on Northern Resource Development," in Chris Southcott, Frances Abele, David Natcher, and Brenda Parlee, eds., *Resources and Sustainable Development in the Arctic* (Oxford: Routledge, 2018), 263. See also Sheena Kennedy Dalseg, Rauna Kuokkanen, Suzanne Mills, and Deborah Simmons, "Gendered Environmental Assessments in the Canadian North: Marginalization of Indigenous Women and Traditional Economies," *The Northern Review* 47 (2018): 135–66.

105 Interestingly, a senior DIAND official, who was generally positive towards the Mackenzie Valley boards, commented that the boards "quite see themselves as equals to the NEB and they are not."

106 MVEIRB, *Report of Environmental Assessment and Reasons for Decision, EA0809–002: Canadian Zinc Corporation Prairie Creek Mine* (Yellowknife, December 8, 2011), 72–77.

107 Kenya Norwegian, presentation to the Seventh Annual Far North Oil and Gas Forum, Calgary, September 28–9, 2005, 14.

108 Katl'odeeche First Nation, "Brief," 2.

Chapter 7: Issues of Board Independence

1 Mackenzie Valley Land and Water Board website, https://mvlwb.com/content/co-management.

2 Nunavut Wildlife Management Board (NWMB), *Governance Manual* (Iqaluit, March 2012), 2.

3 Ibid., 32.

4 Michael d'Eça, "The Relationship between Tribunal Members and Their Appointing Agencies," paper presented to the Administrative Law Conference, Iqaluit, September 19, 2000, 6.

5 An ad in *News/North NWT*, December 8, 2014, sought applications for a Gwich'in Tribal Council nominee to the MVLWB; potential applicants were asked to state "why they would like to serve as a member *representing* the Gwich'in Tribal Council" on the board (emphasis added). A February 12, 2018, post on the NTI website sought applications for appointment to the Nunavut Wildlife Management Board, noting "candidates must be an Inuk enrolled under the Nunavut Agreement, committed to represent the interests of Inuit." The federal and territorial governments also advertise for vacant board positions but the ads are more neutral and inclusive.

Notes to pages 236–50

6 Although the boards are explicitly designed to protect and enhance Indigenous peoples' rights, both claims and boards' enabling legislation typically stipulate that serving on a board does not constitute a conflict of interest for an Indigenous person.

7 Minister of Indian Affairs and Northern Development and Tungavik Federation of Nunavut, *Agreement between the Inuit of the Nunavut Settlement Area and Her Majesty the Queen in Right of Canada* (Ottawa, 1993), Schedule 5–4 (emphasis added).

8 Quoted in Paul Bickford, "Don't Fix What's Not Broken," *News/North NWT*, December 2, 2013, 7.

9 Quoted in SENES Consultants Limited, *Northwest Territories Environmental Audit 2005: Main Report* (Yellowknife: Indian and Northern Affairs Canada, December 2005), 6-2–6-3.

10 Ibid., 6-1–6-2.

11 CBC News, "Imperial Bemoans Permit Delays," September 27, 2006, https://www.cbc.ca/news/canada/north/imperial-bemoans-permit-delays-1.613925.

12 Nathalie Heiberg-Harrison, "NWT Regulatory Boards Running on Empty," *News/North NWT*, August 2, 2011.

13 "Throwing Up Roadblocks" (editorial), *News/North NWT*, August 8, 2011.

14 CBC News, "Empty Seats on Boards Vex Nunavut Regulators," October 24, 2005.

15 CBC North, "Work Short-Handed, Feds Tell Nunavut Boards," October 25, 2005. The official indicated that two NTI nominations were currently being reviewed but that the GN had not yet forwarded nominations.

16 Terriplan Consultants, "Examining and Improving the Relationship between INAC and Resource Management, Advisory and Environmental Assessment Boards in Northern Canada," January 2007, 18.

17 Office of the Auditor General of Canada, *Report of the Auditor General of Canada to the House of Commons*, ch. 3, "Inuvialuit Final Agreement" (Ottawa, October 2007), 21–22.

18 House of Commons, Standing Committee on Aboriginal Affairs and Northern Development, "Northerners' Perspectives for Prosperity," December 2010, 99–100.

19 Mitch Wiles, "Vacant Federal Appointments Slow Decision Making in the North," CBC News, March 30, 2017, http://www.cbc.ca/news/canada/north/vacant-federal-appointments-slow-decision-making-north-1.4047926. A year later, four board positions were still vacant but three of the six alternate positions were filled.

20 Based on confidential interviews.

21 Unsurprisingly, the ethics counsellor declined to discuss this matter.

22 GNWT, "Guidelines for Public Servant Participation on External Boards and Committees," October 2011.

23 *IFA*, s. 1 (23), s. 12 (54), s. 14 (57), s. 18 (10).

24 The quotation and the paraphrase come from an interview held with two DIAND officials; the words were spoken by one person, with the other nodding in agreement.

25 Percy Kabloona, Acting Chairperson, Nunavut Planning Commission, to Bernard Valcourt, Minister of Aboriginal Affairs and Northern Development, July 2, 2014, 1.

26 Nunavut Planning Commission, "Press Release," June 16, 2014.

27 Quoted in "NPC Sues Ottawa, Alleges Broken Promises," *Nunatsiaq News*, August 22, 2014.

28 Lisa Gregoire, "Premier Backs Speedy Remedy for Mary River," *Nunatsiaq News*, June 5, 2015.

29 "NPC Finance Chief Got NPC Private Contracts as Well," *Nunatsiaq News*, December 2, 2016.

30 See, for example, the open letter to the DIAND minister, the premier of Nunavut, and the president of NTI from the chairs of all four active Nunavut claims boards, seeking resolution of "chronic underfunding," July 14, 2014. Settlement of the NTI suit against Ottawa the following May substantially increased Nunavut board funding levels immediately and over a ten-year period.

31 Council of Yukon First Nations, "Changes to YESAA Threaten Our Land, Our Economy, Our Yukon," Whitehorse, n.d. [2014], 3.

32 Ibid., 7.

33 Nancy Thomson, "Bill S-6 Faces Standing Committee Hearing in Whitehorse Today," CBC News, March 30, 2015, http://www.cbc.ca/news/canada/north/bill-s-6-faces-monday -standing -committee-hearing-in-whitehorse-1.3014310.

34 Carolyn Bennett to Grand Chief Ruth Massie, Council of Yukon First Nations, June 25, 2015.

35 John Thompson, "Technical Staff Quits in Protest," *Nunatsiaq News*, April 13, 2007; John Thompson, "Fourth Water Board Employee Quits, *Nunatsiaq News*, April 20, 2017.

Chapter 8: Traditional Knowledge in Claims-Mandated Co-management Boards

1 Fikret Berkes and Thomas Henley, "Co-management and Traditional Knowledge: Threat or Opportunity?" *Policy Options* 18, 3 (March 1997): 30.

2 Henceforth, unless the discussion specifically relates to Inuit Qaujimajatuqangit, "TK" should be understood as encompassing IQ.

3 Stephen Ellis, "Meaningful Consideration? A Review of Traditional Knowledge in Environmental Decision Making," *Arctic* 58 (March 2005): 67.

4 Perhaps the most frequently cited source in support of this position is Arun Agrawal, "Dismantling the Divide between Indigenous and Scientific Knowledge," *Development and Change* 26 (July 1995): 413–39. Its relevance to Northern claims boards, however, is debatable, to some extent because it is addressed to the development literature (no reference is made to Berkes, who had by 1995 published several pieces on TK), but mostly because of its limited conception of TK. Only the most fleeting reference is made in the article to the ethical and cosmological elements of TK.

5 Leonard Tsuji and Elise Ho, "TEK and Western Science: In Search of Common Ground," *Canadian Journal of Native Studies* 22 (2002): 327–60. The empirical setting for this article is Northern Canada.

6 Paul Nadasdy, *Hunters and Bureaucrats: Power, Knowledge, and Aboriginal-State Relations in the Southwest Yukon* (Vancouver: UBC Press, 2003); Thierry Rodon, *En partenariat avec l'État: Les expériences de cogestion des autochtones du Canada* (Quebec: Les Presses de l'Université Laval, 2003).

7 Frances Abele, "Traditional Knowledge in Practice," *Arctic* 50 (March 1997): iv.

8 L.F. Brooke, quoted in Stella Spak, "Canadian Resource Co-management Boards and Their Relationship to Indigenous Knowledge" (PhD diss., University of Toronto, 2001), 9.

9 Henry P. Huntington, "'We Dance around in a Ring and Suppose': Academic Engagement with Traditional Knowledge," *Arctic Anthropology* 42, 1 (2005): 29.

10 Fikret Berkes, *Sacred Ecology: Traditional Ecological Knowledge and Resource Management* (Philadelphia: Taylor and Francis, 1999), 8.

11 Caroline Butler, "Historicizing Indigenous Knowledge," in Charles R. Menzies, ed., *Traditional Ecological Knowledge and Natural Resource Management* (Lincoln: University of Nebraska Press, 2006), 119.

Notes to pages 262–68

12 Ellis, "Meaningful Consideration?" 67.

13 Berkes, *Sacred Ecology,* 164 (emphasis in original).

14 Leanne Simpson, "Anticolonial Strategies for the Recovery and Maintenance of Indigenous Knowledge," *American Indian Quarterly* 28 (Summer/Autumn, 2004): 380.

15 Marc G. Stevenson, "Indigenous Knowledge in Environmental Assessment," *Arctic* 49 (September 1996): 288.

16 Julie Cruikshank, "Uses and Abuses of 'Traditional Knowledge': Perspectives from the Yukon Territory," in D.G. Anderson and Mark Nuttall, eds., *Cultivating Arctic Landscapes: Knowing and Managing Animals in the Circumpolar North* (New York: Berghahn Books, 2005), 17–32; George Wenzel, "Traditional Ecological Knowledge and Inuit: Reflections on TEK Research and Ethics," *Arctic* 52 (June 1999): 113–24.

17 Marie Battiste and James (Sákéj) Youngblood Henderson, *Protecting Indigenous Knowledge and Heritage: A Global Challenge* (Saskatoon: Purich, 2000), 134–35.

18 Quoted in Nadasdy, *Hunters and Bureaucrats,* 63.

19 Battiste and Henderson, *Protecting Indigenous Knowledge,* ch. 2.

20 Ibid., 46.

21 Nadasdy, *Hunters and Bureaucrats,* 120.

22 Nunavut, Department of Culture, Language, Elders and Youth, *The First Annual Report of the Inuit Qaujimajatuqanginnut (IQ) Task Force* (Iqaluit, 2002), 4.

23 George Wenzel, "From TEK to IQ: *Inuit Qaujimajatuqangit* and Inuit Cultural Ecology," *Arctic Anthropology* 41 (2004): 238–50.

24 Erica-Irene Daes, quoted in Battiste and Henderson, *Protecting Indigenous Knowledge,* 19.

25 Frank Duerden and Richard G. Kuhn, "Scale, Context, and Application of Traditional Knowledge of the Canadian North," *Polar Record* 34 (January 1998): 31.

26 Frances Abele, "Between Respect and Control: Traditional Indigenous Knowledge in Canadian Public Policy," in Michael Orsini and Miriam Smith, eds., *Critical Policy Studies: Contemporary Canadian Approaches* (Vancouver: UBC Press, 2007), 236–37.

27 Martha Johnson, "Dene Traditional Knowledge," *Northern Perspectives* 20 (Summer 1992): 3.

28 Ibid.

29 Marc G. Stevenson, "Ignorance and Prejudice Threaten Environmental Assessment," *Policy Options* 20, 3 (March 1997): 26.

30 Cruikshank, "Uses and Abuses," 18.

31 MVEIRB, Paramount Resources Ltd. environmental assessment public hearing transcript, Hay River, NT, February 18, 2004, I, 13, http://reviewboard.ca/registry/ea03-005.

32 MVEIRB, Report of the environmental assessment and reasons for decision on the Paramount Resources Ltd. Cameron Hills Extension Project, EA03–005, 2004, 55–57, http://reviewboard.ca/node/389/documents/B-REA.

33 Ellis, "Meaningful Consideration?," 72.

34 Tsuji and Ho, "TEK and Western Science," 346.

35 Peter J. Usher, "Traditional Ecological Knowledge in Environmental Assessment and Management," *Arctic* 53 (June 2000): 37. See also Ellis, "Meaningful Consideration?," 70.

36 Frank Duerden, Sean Black, and Richard G. Kuhn, "An Evaluation of the Effectiveness of First Nations Participation in the Development of Land-Use Plans in the Yukon," *Canadian Journal of Native Studies* 16 (1996): 120.

37 Stevenson, "Indigenous Knowledge," 287–88.

38 Alan Erlich, Martin Haefele, and Chuck Hubert, "Incorporating TK into EIA," presentation to the International Association for Impact Assessment Conference, Puebla, Mexico, 2011, 8.
39 Ellis, "Meaningful Consideration?," 71.
40 Johnson, "Dene Traditional Knowledge," 5.
41 Natasha Thorpe, "Codifying Knowledge about Caribou: The History of Inuit Qaujimajauqangit in the Kitikmeot Region of Nunavut, Canada," in Anderson and Nuttall, eds., *Cultivating Arctic Landscapes*, 62.
42 The following account, including quotations and paraphrases of participants, is taken from the author's notes of the meeting.
43 Renita Schuh, "Developing Guidelines for Incorporating Traditional Knowledge into the Environmental Impact Assessment Process: The Mackenzie Valley Environmental Impact Review Board Experience," paper presented at the International Association for Impact Assessment Conference, Boston, 2005, 6.
44 Ibid., 6–7.
45 Ibid., 7–8.
46 Ibid., 8–10.
47 Ibid., 10.
48 MVEIRB, *Guidelines for Incorporating Traditional Knowledge in Environmental Impact Assessment* (Yellowknife, 2005), 4.
49 Ibid., 6.
50 Erlich, Haefele, and Hubert, "Incorporating TK into EIA," 5.
51 Ellis, "Meaningful Consideration?"
52 Erlich, Haefele, and Hubert, "Incorporating TK into EIA," 9. Ironically, one of their case studies, on the Prairie Creek Mine access road, was the one that occasioned the dissenting opinion based on board members' dissatisfaction with the weight accorded TK (the paper was presented before the REA was completed).
53 Ibid., 7.
54 MVEIRB, *Guidelines*, 10.
55 MVEIRB, *Status Report and Information Circular: Developing Cultural Impact Assessment Guidelines, a Mackenzie Valley Review Board Initiative* (Yellowknife, May 2009).
56 The substance and the quotations in this paragraph are taken from Mark Cliffe-Phillips, "Mackenzie Valley Environmental Impact Review Board, Technical Sessions on Cultural Impacts – A New Cultural Impact Assessment Tool," presentation to the *MVRMA* Workshop, Yellowknife, February 2018.
57 NWMB, "Inuit Qaujimajatuqangit Workshop March 25th–26th 2014, Iqaluit Nunavut," 8, https://www.nwmb.com/en/public-hearings-a-meetings/workshops/march-2014-inuit-qaujimajatuqangit-workshop.
58 NWMB, "The Inuit Qaujimajatuqangit Wildlife Fund: An Addendum to the NWMB Funding Proposal and Workplan for the Period from 10 July to 31 March 2013," December 21, 2001, 2.
59 The minutes of this meeting contain no reference to the agreement among board members about IQ; however, the author's notes of the meeting are clear on this point.
60 See, for example, Aarluk Consulting, "Phase 2 Scoping Report: Design and Implementation of a Database and Library of Tradition Ecological Knowledge and *Inuit Qaujimajatuqangit*," September 19, 2011.

61 Peter Kilabuk, *Study of Inuit Knowledge of the Southeast Baffin Beluga* (Iqaluit: NWMB, March 1998). Kilabuk subsequently became Nunavut's minister of sustainable development and, therefore, the lead minister in responding to NWMB decisions.

62 NWMB, "Submission of the Nunavut Wildlife Management Board to the Five-Year Independent Review of the *Nunavut Land Claims Agreement* and the Implementation Contract" (Iqaluit, 1999), 4.

63 David C. Natcher and Susan Davis, "Rethinking Devolution: Challenges for Aboriginal Resource Management in the Yukon Territory," *Society and Natural Resources* 20 (January 2007): 272.

64 Kathrin Wessendorf, "Traditional Knowledge and Authority in Nunavut," paper presented at the Fourth International Congress of Arctic Social Sciences, May 16–20, 2001, Quebec City, 1.

65 Nunavut, *Wildlife Act, Statutes of Nunavut, 2003*, c. 26, s. 8 (a).

66 MVEIRB, "Rules of Procedure for Environmental Assessment and Environmental Impact Review Proceedings," 6, http://reviewboard.ca/process_information/guidance_documentation/rules_of_procedure.

67 NWMB, "Rules of Practice for Public Hearings of the Nunavut Wildlife Management Board" (Iqaluit, 1999), 9.

68 Ibid., 1.

69 NWMB, "Meetings Procedures–Public Hearings," https://www.nwmb.com/en/public-hearings-a-meetings/public-hearing-procedures.

70 MVEIRB, "Rules of Procedure," 3.

71 NWMB, *Governance Manual* (Iqaluit, March 2012), 20.

72 Nadasdy, *Hunters and Bureaucrats*, 123–26.

73 NWMB, "Rules of Practice," 10.

74 MVEIRB, *Guidelines*, 26.

75 Ibid., 10.

76 Ibid.

77 Nunavut, *First Annual Report,* 11, 6.

78 Ellis, "Meaningful Consideration?," 75.

79 Julia Christensen and Miriam Grant, "How Political Change Paved the Way for Indigenous Knowledge: The Mackenzie Valley Resource Management Act," *Arctic* 60 (June 2007): 117; Ellis, "Meaningful Consideration?," 74.

80 Tsuji and Ho, "TEK and Western Science," 350.

81 Henry Huntington, "Traditional Knowledge and Resource Development," in Chris Southcott, Frances Abele, David Natcher, and Brenda Parlee, eds., *Resources and Sustainable Development in the Arctic* (Oxford: Routledge, 2018), 245.

82 Carly A. Dokis, *Where the Rivers Meet: Pipelines, Participatory Resource Management, and Aboriginal-State Relations in the Northwest Territories* (Vancouver: UBC Press, 2015), 157.

83 Ibid., 158.

Chapter 9: Indigenous Influence through Claims Boards?

1 Harvey A. Feit, "Self-Management and State-Management: Forms of Knowing and Managing Northern Wildlife," in Milton Freeman and L.N. Carbyn, eds., *Traditional Knowledge and Renewable Resource Management in Northern Regions* (Edmonton: Boreal Institute for Northern Studies, 1988), 74.

2 The following three paragraphs summarize and respond to criticisms offered by the reviewers of the original manuscript. As in other areas, their insightful comments forced me to rethink key arguments more carefully, for which I am grateful. Data on ratification votes are from various web and First Nations sources.

3 Douglas Clark and Jocelyn Joe-Strack, "Keeping the 'Co' in the Co-management of Northern Resources," *Northern Public Affairs* 5 (April 2017): 73.

4 Graham White, "A Fourth Order of Government? Treaty Federalism through Claims-Mandated Co-Management and Regulatory Boards," paper presented at the Annual Meeting of the Canadian Political Science Association, Quebec, June, 2001.

5 Thomas Huegelin, "Exploring Concepts of Treaty Federalism: A Comparative Perspective," paper prepared for the Royal Commission on Aboriginal Peoples, 1994, 4.

6 Paul Nadasdy, *Hunters and Bureaucrats: Power, Knowledge, and Aboriginal-State Relations in the Southwest Yukon* (Vancouver: UBC Press, 2011).

7 H. Høgh, "Bowhead Whale Hunting in Nunavut: A Symbol of Self-Government," in Jens Dahl, Jack Hicks, and Peter Jull, eds., *Nunavut: Inuit Regain Control of Their Lands and Their Lives* (Copenhagen: International Work Group for Indigenous Affairs, 2000), 196–204.

8 Peter Bannon and Will Dunlop, "Building Partnerships in Impact Assessment: A Canadian Approach," paper presented at the International Association of Impact Assessment Conference, April 1998, Christchurch, NZ, 4.

9 Norman M. Simmons and Gladys Netro, "Yukon Land Claims and Wildlife Management: The Cutting Edge," in Valerius Geist and Ian McTaggart-Cowan, eds., *Wildlife Conservation Policy* (Calgary: Detselig, 1995), 171.

10 Peter Usher, "The Beverly-Kaminuriak Caribou Management Board: An Experience in Co-management," in J. Inglis, ed., *Traditional Ecological Knowledge: Concepts and Cases* (Ottawa: Canadian Museum of Nature, 1993), 113.

11 Supreme Court of the Yukon, *The First Nations of Nacho Nyak Dun v. Yukon (Government of)*, 2014, Y.K.S.C., 69, 63, 74.

12 Sara L. Jaremko, "The Peel Watershed Case: Implications for Aboriginal Consultation and Land Use Planning in Alberta," *Canadian Institute of Resources Law, Occasional Paper No. 56*, March 31, 2017 (updated December 1, 2017), 46.

13 Recall that these are raw numbers that do not take into account length of service and that numbers for the Yukon Water Board include only members appointed after the *UFA* came into effect.

14 Thierry Rodon, *En partenariat avec l'État: Les expériences de cogestion des Autochonones du Canada* (Québec: Les Presses de l'Université Laval, 2003), 202–4.

15 Ibid., 217, 227 (my translation).

16 Ibid., 247.

17 Ibid., 277, 274.

18 Ibid., 288 (my translation).

19 Lindsay Staples, *The Inuvialuit Final Agreement: Implementing Its Land, Resource, and Environmental Regimes*. Report prepared for the Royal Commission on Aboriginal Peoples (Ottawa: Indian and Northern Affairs Canada, 1995), 3, 49.

20 Lloyd N. Binder and Bruce Hanbidge, "Aboriginal People and Resource Co-management," in Inglis, ed. *Traditional Ecological Knowledge*, 121–32. It may be worth noting that Binder is an Inuvialuk.

21 John-Erik Kocho-Schellenberg and Fikret Berkes, "Tracking the Development of Co-management: Using Network Analysis in a Case from the Canadian Arctic," *Polar Record* 51 (July 2015): 422–31.

22 Burton Ayles, Redmond Clarke, Kristin Hynes, Robert Bell, and John Noksana, "Co-management of Fisheries Resources in the Western Canadian Arctic," in Claude Rocan, ed., *Building Bridges: Case Studies in Collaborative Governance in Canada* (Ottawa: Invenire, 2018), 168.

23 Leslie Treseder and Jamie Honda-McNeil, "The Evolution and Status of Wildlife Co-management in Canada," in Leslie Treseder, ed., *Northern Eden: Community-Based Wildlife Management in Canada* (Edmonton: Canadian Circumpolar Institute, 1999), 5–20.

24 Fikret Berkes, "Co-Management and the James Bay Agreement," in Evelyn Pinkerton, ed., *Co-operative Management of Local Fisheries: New Directions for Improved Management and Community Development* (Vancouver: UBC Press, 1989), 190.

25 Peter Usher, "Environment, Race and Nation Reconsidered: Reflections on Aboriginal Land Claims in Canada," *Canadian Geographer* 27 (Winter 2003): 379.

26 Lindsay Galbraith, Ben Bradshaw, and Murray B. Rutherford, "Towards a New Supra-regulatory Approach to Environmental Assessment in Northern Canada," *Impact Assessment and Project Appraisal* 25 (March 2007): 36.

27 Thomas Berger, "Keep It Up: Land Use Planning – Land Claims and Canada's North," in Thomas Berger, Steven A. Kennett, and Hayden King, *Canada's North: What's the Plan?* (Ottawa: Conference Board of Canada, 2010), 20.

28 Louise Vertes, David Connelly, and B. Knott, *Implementation of the Nunavut Land Claims Agreement: An Independent 5-Year Review, 1993 to 1998* (Yellowknife: Ile Royale Enterprises, 1999), 4–17, 4–21.

29 Author's meeting notes.

30 Comment by one of the anonymous reviewers.

31 Brenda Parlee, "Finding Voice in a Changing Ecological and Political Landscape – Traditional Knowledge and Resource Management in Settled and Unsettled Claim Areas of the Northwest Territories, Canada," *Aboriginal Policy Studies* 2, 1 (2012): 57–58.

32 Nadasdy, *Hunters and Bureaucrats*, 9.

33 Paul Nadasdy, "The Anti-Politics of TEK: The Institutionalization of Co-management Discourse and Practice," *Anthropologica* 47 (2005): 216.

34 Lars Carlsson and Fikret Berkes, "Co-management: Concepts and Methodological Implications," *Journal of Environmental Management* 75 (April 2005): 71.

35 Nadasdy, "Anti-Politics," 224.

36 Ibid., 225.

37 Berkes, "Co-Management and the James Bay Agreement," 195.

38 Carly Dokis, *Where the Rivers Meet: Pipelines, Participatory Resource Management, and Aboriginal-State Relations in the Northwest Territories* (Vancouver: UBC Press, 2015), xxiii, 9. Based on extensive fieldwork, Dokis presents convincing evidence that, with respect to the Joint Review Panel on the Mackenzie Gas Project, the Sahtu Dene had limited success in having their views and their approach to land and environment issues heard. She also demonstrates serious inadequacies in the project proponents' consultation processes. However, although it did involve one claims board, the Joint Review Panel was a very distinctive exercise that may not be representative of more standard board reviews. As well, she did not examine the inner workings of the Joint Review Panel to assess Indigenous influence at that level.

39 Marc G. Stevenson, "The Possibility of Difference: Rethinking Co-management," *Human Organization* 65 (Summer 2006): 170.

40 Ibid.

41 Ibid., 168, 170, 172.

42 Hayden King, "Give It Up: Land Use and Resource Management in the Canadian North – Illusions of Indigenous Power and Inclusion," in Berger et al., *Canada's North*, 88.

43 Dokis, *Where the Rivers Meet*, 125.

44 Hayden King, "New Treaties, Same Old Dispossession: A Critical Assessment of Land and Resource Management Regimes in the North," in Martin Papillon and André Juneau, eds., *Canada: The State of the Federation 2013 – Aboriginal Multilevel Governance* (Kingston and Montreal: Queen's Institute of Intergovernmental Relations and McGill-Queen's University Press, 2015), 85. See also his "Co-managing the Future?" *Northern Public Affairs* 1 (Special Issue 2013): 27–31. Both these pieces are marred by factual errors.

45 Stevenson, "Possibility of Difference, 169.

46 Nadasdy, "Anti-Politics," 225.

47 Peter Usher, *Contemporary Aboriginal Land, Resource, and Environment Regimes: Origins, Problems, Prospects*. Report prepared for the Royal Commission on Aboriginal Peoples (Ottawa: Indian and Northern Affairs Canada, 1996), 58.

48 Nancy Doubleday, "Co-management Provisions of the Inuvialuit Final Agreement," in Pinkerton, ed., *Co-operative Management of Local Fisheries*, 209–27; Terry Fenge, "Political Development and Environmental Management in Northern Canada: The Case of the Nunavut Agreement," *Etudes/Inuit/Studies* 16 (1992): 115–41.

49 Julie Cruikshank, "Uses and Abuses of 'Traditional Knowledge': Perspectives from the Yukon Territory," in David G. Anderson and Mark Nuttal, eds., *Cultivating Arctic Landscapes: Knowing and Managing Animals in the Circumpolar North* (New York: Berghahn Books, 2004), 31.

50 Stella Spak, "The Position of Indigenous Knowledge in Canadian Co-management Organizations," *Anthropologica* 47 (2005): 233–46.

51 David C. Natcher, Susan Davis, and Clifford G. Hickey, "Co-management: Managing Relationships, Not Resources," *Human Organization* 64 (Fall 2005): 241.

52 Dokis, *Where the Rivers Meet*, 160.

53 "From the Lecture: Conversations and Questions," in Berger et al., *Canada's North*, 133.

54 King, "New Treaties," 96.

55 Nadasdy, *Hunters and Bureaucrats*, 145.

56 Ibid., 145.

57 Eugene S. Hunn, Darryll R. Johnson, Priscilla N. Russell, and Thomas F. Thornton, "Huna Tlingit Traditional Environmental Knowledge and the Management of a 'Wilderness' Park," *Current Anthropology* 44 (December 2003): S80.

58 Nadasdy, "Anti-Politics," 228. Nadasdy's recent book, *Sovereignty's Entailments: First Nation State Formation in the Yukon* (Toronto: University of Toronto Press, 2017), touches upon co-management institutions but does not advance the arguments made in earlier publications.

59 Stevenson, "Possibility of Difference," 176.

60 Usher, "Environment, Race and Nation," 379.

61 Nadasdy, *Hunters and Bureaucrats*, 145.

62 Paul Pierson, "Increasing Returns, Path Dependence and the Study of Politics," *American Political Science Review* 94 (December 2004): 1251–67.

63 Ayles et al., "Co-management of Fisheries Resources," 169.
64 Clark and Joe-Strack, "Keeping the 'Co' in the Co-management of Northern Resources," 73.
65 Thierry Rodon, "Co-management and Self-Determination in Nunavut," *Polar Geography* 22 (April 1998): 132.
66 Feit, "Self-Management," 84–85.

Selected Bibliography

Abele, Frances. "Between Respect and Control: Traditional Indigenous Knowledge in Canadian Public Policy." In Michael Orsini and Miriam Smith, eds., *Critical Policy Studies: Contemporary Canadian Approaches*, 233–56. Vancouver: UBC Press, 2007.

Agrawal, Arun. "Dismantling the Divide between Indigenous and Scientific Knowledge." *Development and Change* 26, 3 (1995): 413–39.

Alcantara, Christopher. *Negotiating the Deal: Comprehensive Land Claims Agreements in Canada*. Toronto: University of Toronto Press, 2013.

Arcadis Design and Consultancy. *2015 Northwest Territories Environmental Audit*, March 2016. https://www.assembly.gov.nt.ca/sites/default/files/td_2015_nwt_environmental_audit_27-june-16.pdf.

Armitage, Derek R. "Collaborative Environmental Assessment in the Northwest Territories, Canada." *Environmental Impact Assessment Review* 25, 3 (2005): 239–58.

–. "Community-Based Narwhal Management in Nunavut, Canada: Change, Uncertainty, and Adaptation." *Society and Natural Resources* 18, 8 (2005): 715–31.

–. "Environmental Impact Assessment in Canada's Northwest Territories: Integration, Collaboration, and the Mackenzie Valley Resource Management Act." In Kevin S. Hanna, ed., *Environmental Impact Assessment: Practice and Participation*, 185–211. Toronto: Oxford University Press, 2005.

Ayles, Burton, Redmond Clarke, Kristin Hynes, Robert Bell, and John Noksana. "Co-management of Fisheries Resources in the Western Canadian Arctic." In Claude M. Rocan, ed., *Building Bridges: Case Studies in Collaborative Management in Canada*, 135–76. Ottawa: Invenire, 2018.

Barsh, Russel Lawrence, and James Youngblood Henderson. *The Road: Indian Tribes and Political Liberty*. Berkeley: University of California Press, 1980.

Battiste, Marie, and James (Sákéj) Youngblood Henderson. *Protecting Indigenous Knowledge and Heritage: A Global Challenge*. Saskatoon: Purich, 2000.

Berger, Thomas R. "Keep It Up: Land Use Planning – Land Claims and Canada's North." In Thomas Berger, Steven A. Kennett, and Hayden King, *Canada's North: What's the Plan?* Ottawa: Conference Board of Canada, 2010.

–. *Nunavut Land Claims Agreement Implementation Contract Negotiations for the Second Planning Period 2003–2013: Conciliator's Interim Report.* August 2005. https://www.tunngavik.com/publication_categories/thomas-berger-conciliation-reports/.

Berkes, Fikret. *Sacred Ecology: Traditional Ecological Knowledge and Resource Management.* Philadelphia: Taylor and Francis, 1999.

Berkes, Fikret, Peter George, and Richard Preston. "Co-management: The Evolution of Theory and Practice of the Joint Management of Living Resources." *Alternatives* 18, 2 (1991): 12–18.

Berkes, Fikret, and Thomas Henley. "Co-management and Traditional Knowledge: Threat or Opportunity?" *Policy Options* 18, 3 (March 1997): 55–56.

Binder Lloyd N., and Bruce Hanbidge. "Aboriginal People and Resource Co-management." In Julian T. Inglis, ed., *Traditional Ecological Knowledge: Concepts and Cases,* 121–32. Ottawa: Canadian Museum of Nature, 1993.

Canada, Department of Indian Affairs and Northern Development. *Comprehensive Land Claim Agreement between Her Majesty the Queen in Right of Canada and the Gwich'in as Represented by the Gwich'in Tribal Council.* Ottawa, 1992.

–. *The Western Arctic Claim: The Inuvialuit Final Agreement.* Ottawa, 1984.

Canada, Minister of Indian Affairs and Northern Development and Tungavik Federation of Nunavut. *Agreement between the Inuit of the Nunavut Settlement Area and Her Majesty the Queen in Right of Canada.* Ottawa, 1993.

Canada, Minister of Supply and Services Canada. *Umbrella Final Agreement between the Government of Canada, the Council for Yukon Indians and the Government of the Yukon.* Ottawa, 1993.

Carlsson, Lars, and Fikret Berkes. "Co-management: Concepts and Methodological Implications." *Journal of Environmental Management* 75, 1 (2005): 65–76.

Christensen, Julia Blythe. "'These Days, We Feel We Have a Say': Indigenous Knowledge, Political Change and Resource Management in the Mackenzie Valley." MA thesis, University of Calgary, 2005.

Christensen, Julia, and Miriam Grant. "How Political Change Paved the Way for Indigenous Knowledge: The Mackenzie Valley Resource Management Act." *Arctic* 60, 2 (2007): 115–23.

Clark, Douglas, and Jocelyn Joe-Strack. "Keeping the 'Co' in the Co-management of Northern Resources." *Northern Public Affairs* 5, 1 (April 2017): 71–74.

Cosentino, Gina. "Treaty Federalism: Challenging Disciplinary Boundaries and Bridging Praxis, Theory, Research and Critical Pedagogy in Canadian Political Science." In Camille Nelson and Charmaine Nelson, eds., *Racism Eh? A Critical Interdisciplinary Anthology of Race and Racism in Canada,* 135–52. Concord, ON: Captus Press, 2004.

Cruikshank, Julie. "Uses and Abuses of 'Traditional Knowledge': Perspectives from the Yukon Territory." In D.G. Anderson and Mark Nuttal, eds., *Cultivating Arctic Landscapes: Knowing and Managing Animals in the Circumpolar North,* 17–32. New York: Berghahn Books, 2005.

Dalseg, Sheena Kennedy, Rauna Kuokkanen, Suzanne Mills, and Deborah Simmons. "Gendered Environmental Assessments in the Canadian North: Marginalization of Indigenous Women and Traditional Economies." *The Northern Review* 47 (2018): 135–66.

d'Eça, Michael. "The Relationship between Tribunal Members and Their Appointing Agencies." Paper presented to the Administrative Law Conference, Iqaluit, September 19, 2000.

Dokis, Carly, A. *Where the Rivers Meet: Pipelines, Participatory Management, and Aboriginal-State Relations in the Northwest Territories.* Vancouver: UBC Press, 2015.

Doubleday, Nancy. "Co-management Provisions of the Inuvialuit Final Agreement." In Evelyn Pinkerton, ed., *Co-operative Management of Local Fisheries: New Directions for Improved Management and Community Development,* 209–27. Vancouver: UBC Press, 1989.

Dowsley, Martha, and George Wenzel. "'The Time of the Most Polar Bears': A Co-management Conflict in Nunavut." *Arctic* 61, 2 (2008): 177–89.

Duerden, Frank, Sean Black, and Richard G. Kuhn, "An Evaluation of the Effectiveness of First Nations Participation in the Development of Land-Use Plans in the Yukon." *Canadian Journal of Native Studies* 16 (1996): 105–24.

Ellis, Stephen. "Meaningful Consideration? A Review of Traditional Knowledge in Environmental Decision Making." *Arctic* 58, 1 (2005): 66–77.

Erlich, Alan, Martin Haefele, and Chuck Hubert. "Incorporating TK into EIA." Paper presented to the International Association for Impact Assessment Conference, Puebla, Mexico, 2011.

Feit, Harvey A. "Self-Management and State-Management: Forms of Knowing and Managing Northern Wildlife." In Milton Freeman and L.N. Carbyn, eds., *Traditional Knowledge and Renewable Resource Management in Northern Regions,* 72–91. Edmonton: Boreal Institute for Northern Studies, 1988.

Fenge, Terry. "Political Development and Environmental Management in Northern Canada: The Case of the Nunavut Agreement." *Études/Inuit/Studies* 16, 1–2 (1992): 115–41.

Galbraith, Lindsay, Ben Bradshaw, and Murray B. Rutherford. "Towards a New Supra-regulatory Approach to Environmental Assessment in Northern Canada." *Impact Assessment and Project Appraisal* 25, 1 (2007): 27–41.

Hayes, Kelly A. "Walking Together: An Evaluation of Renewable Resource Co-management in the Yukon Territory." Master's degree project, Faculty of Environmental Design, University of Calgary, 2000.

Henderson, James [Sákéj]. "Empowering Treaty Federalism." *Saskatchewan Law Review* 58 (1991): 241–329.

Henri, Dominique. "Managing Nature, Producing Cultures: Inuit Participation, Science and Policy in Wildlife Governance in Nunavut Territory, Canada." D. Phil. thesis, University of Oxford, 2012.

Hicks, Jack, and Graham White. *Made in Nunavut: An Experiment in Decentralized Government.* Vancouver: UBC Press, 2015.

Høge, Helle. "Bowhead Whale Hunting in Nunavut: A Symbol of Self-Government." In Jens Dahl, Jack Hicks, and Peter Jull, eds., *Nunavut: Inuit Regain Control of Their Lands and Their Lives,* 196–204. Copenhagen: International Work Group for Indigenous Affairs, 2000.

Huntington, Henry P. "Traditional Knowledge and Resource Development." In Chris Southcott, Frances Abele, David Natcher, and Brenda Parlee, eds., *Resources and Sustainable Development in the Arctic,* 234–50. Oxford: Routledge, 2018.

–. "'We Dance around in a Ring and Suppose': Academic Engagement with Traditional Knowledge." *Arctic Anthropology* 42, 1 (2005): 29–32.

Kafarowski, Joanna. "'Everyone Should Have a Voice, Everyone's Equal': Gender, Decision-Making and Environmental Policy in the Canadian Arctic." *Canadian Woman Studies* 24, 4 (2005): 12–17.

King, Hayden. "New Treaties, Same Old Dispossession: A Critical Assessment of Land and Resource Management Regimes in the North." In Martin Papillon and André Juneau, eds., *Canada: The State of the Federation 2013 – Aboriginal Multilevel Governance*, 83–98. Montreal and Kingston: Institute of Intergovernmental Relations and McGill-Queen's University Press, 2015.

Kocho-Schellenberg, John-Erik, and Fikret Berkes. "Tracking the Development of Co-management: Using Network Analysis in a Case from the Canadian Arctic." *Polar Record* 51, 4 (2015): 422–31.

Ladner, Kiera. "Treaty Federalism: An Indigenous Vision of Canadian Federalisms." In François Rocher and Miriam Smith, eds., *New Trends in Canadian Federalism*, 2nd ed., 167–94. Toronto: University of Toronto Press, 2003.

McCrank, Neil. *Road to Improvement: The Review of the Regulatory Systems across the North.* Ottawa: Minister of Indian Affairs and Northern Development, 2008.

Mills, Suzanne, Martha Dowsley, and David Cox. "Gender in Research on Northern Resource Development." In Chris Southcott, Frances Abele, David Natcher, and Brenda Parlee, eds., *Resources and Sustainable Development in the Arctic*, 251–70. Oxford: Routledge, 2018.

Nadasdy, Paul. "The Anti-Politics of TEK: The Institutionalization of Co-management Discourse and Practice." *Anthropologica* 47, 2 (2005): 215–32.

–. *Hunters and Bureaucrats: Power, Knowledge and Aboriginal-State Relations in the South-west Yukon.* Vancouver: UBC Press, 2003.

–. "Reevaluating the Co-Management Success Story." *Arctic* 56, 3 (2003): 367–80.

–. *Sovereignty's Entailments: First Nation State Development in the Yukon.* Toronto: University of Toronto Press, 2017.

Natcher, David C. "Co-Management: An Aboriginal Response to Frontier Development." *Northern Review* 23 (2001): 146–63.

–. "Gender and Resource Co-Management in Northern Canada." *Arctic* 66, 2 (2013): 218–21.

Natcher, David C., and Susan Davis. "Rethinking Devolution: Challenges for Aboriginal Resource Management in the Yukon Territory." *Society and Natural Resources* 20, 3 (2007): 271–79.

Natcher, David. C., Susan Davis, and Clifford G. Hickey. "Co-Management: Managing Relationships, Not Resources." *Human Organization* 64, 3 (2005): 241.

Notzke, Claudia. "A New Perspective in Aboriginal Natural Resource Management: Co-management." *Geoforum* 26, 2 (1995): 187–209.

Rodon, Thierry. "Co-management and Self-determination in Nunavut." *Polar Geography* 22, 2 (1998): 119–35.

–. *En partenariat avec l'État: Les expériences de cogestion des Autochonones du Canada.* Québec: Les Presses de l'Université Laval, 2003.

Sabin, Jerald. "A Federation within a Federation? Devolution and Indigenous Government in the Northwest Territories." *IRPP Study* 66, Institute for Research on Public Policy, November 2017.

Schmidt, Jeremy, and Martha Dowsley. "Hunting with Polar Bears: Problems with the Passive Properties of the Commons." *Human Ecology* 38, 3 (2010): 377–87.

Schuh, Renita. "Developing Guidelines for Incorporating Traditional Knowledge into the Environmental Impact Assessment Process: The Mackenzie Valley Environmental Impact Review Board Experience." Paper presented at the International Association for Impact Assessment Conference, Boston, 2005.

SENES Consultants Limited. *Northwest Territories Environmental Audit 2005: Main Report.* Yellowknife: Indian and Northern Affairs Canada, 2005.

Simmons, Norman M., and Gladys Netro. "Yukon Land Claims and Wildlife Management: The Cutting Edge." In Valerius Geist and Ian McTaggart-Cowan, eds., *Wildlife Conservation Policy*, 161–73. Calgary: Detselig, 1995.

Simpson, Leanne. "Anticolonial Strategies for the Recovery and Maintenance of Indigenous Knowledge." *American Indian Quarterly* 28, 3–4 (2004): 373–84.

Snook, Jamie, Ashlee Cunsolo, and Robyn Morris. "A Half Century in the Making: Governing Commercial Fisheries through Indigenous Marine Co-management and the Torngat Joint Fisheries Board." In N. Vestergaard, Brooks A. Kaiser, Linda Fernandez, and Joan Nymand Larsen, eds., *Arctic Marine Resource Governance and Development*, 53–73. Cham, CH: Springer, 2018.

Spak, Stella. "Canadian Resource Co-management Boards and Their Relationship to Indigenous Knowledge." PhD diss., University of Toronto, 2001.

–. "The Position of Indigenous Knowledge in Canadian Co-management Organizations." *Anthropologica* 47, 2 (2005): 233–46.

Staples, Kiri, and David C. Natcher. "Gender, Decision Making and Natural Resource Co-management in Yukon." *Arctic* 68, 3 (2015): 356–66.

Staples, Lindsay. *The Inuvialuit Final Agreement: Implementing Its Land, Resource, and Environmental Regimes.* Report prepared for the Royal Commission on Aboriginal Peoples. Ottawa: Indian and Northern Affairs Canada, 1995.

Stevenson, Marc G. "Decolonizing co-management in Northern Canada." *Cultural Survival Quarterly* 28, 1 (March 2004): 68–71.

–. "Ignorance and Prejudice Threaten Environmental Assessment." *Policy Options* 20, 3 (March 1997): 25–28.

–. "Indigenous Knowledge in Environmental Assessment." *Arctic* 49, 3 (1996): 278–91.

–. "The Possibility of Difference: Rethinking Co-management." *Human Organization* 65, 2 (2006): 167–80.

Tapsell, Mary, and Alistair MacDonald. "The 'Awakening' of SEIA in the Northwest Territories, Canada: The Mackenzie Valley Environmental Impact Review Board's Experience." Paper presented to the International Association for Impact Assessment, Seoul, Korea, 2007.

Tester, Frank James, and Peter Irniq. "*Inuit Qaujimajatuqangit*: Social History, Politics and the Practice of Resistance." *Arctic* 61, supp. (2008): 48–61.

Treseder, Leslie, and Jamie Honda-McNeil, "The Evolution and Status of Wildlife Co-management in Canada." In Leslie Treseder, ed., *Northern Eden: Community-Based Wildlife Management in Canada*, 75–87. Edmonton: Canadian Circumpolar Institute, 1999.

Tsuji, Leonard, and Elise Ho. "TEK and Western Science: In Search of Common Ground." *Canadian Journal of Native Studies* 22, 2 (2002): 327–60.

Usher, Peter J. "Devolution of Power in the Northwest Territories: Implications for Wildlife." In *Native People and Renewable Resource Management: The 1986 Symposium of the Alberta Society of Professional Biologists.* Edmonton: Alberta Society of Professional Biologists, 1986.

–. "Traditional Ecological Knowledge in Environmental Assessment and Management." *Arctic* 53, 2 (2000): 183–93.

Wenzel, George. "From TEK to IQ: *Inuit Qaujimajatuqangit* and Inuit Cultural Ecology." *Arctic Anthropology* 41 (2004): 238–50.

–. "Subsistence and Conservation Hunting: A Nunavut Case Study." In Milton M.R. Freeman and Lee Foote, eds., *Inuit, Polar Bears and Sustainable Use: Local, National, and International Perspectives*, 51–63. Edmonton: CCI Press, 2009.

–. "Traditional Ecological Knowledge and Inuit: Reflections on TEK Research and Ethics." *Arctic* 52, 2 (1999): 113–24.

Index

Abele, Frances, 270
Acho Dene Koe First Nation, 232
Action Plan to Improve Northern Regulatory Regimes, 210, 214, 220
Akearok, Jason, 63
Akesuk, Olayuk, 91
Alberta Energy and Utilities Board, 218
Alexie, Robert, Jr., 231, 252
Alfred, Taiaiake, 316
Alternatives North, 233–34, 351n54
Andersen, Chesley, 15
Antoine, Jim, 222
Armstrong, Louis, 268
Arviat, polar bear situation, 94
Association of Yukon Renewable Resources Councils, 133
Auditor General's reports, 172–73, 216, 253
Ayles, Burton, 308, 320

Baffinland project. *See* Mary River project
Barsh, Russel, 8
Basic Needs Level (BNL), 66, 112
Battiste, Marie, 269
Bell, Brendan, 234–35
Bell, Jim, 16
Bennett, Carolyn, 237, 264
Berger, Thomas, 33, 48, 72, 87, 259, 309

Berkes, Fikret, 10, 12, 13, 266, 268, 308, 314, 355n4
Beverly and Qamanirjuaq Caribou Management Board, 15, 267, 302, 304
Bevington, Dennis, 218, 231
BHP Billiton, 179–80, 199. *See also* Ekati mine
Bill C-15: appointment of MVLWB chair, 230, 256–57; Bill C-88, 237; constitutionality, 219, 232, 236; cost recovery, 229; development certificates, 229; devolution elements, 228; federal objectives, 228; fines, 229; GNWT position, 226–28; House of Commons committee hearings, 231–35; Indigenous opposition, 231–34; Katł'odeeche First Nation comments, 243; MVLWB comments, 234; NWT Assembly motion, 227; policy direction to MVEIRB, 229; proposed timelines, 228; quorum changes, 229; restructuring, of MVLWB, 39, 230, 351n54; restructuring, of regional land and water boards, 39, 219–22, 226, 229–30, 232–33, 235–36, 238; Senate committee hearings, 231; significant provisions, 228–29; "superboard," 232, 233, 237; Yellowknife committee meeting, 232–35

Bill C-17, 264
Bill S-6, 39, 124, 263–64
Binder, Lloyd, 308
Blondin-Andrew, Ethel, 181, 200, 222, 231, 233
Board Forum (NWT), 153, 186–87, 216, 341n123
Board Relations Secretariat (NWT), 135–37, 241, 346n76
boards: arbitration, 40; categories, 6; chairs, appointment, 47, 256–57; chairs, influence, 47; and chairs, removal, 47; as co-management, 13; community involvement, 51, 311–12; consensus approach, 250; constitutional status, 6, 39, 73, 84, 172, 219, 236–37, 301–2, 314; criticisms, 16, 18, 313–21; decision-making capacity, 7–8; different from non-claim boards, 12, 15–16, 267, 302, 314; distinctive character, 4; environmental regulatory, 152–55; federal ability to modify, 39; funding, 7, 51, 258–62, 355n30; GNWT appointment policy, 255–56; government response to, 303; *IFA*, 40–41, 307, 320; independence, 17–18, 264–65; independence and co-management, 247–48; Indigenous influence on, 17, 96–97, 148–51, 238–43; 298, 306–13, 321–23; influence, 17, 302–6; honoraria, 244; literature, 5, 15, 307–9; jurisdictions, 6, 36; legal foundations, 38–39; mandates, variations, 40; mandates, relating to environment, 40, 152–53; media attention to, 8; "negative option," 304; numbers, 324n3; origins, 34–35; participant funding, 311; as political compromise, 4; positive assessments, 16, 303–4, 308–9; power, 302–5; as reconciliation, 4, 302; regional offices, 50; restructuring, 262–63; staff, independence from government, 49, 257; staff, numbers, 49; structure, 7; and traditional knowledge, 18; vacancies, 251–52
— members: alternate members, 45; compatible with nominating parties,
250; conflict of interest, 250, 354n6; delay in appointments, 47, 253–54; *IFA* boards, 13; independence, 7, 248–51; nomination process, 26, 249, 254; nominations by CYFN, 46; nominations from government agencies, 45; nominations from Indigenous organizations, 353n5; numbers, 42; numbers of Indigenous members, 42, 44, 306–7; patronage, 254; pay, 48–49; public servants, 45, 255–56; quora, 48, 251, 252, 253; rejection by federal government, 249, 252; residency requirements, 46; vacancies, 47, 354n15; women, 44
— regional land and water (NWT): cooperation, 221; jurisdiction, 161; quorum, 192; relations with MVLWB, 190–92; restructuring (*see* Bill C-15, restructuring); working groups, 351n61
Bowhead whales: hunt, 89–91; and IQ, 275, 283; NWMB decision, 303; population estimates, 85, 91, 275, 283
Bromley, Bob, 227
Burlingame, Todd, 181–83, 200–1, 230, 257, 345n61, 347n92
Butler, Caroline, 268

Calder decision, 29
Callaghan, Pearl, 106
Cameron Hills hearing, 271–74
Campbell, Tracy, 12
Canadian Environmental Assessment Act (*CEAA*), 158, 160, 207, 214, 228, 229
Canadian Environmental Assessment Agency, 48, 343n10, 344n33
Canadian Nuclear Safety Commission, 163
Canadian Wildlife Service, 45, 60–61, 82, 84, 86, 252
Carcross-Tagish First Nation, 300
Carlsson, Lars, 13, 314
Christensen, Julia, 155, 317
Claims and Indian Government Implementation Branch, 217
Clark, Douglas, 300, 320
Cleghorn, Christine, 106
co-management: and board independence, 247–48; definition, 10; differing

370   Index

understandings, 14; ethos, 247; as human process, 14; independence of members, 247–48; literature, 12; natural resources focus, 10–11; as political compromise, 248, 262; as reconciliation, 302

co-management, and indigenous influence: community involvement, 311–12; interview/observation findings, 309–11; measures of, 298; numbers of board members, 306–7; Sahtu experience, 314, 360n38; secondary literature, 307–9; traditional knowledge, 312–13

comprehensive land claims agreements: approval votes, 300; as compromise, 300; constitutional status, 6, 9–10, 30, 172, 219, 301–2; distinction from specific claims, 30; extent, 5; federal policy on, 35, 36; honour of the Crown, 305; implementation contracts/plans, 33; importance, 5–6, 34; Indigenous discontent, 299–300; Inuit strategy on, 35; lack of federal government understanding, 172, 216; mass-elite Indigenous divisions on, 298–99, 311; as modern treaties, 4–6, 30; nature of, 30; in NWT, 156; provisions, 32–33. *See also* treaties

Conservative government. *See* Harper government

Constitution Act, s 35, 30

contribution agreements, 342n129

Convention on International Trade in Endangered Species of Wild Fauna and Flora (CITES), 93

Corntassel, Jeff, 316

Council of Yukon Indians (CYI), 98, 107–8, 337n29. *See also* Council of Yukon First Nations

Council of Yukon First Nations (CYFN), 28–29, 46, 98, 263

Cournoyea, Nellie, 220–21

Cruickshank, Julie, 271

cumulative effects, 158, 176, 343n21

Davis, Susan, 284

De Beers, 164–65, 212, 238

d'Eça, Michael, 63, 86, 248, 264

Dehcho First Nations, 29, 157, 162, 173, 231, 346n82, 352n83

Deh Cho Interim Measures Agreement, 173, 194

Deh Cho Land Use Planning Committee, 343n12

Déline, 343n15

Dene-Métis agreement-in-principle, 34, 156, 221

Dene Nation, 327n9

Deneron, Henry, 232

Deninu K'ue First Nation, 178

devolution, 22–23: in NWT, Indigenous opposition, 228, 231–32; in NWT, process, 225–27, 230

DFO. *See* Fisheries and Oceans Department

DIAND (Department of Indian Affairs and Northern Development): alternative names/acronyms, 20–21; board funding, 73–75, 81, 145, 154, 171, 175–76, 180–81, 193, 203, 259–61; board nomination/appointment issues, 60, 174, 186–87, 219, 252–53; financial control of boards, 73, 180–81, 260; legal name, 21; NWT regional office, 153, 176, 180, 182, 183, 185, 193; participant funding, 206–7; relations with *MVRMA* boards, 154, 161, 163, 165, 169–72, 177–81, 183–86, 194, 197–99, 217, 241, 346n70; relations with NWMB, 26; relations with Yukon RRCs, 132; security deposits, 199; and Treasury Board Secretariat, 74–75, 84, 260

Dokis, Carly, 295, 313–16, 318, 360n38

Donihee, John, 165

Duerden, Frank, 270, 275

Duncan, John, 252

Ecology North, 233–34

Ekati mine, 169, 184, 199. *See also* BHP Billiton

Ellis, Stephen, 266, 268, 274, 280, 294

Environment Department (Yukon), 121

Environment Impact Review Board, 258
environmental audits (NWT), 158–59, 183, 208, 213, 214, 239, 252
environmental resource management, 315–16
Erasmus, Eddie, 231, 233

federal lands, 161, 165, 238, 343n16
Feit, Harvey, 297
Fente, Dennis, 121
Fisheries and Oceans Department (DFO): beluga quotas, 59; bowhead hunt, 90–91; bowhead numbers, 85, 91, 275, 283; community-based management, 67; emergency harvests, 68; failure to consult YFWMB, 124; fish and shrimp quotas, 85–86, 89; integrated fish management plans, 140–41; international activities, 141; oversight of YSSC budget, 141, 145–46; perceptions of YSSC, 143; relations with Fisheries Joint Management Committee, 342n124; relations with NWMB, 57, 69, 71, 84–85, 333n99; relations with YSSC, 142–47, 342n124; staff for YSSC, 49, 140, 144–45
Fisheries Joint Management Committee, 36, 308, 320, 342n124
five-year review (Yukon), 109–10, 133
Frost, Pauline, 122

Gahcho Kué mine, 164–65, 207
Galbraith, Lindsay, 308
Gingell, Judy, 105–6, 337n17
GN. *See* Government of Nunavut (GN)
GNWT. *See* Government of the Northwest Territories (GNWT)
Government of Northwest Territories (GNWT), 23, 39, 47, 154, 160, 161, 165, 166, 168, 174, 177, 182, 183, 185, 187–88, 194, 198, 204–5, 207, 225–27, 228, 229, 232, 239, 241, 255–56, 257–58
Government of Nunavut (GN), 23, 25–26, 37, 46, 57, 60, 62, 64–65, 71–72, 81, 88, 93–95, 97, 253, 294, 354n15
Government of Yukon (YG): 46, 49, 98, 101, 102, 110, 111, 113–16, 118, 119–21, 122–23, 126, 132–33, 135–36, 148, 258, 262, 305, 341n112
Grant, Miriam, 155
Gwich'in Arbitration Panel, 47
Gwich'in Comprehensive Land Claim, 33, 37, 44, 45, 155, 166, 175, 182, 215, 225, 236
Gwich'in Land and Water Board, 38, 159, 190, 201, 252
Gwich'in Land Use Planning Board, 6, 252
Gwich'in Tribal Council, 44, 162, 173, 177, 224, 230, 310

Hagen, Willard, 201, 215
Hanbidge, Bruce, 308
Handley, Joe, 200, 201
Harper government, 209, 217, 226, 263
Hayes, Kelly, 106, 132
Henderson, James Youngblood (Sákéj), 8, 9, 269
Henley, Thomas, 266
Henri, Dominique, 78, 95
Ho, Elise, 275, 295
Hoefer, Tom, 212, 234
Honda-McNeil, Jamie, 308
Huegelin, Thomas, 9, 301
Hunn, Eugene, 318
Hunt, Richard, 270
Hunters and Trappers Organizations (HTOs): accountability, 288; activities, 79; administration, 81; administrative problems, 69, 79–80, 288; capacity, 79; chairs, 93–94; funding, 60, 72, 75, 81–82, 132; opinion on claim, 309; polar bear TAH, 93, 95; quota allocation, 67; relations with NWMB, 56, 80; research, 76; staff, 79; structure, 128; transfer of tags, 68; women in, 79
Hunting, Fishing and Trapping Coordinating Committee, 15, 307
Huntington, Henry, 268, 295
Hutton, Don, 122

Indigenous organizations: activities, 29; importance, 28; organization, 28. *See also specific organizations*

Interim Resources Management Assistance Fund, 207

Inuit: goals for wildlife management, 56; influence on wildlife policy 56; influence through NWMB, 96–97; and polar bears, 92, 94, 97; role in wildlife management, 57; skepticism about Western science, 78, 94–95, 336n145

Inuit Bowhead Knowledge Study, 76–77

Inuit Qaujimajatuqangit (IQ): concept, 270; GN policy, 25; GN Task Force, 294; at Nunavut Wildlife Management Board, 77–78, 281–84; wildlife studies, 283

Inuvialuit Final Agreement (IFA): Arbitration Board, 258, 338n33; board chairs, 47; board staff, 49–50, 257; boards, 13, 38, 40–41, 45–46, 256, 307, 326n23; co-management, 12, 308, 320; outside *MVRMA*, 156; and *UFA*, 99, 327n20; wildlife management advisory councils, 99, 258, 327n20

Inuvialuit Regional Corporation (IRC), 28, 221, 352n81

Inuvialuit Water Board, 38, 50, 341n123, 352n81. *See also* Northwest Territories Water Board

IQ. *See* Inuit Qaujimajatuqangit (IQ)

IQ Task Force, 294

James Bay and Northern Quebec Agreement (JBNQA), 12, 29, 156, 307

Joe, Dave, 147

Joint Review Panel on Mackenzie Gas Project, 162, 164, 175, 177, 215, 313, 344n26, 360n38

Joint Secretariat (*IFA*), 50, 258, 324n3

Johnson, Martha, 270, 274

Kadlak, Noah, 91–92

Kadlun, Bob, 36

Kakfwi, Stephen, 91, 200

Kakisa, 272

Katł'odeeche First Nation, 231, 243, 351n54

Kilabuk, Peter, 91, 358n61

Kilpatrick, Robert, 91

Kitikmeot Inuit Association, 264

King, Hayden, 16, 315–16, 318

Kocho-Schellenberg, 308

Koe-Strack, Jocelyn, 300, 320

Kormendy, Ed, 121

Koshinsky, Gordon, 82

Kovic, Ben, 61, 62, 63, 80, 82, 90

Kusugak, Jose, 90

Kwanlin Dün First Nation, 129, 300, 340n85

Labrador Inuit Land Claims Agreement, 332n67

Ladner, Kiera, 9

land claims, negotiation of, 29

Land Claims Agreements Coalition, 34

Leas, Dayrn, 130

LeBlanc, Dominic, 85

Lennie, Gordon, 181

Łíídlįį Kų́ę́ First Nation, 242

MacDonald, Graham, 106

Mackenzie Gas Project, 162, 164, 175, 177, 344n26

Mackenzie Valley, resource management regime: board funding, 203; board staff, 238; criticisms of DIAND, 217; different by design, 223; honoraria, 203; Indigenous influence, 238–43; initial projected costs, 171; land use planning, 343n12; participant funding, 206–7; relations with DIAND, 154, 169–77, 240–41; relations with GNWT, 154; traditional knowledge, 239–40, 241

Mackenzie Valley Environmental Impact Review Board (MVEIRB): appointments, delay in, 184; BHP Billiton Environmental Assessment (EA), 179–80; Cameron Hills EA, 271–74; chair, 174; consult to modify process, 167, 184, 346n72; criticisms, 310; cultural impact assessment, 280–81; cumulative effects, 162; Dehcho Geotechnical EA, 346n72; delays, 214; development certificates, 204; Drybones Bay EA, 184, 215; duty to consult (Crown),

Index   **373**

166, 344n29; early days, 177–79; environmental assessment, 162–63 (*see also specific EAs*); environment impact review (EIR), 164–65; federal policy directives, 174, 229; formality, 286; funding, 174–76, 180–81; independence of members, 173; influence, 166; "measures," 345n53; office, 176; powers, 176; Prairie Creek EA, 205, 241–42, 357n52; public registry, 176; quorum, 173, 249; Ranger Oil/Canadian Forest Oil/Chevron EA, 178–79; "recommendations," 345n53; relations with DIAND, 175, 177–81, 183–86; relations with GNWT, 187–88; relations with Indigenous peoples, 188–90; relations with MVLWB, 178, 206; Screech Lake EA, 238; Snap Lake EA, 238; socioeconomic impact assessment, 189; staff, 174; structure, 173; "suggestions," 205; Tlicho Government, 165–66; and Todd Burlingame, 181–83, 345n61; traditional knowledge, 184, 189, 277–81, 346n77; traditional knowledge, *Guidelines*, 278–80, 292, 293; traditional knowledge, in decision making, 280; Whitebeach Point EA, 212; workload, 176–77; Yellowknife TK workshop, 277–78, 287–88, 310

Mackenzie Valley Land and Water Board (MVLWB): BHP Billiton Ekati mine, 199; Cameron Hills hearing, 273; chair, 191, 347n92; co-management statement, 248; compensation awards, 195, 347n86; conditions imposed, 167; de Beers threat, 212; early days, 196–97; engagement and consultation policy, 195; funding, 193–94, 217, 346n82; hearings, 161–62, 194–95; implementation/enforcement of conditions, 203; internal tensions, 197; jurisdiction, 161, 191; meetings, 191–92; policy direction to, 194; powers, 161, 194; relations with DIAND, 197–99; relations with Indigenous peoples, 195, 198; relations with MVEIRB, 178, 202, 206; relations with regional land

and water boards, 190–92; renewal of licences/permits, 168, 194–95, 199; section 99(4) board, 191–92; security deposits, 195–96; staff, 192–93, 198; structure, 191; timelines, 194; Tlicho Government, 191, 194; and Todd Burlingame, 200–1, 347n92; traditional knowledge, 197; "unsettled areas," 191, 192, 201, 230; workload, 196. *See also* boards, regional land and water (NWT); Bill C-15, restructuring

Mackenzie Valley Land and Water Working Group, 196

Mackenzie Valley Resource Management Act (MVRMA): 2014 amendments, 8, 224–30, 346n81; assessments, of, 213–15; complexity, 160, 202, 286; creation of boards, 38, 155–56; development, 157; "different by design," 156; environment, definition, 160, 163; environmental impact review, 164–65; federal appointment power, 229; funding, 202; Indigenous opposition, 157; industry complaints, 210–13; initial DIAND response, 169–70; inspection/enforcement, 223; inspectors, 205; jurisdiction, 156; main features, 158; need for revision, 209, 216, 224; orphan measures, 204; participant funding, 223; process, deadlines, 167–68; process, land use planning, 159; process, restrictions on minister, 166–67; process, screening, 159; "public concern," 164, 210, 229, 234; revision process, 224–26; significance in NWT development, 155; "significant public concern," 164, 229; traditional knowledge, 312

Mackenzie-Scott, Gabrielle, 165, 240

Makivik, 62

Mary River project, 261

McCormick, Kevin, 62, 82–83

McCrank, Neil, 218, 232

McCrank report, 215, 218–20, 223

McLeod, Bob, 227, 229, 230, 232, 352n74

McLeod, Melody, 199

Meyers, Rick, 234–35

Miltenberger, Michael, 226

Mining Association of Canada, 211, 234
Moore, Jim, 213

Nadasdy, Paul, 125, 133, 150, 262, 269,
    302, 313, 316–20
Nadli, Mike, 157
Natcher, David, 11, 12, 14, 138, 284, 317
National Energy Board, 163, 178, 186
natural resource management: Indigenous
    system, 11; integrated fish and wildlife,
    140–41; "managing" wildlife, 290;
    melding Indigenous and state systems,
    12, 15; state system, 11
Nault, Robert, 181, 182
Netro, Gladys, 303
News/North NWT, 212, 213, 252
Neyelle, Michael, 253
Nickerson, Dave, 210
Nielsen, Stephen, 201
Noble, Jim, 63, 73, 74, 330n27
North Slave Métis Alliance, 232
Northern Affairs Program, 217
Northern Participant Funding Program,
    207–8
Northern Regulatory Improvement
    Initiative, 209, 215, 216, 218
Northwest Territories (NWT): cultural
    divisions, 27; demographics, 27; gov-
    ernment structure, 28; political de-
    velopment, 27; "unsettled areas," 28,
    29. *See also* Government of Northwest
    Territories (GNWT)
Northwest Territories Devolution Act. See
    Bill C-15
Northwest Territories Water Act, 38, 50,
    225
Northwest Territories Water Board, 38,
    50, 158, 181, 182, 193, 196, 197, 198,
    217, 344n33, 352n81. *See also* Inuvi-
    aluit Water Board
Norwegian, Herb, 157
Norwegian, Kenya, 242
Nunavik, 62
Nunavik Marine Region Wildlife Board,
    62
Nunavut: demographics, 24; economy, 25;
    government, 25, 253; decentralization,

26; structure, 25; regions within, 24.
    See also Government of Nunavut (GN)
Nunavut Arbitration Board, 329n1
Nunavut Harvest Study, 76–77
Nunavut Impact Review Board, 8, 204–5,
    223
Nunavut Implementation Panel, 72, 75, 87
Nunavut Inuit Wildlife Secretariat (NIWS),
    79, 80–81, 135, 288, 333n87
Nunavut Land Claims Agreement: Article
    5, 56–57; federal government oppos-
    ition to terms, 56–57; implementation
    contract, 258. *See also* Nunavut Wild-
    life Management Board (NWMB)
Nunavut Land Claims Agreement Act, 66
*Nunavut Planning and Project Assessment
    Act,* 37, 229
Nunavut Planning Commission, 37, 42,
    45, 46, 47, 49, 50, 55, 255, 260–62
Nunavut Settlement Area, 66, 331n34
Nunavut Surface Rights Tribunal, 328n25,
    329n1
Nunavut Tunngavik Incorporated (NTI):
    board appointments, 60, 253; bowhead
    hunt, 90–91; and devolution, 23; and
    HTOs, 80–81; lawsuit against federal
    government, 33, 51, 72, 259, 261,
    329n1, 355n30; polar bear quotas and
    traditional hunt, 91–94; relations with
    NWMB, 55, 62–63, 65–66, 70–71, 73,
    86–89
Nunavut Water Board, 37, 55, 68, 253, 264
*Nunavut Waters and Nunavut Surface
    Rights Tribunal Act,* 38
Nunavut Wildlife Management Advisory
    Board, 59–60
Nunavut Wildlife Management Board
    (NWMB): activities, 66–69; adminis-
    trative support to other agencies, 69;
    BNL, 67; Bowhead hunt, 89–91, 303,
    334n125; chair, 60–61; co-management
    statement, 248; co-management orien-
    tation, 58–59, 83; community-based
    management, 67, 331n37; conference
    calls, 71; conflict with PCO, 86–88;
    conservation education, 69; and DFO,
    84–85; donations by, 75; elders, respect

Index

for, 290; fish and shrimp quotas, 85–86; *Governance Manual,* 58, 71, 288; hearing procedures, 286–87; independent reviews of, 55; Inuit character, 96; Inuit influence through, 96–97, 322; Inuktitut, use of, 57, 61–62, 64–65, 77, 95–96; IQ, 58, 77–78, 93, 281–84; IQ Research Fund, 78, 283; live capture of animals, 67–68; office, 62; relations with DFO, 67–69, 84–86, 89–90, 333n99; relations with GN, 88; relations with NIWS, 81; relations with NTI, 88–89; reluctance to act against Inuit organizations, 80; research funding, 76; and *SARA,* 68–69, 84, 334n108; screening of applications and research, 68; staff, 63; start-up, 59; TAH, 67; translation, 65, 95–96, 331n32; traditional polar bear hunt, 91–92
— decision-making process: confidentiality, 69–70; "final decision," 70; ministerial response, 70; "negative option," 58; role of federal ministers, 69; role of GN minister, 69; time limits, 69; website registry, 71
— funding: conflict with DIAND, 73–74, 84; contribution agreements, 73; flexible transfer payments, 74–75; initial, 72; "reprofiling" funds, 75
— mandate: habitat, 57; Inuit interests, 88; not an agent of the Crown, 66
— meetings: attendance by officials, 65–66; conference calls, 71; frequency, 64; "internal in camera," 66; location, 64; "non-voting observers," 66, 69, 330n22; polar bear quotas, 93–95; public hearings, 64; public interest in, 66
— members: appointing agencies, 60; characteristics, 61–62; honoraria, 86–87, 334n116; independence, 82–83; Nunavik, 62; vacancies, 61
— polar bears: defence kills, 335n143; "Manitoba bears" 94, 335n143; numbers, 335n134; quotas, 92–95
Nunavut Wildlife Research Trust, 60, 76

NWT Chamber of Commerce, 211, 220, 234
NWT Chamber of Mines, 210
NWT and Nunavut Chamber of Mines, 211, 212, 234
NWT Federation of Labour, 233
NWT Treaty 8 Tribal Corporation, 231

Okalik, Paul, 34
Overvold, Bob, 25

Pan-Territorial Assessment and Regulatory Board Forum, 187
Paramount Resources, 271–74
Peary Caribou, 86, 334n108
Peel Watershed Planning Commission, 305
Penikett, Tony, 128, 131
"Perspectives on Regulatory Reform in the NWT," 223
Pollard, John, 220–22, 232, 351n54
Pollard Mission, 220–22, 351n54
Pope, Frank, 182, 183
Porcupine Caribou Management Board, 99
Prentice, Jim, 201, 210, 211
Prime Minister's Office, 220
Privy Council Office (PCO), 21, 48, 86
Prospectors and Developers Association of Canada, 211

Quassa, Paul, 91–92

Redfern, Madeleine, 44
regional wildlife organizations (Nunavut), 79–80
regulations, 338n49
Renewable Resources Councils (RRCs) (Yukon): activities, 130, 131–32; as co-management, 128; bylaw authority, 130; capacity, 130; chairs, appointment of, 129; chairs, invited to YFWMB meetings, 116; challenges, 128; demands on, 130; differences from Nunavut HTOs, 127–28, 132–33; effectiveness, 138; First Nation influence through, 138; local focus, 128;

"local knowledge," 132; mandate, 129–31, 133; meetings, 129; offices, 129; origin, 128; policy influence, 148; political interference, 136; relations with federal government, 133; relations with YFWMB, 134–35; relations with YG, 135–36; *Renewable Resources Council Training Handbook,* 340n84; resources, 131, 134; staff, 129; structure, 129; traditional knowledge, 132; "traditional territories," 136–38
— funding: fundraising, 133; increases, 134; initial level, 133, 341n99; review by YG, 133–34, 262; reviews of, 133
— members: appointments, 129, 136; demands on, 130; difficulty recruiting, 130; residency requirement, 129; term, 129; women, 129, 340n89
Road to Improvement. See McCrank report
Rodon, Thierry: assessment of NWMB, 96, 307, 322; models of co-management, 14–15
Ross River Dena Council, 151, 342n135
Royal Commission on Aboriginal Peoples (RCAP), 3, 9
Ruby Range Sheep Steering Committee, 267, 302, 313–14

Sahtu Dene and Métis Comprehensive Land Claim, 225, 227, 236
Sahtu Renewable Resources Board, 253
Sahtu Secretariat, 44, 162, 173, 177, 181, 222, 230, 231
Schryer, Rick, 215
Scott, Andy, 200–1
Scottie, Joan, 79
"self-management" (Indigenous), 297
Shaner, Karan, 237
Shewchuk, Daniel, 61
Simmons, Norman, 303
Simpson, Leanne, 269
Species at Risk Act (*SARA*), 64, 68–69, 82, 84, 86, 334n108
specific claims, 30
Staples, Kiri, 138
Staples, Lindsay, 308

Stevenson, Marc, 269, 275, 313, 315–17, 319–20
Strahl, Chuck, 211, 218, 220
Supreme Court of Canada, 29, 305
Supreme Court of the Northwest Territories, 164, 236–37
Supreme Court of Yukon, 305

Ta'an Kwächän Council, 129, 340n85
Taptuna, Peter, 261
ten-year review (Yukon), 133, 136, 145
Terriplan Consultants, 217
territorial formula finance, 345n58
territories: devolution, 22–23; differences from provinces, 21; funding, 21, 24, 345n58; relation to federal government, 21
Thorpe, Natasha, 276
Tlicho Agreement, 32, 46, 155, 162, 164, 191, 199, 236, 237
Tlicho Government, 46, 165–66, 173, 191, 194, 224, 230, 231, 236, 239
Tootoo, Hunter, 85, 261, 262
Torngat Secretariat, 332n67
total allowable harvest (TAH), 66, 112
traditional knowledge (TK): and co-management, 266; context, importance of, 275–76; decision making, 280, 294; definition, 268; and language, 269, 276–78, 287–88; misuse, 269, 271; at MVEIRB, 277–81; nature, 268–69, 270; oral evidence, 287; public availability, 292–93; Sahtu experience, 295; significance, 268; spiritual element, 270–71; traditional ecological knowledge, 270; traditional element, 269–70; and Western governance, 267, 284–93; and Western science, 266–67, 269, 274–75; Yellowknife workshop, 277–78, 287–88. *See also* Inuit Qaujimajatuqangit
"traditional territory" (Yukon): areas without, 137–38; artificial nature, 137; overlap, 137, 341n115; variations, 137
Treasury Board Secretariat (TBS), 74, 75, 84, 146, 260
treaties: honour of the Crown, 305; importance of, 3–4; as reconciliation,

305. *See also* comprehensive land claims agreements

treaty federalism: and co-management, 301–2; and comprehensive claims, 9; as constitution, 3, 8–9; Indigenous understanding of, 10; literature on, 9–10; as reconciliation, 302

Treseder, Leslie, 308

Tsuji, Leonard, 275, 295

Tungavik Federation of Nunavut, 59. *See also* Nunavut Tunngavik Incorporated

Type C licences/permits, 343n 15

Umbrella Final Agreement (Yukon) (*UFA*): Bill S-6, 124; board staffing, 49, 104, 143; boards, 44, 46, 101–2, 111, 118, 136; Chapter 16, 99–100, 108–9, 112, 124, 340n84; coming into force, 104; DFO not respecting, 124; finalized claims under, 32; First Nations influence, 148–49, 310; five-year review, 109–10, 144; government implementation of YFWMB recommendations, 115; land use planning commissions, 305, 324n3; not finalized land claim, 26, 98–99; Renewable Resources Councils, 127–30, 132, 134–35; reshaping Yukon governance, 27; resistance to, 101, 119; as social contract, 138, 149–51; traditional knowledge, 124; trapline allocations, 132; Yukon Fish and Wildlife Enhancement Trust, 125–26; Yukon Salmon Subcommittee, 139, 143, 146–48

United Nations Declaration of the Rights of Indigenous Peoples, 4

"unsettled areas," 28, 162, 191, 207, 242, 309. *See also* Mackenzie Valley Land and Water Board (MVLWB), "unsettled areas"

Urquhart, Doug, 340n84

Usher, Peter, 11, 275, 308, 317, 319

Valcourt, Bernard, 226, 229, 230

van Tighem, Graham, 107, 117, 339n56

Veale, R.S., 305

Wek' éezhii Land and Water Board, 50, 159, 174, 185, 191, 194, 196, 199, 203, 212, 235, 236, 237, 239

Wenzel, George, 95

Western Governance Model and TK/IQ: adversarial nature, 291–92; compartmentalization, 289–90; concentration of power, 285; hierarchical, 285; merit, 290–91; office holding, 289; release of information, 292–93; rules and procedures, 285–88; Weberian bureaucracy, 284

Wildlife Act (Nunavut) 38, 88, 286, 328n22, 330n11

Wildlife Act (Yukon), 99

— regulations: board dissatisfaction, 116; board recommendations, 114, 338n50; board review, 114; government response, 115; ministerial response, 114; process, 113–15; public review, 114

Wildlife Management Advisory Council (North Slope), 99

Wildlife Management Advisory Council (NWT), 104–5

Wooley, Bob, 201

Wray, Gordon, 182, 183, 345n63

Yakela, Norman, 228

Yukon: demographics, 26; government structure, 27; political parties, 26. *See also* Government of Yukon (YG)

Yukon Court of Appeal, 305

Yukon Environmental and Socio-economic Assessment Act, 38, 124, 263

Yukon Environmental and Socio-economic Assessment Board (YESAB), 38, 39, 40, 46, 49, 50, 111, 141, 229, 249, 263

Yukon Fish and Wildlife – A 20:20 Vision, 121–22

Yukon Fish and Wildlife Enhancement Trust: activities, 103–4; application review process, 125–26; grants, 125–26; initial funding, 125; YFWMB members as trustees, 12

Yukon Fish and Wildlife Management Board (YFWMB): activities, 111–16; aversion to legalism, 107, 337n25; Bill S-6, 124, 339n72; catch-and-release fishing, 150, 312; community stewards program, 104; Committee on the Status of Endangered Wildlife in Canada (COSEWIC), 124; decisions by consensus, 107; differences from NWMB, 98, 101; early activities, 109; executive, 103; "exotic species," 99; First Nations empowerment, 149; First Nations influence through, 149; *Fisheries Act* revisions, 116–17; funding approval, 110; funding level, 110; fundraising, 110–11; game farming, 108, 120; jurisdiction, 99; mandate, 100–1; non-Indigenous empowerment, 149; office, 104, 106; outfitting, 108; policy against recommendations to First Nations, 99–100, 150–51; policy influence, 148; political interference, 120–23; pre-implementation board, 104–5; regulations, proposed, 338n50; relations with federal government, 123–24, 341n111; relations with RRCs, 108, 134–35; relations with YESAB, 112; relations with YG, 108–9; relations with YG bureaucrats, 123; reluctance to intervene with RRCs, 135; review by Yukon Forum, 126–27; staff, 104, 106–7, 337n8; structure, 101; traditional knowledge, 124–25, 339n74; transparency, 107; "transplanted populations," 99; working groups, 103; YG director of Fish and Wildlife, 104, 116
— chair: appointment of, 103; First Nation–non-Indigenous alternation, 103, 107; meeting management, 117
— meetings: atmosphere, 117; attendance by media, 117; attendance by public,

117; frequency, 103; initial, 105–6; location, 103, 116; quorum, 116; regular attendees, 116–17; with RRC chairs, 134
— members: appointment of, 101; CYFN appointments, 102; CYFN staff, 102; differing views, 109; experience, 117, 119; independence, 118; mutual respect, 117, 119, 339n57; no public servants, 102; removal, 102, 337n6; as "representatives," 118; residency requirements, 101–2; trustees on trust, 125; turnover, 102; women, 102–3
Yukon Forum, 126
"Yukon Indian People," 100–1, 124, 137, 150, 339n74
Yukon Salmon Sub-Committee (YSSC): activities, 140–41; as subcommittee of YFWMB, 139; chair, 139, 142; habitat, 141; integrated fish management plans, 140–41; meetings, 140; *Pacific Salmon Treaty,* 139; policy influence, 148; public education, 141; relations with First Nations, 148; relations with RRCs, 141; relations with YFWMB, 142; traditional knowledge, 141–42; Yukon River Drainage Fisheries Association, 147; Yukon River Panel, 139; *Yukon River Salmon Agreement,* 139
— funding, 142: contribution agreement, 145–46; DFO oversight, 145; level, 145; loan from YFWMB, 145; source, 145
— members: basis of appointment, 139; numbers, 139; term, 139
— staff: complement, 140; DFO employees, 140; independence, 145
Yukon Water Board, 38, 44, 46, 49, 141, 258, 359n13
Yukon Wildlife Management Board, 104–5

Printed and bound in Canada

Set in Myriad and Minion by Artegraphica Design Co. Ltd.

Copy editor: Joanne Richardson

Proofreader: Judith Earnshaw

Cartographer: Eric Leinberger